Beginning Perl, Second Edition

JAMES LEE
with SIMON COZENS and PETER WAINWRIGHT

Apress®

Beginning Perl, Second Edition

Copyright © 2004 by James Lee, Simon Cozens, Peter Wainwright

ISBN-13 (pbk): 978-1-59059-391-2
ISBN-10 (pbk): 1-59059-391-X
eISBN-13: 978-1-4302-0665-1

Printed and bound in the United States of America (POD)

Lead Editor: Chris Mills
Technical Reviewer: Sam Tregar
Editorial Board: Steve Anglin, Dan Appleman, Ewan Buckingham, Gary Cornell, Tony Davis, Jason Gilmore, Jonathon Hassell, Chris Mills, Dominic Shakeshaft, Jim Sumser
Project Manager: Kylie Johnston
Copy Edit Manager: Nicole LeClerc
Copy Editor: Ami Knox
Production Manager: Kari Brooks
Production Editor: Katie Stence
Compositor and Artist: Kinetic Publishing Services, LLC
Proofreader: Elizabeth Berry
Indexer: John Collin
Cover Designer: Kurt Krames
Manufacturing Manager: Tom Debolski

Distributed to the book trade in the United States by Springer-Verlag New York, LLC, 233 Spring Street, 6th Floor, New York, NY 10013, and outside the United States by Springer-Verlag GmbH & Co. KG, Tiergartenstr. 17, 69112 Heidelberg, Germany.

In the United States: phone 1-800-SPRINGER, e-mail orders@springer-ny.com, or visit http://www.springer-ny.com. Outside the United States: fax +49 6221 345229, e-mail orders@springer.de, or visit http://www.springer.de.

For information on translations, please contact Apress directly at 2855 Telegraph Avenue, Suite 600, Berkeley, CA 94705. Phone 510-549-5930, fax 510-549-5939, e-mail info@apress.com, or visit http://www.apress.com.

The source code for this book is available to readers at http://www.apress.com in the Source Code/Downloads/Source Code section.

To Kelli, Ryan, Christian, and Madeline

Contents at a Glance

Contents

■CHAPTER 7   **Regular Expressions** 149

■CHAPTER 8   **Files and Data** 177

About the Author

JAMES LEE is a hacker and open-source advocate based in Illinois. He has a masters degree from Northwestern University, where he can often be seen rooting for the Wildcats during football season. The founder of Onsight, he has worked as a programmer, trainer, manager, writer, and open-source advocate. He is the author of *Open Source Web Development with LAMP* published by Addison-Wesley and a coauthor of *Hacking Linux Exposed, Second Edition* published by McGraw-Hill/Osborne. He has also written a number of articles on Perl for *Linux Journal*. Mr. Lee enjoys hacking Perl, developing software for the web, listening to music on his iPod, reading, traveling, and most of all playing with his kids, who are too young to know why Dad's favorite animals are penguins and camels. You can reach James at james@onsight.com.

Acknowledgments

Thanks to Simon Cozens for writing an excellent book that I had the privilege of revising for this latest edition. You set the bar extremely high—I hope that my work has not lowered it.

I am indebted to Sam Tregar, the technical editor for this edition. Sam, you caught my mistakes, made excellent suggestions, and put up with me when I knew I was right (when I was really wrong)—this book is better as a result of your input. Any mistakes that remain are all mine. Also, thanks for the ideas for the creative examples—your suggestions have helped me to become a better writer.

Thanks to all the folks at Apress: Chris Mills, Kylie Johnston, Ami Knox, and Katie Stence. You were all a pleasure to work with.

Thanks to Larry Wall for creating Perl, the language that has brought me great joy for the last 12 years. I don't think I would like my job as much as I do if I never had Perl to play with. Thanks also to the Perl community for all the selfless work making Perl what it is, especially Lincoln Stein for `CGI.pm` and Tim Bunce for `DBI`.

And finally, my deepest appreciation for those in my life that help make it worth living: Kelli and the kids, Polly and Dave Pistole, Keith Lewis, and all my friends—I'd list you all by name, but I have no idea who to start with. Besides, you know who you are.

Introduction

Perl was originally written by Larry Wall while he was working at NASA's Jet Propulsion Labs. Larry is an Internet legend, known not just for Perl, but as the author of the UNIX utilities rn, one of the original Usenet newsreaders, and patch, a tremendously useful utility that takes a list of differences between two files and allows you to turn one into the other. The word *patch* used for this activity is now widespread.

Perl started life as a "glue" language, allowing one to "stick" different tools together by converting between their various data formats, for the use of Larry and his officemates. It pulled together the best features of several languages: the powerful regular expressions from sed (the Unix stream editor), the pattern-scanning language awk, and a few other languages and utilities. The syntax was further made up out of C, Pascal, Basic, Unix shell languages, English, and maybe a few other things along the way.

While Perl started its life as glue, it is now more often referred to as another handy multiuse tool: duct tape. A common statement heard in cyberspace is that Perl is the duct tape that holds the Internet together.

Version 1 of Perl hit the world on December 18, 1987, and the language has been steadily evolving since then with contributions from a whole bunch of people (see the file AUTHORS in the latest stable release tarball). Perl 2 expanded the regular expression support, while Perl 3 allowed Perl to deal with binary data. Perl 4 was released so that the "Camel Book" (also known as *Programming Perl* by Larry Wall [O'Reilly & Associates, 2000]) could refer to a new version of Perl.

Perl 5 has seen some rather drastic changes in syntax, and some pretty fantastic extensions to the language. Perl 5 is (more or less) backwardly compatible with previous versions of the language, but at the same time makes a lot of the old code obsolete. Perl 4 code may still run, but Perl 4 style is definitely frowned upon these days.

At the time of writing, the current stable release of Perl is 5.8.3, which is what this book will describe. That said, the maintainers of Perl are very careful to ensure that old code will run, perhaps all the way back to Perl 1—changes and features that break existing programs are evaluated extremely seriously. Everything you see here will continue to function in the future.

We say "maintainers" because Larry no longer looks after Perl by himself—there is a group of "porters" who maintain the language and produce new releases. The perl5-porters mailing list is the main development list for the language, and you can see the discussions archived at www.xray.mpe.mpg.de/mailing-lists/perl5-porters. For each release, one of the porters will carry the "patch pumpkin"—the responsibility for putting together and releasing the next version of Perl.

The Future of Perl—Developers Releases and Perl 6

Perl is a living language, and continues to be developed and improved. The development happens on two fronts. Stable releases of Perl, intended for the general public, have a version number *x.y.z* where *z* is less than 50. Currently, we're at 5.8.3; the next major stable release is going to be 5.10.0 (if there is another major release before version 6.0.0). Cases where *z* is more than 0 are maintenance releases issued to fix any overwhelming bugs. This happens extremely infrequently—for example, the 5.5 series had three maintenance releases in approximately a year of service.

Between stable releases, the porters work on the development track (where *y* is odd); when 5.6.0 was released, work began on 5.7.0 (the development track) to eventually become 5.8.0. Naturally, releases on the development track happen much more frequently than those on the stable track, but don't think that you should be using a development Perl to get the latest and greatest features, or just because your stable version of last year seems old in comparison to the bright and shiny Perl released last week—no guarantees whatsoever are made about a development release of Perl. Releases are coordinated by a "patch pumpkin holder," or "pumpking"—a programmer of discernment and taste who, with help from Larry, decides which contributions make the grade and when, and bears the heavy responsibility of releasing a new Perl to the world. They maintain the most current and official source to Perl, which they sometimes make available to the public: you can find the latest Perl at ftp://ftp.linux.activestate.com/pub/staff/gsar/APC/perl-current/.

Why a pumpkin? To allow people to work on various areas of Perl at the same time and to avoid two people changing the same area in different ways, one person has to take responsibility for bits of development, and all changes are to go through them. Hence, the person who has the patch pumpkin is the only person who is allowed to make the change. Chip Salzenburg explains: "David Croy once told me that at a previous job, there was one tape drive and multiple systems that used it for backups. But instead of some high-tech exclusion software, they used a low-tech method to prevent multiple simultaneous backups: a stuffed pumpkin. No one was allowed to make backups unless they had the 'backup pumpkin'."

So what development happens? As well as bug fixes, the main focus of development is to allow Perl to build more easily on a wider range of computers and to make better use of what the operating system and the hardware provides—support for 64-bit processors, for example. The Perl compiler is steadily getting more useful but still has a way to go. There's also a range of optimizations to be done to make Perl faster and more efficient, and work progresses to provide more helpful and more accurate documentation. Finally, there are a few enhancements to Perl syntax that are being debated—the Todo file in the Perl source kit explains what's currently on the table.

The future of Perl lies in Perl 6, a complete rewrite of Perl. The purpose of Perl 6 is to address the problems with Perl 5 and to create a language that will continue to grow and change in the future. Larry Wall has this to say about Perl 6:

> *Perl 5 was my rewrite of Perl. I want Perl 6 to be the community's rewrite of Perl and of the community.*

There are several changes to the Perl language that are in the works for Perl 6 including enhanced and improved regular expression syntax, more powerful function definitions, some changes to the constructs (including the addition of a switch statement), new object-oriented syntax, and more. Stay tuned for more information—it is definitely a work in progress.

A big change in Perl 6 is the introduction of Parrot (www.parrotcode.org). Parrot is the new runtime environment that is being developed from scratch for Perl 6, but it will not be limited to Perl 6—any bytecode-compiled language such as Tcl and Python can use it.

You can read all about the future of Perl at http://dev.perl.org/perl6/. Stay informed, and get involved!

Why Perl?

The name "Perl" isn't really an acronym. People like making up acronyms though, and Larry has two favorite expansions. Perl is, according to its creator, the Practical Extraction and Report Language, or the Pathologically Eclectic Rubbish Lister. Either way, it doesn't really matter. Perl is a language for doing what you want to do easily and quickly.

The Perl motto is "There's More Than One Way To Do It," emphasizing both the flexibility of Perl and the fact that Perl is about getting the job done. This motto is so important someone has created an acronym for it: TMTOWTDI (pronounced "TimToeDee"). This acronym will come up again and again in this book since we often talk about many ways of doing the same thing. We can say that one Perl program is faster, or more idiomatic, or more efficient than another, but if both do the same thing, Perl isn't going to judge which one is "better." It also means that you don't need to know every last little detail about the language in order to do what you want with it. You'll probably be able to achieve a lot of the tasks you might want to use Perl for after the first four or five chapters of this book.

Perl has some very obvious strengths:

- It's easy to learn, and learning a little Perl can get you a long way. Perl is a lot like English in this regard—you don't need to know a lot of English to get your point across (as evidenced by a three year old who wants a particular toy for her birthday), but if you know quite a bit about the English language, you can say a lot with a little.

- Perl was designed to be easy for humans to write, rather than easy for computers to understand—the syntax of the language is a lot more like a human language than the strict, rigid grammars and structures of other languages, and so it doesn't impose any particular way of thinking upon you.

- Perl is very portable. That means what it sounds like—you can pick up a Perl program and carry it around between computers. Perl is available for a huge variety of operating systems and computers, and properly written programs should be able to run almost anywhere that Perl does without any change.

- Perl talks text. It can think about words and sentences, where other languages see a character at a time. It can think about files in terms of lines, not individual bytes. Its regular expressions allow you to search for and transform text in innumerable ways with ease and speed.

- Perl is what is termed a "high-level language." Some languages like C concern you with unnecessary, low-level details about the computer's operation: making sure you have enough free memory, making sure all parts of your program are set up properly before you try to use them, and leaving you with strange and unfriendly errors if you don't do so. Perl cuts you free from all this.

However, since Perl is so easy to learn and to use, especially for quick little administrative tasks, "real" Perl users in practice tend to write programs to achieve small, specific jobs. In these cases, the code is meant to have a short lifespan, and be for the programmer's eyes only. The problem is, these programs may live a little longer than the programmer expects, and be seen by other eyes too. The result is a cryptic one-liner that is incomprehensible to everyone but the original programmer (and sometimes incomprehensible to him a year later). Because of the proliferation of these rather concise and confusing programs, Perl has developed a reputation for being arcane and unintelligible, one that will hopefully be dispelled during the course of this book.

For starters, this reputation is unfair. It's possible to write code that is tortuous and difficult to follow in any programming language, and Perl was never meant to be difficult. In fact, one could say that Perl is one of the easiest languages to learn, especially given its scope and flexibility.

Throughout this book will be examples showing you how to avoid the stereotypical "spaghetti code" and how to write programs that are both easy to write and easy to follow.

It's Open Source

Larry started (and indeed, continued) Perl with the strong belief that software should be free—freely available, freely modifiable, and freely distributable. It is part of a collection of programs known as open source (see www.opensource.org for details). Perl is developed and maintained by the porters, who are volunteers from the Perl user community, all of who strive to make Perl as good as possible.

This has a few nice side effects—the porters are working for love, rather than merely because it's their job, and they're motivated solely by their desire to see a better Perl. It also means Perl will continue to be free to use and distribute.

This doesn't mean that Perl is part of the GNU suite of utilities. The GNU project was set up to produce a freely usable, distributable, and modifiable version of the Unix operating system and its tools, and now produces a lot of helpful, free utilities. Perl is included in distributions of GNU software, but Perl itself is not a product of the Free Software Foundation, the body that oversees GNU.

While Perl can be distributed under the terms of the GNU Public License (which you can find at www.gnu.org), it can also be distributed under the Artistic License (found either with the Perl sources or at www.opensource.org/licenses), which purports to give more freedom to users and more security to developers than the GPL.

Of course, those wanting to use Perl at work might be a little put off by this—managers like to pay money for things and have pieces of paper saying that they can get irate at someone if it all stops working. There's a question in the Perl Frequently Asked Questions (FAQ) about how to get a commercial version or support for Perl, and we'll see how you can find out the answer for yourself pretty soon.

When we say, "Anyone can help," we don't mean anyone who can understand the whole of the Perl source code. Of course, people who can knuckle down and attack the source files are useful, but equally useful work is done by the army of volunteers who offer their services as testers, documenters, proofreaders, and so on. Anyone who can take the time to check the spelling or grammar of some of the core documentation can help, as can anyone who can think of a new way of explaining a concept, or anyone who can come up with a more helpful example for a function.

Perl development is done in the open, on the perl5-porters mailing list. The `perlbug` program, shipped with Perl, can be used to report problems to the list, but it's a good idea to check with someone first to make sure that it really is a problem and that it isn't fixed in a later or development release of Perl.

Perl on the Web and the Network

One of the most popular uses of Perl is CGI programming—that is, dynamically generating web pages. This is introduced in Chapter 14. Perl is the power behind some of the most popular sites on the web: Slashdot (www.slashdot.org), Amazon (www.amazon.com), and many others besides are almost entirely Perl driven.

Of course, Perl is still widely used for its original purpose: extracting data from one source and translating it to another format. This covers everything from processing and summarizing system logs, through manipulating databases, reformatting text files, and simple search-and-replace operations, to something like `alien`, a program to port Linux software packages between different distributors' packaging formats. Perl even manages the data from the Human Genome Project, a task requiring massive amounts of data manipulation.

For system administrators, Perl is certainly the "Swiss Army chainsaw" that it claims to be. It's great for automating administration tasks, sending automatically generated mails, and generally tidying up the system. It can process logs, report information on disk usage, produce reports on resource use, and watch for security problems. There are also extensions that allow Perl to deal with the Windows registry and run as a Windows NT service, not to mention functions built into it that allow it to manipulate UNIX `passwd` and `group` file entries.

However, as you might expect, that's not all. Perl is becoming the de facto programming language of the Internet—its networking capabilities have allowed it to be used to create clients, servers, and proxies for things such as IRC, WWW, FTP, and practically every other protocol you wish to think of. It's used to filter mail, automatically post news articles, mirror websites, automate downloading and uploading, and so on. In fact, it's hard to find an area of the Internet in which Perl isn't used. This is kind of like duct tape, really. When was the last time you used duct tape to tape a duct?

Windows, Unix, and Other Operating Systems

Perl is one of the most portable, if not the most portable, programming languages around. It can be compiled on over 70 operating systems, and you can get binary distributions for most common platforms. Most of the programs in this book can run equally well on almost any operating system.

When we're setting up Perl and running our examples, we'll concentrate particularly on Unix and Windows. The term *Unix* describes any commercial or free Unix-like implementation—Solaris; Linux; Net-, Free-, and OpenBSD; HP/UX; A/IX; and so on. Perl's home platform is Unix, and 90% of the world uses Windows. That said, the Perl language is the same for everyone. If you need help with your particular platform, you will probably be able to find a README file for it in the Perl source distribution.

You can also get more information on portable Perl programming from the `perlport` documentation. Again, you'll see how to access this documentation very soon.

Program Names

Perl doesn't care what we programmers name our scripts, but this book uses the conventional filename extension .pl. For instance, one of our first programs will be named helloworld.pl.

The Prompt

If you're primarily using your computer in a graphical environment like Windows or X, you may not be familiar with using the command line interface, or *shell*. Before these graphical environments came into common use, users had to start a new program not by finding its icon and clicking it, but by typing its name. The shell is the program that takes the name from you—the *shell prompt* (or just *prompt*) refers specifically to the text that prompts you to enter a new program name, and more generally to working with the shell instead of using a graphical interface. Some people still find working with the shell much easier, and sophisticated shells have developed to simplify common tasks. In fact, on Unix, the shell is programmable, and Perl takes some of its inspiration from standard "Bourne Shell" programming practices.

To get to a prompt in Windows, look for Command Prompt or DOS Prompt in the Start menu. Unix users should look for a program called something like console, terminal, konsole, xterm, eterm, or kterm. You'll then be faced with a usually black screen with a small amount of text on it that says various things like

```
$
%
C:\>
#
bash$
```

If your shell prompt is #, chances are you are running the shell as the root user. This is usually a bad idea—use with caution!

For the purposes of this book, however, we'll use a prompt that looks like this:

```
$
```

We'll show text that you type in using a bold font, and the text the computer generates in normal typeface, like this:

```
$ perl helloworld.pl
Hello, world!
```

More on what this program looks like in just a few pages.

The command line may look scary at first, but you'll quickly get used to it as we go through the following examples and exercises.

A note to Unix/Linux/OpenBSD/etc. users: a Perl program can be executed from the shell with

```
$ perl -w helloworld.pl
Hello, world!
```

Or, if the first line of the file resembles

```
#! /usr/bin/perl -w
```

and the file has the proper executable permissions set, then it can be executed as

```
$ ./helloworld.pl
Hello, world!
```

Since both methods of invoking the program work in Unix/Linux/OpenBSD/etc., and only the first will work in Windows, the examples in this book will be executed using the first style.

What Do I Need to Use This Book?

First, you'll need Perl. As mentioned previously, Perl is available for almost any kind of computer that has a keyboard and a screen, but we will be concentrating on Perl for Windows and Unix. Perl 5.8.3 will run on Windows NT, 2000, and XP. It'll run on more or less any Unix, although you may find compilation is difficult if you don't have the latest C libraries. Any 2.x Linux kernel should be fine, likewise Solaris 2.6 or higher. Perl is also available on Apple Macintosh computers—see www.macperl.com for Mac OS 9 and below; for Mac OS X, it is found in /usr/bin/perl.

As well as Perl itself, you'll need a text editor to write and edit Perl source files. We look at a couple of options later in this introduction.

To get the most out of some chapters, you'll also need to have an Internet connection. A helpful place to start on the Internet is www.apress.com, where you can download all the source code for the examples found in the book.

For Chapter 14, you'll need a web server that supports CGI scripting. Apache is a good bet on Unix machines (and it's included in most Linux distributions). Windows users should also use Apache; check it out at www.apache.org.

How Do I Get Perl?

Perl has been ported to many, many platforms. It will almost certainly build and run on anything that looks like (or pretends to be) Unix, such as Linux, Solaris, A/IX, HP/UX, FreeBSD, or even the Cygwin32 UNIX environment for Windows. Most other current operating systems are supported: Windows, OS/2, VMS, DOS, BeOS, the Apple Mac OS, and AmigaOS, to name but a few.

- You can get the source to the latest stable release of Perl from www.perl.com/ CPAN-local/src/stable.tar.gz.

- Binary distributions for some ports will appear in www.perl.com/CPAN-local/ports/. These ports may differ in implementation from the original sources.

- You can get binary packages of Perl for Linux, Solaris, and Windows from ActiveState at www.activestate.com/ActivePerl/download.htm.

- Linux users should be able to get binary packages from the `contrib` section of their distributor's FTP site.

Installing Perl is well documented at the websites mentioned, so we won't go through the steps here. Go and install Perl now—reading this book will be much more fun if you can try the examples.

How to Get Help

Perl comes with an excellent set of documentation. The interface to this system is through the perldoc command, itself a Perl program. Unix users can also use the man command to get at the same information, but perldoc allows you to do interesting things, as you're about to see.

Perldoc

Typing perldoc perl from a command prompt presents the Perl documentation table of contents and some basic information about Perl.

The pages you're probably going to use the most are the Perl FAQ and perlfunc, which describes the built-in functions. Because of this, perldoc has a special interface to these two pages. perldoc -f allows you to see information about a particular function, like this (the output has been snipped—try it yourself!):

```
$ perldoc -f print
print FILEHANDLE LIST
print LIST
print   Prints a string or a list of strings.  Returns true if success-
        ful.  FILEHANDLE may be a scalar variable name, in which case

        [output snipped]...
```

Similarly, perldoc -q allows you to search the Perl FAQ for any regular expression or keyword.

```
$ perldoc -q reverse
Found in /usr/lib/perl5/5.8.3/pod/perlfaq4.pod
  How do I reverse a string?
     Use reverse() in scalar context, as documented in the reverse
     entry in the perlfunc manpage

     $reversed = reverse $string;
```

As well as the documentation pages for the language itself, whose names all start with "perl", there's an awful lot of other documentation out there too. The reason for this is modules: files containing Perl code that can be used to help with a certain task. We'll examine what modules are available and what they can help us do later on, but you should know that each Perl module, whether a core module that comes with the Perl distribution, or one you download from the Internet, should contain its own documentation. We'll see how that's constructed later—for now though, know that you can use perldoc to get at this too. Here's the beginning of the documentation for the Text::Wrap module, which is used to wrap lines into paragraphs:

```
$ perldoc Text::Wrap
5.8.3::Text  User Contributed Perl Documentation  Text::Wrap(3)


NAME
      Text::Wrap - line wrapping to form simple paragraphs

...
```

Perl Resources

There is truly a wealth of Perl information available out there, and especially on the Internet. Let's have a look at some of the more prominent ones.

Websites

On the web, the first port of call is www.perl.com, the main Perl community site. This site contains some good articles of interest to the Perl community and news from Perl's major developers, as well as a wealth of links, tips, reviews, and documentation.

The next stop is CPAN, the Comprehensive Perl Archive Network (www.cpan.org), a collection of ready-made programs, documents, notably the latest edition of the FAQ, some tutorials, and the Far More Than Everything You Wanted To Know About[1] series of more technical notes. Most useful of all, this site contains a huge (and they don't call it comprehensive for nothing!) collection of those Perl modules mentioned previously.

Other important Perl sites are listed here:

- www.perl.org: A site with tons of information about Perl

- www.pm.org: The Perl Mongers, a worldwide umbrella organization for Perl user groups

- www.theperlreview.com: The home of the *Perl Review*, an online Perl magazine

- www.activestate.com: The home of Perl on Windows

- www.perlarchive.com: Another great source of articles, tutorials, and information

Newsgroups

Perl has its own Usenet hierarchy, comp.lang.perl.*. The groups in it are listed here:

- comp.lang.perl.announce for Perl-related announcements: new modules, new versions of Perl, conferences and so on

- comp.lang.perl.misc for general Perl chat and questions

---

1. Yup, there is an acronym for this phrase—FMTEYWTKA.

- comp.lang.perl.moderated, which requires prior registration before posting, but is excellent for sensible questions and in-depth discussion of Perl's niggly bits

- comp.lang.perl.modules, for discussion and queries relating to creating and using Perl modules

- comp.lang.perl.tk, for discussion and queries relating to the Tk graphical extensions

IRC

If you've got a more urgent mindbender, or just want to hang around like-minded individuals, come join #perl on Efnet (www.efnet.org). Make sure you read the channel rules (at http://pound.perl.org/RTFM/) and the Perl documentation thoroughly first. Asking questions about CGI or topics covered in the FAQ or the perldoc documentation is highly inflammatory behavior.

Books

Of course, reading stuff from the Net is a great way to learn, but it is difficult to curl up in bed with a good website (unless you have a WiFi-enabled laptop).

In the meantime, there are a few good treeware resources available too. Check out the book reviews pages housed at the www.perl.com and www.perl.org sites.

As for the best book for teaching yourself Perl, just keep reading . . .

Downloading This Book's Example Source Code

As you work through the examples in this book, you might decide that you prefer to type all the code in by hand. Many readers prefer this because it's a good way to get familiar with the coding techniques that are being used.

Whether you want to type the code in or not, we have made all the source code for this book available at our website, at the following address: www.apress.com.

If you're one of those readers who likes to type in the code, you can use our files to check the results you should be getting—they should be your first stop if you think you might have typed in an error. If you're one of those readers who doesn't like typing, then downloading the source code from our website is a must!

Either way, it'll help you with updates and debugging.

Exercises

At the end of most of this book's chapters, you'll find a number of exercises that we highly recommend you work through. This book will give you the knowledge you need—but it is only through practice that you will hone your skills and get a true feel for what Perl can help you achieve. You can find our suggested solutions to the exercises in the Appendix at the back of the book and also for download from www.apress.com, but remember, TMTOWTDI, so they're not the only ways to solve the exercises.

Who This Book Is For

This book is written for the novice programmer and the experienced programmer alike. Using extensive use of examples, the features of Perl are introduced and discussed in a way that is easy to learn for the newcomer and useful for the veteran.

If you are looking to learn Perl and get an introduction to its power, this book is for you.

How This Book Is Organized

Chapter 1—"First Steps in Perl": The basics of Perl are introduced, including how to execute Perl code. A simple first program is developed.

Chapter 2—"Scalars": The most basic Perl data type, the scalar, is described. Perl's arithmetic, logical, and string operators are explained, as are a few of Perl's simplest control flow constructs: if and while. Several functions are discussed including chop(), chomp(), exit(), and die().

Chapter 3—"Control Flow Constructs": The control flow constructs are discussed. These include if, unless, while, until, do .. while, do .. until, for, and foreach. We also talk about expression modifiers and short-circuited operators as alternative ways of writing constructs.

Chapter 4—"Lists and Arrays": We talk about the array data type—a collection of 0 or more scalars. Lists and list operators are also discussed. The array functions push(), pop(), shift(), unshift(), reverse(), and sort() are described as well as the foreach loop.

Chapter 5—"Hashes": Hashes, the third major data type, are discussed. We describe what hashes are, why we need them, and how to operate upon them. We talk about the hash functions keys(), values(), each(), delete(), and exists().

Chapter 6—"Subroutines/Functions": This chapter talks about user-defined functions. Function definitions are discussed, as well as function invocation, return values, and passing arguments.

Chapter 7—"Regular Expressions": One of Perl's features that makes it a powerful text processing language is discussed. The basics of regular expressions are introduced, including creating character classes and regex quantifiers. Regex memory, a powerful feature allowing the programmer to extract text, is covered. Several operators including the match operator and the substitute operator are introduced.

Chapter 8—"Files and Data": Opening files for reading and writing data are discussed. Following this, the topic of reading from files that are provided on the command line using the diamond is covered. Pipes to external processes and pipes from processes are described. File test operators, which test certain qualities of files such as readability and writability, are introduced.

Chapter 9—"String Processing": String manipulation functions and operators are introduced including length(), index(), rindex(), substr(), and tr///.

Chapter 10—"Interfacing to the Operating System": Functions such as chdir(), mkdir(), rename(), and others are discussed. Also, executing external programs with system() and backquotes are introduced. Reading the contents of a directory using directory streams are also covered.

Chapter 11—"References": A reference is a scalar that refers to another variable in memory. The topics covered include creating references, dereferencing references, creating anonymous variables, and complex data types.

Chapter 12—"Object-Oriented Perl": The basics of creating a class definition in Perl are described, including creating objects with attributes and methods. Inheritance is briefly introduced.

Chapter 13—"Modules": Using existing modules to easily solve complex problems is described. Several useful modules are discussed and demonstrated. Creating a module from scratch is illustrated.

Chapter 14—"Introduction to CGI": Perl is a popular language to do CGI, or web, programming. This chapter introduces CGI.pm, a popular Perl module to make writing CGI programs easy.

Chapter 15—"Perl and DBI": The useful DBI module enables a Perl programmer to easily write powerful scripts that connect to and query an SQL database. This chapter introduces the idea of relational databases and SQL. Several Perl scripts to administer a database are described. Then a detailed example is discussed that shows how to use CGI.pm and the DBI module to web-enable SQL access.

## CHAPTER 1

First Steps in Perl

Every programming language has a number of things in common. The fundamental concepts of programming are going to be the same, no matter what language in which you do them. In this chapter, we'll investigate the things you need to know before you start writing any programs at all. For instance:

- What is programming anyway? What does it mean to program?

- How do we structure programs, and make them easy to understand?

- How do computers see numbers and letters?

- How do we find and eliminate errors in our programs?

Of course, we'll be looking at these from a Perl perspective, and we'll look at a couple of basic Perl programs, and see how they're constructed and what they do. At the end of this chapter, you will be asked to write a couple of trivial Perl programs of your own.

Programming Languages

The first question we should ask ourselves when we're learning programming is, "What is programming?" That may sound particularly philosophical, but the answer is easy. Programming is telling a computer what you want it to do; and we do this by writing it a program. The only trick, then, is making sure that the program is written in a way the computer can understand, and to do this, we need to write it in a language that it can comprehend—a programming language, such as Perl.

There's nothing magical about writing a program, but it does call for a particular way of thinking. When you're telling a human what you want them to do, you take certain things for granted.

- The human can ask questions if they don't understand your instructions.

- They can break up tasks into smaller tasks by themselves.

- They can draw parallels between the current task and a task they have completed in the past.

- Perhaps most importantly, they can learn from demonstrations and from their own mistakes.

Computers can't yet do any of these things very well—it's still much easier to explain to someone how to tie their shoelaces than it is to set the clock on the VCR.

The most important thing you need to bear in mind, though, is that you're never going to be able to express a task to a computer if you can't express it to yourself. Computer programming leaves little room for vague specifications and hand waving. If you want to write a program to, say, remove useless files from your computer, you need to be able to explain how to determine whether a file is useless or not. You need to examine and break down your own mental processes when carrying out the task for yourself—do you mean a file that hasn't been accessed for a long time? How long, precisely? Then do you delete it immediately, or do you examine it? If you examine it, how much of it? And what are you examining it for?

The first step in programming is to stop thinking in terms of "I want a program that removes useless files," but instead think "I want a program that looks at each file on the computer in turn and deletes the file if it is over six months old, and if the first five lines do not contain any of the words 'Simon', 'Perl', or 'Camel'"—in other words, you have to specify your task precisely.

When you're able to do that, you need to translate that into the programming language you're using. Unfortunately, like any human language, the programming language may not have a direct equivalent for what you're trying to say. So, you have to get your meaning across using the parts of the language that are available to you, and this may well mean breaking down your task further. For instance, there's no way of saying "if the first five lines do not contain any of the following words" in Perl. However, there is a way of saying "if a line contains this word," a way of saying "get another line," and "do this five times." Programming is the art of putting those elements together to get them to do what you want.

So much for what you have to do—what does the computer have to do? Once we have specified the task in our programming language, the computer takes our instructions and performs them. This is called *running* or *executing* the program. Usually, we'll specify the instructions in a file, which we edit with an ordinary text editor; sometimes, if we have got a small program, we can get away with typing the whole thing in at the command line. Either way, the instructions that we give to the computer—in this case, written in Perl—are collectively called the *source code* (or sometimes just *source*) to our program.

Our First Perl Program

Assuming that you now have a copy of Perl installed on your machine (perhaps having followed the instructions in the Introduction), you are ready to start using Perl. If not, go back and follow the instructions. The next step is to set up a directory for all the examples used in the rest of the book, and to write our first Perl program.

Here's what it will look like:

```
#!/usr/bin/perl -w

print "Hello, world!\n";
```

We highly suggest that you type this example in and try to make it work, so before we go any further, a quick note on editors. Perl source code is just plain text, and should be written with a plain text editor, rather than a word processor. Your operating system, whether Unix or Windows, comes with a selection of text editors. You may have a favorite already, so feel free to use it. If not, may we suggest. vi (www.vim.org), emacs (www.xemacs.org), and nedit (www.nedit.org). Windows provides WordPad and Notepad, but they lack many features of modern text editors, so they should be avoided. nedit is the most WordPad- and Notepad-like, so give it a try.

After an editor is chosen, we need to create a new directory for our work. If you are in Windows, a simple way to do this is to start up a command shell (Start ➤ Run ➤ cmd) and enter

```
c:> mkdir begperl
c:> cd begperl
```

If you are working in any Unix variant, start a shell and enter

```
$ mkdir begperl
$ cd begperl
```

This directory will hold all the examples that we will do as we go through this book.

The next step is to fire up your editor of choice, type in the code shown previously, and save it into a file named helloworld.pl in the directory we just made. Then, to execute it, type

```
$ perl helloworld.pl
Hello, world!
$
```

Congratulations. You have successfully written and executed your first Perl program!

Note Note that from this point on, we'll not run through these steps again. Instead, the name we've given the file will be shown as a comment on the second line of the program.

You may also have noticed that the output for helloworld.pl on Windows and Unix differs in that Windows adds a blank line at the end of the output for all its Perl programs. From now on, we'll only print the Unix output that is without the additional blank line. Windows users please be aware of this.

Let's look at this program in detail by going through it a line at a time. The first line is

```
#!/usr/bin/perl -w
```

Normally, Perl treats a line starting with # as a comment, and ignores it. However, the # and ! characters together at the start of the first line tell Unix how the file should be run—in this case the file should be executed by the Perl interpreter, which lives in /usr/bin/perl in this example. In the Unix world, this line is known as the *shebang* (short for "hash bang"), and it must be located on the first line starting in the first column.

▓**Note** Note to Unix users: your version of Perl may reside in a different location than /usr/bin/perl. Common alternative locations are /usr/local/bin/perl and /opt/bin/perl. If your version of Perl resides somewhere other than /usr/bin/perl, you will have to adjust your shebang line to point to it.

Unix users can use the invocation shown previously to execute Perl programs:

```
$ perl helloworld.pl
```

But they can also execute Perl programs by making the file executable with the chmod command and executing it by name like this:

```
$ chmod +x helloworld.pl
$ ./helloworld.pl
```

Perl also reads the shebang line regardless of whether you are on Unix, Windows, or any other system. The reason for this is to see if there are any special options it should turn on. In this case, -w is present and it instructs Perl to turn on the reporting of warnings (we'll talk more about warnings later in this chapter).

The second line of this program is a blank line. Perl, like C, C++, and many other programming languages, treats blank lines, extra spaces, and tabs as *whitespace*. In Perl, whitespace can be added to the program to make it more readable.

The third line of the program is

```
print "Hello, world!\n";
```

The print() function tells Perl to display the given text, without the quotation marks. The text inside the quotes is not interpreted as code, and is called a *string*. As we'll see later, strings start and end with some sort of quotation mark. The \n at the end of the quote is a type of escape sequence which stands for "new line." This instructs Perl to finish the current line and take the prompt to the start of a new one.

You may be wondering why -w is so helpful. Suppose we altered our program to demonstrate this, and made two mistakes by leaving out -w and modifying our code so it looks like this:

```
#!/usr/bin/perl

print "Hello, $world!\n";
```

The string that we are printing now contains the text $world. As we will see in the next chapter, $world is a variable, and this variable has not been assigned a value. If we attempt to print a variable that has no value, we simply print nothing.

Save these changes in helloworld2.pl before exiting your editor. Now let's get back to the command prompt, and type the following:

```
$ perl helloworld2.pl
```

Instead of getting the expected

```
Hello, world!
$
```

the output would be

```
Hello, !
$
```

If we now correct one of the mistakes by including -w in our program, then helloworld2.pl looks like this:

```
#!/usr/bin/perl -w

print "Hello, $world!\n";
```

Once we have saved this new change into the program, we can run it again. The output that we get now contains a warning as well as the text printed, so the screen looks like this:

```
$ perl helloworld2.pl
Use of uninitialized value in concatenation (.) or string at helloworld2.pl line 3.
Hello, !
```

On the surface of things, it may seem that we have just given ourselves another line of output, but bear in mind that the first line is now a *warning message*, and is informing us that Perl has picked something up that may (or may not) cause problems later on in our program. Don't worry if you don't understand everything in the error message at the moment, just so long as you are beginning to see the usefulness of having an early warning system in place.

For Perl versions 5.6.x and higher, the -w switch can be replaced with a use warnings directive that follows *after* the shebang line:

```
#!/usr/bin/perl
use warnings;

print "Hello, world!\n";
```

However, this code will not turn on warnings in Perl for versions pre-5.6. For backward compatibility, we will stick with the -w option.

Program Structure

One of the things we want to develop throughout this book is a sense of good programming practice. Obviously this will not only benefit you while using Perl, but in almost every other programming language too. The most fundamental notion is how to structure and lay out the code in your source files. By keeping this tidy and easy to understand, you'll make your own life as a programmer easier.

Documenting Your Programs

As we mentioned earlier, a line starting with a hash, or pound sign (#), is treated as a comment, and ignored. This allows you to provide comments about what your program is doing, something that will become extremely useful to you when working on long programs, or when someone else is looking over your code. For instance, you could make it quite clear what the preceding program was doing by saying something like this:

```
#!/usr/bin/perl -w
```

```
# print a short message
print "Hello, world!\n";
```

A line may contain some Perl code, and be followed by a comment. This means that we can document our program "inline" like this:

```
#!/usr/bin/perl -w
```

```
print "Hello, world!\n"; # print a short message
```

When we come to write more advanced programs, we'll take a look at some good and bad commenting practice.

Keywords

A *keyword* is a term in Perl that has a predefined meaning. One example would be the term use as we saw in the statement

```
use warnings;
```

Other types of keywords include built-in functions such as print() and control flow constructs such as if and while. We will talk about many built-in functions and control flow constructs in detail as we progress in our discussion of Perl.

It's a good idea to respect keywords and not give anything else the same name as one. For example, a little later on we'll learn that you can create and name a variable, and that calling your variable $print is perfectly allowable. The problem with this is that it leads to confusing and uninformative statements like print $print. It is always a good idea to give a variable a meaningful name, one that relates to its content in a logical manner. For example, $my_name, @telephone_numbers, %account_info, and so on, rather than $a, @b, and %c.

Statements and Statement Blocks

If functions are the verbs of Perl, then *statements* are the sentences. Instead of a period, a statement in Perl usually ends with a semicolon, as we saw earlier:

```
print "Hello, world!\n";
```

To print some more text, we can add another statement:

```
print "Hello, world!\n";
print "Goodbye, world!\n";
```

We can also group together a bunch of statements into a *block*—which is a bit like a paragraph—by surrounding them with curly braces { . . . }. We'll see later how blocks are used to specify a set of statements that must happen at a given time, and also how they are used to limit the effects of a statement. Here's an example of a block:

```
{
    print "This is ";
    print "a block ";
    print "of statements.\n";
}
```

Notice how indentation is used to separate the block from its surroundings. This is because, unlike paragraphs, you can put blocks inside of blocks, which makes it easier to see on what level things are happening. This:

```
print "Top level\n";
{
    print "2nd level\n";
    {
        print "3rd level\n";
    }
    print "Where are we?";
}
```

is easier to follow than this:

```
print "Top level\n";
{
print "2nd level\n";
{
print "3rd level\n";
}
print "Where are we?";
}
```

As well as curly braces to mark out the territory of a block of statements, you can use parentheses to mark out what you're giving a function. The set of things given to a function are the *arguments*; and you *pass* the arguments to the function. For instance, you can pass a number of arguments to the print() function by separating them with commas:

```
print "here ", "we ", "print ", "several ", "strings.\n";
```

The print() function happily takes as many arguments as it is given, and it produces the expected answer:

```
here we print several strings.
```

Surrounding the arguments with parentheses clears things up a bit:

```
print("here ", "we ", "print ", "several ", "strings.\n");
```

In the cases where parentheses are optional, the important thing to do is to use your judgment. Sometimes something will look perfectly understandable without the parentheses, but when you've got a complicated statement and you need to be sure of which arguments belong to which function, putting in the parentheses is useful. Always aim to help the readers of your code, and remember that these readers will more than likely include you.

Escape Sequences

UTF8 gives us 65536 characters, and ASCII gives us 256 characters, but on the average keyboard, there's only a hundred or so keys. Even using the shift keys, there will still be some characters that you aren't going to be able to type. There'll also be some things that you don't want to stick in the middle of your program, because they would make it messy or confusing. However, you'll want to refer to some of these characters in strings that you output. Perl provides us with mechanisms called *escape sequences* as an alternative way of getting to them. We've already seen the use of \n to start a new line. Table 1-1 lists the more common escape sequences.

Table 1-1. *Escape Sequences*

Escape Sequence	Meaning
\t	Tab
\n	Start a new line (usually called *newline*)
\r	Carriage return
\b	Back up one character (*backspace*)
\a	Alarm (rings the system bell)
\x{1F18}	Unicode character

In the last example, 1F18 is a hexadecimal number (see the upcoming section "Number Systems") referring to a character in the Unicode character set, which runs from 0000-FFFF. As another example, \x{2620} is the Unicode character for a skull-and-crossbones!

Whitespace

As mentioned previously, *whitespace* is the name we give to tabs, spaces, and newlines. Perl is very flexible about where you put whitespace in your program. We have already seen how we're free to use indentation to help show the structure of blocks. You don't need to use any whitespace at all, if you don't want to. If you'd prefer, your programs can all look like this:

```
print"Top level\n";{print"2nd level\n";{print"3rd level\n";}print"Where are we?";}
```

This is considered a bad idea. Whitespace is another tool we have to make our programs more understandable; let's use it as such.

Number Systems

If you thought the way computers see characters was weird, we have a surprise for you.

The way most humans count is using the decimal system, or what is called base 10; we write 0, 1, 2, 3, 4, 5, 6, 7, 8, 9, and then when we get to 10, we carry 1 in the 10s column and start from 0 again. Then when the 10s column gets to 9 and the 1s column gets to 9, we carry 1 in the 100s column and start again. Why 10? We used to think it's because we have 10 fingers, but then we found out that the Babylonians counted up to 60, which stopped that.

On the other hand, computers count by registering whether or not electricity flows in a certain part of the circuit. For simplicity's sake, we'll call a flow of electricity a 1, and no flow a 0. So, we start off with 0, no flow. Then we get a flow, which represents 1. That's as much as we can do with that part of the circuit. 0 or 1, off or on. Instead of base 10, the decimal system, this is *base 2, the binary system*. In the binary system, one digit represents one unit of information: one **binary digit**, or *bit*.

When we join two parts of the circuit together, things get more interesting. Look at them both in a row, when they are both off, the counter reads 00. Then one comes on, so we get 01. Then what? Well, humans get to 9 and have to carry 1 to the next column, but computers only get to 1. The next number, number 2, is represented as 10. Then 11. And we need some more of our circuit. Number 4 is 100, 5 is 101, and so ad infinitum. If we got used to it, and we used the binary system naturally, we could count up to 1023 on our fingers.

This may sound like an abnormal way to count, but even stranger counting mechanisms are all around us. As this is being written, it's 7:59 p.m. In one minute, it'll be 8:00 p.m., which seems unremarkable. But that's a base 60 system. In fact, it's worse than that—it doesn't stay in base 60, because hours carry at 24 instead of 60. Anyone who's used the Imperial measurement system, a Chinese abacus, or pounds, shillings, and pence knows the full horror of mixed base systems, which are far more complicated than what we're dealing with here.

As well as binary, there are two more important sequences we need to know about when talking to computers. We don't often get to deal with binary directly, but the following two sequences have a logical relationship to base 2 counting. The first is *octal, base 8*.

Eight is an important number in computing; bits are organized in groups of eight to form *byte*s, giving you the range of 0–255 we saw earlier with ASCII. Each ASCII character can be represented by one byte. Octal is therefore a good way of counting bits, although it has fallen out of fashion these days. Octal numbers all start with 0 (that's a zero, not an oh), so we know they're octal, and proceed as you'd expect: 00, 01, 02, 03, 04, 05, 06, 07, carry one, 010, 011, 012 . . . 017, carry one, 020, and so on. Perl recognizes octal numbers if you're certain to put that zero in front, like this:

```
print 06301;
```

which prints out the decimal number

```
3265
```

The second is called the hexadecimal system, as mentioned previously. Of course, programmers are lazy, so they just call it *hex*. (They like the wizard image.)

Decimal is base 10, and hexagons have six sides, so this system is base 16. As you might have guessed from the number 1F18 shown previously, digits above 9 are represented by letters, so A is 10, B is 11, and so on, all the way through to F, which is 15. We then carry one and start with 10 (which, in decimal, is 16) all the way up through 19, 1A, 1B, 1C, 1D, 1E, 1F, and carry one again to get 20 (which in decimal is 32). The magic number 255, the maximum number we can store in one byte, is FF. Two bytes next to each other can get you up to FF FF, better known as 65535. We met 65535 as the highest number in the Unicode character set, and you guessed it, a Unicode character can be stored as a pair of bytes.

To get Perl to recognize hex, place 0x in front of the digits so that

```
print 0xBEEF;
```

gives the answer

```
48879
```

The Perl Debugger

One thing you'll soon notice about programming is that you'll make mistakes; mistakes in programs are called *bugs*. Bugs are almost entirely unavoidable, and creating bugs does not mean you're a bad programmer. Windows 2000 allegedly shipped with 65,000 bugs, but then that's a special case, and even the greatest programmers in the world have problems with bugs. Donald Knuth's typesetting software TeX has been in use for more than 20 years, and Professor Knuth was still finding bugs until a couple of years ago. Who can tell when all the bugs are out anyway?

While we will be showing you ways to avoid getting bugs in your program, Perl provides you with a tool to help find and trace the causes of bugs. Naturally, any tool for getting rid of bugs in your program is called a *debugger*. Mundanely enough, the corresponding tool for putting bugs into your program is called a "programmer."

To use the debugger, start your program with the -d option as in

```
$ perl -d myprogram.pl
```

See perldoc perldebug for information about the debugger.

Summary

We've started on the road to programming in Perl, and programming in general. We've seen our first piece of Perl code, and hopefully, you were able to get it to run.

Programming is basically telling a computer what to do in a language it comprehends. It's about breaking down problems or ideas into byte-sized chunks (as it were), and examining what needs to be done in order to communicate them clearly to the machine.

Thankfully, Perl is a language that allows us a certain degree of freedom in our expression, and, so long as we work within the bounds of the language, it won't enforce any particular method of expression on us. Of course, it may judge what we're saying to be wrong, because we're not speaking the language correctly, and that's how the majority of bugs are born. Generally though, if a program does what we want, that's enough—TMTOWTDI.

We've also seen a few ways of making it easy for ourselves to spot potential problems, and we know there are tools that can help us if we need it. We have examined a little bit of what goes on inside a computer, how it sees numbers, and how it sees characters, as well as what it does to our programs when and as it executes them.

Exercises

1. Create a program `newline.pl` containing `print "Hi Mom.\nThis is my second program.\n"`. Run this and then replace `\n` with a space or a return and compare the results.

2. Download the code for this book from the publisher's website at www.apress.com.

3. Have a look around the Perl homepage at www.perl.com.

CHAPTER 2

■■■

Scalars

The essence of programming is computation—we want the computer to do some work with the input (the data we give it). Very rarely do we write programs that tell us something we already know. Even more rarely do we write programs that do nothing interesting with our data at all. So, if we're going to write programs that do more than say hello to us, we're going to need to know how to perform computations, or operations on our data.

In this chapter, we will discuss several important basic ideas of programming in Perl:

- *Scalars:* Single values, either numbers or strings.

- *Variables:* A place to store a value.

- *Operators:* Symbols such as + and – that operate upon data.

- *Reading data from the user:* We will read from standard input, also known as the keyboard.

Types of Data

A lot of programming jargon is about familiar words in an unfamiliar context. We've already seen a string, which was a series of characters. We could also describe that string as a *scalar literal constant.* What does that mean?

By calling a value a *scalar,* we're describing the type of data it contains. If you remember your math (and even if you don't), a *scalar* is a plain, simple, one-dimensional value. In math, the word is used to distinguish it from a vector, which is expressed as several numbers. Velocity, for example, has a pair of coordinates (speed and direction), and so must be a vector. In Perl, a scalar is the fundamental, basic unit of data of which there are two kinds—numbers and strings.

A *literal* is value that never changes. The value 5 is a scalar literal—and is literally 5; it can never be 4. Perl has three types of scalar literals: integers (such as 5), floating point numbers (like 3.14159), and strings (for example "hello, world"). To put it another way, a literal is a *constant*—it never changes.

As opposed to a *variable* which is a piece of memory that can hold a scalar value. Variables are so named because the value stored within them can vary. For instance, $number can be assigned 5, and then later can be changed to the value 6. We will talk more about variables later in this chapter.

Numbers

There are two types of number that we are interested in as Perl programmers: integers and floating point numbers. The latter we'll come to in a minute, but let's work a bit with integers right now. Integers are whole numbers with no numbers after the decimal point like 42, –1, or 10. The following program prints a couple of integer literals in Perl.

```
#!/usr/bin/perl -w
# number1.pl

print 25, -4;
```

```
$ perl number1.pl
25-4$
```

Well, that's what you see, but it's not exactly what we want. Fortunately, this is pretty easy to fix. Firstly, we didn't tell Perl to separate the numbers with a space, and secondly, we didn't tell it to put a new line on the end. Let's change the program so it does that:

```
#!/usr/bin/perl -w
# number2.pl

print 25, " ", -4, "\n";
```

This will do what we were thinking of:

```
$ perl number2.pl
25 -4
$
```

For the purpose of human readability, we often write large integers such as 10000000 by splitting up the number with commas: 10,000,000. This is sometimes known as *chunking*. While we might write 10 million with a comma if we wrote a check for that amount, don't use the comma to chunk in a Perl program. Instead, use the underscore: 10_000_000. Change your program to look like the following:

```
#!/usr/bin/perl -w
# number3.pl

print 25_000_000, " ", -4, "\n";
```

Notice that those underscores don't appear in the output:

```
$ perl number3.pl
25000000 -4
$
```

As well as integers, there's another type of number—floating point numbers. These contain everything else, like 0.5, –0.01333, and 1.1.

Note that **floating point numbers are accurate to a certain number of digits**. For instance, the number 15.39 may in fact be stored in memory as 15.3899999999999. This is accurate enough for most scientists, so it will have to be for us programmers as well.

Here is an example of printing the approximate value of pi:

```perl
#!/usr/bin/perl -w
# number4.pl

print "pi is approximately: ", 3.14159, "\n";
```

Executing this program produces the following result:

```
$ perl number4.pl
pi is approximately: 3.14159
$
```

Binary, Hexadecimal, and Octal Numbers

As we saw in the previous chapter, we can express numbers as binary, hexadecimal, or octal numbers in our programs. Let's look at a program to demonstrate how we use the various number systems. Type in the following code, and save it as goodnums.pl:

```perl
#!/usr/bin/perl -w
# goodnums.pl

print 255,        "\n";
print 0377,       "\n";
print 0b11111111, "\n";
print 0xFF,       "\n";
```

All of these are representations of the number 255, and accordingly, we get the following output:

```
$ perl goodnums.pl
255
255
255
255
$
```

When Perl reads your program, it reads and understands numbers in any of the allowed number systems, 0 for octal, 0b for binary, and 0x for hex.

What happens, you might ask, if you specify a number in the wrong system? Well, let's try it out. Edit goodnums.pl to give you a new program, badnums.pl, that looks like this:

```perl
#!/usr/bin/perl -w
# badnums.pl
```

```
print 255,        "\n";
print 0378,       "\n";
print 0b11111112, "\n";
print 0xFG,       "\n";
```

Since octal digits only run from 0 to 7, binary digits from 0 to 1, and hex digits from 0 to F, none of the last three lines make any sense. Let's see what Perl makes of it:

```
$ perl badnums.pl
Bareword found where operator expected at badnums.pl line 7, near "0xFG"
        (Missing operator before G?)
Illegal octal digit '8' at badnums.pl line 5, at end of line
Illegal binary digit '2' at badnums.pl line 6, at end of line
syntax error at badnums.pl line 7, near "0xFG"
Execution of badnums.pl aborted due to compilation errors.
$
```

Now, let's match those errors up with the relevant lines:

```
Illegal octal digit '8' at badnums.pl line 5, at end of line
```

And line 5 is

```
print 0378,       "\n";
```

As you can see, Perl thought it was dealing with an octal number, but then along came an 8, which stopped making sense, so Perl quite rightly complained. The same thing happened on the next line:

```
Illegal binary digit '2' at badnums.pl line 6, at end of line
```

And line 4 is

```
print 0b11111112, "\n";
```

The problem with the next line is even bigger:

```
Bareword found where operator expected at badnums.pl line 7, near "0xFG"
        (Missing operator before G?)
syntax error at badnums.pl line 7, near "0xFG"
```

The line starting "Bareword" is a warning (since we are using the -w option). Then it is followed by a syntax error. A *bareword* is a series of characters outside of a string that Perl doesn't recognize. The word could mean a number of things, and Perl is usually quite good about knowing what you mean. In this case, the bareword was G: Perl had understood 0xF, but couldn't see how the G fitted in. We might have wanted an operator do something with it, but there was no operator there. In the end, Perl gave us a *syntax error*, which is the equivalent of it giving up and saying, "How do you expect me to understand this?"

Strings

The other type of scalar available to us is the string, and we've already seen a few examples of them. In the last chapter, we met the string "Hello, world!\n". A string is a series of characters surrounded by some sort of quotation marks. Strings can contain ASCII (or Unicode) data and escape sequences such as the \n of our example, and there is no maximum length restriction on a string imposed by Perl. Practically speaking there is a limit imposed by the amount of memory in your computer, but it's quite hard to hit.

Single- vs Double-Quoted Strings

The quotation marks you choose for your string are significant. So far we've only seen *double-quoted* strings, like this: "Hello, world!\n". There is another type of string—one which has been *single-quoted*. Predictably, they are surrounded by single quotes: ' '. The important difference is that no processing is done within single-quoted strings, except on \\ and \' . We'll also see later that variable names inside double-quoted strings are replaced by their contents, whereas single-quoted strings treat them as ordinary text. We call both these types of processing *interpolation*, and say that single-quoted strings are not interpolated.

Consider the following program, bearing in mind that \t is the escape sequence that represents a tab:

```
#!/usr/bin/perl -w
# quotes.pl

print '\tThis is a single quoted string.\n';
print "\tThis is a double quoted string.\n";
```

The double-quoted string will have its escape sequences processed, and the single-quoted string will not. The output is

```
$ perl quotes.pl
\tThis is a single quoted string.\n    This is a double quoted string.
$
```

What do we do if we want to have a backslash in a string? This is a common concern for Windows users, as a Windows path looks something like this: C:\WINNT\Profiles\ . . . In a double-quoted string, a backslash will start an escape sequence, which is not what we want it to do.

There is, of course, more than one way to do it. We can either use a single-quoted string, as shown previously, or we can *escape* the backslash. One principle that we'll see often in Perl, and especially when we get to regular expressions, is that we can use a backslash to turn off any special effect a character may have. This operation is called *escaping*, or more commonly, *backwhacking*.

In this case, we want to turn off the special effect a backslash has, and so we escape it:

```
#!/usr/bin/perl -w
# quotes2.pl

print "C:\\WINNT\\Profiles\\\n";
print 'C:\WINNT\Profiles\ ', "\n";
```

This prints the following:

```
$ perl quotes2.pl
C:\WINNT\Profiles\
C:\WINNT\Profiles\
$
```

Aha! Some of you may have got this message instead:

```
Can't find string terminator " ' " anywhere before EOF at quotes2.pl line 5.
```

The reason for this is that you have probably left out the space character in line 5 before the second single quote. Remember that `\'` tells Perl to escape the single quote, and so it merrily heads off to look for the next quote, which of course is not there. Try this program to see how Perl treats these special cases:

```
#!/usr/bin/perl -w
# aside1.pl

print 'ex\\ er\\' , ' ci\' se\'' , "\n";
```

The output you get this time is

```
$ perl aside1.pl
ex\ er\ ci' se'
$
```

Can you see how Perl did this? Well, we simply escaped the backslashes and single quotes. It will help you to sort out what is happening if you look at each element individually. Remember, there are three arguments in this example. Don't let all the quotes confuse you.

Actually, there's an altogether sneakier way of doing it. Internally, Windows allows you to separate paths in the Unix style with a forward slash, instead of a backslash. If you're referring to directories in Perl on Windows, you may find it easier to say `C:/WINNT/Profiles/` instead. This allows you to get the variable interpolation of double-quoted strings without the "Leaning Toothpick Syndrome" of multiple backslashes.

So much for backslashes, what about quotation marks? The trick is making sure Perl knows where the end of the string is. Naturally, there's no problem with putting single quotes inside a double-quoted string, or vice versa:

```
#!/usr/bin/perl -w
# quotes3.pl

print "It's as easy as that.\n";
print '"Stop," he cried.', "\n";
```

This will produce the quotation marks in the right places:

```
$ perl quotes3.pl
It's as easy as that.
"Stop," he cried.
$
```

The trick comes when we want to have double quotes inside a double-quoted string or single quotes inside a single-quoted string. As you might have guessed, though, the solution is to escape the quotes on the inside. Suppose we want to print out the following quote, including both sets of quotation marks:

```
'"Hi," said Jack. "Have you read Slashdot today?"'
```

Here's a way of doing it with a double-quoted string:

```
#!/usr/bin/perl -w
# quotes4.pl

print "'\"Hi,\" said Jack. \"Have you read Slashdot today?\"'\n";
```

Now see if you can modify this to make it a single-quoted string—don't forget that \n needs to go in separate double quotes to make it interpolate.

q// and qq//

It would be nice if you could select a completely different set of quotes so that there would be no ambiguity and no need to escape any quotes inside the text. The first operators we're going to meet are the *quote-like operators* that do this for us. They're written as q// and qq//, the first acting like a single-quoted string, and the second like a double-quoted string. Now instead of the preceding, we can write

```
#!/usr/bin/perl -w
# quotes5.pl

print qq/'"Hi," said Jack. "Have you read Slashdot today?"'\n/;
```

Alternative Delimiters

That's all very well, of course, until we want a / in the string. Suppose we want to replace "Slashdot" with "/."—now we're back where we started, having to escape things again. Thankfully, Perl allows us to choose our own delimiters so we don't have to stick with //. Any nonalphanumeric (that is, nonalphabetic and nonnumeric) character can be used as a delimiter, provided it's the same on both sides of the text. Furthermore, you can use {}, [], (), and <> as left and right delimiters. Here's a few ways of doing the print qq/.../;, all of which have the same effect:

```
#!/usr/bin/perl -w
# quotes6.pl

print qq|'"Hi," said Jack. "Have you read /. today?"'\n|;
print qq#'"Hi," said Jack. "Have you read /. today?"'\n#;
print qq('"Hi," said Jack. "Have you read /. today?"'\n);
print qq<'"Hi," said Jack. "Have you read /. today?"'\n>;
```

We'll see more of these alternative delimiters when we start working with regular expressions.

Here-Documents

There's one final way of specifying a string—by means of a *here-document*. This idea was taken from the Unix shell, and works on any platform. Effectively, it means that you can write a large amount of text within your program, and it will be treated as a string provided it is identified correctly. Here's an example:

```
#!/usr/bin/perl -w
# heredoc.pl

print <<EOF;

This is a here-document. It starts on the line after the two arrows,
and it ends when the text following the arrows is found at the beginning
of a line, like this:

EOF
```

A here-document must start with << and then a label. The label can be anything, but is traditionally EOF (end of file) or EOT (end of text). The label must immediately follow the arrows with no spaces between, unless the same number of spaces precedes the end marker. It ends when the label is found at the beginning of a line. In our case, the semicolon does not form part of the label, because it marks the end of the print() function call.

By default, a here-document works like a double-quoted string. In order for it to work like a single-quoted string, surround the label in single quotes. This will become important when variable interpolation comes into play, as we'll see later on.

Converting Between Numbers and Strings

Perl treats numbers and strings on an equal footing, and where necessary, Perl converts between strings, integers, and floating point numbers behind the scenes. There is a special term for this: *automatic conversion of scalars*. This means that you don't have to worry about making the conversions yourself, like you do in other languages. If you have a string literal "0.25", and multiply it by four, Perl treats it as a number and gives you the expected answer, 1. For example:

```
#!/usr/bin/perl -w
# autoconvert.pl

print "0.25" * 4, "\n";
```

The asterisk (*) is the multiplication operator. All of Perl's operators, including this one, will be discussed in the next section.

There is, however, one area where this automatic conversion does not take place. Octal, hex, and binary numbers in string literals or strings stored in variables don't get converted automatically.

```
#!/usr/bin/perl -w
# octhex1.pl
```

```
print "0x30\n";
print "030\n";
```

gives you

```
$ perl octhex1.pl
0x30
030
$
```

If you ever find yourself with a string containing a hex or octal value that you need to convert into a number, you can use the hex() or oct() functions accordingly:

```
#!/usr/bin/perl -w
# octhex2.pl

print hex("0x30"), "\n";
print oct("030"), "\n";
```

This will now produce the expected answers, 48 and 24. Note that for hex() or oct(), the prefix 0x or 0 respectively is not required. If you know that what you have is definitely supposed to be a hex or octal number, then hex(30) and oct(30) will produce the preceding results. As you can see from that, the string "30" and the number 30 are treated as the same.

Furthermore, these functions will stop reading when they get to a digit that doesn't make sense in that number system:

```
#!/usr/bin/perl -w
# octhex3.pl

print hex("FFG"), "\n";
print oct("178"), "\n";
```

These will stop at FF and 17 respectively, and convert to 255 and 15. Perl will warn you, though, since those are illegal characters in hex and octal numbers.

What about binary numbers? Well, there's no corresponding bin() function but there is actually a little trick here. If you have the correct prefix in place for any of the number systems (0, 0b, or 0x), you can use oct() to convert it to decimal. For example, print oct("0b11010") prints 26.

Operators

Now we know how to specify our strings and numbers, let's see what we can do with them. The majority of the things we'll be looking at here are numeric operators (operators that act on and produce numbers) like plus and minus, which take two numbers as *arguments*, called *operands*, and add or subtract them. There aren't as many string operators, but there are a lot of string functions. Perl doesn't draw a very strong distinction between functions and operators, but the main difference between the two is that operators tend to go in the middle of their arguments— for example: 2 + 2. Functions go before their arguments and have them separated by commas.

Both of them take arguments, do something with them, and produce a new value; we generally say they *return* a value, or *evaluate* to a value. Let's take a look.

Numeric Operators

The numeric operators take at least one number as an argument, and evaluate to another number. Of course, because Perl automatically converts between strings and numbers, the arguments may appear as string literals or come from strings in variables. We'll group these operators into three types: arithmetic operators, bitwise operators, and logic operators.

Arithmetic Operators

The arithmetic operators are those that deal with basic mathematics like adding, subtracting, multiplying, dividing, and so on. To add two numbers together, we would write something like this:

```
#!/usr/bin/perl -w
# arithop1.pl

print 69 + 118, "\n";
```

And, of course, we would see the answer 187. Subtracting numbers is easy too, and we can subtract at the same time:

```
#!/usr/bin/perl -w
# arithop2.pl

print "21 from 25 is: ", 25 - 21, "\n";
print "4 + 13 - 7 is: ", 4 + 13 - 7, "\n";
```

```
$ perl arithop2.pl
21 from 25 is: 4
4 + 13 - 7 is: 10
$
```

Our next set of operators (multiplying and dividing) is where it gets interesting. We use the * and / operators to multiply and divide respectively.

```
#!/usr/bin/perl -w
# arithop3.pl

print "7 times 15 is ", 7 * 15, "\n";
print "249 divided by 3 is ", 249 / 3, "\n";
```

The fun comes when you want to multiply something and then add something, or add then divide. Here's an example of the problem:

```
#!/usr/bin/perl -w
# arithop4.pl

print 3 + 7 * 15, "\n";
```

This could mean one of two things: either Perl must add the 3 and the 7, and then multiply by 15, or multiply 7 and 15 first, and then add. Which does Perl do? Try it and see . . .

Perl should have given you 108, meaning it did the multiplication first. The order in which Perl performs operations is called *operator precedence*. Multiply and divide have a higher precedence than add and subtract, and so they get performed first. We can start to draw up a list of precedence as follows:

```
* /
```

```
+ -
```

To force Perl to perform an operation of lower precedence first, we need to use parentheses, like so:

```
#!/usr/bin/perl -w
# arithop5.pl

print (3 + 7) * 15, "\n";
```

Unfortunately, if you run that, you'll get a warning and 10 is printed. What happened? The problem is that print() is a function and the parentheses around 3 + 7 are treated as the only argument to print().

print() as an operator takes a list of arguments, performs an operation (printing them to the screen), and returns a 1 if it succeeds, or no value if it does not. Perl calculated 3 plus 7, printed the result, and then multiplied the result of the returned value (1) by 15, throwing away the final result of 15.

To get what we actually want, then, we need another set of parentheses:

```
#!/usr/bin/perl -w
# arithop6.pl

print((3 + 7) * 15, "\n");
```

This now gives us the correct answer, 150, and we can put another entry in our list of precedence:

List operators

```
* /
```

```
+ -
```

Next we have the exponentiation operator, **, which simply raises one number to the power of another—squaring, cubing, and so on. Here's an example of some exponentiation:

```
#!/usr/bin/perl -w
# arithop7.pl

print 2**4, " ", 3**5, " ", -2**4, "\n";
```

That's 2*2*2*2, 3*3*3*3*3, and −2*−2*−2*−2. Or is it?

The output we get is

```
$ perl arithop7.pl
16 243 -16
$
```

Hmm, the first two look OK, but the last one's a bit wrong. −2 to the 4th power should be positive. Again, it's a precedence issue. Turning a number into a negative number requires an operator, the *unary minus operator*. It's called unary because unlike the ordinary minus operator, it only takes one argument. Although unary minus has a higher precedence than multiply and divide, it has a lower precedence than exponentiation. What's actually happening, then, is -(2**4) instead of (-2)**4. Let's put these two operators in our list of precedence as well:

List operators

**

Unary minus

* /

\+ -

The last arithmetic operator is %, the *remainder*, or *modulo operator*. This calculates the remainder when one number divides another. For example, 6 divides into 15 twice, with a remainder of 3, as our next program will confirm:

```
#!/usr/bin/perl -w
# arithop8.pl

print "15 divided by 6 is exactly ", 15 / 6, "\n";
print "That's a remainder of ", 15 % 6, "\n";
```

```
$ perl arithop8.pl
15 divided by 6 is exactly 2.5
That's a remainder of 3
$
```

The modulo operator has the same precedence as multiply and divide.

Bitwise Operators

Up to this point, the operators worked on numbers in the way we think of them. However, as we already know, computers don't see numbers the same as we do; they see them as a string of bits. These next few operators perform operations on numbers one bit at a time—that's why we call them *bitwise operators*. These aren't used quite so much in Perl as in other languages, but we'll see them when dealing with things like low-level file access.

First, let's have a look at the kind of numbers we're going to use in this section, just so we get used to them:

- 0 in binary is 0, but let's write it as 8 bits: 00000000.

- 51 in binary is 00110011.

- 85 in binary is 01010101.

- 170 in binary is 10101010.

- 204 in binary is 11001100.

- 255 in binary is 11111111.

Does it surprise you that 10101010 (170) is twice as much as 01010101 (85)? It shouldn't, when we multiply a number by 10 in base 10, all we do is slap a 0 on the end, so 21 becomes 210. Similarly, to multiply a number by 2 in base 2, we do exactly the same.

People think of bitwise operators as working from right to left; the rightmost bit is called the *least significant bit* and the leftmost is called the *most significant bit*.

The AND Operator

The easiest bitwise operator to fathom is called the *and* operator, and is written &. This compares pairs of bits as follows:

- 1 and 1 gives 1.

- 1 and 0 gives 0.

- 0 and 1 gives 0.

- 0 and 0 gives 0.

For example, 51 & 85 looks like this:

```
51      00110011
85      01010101
---------------
17      00010001
```

Sure enough, if we ask Perl the following:

```
#!/usr/bin/perl -w
# bitop1.pl

print "51 ANDed with 85 gives us ", 51 & 85, "\n";
```

it'll tell us the answer is 17. Notice that since we're comparing one pair of bits at a time, it doesn't really matter which way around the arguments go, 51 & 85 is exactly the same as 85 & 51. Operators with this property are called *associative operators*. Addition (+) and multiplication (*) are also associative: 5 * 12 produces the same result as 12 * 5. Subtraction (−) and division (/) are not associative: 5 − 12 does not produce the same result as 12 − 5.

Here's another example—look at the bits, and see what you get:

```
51     00110011
170    10101010
---------------
34     00100010
```

The OR Operator

As well as checking whether the first *and* the second bits are 1, we can check whether one *or* another is 1, the *or* operator in Perl is |. This is how we would calculate 204 | 85:

```
204    11001100
85     01010101
---------------
221    11011101
```

Now we produce 0s only if both the bits are 0; if either or both are 1, we produce a 1. As a quick rule of thumb, X & Y will always be smaller or equal to the smallest value of X and Y, and X | Y will be bigger than or equal to the largest value of X or Y.

The XOR Operator

What if you really want to know if one or the other, but not both, are one? For this, you need the *exclusive or* operator, written as the ^ operator:

```
204    11001100
170    10101010
---------------
102    01100110
```

The NOT Operator

Finally, you can flip the number completely, and replace all the 1s by 0s and vice versa. This is done with the *not*, or ~, operator:

```
85     01010101
170    10101010
```

Let's see, however, what happens when we try this in Perl:

```
#!/usr/bin/perl -w
# bitop2.pl

print "NOT 85 is ", ~85, "\n";
```

Depending on the computer, the answer might be

```
$ perl bitop2.pl
NOT 85 is 4294967210
$
```

Your answer might be different, and we'll explain why in a second.

Why is it so big? Well, let's look at that number in binary to see if we can find a clue as to what's going on:

4294697210   11111111111111111111111110101010

Aha! The last part is right, but it's a lot wider than we're used to. That's because the previous examples only used 8 bits across, whereas many computers store integers as 32 bits across, so what's actually happened is this:

85   00000000000000000000000001010101
4294697210   11111111111111111111111110101010

If you get a much bigger number, it's because your computer represents numbers internally with 64 bits instead of 32, and Perl has been configured to take advantage of this.

Truth and Falsehood

True and false are important in Perl. In Perl, false is defined as

- 0

- "0"

- "" (also known as the *empty string*)

- Undefined

- Empty list (we'll discuss this in Chapter 4)

Later, we will want to perform actions based on whether something is true or false, like if one number is bigger than another, or unless a problem has occurred, or while there is data left to examine. We will use *comparison operators* to evaluate whether these things are true or false so that we can make decisions based on them.

Some programming languages represent false as 0 and true as 1, and this allows us to use operators very similar to those bitwise operators we've just met to combine our comparisons, and to say "if this *or* this is true," "if this is *not* true," and so on. The idea of combining values that represent truth and falsehood is called *Boolean logic*, after George Boole, who invented the concept in 1847, and we call the operators that do the combining *Boolean operators*.

Comparing Numbers for Equality

The first simple comparison operator is ==. Two equals signs tells Perl to "return true if the two numeric arguments are equal." If they're not equal, return false. Boolean values of truth and falsehood aren't very exciting to look at, but let's see them anyway:

```
#!/usr/bin/perl -w
# bool1.pl

print "Is two equal to four? ",          2 == 4, "\n";
print "OK, then, is six equal to six? ", 6 == 6, "\n";
```

This will produce

```
$ perl bool1.pl
Is two equal to four?
OK, then, is six equal to six? 1
$
```

This output shows that in Perl, operators that evaluate to false evaluate to the empty string ("") and when true evaluate to 1.

The obvious counterpart to testing whether things are equal is testing whether they're not equal, and the way we do this is with the != operator. Note that there's only one = this time; we'll find out later why there had to be two before.

```
#!/usr/bin/perl -w
# bool2.pl

print "So, two isn't equal to four? ", 2 != 4, "\n";
```

```
$ perl bool2.pl
So, two isn't equal to four? 1
$
```

There you have it, irrefutable proof that two is not four. Good.

Comparing Numbers for Inequality

So much for equality, let's check if one thing is bigger than another. Just like in mathematics, we use the greater-than and less-than signs to do this: < and >.

```
#!/usr/bin/perl -w
# bool3.pl

print "Five is more than six? ",        5 >  6, "\n";
print "Seven is less than sixteen? ", 7 < 16, "\n";
print "Two is equal to two? ",           2 == 2, "\n";
print "One is more than one? ",          1 >  1, "\n";
print "Six is not equal to seven? ",  6 != 7, "\n";
```

The results should hopefully not be very new to you:

```
$ perl bool3.pl
Five is more than six?
Seven is less than sixteen? 1
Two is equal to two? 1
One is more than one?
Six is not equal to seven? 1
$
```

Let's have a look at one last pair of comparisons: we can check **greater-than-or-equal-to** **and less-than-or-equal-to with the** >= **and** <= **operators** respectively.

```
#!/usr/bin/perl -w
# bool4.pl

print "Seven is less than or equal to sixteen? ", 7 <= 16, "\n";
print "Two is more than or equal to two? ",      2 >= 2,  "\n";
```

As expected, Perl faithfully prints out

```
$ perl bool4.pl
Seven is less than or equal to sixteen? 1
Two is more than or equal to two? 1
$
```

There's also a special operator that isn't really a Boolean comparison because it doesn't give us a true-or-false value; instead it returns 0 if the two are equal, –1 if the right-hand side is bigger, and 1 if the left-hand side is bigger—it is denoted by <=>.

```
#!/usr/bin/perl -w
# bool5.pl

print "Compare six and nine? ",   6 <=> 9, "\n";
print "Compare seven and seven? ", 7 <=> 7, "\n";
print "Compare eight and four? ",  8 <=> 4, "\n";
```

gives us

```
$ perl bool5.pl
Compare six and nine? -1
Compare seven and seven? 0
Compare eight and four? 1
$
```

The <=> operator is also known as the *spaceship operator* or the *shuttle operator* due to its shape.

We'll see this operator used when we look at sorting things, where we have to know whether something goes before, after, or in the same place as something else.

Boolean Operators

As well as being able to evaluate the truth and falsehood of some statements, we can also combine such statements. For example, we may want to do something if one number is bigger than another and another two numbers are the same. The combining is done in a very similar manner to the bitwise operators we saw earlier. We can ask if one value *and* another value are both true, or if one value *or* another value are true, and so on.

The operators even resemble the bitwise operators. To ask if both truth values are true, we would use && instead of &.

So, to test whether 6 is more than 3 *and* 12 is more than 4, we can write

```
6 > 3 && 12 > 4
```

To test if 9 is more than 7 *or* 8 is less than 6, we use the doubled form of the | operator, ||:

```
9 > 7 || 6 > 8
```

To negate the sense of a test, however, use the slightly different operator !; this has a higher precedence than the comparison operators, so use parentheses. For example, this tests whether 2 is not more than 3:

```
!(2>3)
```

while this one tests whether !2 is more than 3:

```
!2>3
```

2 is a true value. !2 is therefore a false value, which gets converted to 0 when we do a numeric comparison. We're actually testing if 0 is more than 3, which has the opposite effect to what we wanted.

Instead of those forms, &&, ||, and !, we can also use the slightly easier-to-read versions, and, or, and not. There's also xor, for *exclusive or* (one or the other but not both are true), which doesn't have a symbolic form. However, you need to be careful about precedence again:

```
#!/usr/bin/perl -w
# bool6.pl

print "Test one: ", 6 > 3 && 3 > 4, "\n";
print "Test two: ", 6 > 3 and 3 > 4, "\n";
```

This prints, somewhat surprisingly, the following:

```
$ perl bool6.pl
Useless use of a constant in void context at bool6.pl line 5.
Test one:
Test two: 1$
```

We can tell from the presence of the warning about line 5 and from the position of the prompt that something is amiss (or least Unix users can—Windows users need to be a bit more alert since Windows automatically adds a newline character at the end of the program so the system prompt will be on the next line, but the blank line that is expected will not be there). Notice the second newline did not get printed. The trouble is, and has a lower precedence than &&. What has actually happened is this:

```
print("Test two: ", 6 > 3) and (3 > 4, "\n");
```

Now, 6 is more than 3, so that returned 1, print() then returned 1, and the rest was irrelevant.

String Operators

After that lot, there are surprisingly few string operators. Actually, for the moment, we're only going to look at two.

The first one is the *concatenation operator*, which glues two strings together into one. Instead of saying

```
print "Print ", "several ", "strings ", "here", "\n";
```

we could say

```
print "Print " . "one ". "string " . "here" . "\n";
```

As it happens, printing several strings is slightly more efficient, but there will be times you really do need to combine strings together, especially if you're putting them into variables.

What happens if we try and join a number to a string? The number is evaluated and then converted:

```
#!/usr/bin/perl -w
# string1.pl

print "Four sevens are ". 4*7 ."\n";
```

which tells us, reassuringly, that

```
$ perl string1.pl
Four sevens are 28
$
```

The other string operator is the *repetition operator,* marked with an x. This repeats a string a given number of times:

```
#!/usr/bin/perl -w
# string2.pl

print "GO! " x 3, "\n";
```

will print

```
$ perl string2.pl
GO! GO! GO!
$
```

We can, of course, use it in conjunction with concatenation. Its precedence is higher than the concatenation operator's, as we can easily see for ourselves:

```
#!/usr/bin/perl -w
# string3.pl

print "Ba" . "na" x 4 ,"\n";
```

On running this, we'll get

```
$ perl string3.pl
Banananana
$
```

In this case, the repetition is done first ("nananana") and then it is concatenated with the "Ba". The precedence of the repetition operator is the same as the arithmetic operators, so if you're working out how many times to repeat something, you're going to need parentheses:

```
#!/usr/bin/perl -w
# string4.pl

print "Ba" . "na" x 4*3 ,"\n";
print "Ba" . "na" x (4*3) ,"\n";
```

Compare:

```
$ perl string4.pl
Argument "nananana" isn't numeric in multiplication (*) at string4.pl line 4.
Ba0
Banananananananananananananana
$
```

Why was the first one Ba0? The first thing was the repetition, giving us "nananana". Then the multiplication—What's "nananana" times three? When Perl converts a string to a number, it takes any spaces, an optional minus sign, and then as many digits as it can from the beginning of the string, and ignores everything else. Since there were no digits here, the number value of "nananana" was 0. Also note that if the string that is converted to a number contains no numeric characters, Perl will warn you about it as shown previously.

That 0 was then multiplied by 3, to give 0. Finally, the 0 was turned back into a string to be concatenated onto the "Ba".

Here is an example showing how strings automatically convert to numbers by adding 0 to them:

```
#!/usr/bin/perl -w
# str2num.pl

print "12 monkeys"    + 0,  "\n";
print "Eleven to fly" + 0,  "\n";
print "UB40"          + 0,  "\n";
print "-20 10"        + 0,  "\n";
print "0x30"          + 0,  "\n";
```

You get a warning for each line saying that the strings aren't "numeric in addition (+)," but what can be converted is:

```
$ perl str2num.pl
Argument "12 monkeys" isn't numeric in addition (+) at str2num.pl line 4.
Argument "Eleven to fly" isn't numeric in addition (+) at str2num.pl line 5.
```

```
Argument "UB40" isn't numeric in addition (+) at str2num.pl line 6.
Argument "-20 10" isn't numeric in addition (+) at str2num.pl line 7.
Argument "0x30" isn't numeric in addition (+) at str2num.pl line 8.
12
0
0
-20
0
$
```

Notice how for each of these strings, when converted to numeric values, Perl complains that the string is not numeric. This happens because the string is not a simple numeric value. But also note that Perl does convert the strings to numbers (in the case of three of the strings, the value is 0).

Our first string, "12 monkeys", did pretty well. Perl understood the 12, and stopped after that. The next one was not so brilliant—English words don't get converted to numbers. Our third string was also a nonstarter as Perl only looks for a number at the beginning of the string. If there's something there that isn't a number, it's evaluated as a 0. Similarly, Perl only looks for the first number in the string. Any numbers after that are discarded. Finally, Perl doesn't convert binary, hex, or octal to decimal when it's stringifying a number, so you have to use the hex() or oct() functions to do that. On our last effort, Perl stopped at the x, returning 0. If we had an octal number, such as 030, that would be treated as the decimal number 30.

Therefore, conversion from strings to numbers can be summed up with these rules:

- A string that is purely a number is automatically converted to the number ("21.42" is converted to 21.42).

- Leading whitespace is ignored (" 12" is converted to 12).

- Trailing nonnumerics are discarded ("12perl" is converted to 12).

- Strings that do not start with numeric values are treated as 0 ("perl12" is converted to 0).

The last three conversions listed will produce a warning message if the -w option is used.

String Comparison

As well as comparing the value of numbers, we can compare the value of strings. This does not mean we convert a string to a number, although if you say something like "12" > "30", Perl will convert to numbers for you. This means we can compare the strings alphabetically: "Bravo" comes after "Alpha" but before "Charlie", for instance.

In fact, it's more than alphabetical order; the computer is using either ASCII or Unicode internally to represent the string, and so has converted it to a series of numbers in the relevant sequence. This means, for example, "Fowl" comes before "fish", because a capital "F" has a smaller ASCII value (70) than a lowercase "f" (102).[1]

---

1. This is not strictly true, though. Locales can define nonnumeric sorting orders for ASCII or Unicode characters that Perl will respect.

We can find a character's value by using the ord() function, which tells us where in the (ASCII) order it comes. Let's see which comes first, a # or a *?

```
#!/usr/bin/perl -w
# ascii.pl

print "A # has ASCII value ", ord("#"), "\n";
print "A * has ASCII value ", ord("*"), "\n";
```

This should say

```
$ perl ascii.pl
A # has ASCII value 35
A * has ASCII value 42
$
```

If we're only concerned with a character at a time, we can compare the return values of ord() using the < and > operators. However, when comparing entire strings, it may get a bit tedious. If the first character of each string is the same, you would move on to the next character in each string, and then the next, and so on.

Instead, there are string comparison operators that do this for us. Whereas the comparison operators for numbers are mathematical symbols, the operators for strings are abbreviations. To test whether one string is less than another, use lt. "Greater than" becomes gt, "equal to" becomes eq, and "not equal to" becomes ne. There's also ge and le for "greater than or equal to" and "less than and equal to." The three-way-comparison becomes cmp.

Here are a few examples of these:

```
#!/usr/bin/perl -w
# strcomp1.pl

print "Which came first, the chicken or the egg? ";
print "chicken" cmp "egg", "\n";
print "Are dogs greater than cats? ";
print "dog" gt "cat", "\n";
print "Is ^ less than + ? ";
print "^" lt "+", "\n";
```

And the results:

```
$ perl strcomp1.pl
Which came first, the chicken or the egg? -1
Are dogs greater than cats? 1
Is ^ less than + ?
$
```

The last line prints nothing as a result of "^" lt "+" since this operation returns the empty string indicating false.

Be careful when comparing strings with numeric comparison operators (or numeric values with string comparison operators):

```
#!/usr/bin/perl -w
# strcomp2.pl

print "Test one: ", "four" eq "six", "\n";
print "Test two: ", "four" == "six", "\n";
```

This code produces

```
$ perl strcomp2.pl
Argument "six" isn't numeric in numeric eq (==) at strcmp2.pl line 5.
Argument "four" isn't numeric in numeric eq (==) at strcmp2.pl line 5.
Test one:
Test two: 1
$
```

Is the second line really claiming that "four" is equal to "six"? Yes, when treated as numbers. If you compare them as numbers, they get converted to numbers. "four" converts to 0, "six" converts to 0, and the 0s are equal, so our test returns true and we get a couple of warnings telling us that they were not numbers to begin with. The moral of this story is, compare strings with string comparison operators and compare numbers with numeric comparison operators. Otherwise, your results may not be what you anticipate.

Operators to Be Seen Later

There are a few operators left that we are not going to go into in detail right now. Don't worry, we will eventually come across the more important ones.

- The conditional operator looks like this: a?b:c. It returns b if a is true, and c if it is false.

- The range operators, .. and ..., make a range of values. For instance, (0..5) is short-hand notation for (0,1,2,3,4,5).

- We've seen the comma for separating arguments to functions like print(). In fact, the comma is an operator that builds a list, and print() works on a list of arguments. The operator => works like a comma with certain additional properties.

- The =~ and !~ operators are used to "apply" a regular expression to a string. More on these operators in Chapter 7.

- As well as providing an escape sequence and backwhacking special characters, \ is used to take a reference to a variable, to examine the variable itself rather than its contents. We will discuss this operator in Chapter 11.

- The >> and << operators "shift" a binary number right and left a given number of bits.

- -> is an operator used when working with references, covered in Chapter 11.

Operator Precedence

Table 2-1 provides the precedence for all the operators we've seen so far, listed in descending order of precedence.

Table 2-1. *Operator Precedence*

Operator	Description
List operators	Functions that take list arguments
->	Infix dereference operator
++ --	Increment, decrement
**	Exponentiation
! ~ \	Logical not, bitwise not, reference of
=~ !~	Regex match, negated regex match
* / % x	Multiplication, division, modulus, replication
+ - .	Addition, subtraction, concatenation
<< >>	Left shift, right shift
< > <= >= lt gt le ge	Comparison operators
== != <=> eq ne cmp	More comparison operators
&	Bitwise and
| ^	Bitwise or, bitwise xor
&&	Logical and
||	Logical or
.. ...	Range
?:	Conditional
, =>	List separator
not	Logical not
and	Logical and
or xor	Logical or, xor

Remember that if you need to get things done in a different order, you will need to use parenthesis. Also remember that you can use parenthesis even when they're not strictly necessary, and you should certainly do so to help keep things readable. While Perl knows full well what order to do 7+3*2/6-3+5/2&3 in, you may find it easier on yourself to spell it out, because next week you may not remember everything you have just written.

Variables

Now it is time to talk about variables. As explained earlier, a variable is storage for your scalars. Once you've calculated 42*7, it's gone. If you want to know what it was, you must do the calculation again. Instead of being able to use the result as a halfway point in more complicated calculations, you've got to spell it all out in full. That's no fun. What we need to be able to do, and what variables allow us to do, is store a scalar away and refer to it again later.

A scalar variable name starts with a dollar sign, for example: $name. Scalar variables can hold either numbers or strings, and are only limited by the size of your computer's memory. To put data into our scalar, we assign the data to it with the assignment operator =. (Incidentally, this is why numeric comparison is ==, because = was taken to mean the assignment operator.)

What we're going to do here is tell Perl that our scalar contains the string "fred". Now we can get at that data by simply using the variable's name:

```
#!/usr/bin/perl -w
# vars1.pl

$name = "fred";
print "My name is ", $name, "\n";
```

Lo and behold, our computer announces to us that

```
$ perl vars1.pl
My name is fred
$
```

Now we have somewhere to store our data, and some way to get it back again. The next logical step is to be able to change it.

Modifying a Variable

Modifying the contents of a variable is easy, just assign something different to it. We can say

```
#!/usr/bin/perl -w
# vars2.pl

$name = "fred";
print "My name is ",            $name, "\n";
print "It's still ",            $name, "\n";
$name = "bill";
print "Well, actually, now it's ", $name, "\n";
$name = "fred";
print "No, really, now it's ",  $name, "\n";
```

And watch our computer have an identity crisis:

```
$ perl vars2.pl
My name is fred
It's still fred
```

```
Well, actually, now it's bill
No, really, now it's fred
$
```

We can also do a calculation in several stages:

```
#!/usr/bin/perl -w
# vars3.pl

$a = 6 * 9;
print "Six nines are ", $a, "\n";
$b = $a + 3;
print "Plus three is ", $b, "\n";
$c = $b / 3;
print "All over three is ", $c, "\n";
$d = $c + 1;
print "Add one is ", $d, "\n";
print "\nThose stages again: ", $a, " ", $b, " ", $c, " ", $d, "\n";
```

This code prints

```
$ perl vars3.pl
Six nines are 54
Plus three is 57
All over three is 19
Add one is 20
Those stages again: 54 57 19 20
$
```

While this works perfectly fine, it's often easier to stick with one variable and modify its value, if you don't need to know the stages you went through at the end:

```
#!/usr/bin/perl -w
# vars4.pl

$a = 6 * 9;
print "Six nines are ", $a, "\n";
$a = $a + 3;
print "Plus three is ", $a, "\n";
$a = $a / 3;
print "All over three is ", $a, "\n";
$a = $a + 1;
print "Add one is ", $a, "\n";
```

The assignment operator =, has very low precedence. This means that Perl will do the calculations on the right-hand side of it, including fetching the current value, before assigning the new value. To illustrate this, take a look at the sixth line of our example. Perl takes the current value of $a, adds three to it, and then stores it back in $a.

Operating and Assigning at Once

Operations, like fetching a value, modifying it, or storing it, are very common, so there's a special syntax for them. Generally

```
$a = $a <some operator> $b;
```

can be written as

```
$a <some operator>= $b;
```

For instance, we could rewrite the preceding example as follows:

```
#!/usr/bin/perl -w
# vars5.pl

$a = 6 * 9;
print "Six nines are ", $a, "\n";
$a += 3;
print "Plus three is ", $a, "\n";
$a /= 3;
print "All over three is ", $a, "\n";
$a += 1;
print "Add one is ", $a, "\n";
```

This works for **=, *=, +=, -=, /=, .=, %=, &=, |=, ^=, <<=, >>=, &&=, and ||=. These all have the same precedence as the assignment operator =.

Autoincrement and Autodecrement

There are also two more operators, ++ and --. They add and subtract one from the variable, but their precedence is a little strange. When they precede a variable, they act before everything else. If they come afterwards, they act after everything else. Let's examine these in the following example:

```
#!/usr/bin/perl -w
# auto1.pl

$a = 4;
$b = 10;
print "Our variables are ", $a, " and ", $b, "\n";
$b = $a++;
print "After incrementing, we have ", $a, " and ", $b, "\n";
$b = ++$a * 2;
print "Now, we have ", $a, " and ", $b, "\n";
$a = --$b + 4;
print "Finally, we have ", $a, " and ", $b, "\n";
```

You should see the following output:

```
$ perl auto1.pl
Our variables are 4 and 10
After incrementing, we have 5 and 4
Now, we have 6 and 12
Finally, we have 15 and 11
$
```

Let's work this through a piece at a time. First we set up our variables, giving the values 4 and 10 to $a and $b respectively:

```
$a = 4;
$b = 10;
print "Our variables are ", $a, " and ", $b, "\n";
```

In the following line, the assignment happens before the increment—this is known as a *post-increment*. So $b is set to $a's current value, 4, and then $a is autoincremented, becoming 5.

```
$b = $a++;
print "After incrementing, we have ", $a, " and ", $b, "\n";
```

In the next line however, the incrementing takes place first—this is known as a *pre-increment*. $a is now 6, and $b is set to twice that, 12.

```
$b= ++$a * 2;
print "Now, we have ", $a, " and ", $b, "\n";
```

Finally, $b is decremented first (a *pre-decrement*), and becomes 11. $a is set to $b plus 4, which is 15.

```
$a= --$b + 4;
print "Finally, we have ", $a, " and ", $b, "\n";
```

The autoincrement operator actually does something interesting if the variable contains a string of only alphabetic characters, followed optionally by numeric characters. Instead of converting to a number, Perl "advances" the variable along the ranges a–z, A–Z, and 0–9. This is more easily understood from a few examples:

```
#!/usr/bin/perl -w
# auto2.pl

$a = "A9"; print ++$a, "\n";
$a = "bz"; print ++$a, "\n";
$a = "Zz"; print ++$a, "\n";
$a = "z9"; print ++$a, "\n";
$a = "9z"; print ++$a, "\n";
```

should produce

```
$ perl auto2.pl
B0
ca
AAa
aa0
10
$
```

This shows that a 9 turns into a 0 and increments the next digit left. A z turns into an a and increments the next digit left, and if there are no more digits to the left, either an a or an A is created depending on the case of the current leftmost digit.

Multiple Assignments

We've said that = is an operator, but does that mean it returns a value? Well, actually it does, it returns whatever was assigned. This allows us to set several variables up at once. Here's a simple example of this; read it from right to left:

```
$d = $c = $b = $a = 1;
```

First we set $a to 1, and the result of this is 1. $b is set with that, the result of which is 1. And so it goes on.

Scoping

All the variables we've seen so far in our programs have been *global* variables. That is, they can be seen and changed from anywhere in the program. For the moment, that's not too much of a problem, since our programs are very small, and we can easily understand where things get assigned and used. However, when we start writing larger programs, this becomes a problem.

Why is this? Well, suppose one part of your program uses a variable, $counter. If another part of your program wants a counter, it can't call it $counter as well for fear of clobbering the old value. This becomes more of an issue when we get into *subroutines*, which are little sections of code we can temporarily call upon to accomplish something for us before returning to what we were previously doing. Currently, we'd have to make sure all the variables in our program had different names, and with a large program that's not desirable. It would be easier to restrict the life of a variable to a certain area of the program.

To achieve this, Perl provides another type of variable, called *lexical* variables. These are constrained to the enclosing block and all blocks inside it. If they're not currently inside a block, they are constrained to the current file. To tell Perl that a variable is *lexical*, we say my $variable;. This creates a brand-new lexical variable for the current block, and sets it to the undefined value. Here's an example:

```
#!/usr/bin/perl -w
# scope1.pl

$record = 4;
print "We're at record ", $record, "\n";
```

```
{
    my $record;
    $record = 7;
    print "Inside the block, we're at record ", $record, "\n";
}

print "Outside, we're still at record ", $record, "\n";
```

And this should tell you

```
$ perl scope1.pl
We're at record 4
Inside the block, we're at record 7
Outside we're still at record 4
$
```

Let's look at how this program works. Firstly, we set our global variable $record to 4.

```
$record = 4;
print "We're at record ", $record, "\n";
```

Now we enter a new block, and create a new lexical variable. Important! This is completely and utterly unrelated to the global variable $record as my() creates a *new* lexical variable. This exists for the duration of the block only, and has the undefined value.

```
{
    my $record;
```

Next, the lexical variable is set to 7, and printed out. The global $record is unchanged.

```
    $record = 7;
    print "Inside the block, we're at record ", $record, "\n";
```

Finally, the block ends, and the lexical copy ends with it. We say that it has gone *out of scope*. The global remains however, and so $record has the value 4.

```
}

print "Outside, we're still at record ", $record, "\n";
```

In order to make us think clearly about our programming, we will ask Perl to be strict about our variable use. The statement use strict; checks that, amongst other things, we've declared all our variables. We declare lexicals with the my() function. Here's what happens if we change our program to use strict format:

```
#!/usr/bin/perl -w
# scope2.pl
```

```
use strict;

$record = 4;
print "We're at record ", $record, "\n";

{
    my $record;
    $record = 7;
    print "Inside the block, we're at record ", $record, "\n";
}

print "Outside, we're still at record ", $record, "\n";
```

Now, the global $record is not declared. So sure enough, Perl complains about it, generating this output:

```
$ perl scope2.pl
Global symbol "$record" requires explicit package name at scope2.pl line 6.
Global symbol "$record" requires explicit package name at scope2.pl line 7.
Global symbol "$record" requires explicit package name at scope2.pl line 15.
Execution of scope2.pl aborted due to compilation errors.
$
```

We'll see exactly what this means in later chapters, but for now it suffices to declare $record as a my() variable:

```
#!/usr/bin/perl -w
# scope3.pl

use strict;

my $record;
$record = 4;
print "We're at record ", $record, "\n";

{
    my $record;
    $record = 7;
    print "Inside the block, we're at record ", $record, "\n";
}

print "Outside, we're still at record ", $record, "\n";
```

Now Perl is happy, and we get the same output as before. You should almost always start your programs with a use strict. Of course, nobody's going to force you, but it will help you avoid a lot of mistakes, and will certainly give other people who have to look at your code more confidence in it.

Variable Names

We've not really examined yet what the rules are regarding what we can call our variables. We know that scalar variables have to start with a dollar sign, but what next? The next character must be a letter (uppercase or lowercase) or an underscore, and after that, any combination of numbers, letters, and underscores is permissible.

Note that Perl's variable names, like the rest of Perl, are case-sensitive, so $user is different from $User, and both are different from $USER.

The following are legal variable names: $I_am_a_long_variable_name, $simple, $box56, $__hidden, $B1.

The following are not legal variable names: $10c (doesn't start with letter or underscore), $mail-alias (- is not allowed), $your name (spaces not allowed).

The Special Variable $_

There are certain variables, called *special variables*, which Perl provides internally that you either are not allowed to or do not want to overwrite. One which is allowed by the preceding rules is $_, a very special variable indeed. $_ is the *default variable* that a lot of functions read from, write to, and operate upon if no other variable is given. We'll see plenty of examples of it throughout the book. For a complete list of all the special variables that Perl uses and what they do, type perldoc perlvar at the command line.

Variable Interpolation

We said earlier that double-quoted strings interpolate variables. What does this mean? Well, if you mention a variable, say $name, in the middle of a double-quoted string, you get the value of the variable, rather than the actual characters. As an example, see what Perl does to this:

```
#!/usr/bin/perl -w
# varint1.pl
use strict;

my $name = "fred";
print "My name is $name\n";
```

This produces

```
$ perl varint1.pl
My name is fred
$
```

Perl interpolates the value of $name into the string. Note that this doesn't happen with single-quoted strings, just like escape sequence interpolation:

```
#!/usr/bin/perl -w
# varint2.pl

use strict;
```

```perl
my $name = "fred";
print 'My name is $name\n';
```

Here we get

```
$ perl varint2.pl
My name is $name\n$
```

Notice that the system prompt is printed at the end of that line because \n is not a newline character within the single quotes. This doesn't just happen in things we print, it happens every time we construct a string:

```perl
#!/usr/bin/perl -w
# varint3.pl

use strict;

my $name = "fred";
my $salutation = "Dear $name,";
print $salutation, "\n";
```

This gives us

```
$ perl varint3.pl
Dear fred,
$
```

This has exactly the same effect as

```perl
my $salutation = "Dear " . $name . ",";
```

but is more concise and easier to understand.

If you need to place text immediately after the variable, you can use curly braces to delimit the name of the variable. Take this example:

```perl
#!/usr/bin/perl -w
# varint4.pl

use strict;

my $times = 8;
print "This is the $timesth time.\n";
```

This is syntactically incorrect, because Perl looks for a variable $timesth which hasn't been declared. In this case, we have to change the last line by wrapping the variable name in curly braces to this:

```perl
print "This is the ${times}th time.\n";
```

Now we get the right result:

```
$ perl varint4.pl
This is the 8th time.
$
```

Currency Converter

Let's begin to wind up this chapter with a real example—a program to convert between currencies. This is our very first version, so we won't make it do anything too clever. As we get more and more advanced, we'll be able to hone and refine it.

```perl
#!/usr/bin/perl -w
# currency1.pl

use strict;

my $yen = 105.6;    # as of 02 February 2004
print "49518 Yen is ", (49_518/$yen), " dollars\n";
print "360 Yen is   ", (   360/$yen), " dollars\n";
print "30510 Yen is ", (30_510/$yen), " dollars\n";
```

Save this, and run it through Perl. You should see something like this:

```
$ perl currency1.pl
49518 Yen is 468.920454545455 dollars
360 Yen is   3.40909090909091 dollars
30510 Yen is 288.920454545455 dollars
$
```

First, we declare the exchange rate to be a lexical variable and set it to 105.6.

```perl
my $yen = 105.6;
```

Notice that we can declare and assign a variable at the same time. Now we do some calculations based on that exchange rate:

```perl
print "49518 Yen is ", (49_518/$yen), " dollars\n";
print "360 Yen is   ", (   360/$yen), " dollars\n";
print "30510 Yen is ", (30_510/$yen), " dollars\n";
```

Of course, this is currently of limited use, because the exchange rate changes, and we might want to change some different amounts at times. To do either of these things, we need to be able to ask the user for additional data when we run the program.

Introducing <STDIN>

Perl reads from *standard input* (the keyboard) with <STDIN>. It reads *up to and including* the newline character, so the newline is part of the string read in. To read a single line of input from the user we can say something like

```
print "Please enter something interesting\n";
$comment = <STDIN>;
```

This will read one line from the user, including the newline character, and assign the string that was read to the variable $comment. Let's use this to get the exchange rate from the user when the program is run. This example will read the exchange rate from the user's keyboard, storing it in $yen:

```
#!/usr/bin/perl -w
# currency2.pl

use strict;

print "Currency converter\n\nPlease enter the exchange rate: ";
my $yen = <STDIN>;
print "49518 Yen is ", (49_518/$yen), " dollars\n";
print "360 Yen is    ", (   360/$yen), " dollars\n";
print "30510 Yen is ", (30_510/$yen), " dollars\n";
```

Now when you run the program, you'll be asked for the exchange rate. The currency values will be calculated using the rate you entered:

```
$ perl currency2.pl
Currency converter

Please enter the exchange rate: 100
49518 Yen is 495.18 dollars
360 Yen is    3.6 dollars
30510 Yen is 305.1 dollars
$
```

Note that this time we read the exchange rate from the user's keyboard and it was read in as a string. Perl converts the string to a number in order to perform the calculation.

So far, we haven't done any checking to make sure that the exchange rate given makes sense; this is something we'll need to think about in the future.

The chomp() and chop() Functions

<STDIN> reads up to and including the newline character. Sometimes we don't want to include the newline in the text we have read, so we can chomp() the newline off the string.

The chomp() function removes the last character of a string if and only if it is the newline character. For instance:

```
$string = "testing 1, 2, 3\n";
chomp($string);                # $string is now "testing 1, 2, 3"
```

Since <STDIN> reads up to and including the newline character, this code reads and then removes the newline:

```
my $input = <STDIN>;
chomp($input);
```

Those two statements can be combined into one:

```
chomp(my $input = <STDIN>);
```

A related function is chop(). It removes the last character of a string, regardless of what character it is. Here is an example:

```
$string = "testing, 1, 2, 3";
chop($string);                    # $string is now "testing 1, 2, "
```

Two Miscellaneous Functions

Before we end our discussion of scalars, we should discuss two functions that are often used to terminate Perl programs: exit() and die().

The exit() Function

The exit() function exits the program. If an argument is provided, it returns that value back to the calling program (or shell). If no argument is provided, it returns back the value 0. In the shell, the value 0 means that the program terminated normally, so we can report that all is well with

```
exit(0);
```

or

```
exit;
```

If the program exits abnormally due to some error condition, simply return back a nonzero value to tell the calling program that all is not well:

```
exit(1);
```

Here is an example of using the exit() function:

```
#!/usr/bin/perl -w
# exit.pl

use strict;

print "enter value to return back to the calling program: ";
chomp(my $value = <STDIN>);

exit($value);
```

In Unix, we can echo out the value $? to see the return value of the most recent command:

```
$ perl exit.pl
enter value to return back to the calling program: 0
$ echo $?
0
$ perl exit.pl
enter value to return back to the calling program: 255
$ echo $?
255
$
```

The die() Function

The die() function is how we handle severe errors in Perl. It takes a character string argument and prints it to standard error output (this normally prints to the screen like standard output does). If the argument string does not end in newline, the \n character, die() automatically appends to the output string the name of the Perl program and the line number of the program where the die() was executed; this is very helpful—it tells us right where the error took place. Then die() cleans up the program and exits with a non-0 exit status. Therefore, die() is a permanent solution—the program terminates:

```
die "there was an error";
```

Here is an example of using die():

```
#!/usr/bin/perl -w
# die.pl

use strict;

print "please enter a string to pass to die: ";
chomp(my $string = <STDIN>);

die($string);
print "didn't make it this far...\n";
```

Executing this code would resemble

```
$ perl die.pl
please enter a string to pass to die: this is the end
this is the end at die.pl line 9, <STDIN> line 1.
$
```

Notice that the name of the script and the line number is automatically added to the output of die() because the argument to die() did not end in the newline character. Also notice that the last print() is not executed because the program terminated when die() executed.

Summary

Perl's basic data type is a scalar. A scalar can be either an integer, floating point number, or string. Perl converts between these three automatically when necessary.

Double- and single-quoted strings differ in the way they process the text inside them. Single-quoted strings do little to no processing at all, whereas double-quoted strings interpolate escape sequences and variables.

We can operate on these scalars in a number of ways—ordinary arithmetic, bitwise arithmetic, string manipulation, and logical comparison. We can also combine logical comparisons with Boolean operators. These operators vary in precedence, which is to say that some take effect before others, and as a result we must use parentheses to enforce the precedence we want.

Scalar variables are a way of storing scalars so that we can get at them and change their values. Scalar variable names begin with a dollar sign ($) and are followed by one or more alphanumeric characters or underscores. There are two types of variables—lexical and global. Globals exist all the way through the program, and so can be troublesome if we don't keep very good track of where they are being used. Lexicals have a life span of the current block, and so we can use them safely without worrying about clobbering similarly named variables somewhere else in the program.

<STDIN> reads in from standard input, which is normally the user's keyboard. We can store this input in a variable and then operate upon it, making our programs more flexible. <STDIN> reads up to and including the newline character, and we normally chomp() off the newline.

Two ways to terminate our programs are by using exit() and die(). die() is helpful because it prints its argument, and if that argument does not end in \n, it magically adds the script name and line number to the output which helps us locate the error.

Exercises

1. Change the currency conversion program so that it asks for an exchange rate and three prices to convert.

2. Write a program that asks for a hexadecimal number and converts it to decimal. Then change it to convert an octal number to decimal.

3. Write a program that asks for a decimal number less than 256 and converts it to binary. (Hint: You may want to use the bitwise and operator 8 times.)

4. Without the aid of the computer, work out the order in which each of the following expressions would be computed, and their value. Put the appropriate parentheses in to reflect the normal precedence:

   - 2+6/4-3*5+1

   - 17+-3**3/2

   - 26+3^4*2

   - 4+3>=7||2&4*2<4

CHAPTER 3

■■■

Control Flow Constructs

Most of the programs we have seen so far have been very simply structured—they've done one statement after another in turn. If we were to represent statements by boxes, our programs would look like this:

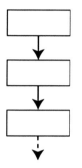

This sort of diagram is called a *flow chart*, and programmers have used them for a long time to help design their programs. They're considered a bit passé these days, but they're still useful. The path Perl (or any other language) takes by following the arrows is called the *flow of execution* of the program. Boxes denote statements (or a single group of statements), and diamonds denote tests. There are also a whole host of other symbols for magnetic tapes, drum storage, and all sorts of wonderful devices, now happily lost in the mists of time.

We can choose our path through the program depending on certain things. For instance, we'll do something *if* two strings are equal:

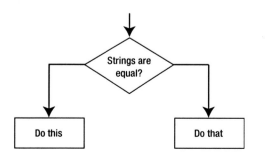

We can also iterate, or loop, through a number of things by executing a block of statements again and again for each element of the list:

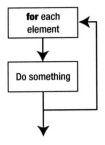

We'll take a look at the other sorts of control structures we have in Perl. For example, structures that do things *if* or *unless* something is true. We'll see structures that do things *while* something is true, or *until* it is true. Structures that loop *for* a certain number of times, or *foreach* element in a list. Each of the words in italic in this paragraph is a Perl keyword, and we'll examine them in this chapter.

The if Statement

In programming, we often need to test a condition, and if that condition is true, take some action. This can be performed using an *if statement*. The if has the general syntax:

```
if ( condition ) {
    statements
}
```

Don't type this in and try to make it run—it is meant to be a general structure of the construct.

An important note: those curly braces around the body (the *statements*) are *required*. You must use them, even if the body is one line of code.

For instance, let's say we want to divide by a number unless that number is 0. We can first check to see if the number is not 0, and if it is not, perform the division.

```
if ($number != 0) {
    $result = 100 / $number;
}
```

Let's create a program to use the if statement. It will prompt the user to enter a number. If the number is not 0, then 100 is divided by that number and the result is stored in $result. If the number is 0, the result will remain the default value of 0:

```
#!/usr/bin/perl -w
# if.pl

use strict;
```

```
print "please enter a number: ";
chomp(my $number = <STDIN>);
my $result = 0;
if ($number != 0) {
    $result = 100 / $number;
}

print "the result is: $result\n";
```

Recall that the statement

```
chomp(my $number = <STDIN>);
```

is shorthand for the two statements that read from standard input and then remove the newline:

```
my $number = <STDIN>;
chomp $number;
```

Now let's execute the program, once with a nonzero value and once with 0:

```
$ perl if.pl
please enter a number: 8
the result is: 12.5
$ perl if.pl
please enter a number: 0
the result is: 0
$
```

Operators Revisited

The if statement, and all the other control structures we're going to visit in this chapter, test to see if a condition is true or false. They do this using the Boolean logic mentioned in Chapter 2, together with Perl's ideas of true and false. To remind you of these:

- An empty string, "", is false.

- The number 0 and the string "0" are both false.

- An empty list, (), is false.

- The undefined value is false.

- Everything else is true.

However, you need to be careful for a few traps here. A string containing invisible characters, like spaces or newlines, is true. A string that isn't "0" is true, even if its numerical value is 0, so "0.0" for instance, is true.

Larry Wall has said that programming Perl is an empirical science—you learn things about it by trying them out. Is (()) a true value? You can look it up in books and the online documentation, or you can spend a few seconds writing a program like this:

```perl
#!/usr/bin/perl -w
# emptylist.pl

use strict;

if ( (()) ) {
    print "Yes, it is.\n";
}
```

This way you get the answer straight away, with the minimum of fuss. (If you're interested, it isn't a true value.) We've also seen that conditional operators can test things out, returning 1 if the test was successful and empty string if it was not. Let's see more of the things we can test.

Comparing Numbers

We can test whether one number is bigger, smaller, or the same as another. Assuming we have two numbers stored in the variables $x and $y, Table 3-1 shows the operators we can use for this.

Table 3-1. *Numeric Comparison Operators*

Operator	Description
$x > $y	$x is greater than $y.
$x < $y	$x is less than $y.
$x >= $y	$x is greater than or equal to $y.
$x <= $y	$x is less than or equal to $y.
$x == $y	$x has the same numeric value as $y.
$x != $y	$x does not have the same numeric value as $y.

Don't forget that the numeric comparison needs a doubled equals sign (==) so that Perl doesn't think you're trying to set $x to the value of $y.

Also remember that Perl converts $x and $y to numbers in the usual way. It reads numbers or decimal points from the left for as long as possible, ignoring initial spaces, and then drops the rest of the string. If no numbers were found, the value is set to 0.

Let's see an example—a very simple guessing game. The computer has a number, and the user has to guess what it is. If the user doesn't guess correctly, the computer gives a hint. As we learn more about Perl, we'll add the opportunity to give more than one try, and to pick a different number each game.

```perl
#!/usr/bin/perl -w
# guessnum1.pl

use strict;

my $target = 12;
print "Guess my number!\n";
print "Enter your guess: ";
my $guess = <STDIN>;
```

```perl
if ($target == $guess) {
   print "That's it! You guessed correctly!\n";
   exit;
}
if ($guess > $target) {
   print "Your number is more than my number\n";
   exit;
}
if ($guess < $target){
   print "Your number is less than my number\n";
   exit;
}
```

Let's have a few goes at it:

```
$ perl guessnum1.pl
Guess my number!
Enter your guess: 3
Your number is less than my number
$ perl guessnum1.pl
Guess my number!
Enter your guess: 15
Your number is more than my number
$ perl guessnum1.pl
Guess my number!
Enter your guess: 12
That's it! You guessed correctly!
$
```

The first thing we do in this program is set up our secret number. OK, at the moment it's not very secret, since it's right there in the source code, but we can improve on this later. After this, we get a number from the user:

```perl
my $guess = <STDIN>;
```

Then we do three sorts of comparisons with the numeric operators we've just seen. We use the basic pattern of the if statement again: if (*condition*) { *action* }.

```perl
if ($target == $guess) {
   print "That's it! You guessed correctly!\n";
   exit;
}
```

Since only one of the tests can be true—the user's number can't be both smaller than our number and the same as it—we may as well stop work after a test was successful. The exit() function tells Perl to stop the program completely.

Comparing Strings

When we're comparing strings, we use a different set of operators to do the comparisons as listed in Table 3-2.

Table 3-2. *String Comparison Operators*

Operator	Description
$x gt $y	$x is string greater than $y.
$x lt $y	$x is string less than $y.
$x ge $y	$x is string greater than or equal to $y.
$x le $y	$x is string less than or equal to $y.
$x eq $y	$x is the same as $y.
$x ne $y	$x is not the same as $y.

Here's a very simple way of testing if a user knows a password. Note: don't use a good password in this program since the user can just read the source code to find it!

```
#!/usr/bin/perl -w
# password.pl

use strict;

my $password = "foxtrot";
print "Enter the password: ";
my $guess = <STDIN>;
chomp $guess;
if ($password eq $guess) {
    print "Pass, friend.\n";
}
if ($password ne $guess) {
    die "Go away, imposter!\n";
}
```

Here's our security system in action:

```
$ perl password.pl
Enter the password: abracadabra
Go away, imposter!
$ perl password.pl
Enter the password: foxtrot
Pass, friend.
$
```

This program starts by asking the user for input:

```
my $guess = <STDIN>;
```

Just a warning: this is a horrendously bad way of asking for a password, since it's echoed to the screen, and everyone looking at the user's computer would be able to read it. Even though you won't be using a program like this, if you ever do need to get a password from the user, the Perl FAQ provides a better method in perlfaq8. Type `perldoc -q password` to find it.

```
chomp $guess;
```

This statement chomps the newline off of `$guess`. We must never forget to remove the newline from the end of the user's data. We didn't need to do this for numeric comparison, because Perl would remove that for us anyway during conversion to a number. Otherwise, even if the user had entered the right password, Perl would have tried to compare `"foxtrot"` with `"foxtrot\n"` and it could never be the same.

```perl
if ($password ne $guess) {
    die "Go away, imposter!\n";
}
```

Then if the password we have isn't the same as the user's input, we send out a rude message and terminate the program.

Other Tests

What other tests can we perform? We can test if a variable is defined (it must contain something other than the undefined value) using `defined()`.

```perl
#!/usr/bin/perl -w
# defined.pl

use strict;

my ($a, $b);
$b = 10;

if (defined $a) {
    print "\$a has a value.\n";
}
if (defined $b) {
    print "\$b has a value.\n";
}
```

Not surprisingly, the result we get is this:

```
$ perl defined.pl
$b has a value.
$
```

You can use this to avoid the warnings you get when you try and use a variable that doesn't have a value. If we'd tried to say if (`$a == $b`), Perl would have said

```
Use of uninitialized value in numeric eq (==)
```

So we have our basic comparisons. Don't forget that some functions will return a true value if they were successful and false if they were not. You will often want to check whether the return value of an operation (particularly one that relates to the operating system) is true or not.

Logical Operators

We also saw in Chapter 2 that we can join together several tests into one by the use of the logical operators. Table 3-3 provides a summary of those.

Table 3-3. *Logical Operators*

Operator	Description
$x and $y $x && $y	True if both $x and $y are true
$x or $y $x || $y	True if either of $x or $y, or both are true
not $x ! $x	True if $x is not true

The operators and, or, and not are usually used instead of &&, ||, and ! mainly due to their readability. The operator not means not, after all. Don't forget there is a difference in precedence between the two—and, or, and not all have lower precedence than their symbolic representations.

Multiple Choice: if . . . else

Consider these two if statements:

```
if ($password eq $guess) {
    print "Pass, friend.\n";
}
if ($password ne $guess) {
    die "Go away, imposter!\n";
}
```

We know that if the first test condition is true, then the second one will not be—we're asking exactly opposite questions: Are these the same? Are they not the same?

In which case, it seems wasteful to do two tests. It'd be much nicer to be able to say, "If the strings are the same, do this. Otherwise, do that." And in fact we can do exactly that, although the keyword is not *otherwise* but *else*:

```
if ($password eq $guess) {
    print "Pass, friend.\n";
} else {
    die "Go away, imposter!\n";
}
```

That's

```
if ( condition ) { action } else { alternative action }
```

Like the if statement, those **curly braces are** *required* **in the** else part.

Even More Choices: if . . . elsif . . . else

Some things in life aren't clear-cut. In some cases, we'll want to test more than one condition. When looking at several related possibilities, we'll want to ask questions like "Is this true? If this isn't, then is that true? If that's not true, how about the other?" Note that this is distinct from asking three independent questions; whether we ask the second depends on whether or not the first was true. In Perl, we could very easily write something like this:

```
if ( condition1 ) {
    action1
} else {
    if ( condition2 ) {
        action2
    } else {
        if ( condition3 ) {
            action3
        } else {
            action4
        }
    }
}
```

You might agree that this looks pretty messy. To make it nicer, we can combine the else and the next if into a single word, elsif. Here's what the preceding would look like when rephrased in this way:

```
if ( condition1) {
    action1
} elsif ( condition2 ) {
    action2
} elsif ( condition3 ) {
    action3
} else {
    action4
}
```

Much neater! We don't have an awful cascade of closing curly braces at the end, and it's easier to see what we're testing, and when we're testing it.

Let's look at an example. Most of us will not go outside if it's raining, but we'll always go out for a walk in the snow. We will not go outside if it's less than 18 degrees Celsius. Otherwise, we'll probably go out unless we've got too much work to do. Do we want to go for a walk?

```
#!/usr/bin/perl -w
# walking.pl

use strict;
```

```
print "What's the weather like outside? ";
chomp(my $weather = <STDIN>);
print "How hot is it, in degrees? ";
chomp(my $temperature = <STDIN>);
print "And how many emails left to reply to? ";
chomp(my $work = <STDIN>);

if ($weather eq "snowing") {
    print "It's snowing, let's go!\n";
} elsif ($weather eq "raining") {
    print "No way, sorry, it's raining so I'm staying in.\n";
} elsif ($temperature < 18) {
    print "Too cold for me!\n";
} elsif ($work > 30) {
    print "Sorry - just too busy.\n";
} else {
    print "Well, why not?\n";
}
```

Let's say it is 20[1] degrees, we've got 27 emails to reply to, and it's cloudy out there:

```
$ perl walking.pl
What's the weather like outside? cloudy
How hot is it, in degrees? 20
And how many emails left to reply to? 27
Well, why not?
$
```

Looks like we can fit a walk in after all.

The point of this rather silly little program is that once it has gathered the information it needs, it runs through a series of tests, each of which could cause it to finish. First, we check to see if it's snowing:

```
if ($weather eq "snowing") {
    print "It's snowing, let's go!\n";
```

If so, then we print our message and, this is the important part, do no more tests. If not, then we move on to the next test:

```
} elsif ($weather eq "raining") {
    print "No way, sorry, it's raining so I'm staying in.\n";
```

Again, if this is true, we stop testing; otherwise, we move on. Finally, if none of the tests are true, we get to the else:

```
} else {
    print "Well, why not?\n";
}
```

---

1. Celsius, that is.

Please remember that this is very different to what would happen if we used four separate if statements. The tests overlap, so it is possible for more than one condition to be true at once. For example, if it was snowing and we had over 30 emails to reply to, we'd get two conflicting answers. elsif tests should be read as "Well, how about if . . . ?"

Another example of using an if/elsif/else is the program we saw earlier, guessnum1.pl. The decision we made in that program was implemented with three if statements:

```
if ($target == $guess) {
    print "That's it! You guessed correctly!\n";
    exit;
}
if ($guess > $target) {
    print "Your number is more than my number\n";
    exit;
}
if ($guess < $target){
    print "Your number is less than my number\n";
    exit;
}
```

Notice that in each if statement we execute the exit() function since, if the condition is true, there is no reason to check any of the following conditions. Instead of using the exit() function in each of the if blocks, this would be better written with an if/elsif/else as shown in guessnum2.pl:

```
#!/usr/bin/perl -w
# guessnum2.pl

use strict;

my $target = 12;
print "Guess my number!\n";
print "Enter your guess: ";
my $guess = <STDIN>;

if ($target == $guess) {
    print "That's it! You guessed correctly!\n";
} elsif ($guess > $target) {
    print "Your number is more than my number\n";
} elsif ($guess < $target) {
    print "Your number is less than my number\n";
}
```

The unless Statement

There's another way of saying if (not $a). As always in Perl, there's more than one way to do it.[2] Some people prefer to think "If this is not true, then { ... }," but other people think "Unless

---

2.　TMTOWTDI—our favorite acronym!

this is true, then { … }." Perl caters to both sets of thought patterns, and we could just as easily have written this:

```
unless ($a) {
    print "\$a is not true\n";
}
```

The psychology is different, but the effect is the same. We'll see later how Perl provides a few alternatives for these control structures to help them more effectively fit the way you think.

Expression Modifiers

When we're talking in English, it's quite normal for us to say

- If this is not true, then this happens, or

- Unless this is true, this happens.

Similarly, it's also quite natural to reverse the two phrases, saying

- This happens if this is not true, or

- This happens unless this is true.

In Perl-speak, we can take this if statement:

```
if ($number == 0) {
    die "can't divide by 0";
}
```

and rewrite it using expression modifiers as follows:

```
die "can't divide by 0" if $number == 0;
```

Notice how the syntax here is slightly different, it's *action* if *condition*. There is no need for parentheses around the condition, and there are no curly braces around the action. Indeed, the indentation isn't part of the syntax, so we could even put the whole statement on one line. Only a single statement will be covered by the condition. This form of the if statement is called an *expression modifier*.

We can turn unless into an expression modifier too, so, instead of this:

```
if (not $name) {
    die "\$name has a false value";
}
```

you may find it more natural to write this:

```
die "\$name has a false value" unless $name;
```

Using Short-Circuited Evaluation

There is yet another way to do something if a condition is true. By using the fact that Perl stops processing a logical operator when it knows the answer, we can create a sort of unless conditional:

```
$name or die "\$name has a false value";
```

How does this work? Well, it's reliant on the fact that Perl uses short-circuited, or lazy, evaluation to give a logical operator its value. If we have the statement X or Y, then if X is true, it doesn't matter what Y is, so Perl doesn't look at it. If X isn't true, Perl has to look at Y to see whether or not that's true. So if $name has a true value, then the die() function will not be executed. Instead, it will do nothing and continue on executing the next statement.

This form of conditional is most often used when checking that something we did succeeded or returned a true value. We will see it often when we're handling files.

To create a positive if conditional this way, use and instead of or. For example, to add one to a counter if a test is successful, you may say

```
$success and $counter++;
```

If you'll recall, and statements are reliant on both substatements being true. So, if $success is not true, Perl won't bother evaluating $counter++ and upping its value by 1. If $success was true, then it would.

Looping Constructs

Now we know how to do everything once. What about if we need to repeat an operation or series of operations? Of course, there are constructs available to do this in Perl, too.

In programming, there are various types of loops. Some loop forever, and are called *infinite loops*, while most, in contrast, are *finite loops*. We say that a program "gets into" or "enters" a loop, and then "exits" or "falls out" when finished. Infinite loops may not sound very useful, but they certainly can be—particularly because most languages, Perl included, provide you with a way by which you can exit the loop. They will also be useful for situations when you just want the program to continue running until the user stops it manually, the computer powers down, or the heat death of the universe occurs, whichever is sooner.

There's also a difference between *definite loops* and *indefinite loops*. In a definite loop, you know how many times the block will be repeated in advance. An indefinite loop will check a condition in each iteration to determine whether it should do another or not.

There's also a difference between an indefinite loop that checks before the iteration, and one that checks afterward. The latter will always go through at least one iteration, in order to get to the check, whereas the former checks first and so may not go through any iterations at all.

Perl supports ways of expressing all of these types of loops. First, let's examine the while loop.

The while Loop

Let's start with the indefinite loops. These check a condition, then do an action, then go back and check the condition again. The first one is the while loop. As you might be able to work out from the name, this keeps doing something while a condition is true. The syntax of while is much like the syntax of if:

while (*condition*) { *action* }

Once again, those curly braces are required. Here's a very simple while loop:

```perl
#!/usr/bin/perl -w
# while1.pl

use strict;

my $countdown = 5;

while ($countdown > 0) {
    print "Counting down: $countdown\n";
    $countdown--;
}
```

And here's what it produces:

```
$ perl while1.pl
Counting down: 5
Counting down: 4
Counting down: 3
Counting down: 2
Counting down: 1
$
```

Let's see a flow chart for this program:

While there's still a value greater than 0 in the $counter variable, we do these two statements:

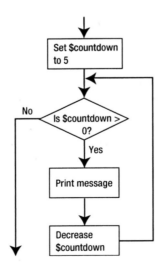

```
print "Counting down: $countdown\n";
$countdown--;
```

Perl goes through the loop a first time when $countdown is 5—the condition is met, so a message gets printed, and $countdown gets decreased to 4. Then, as the flow chart implies, back we go to the top of the loop. We test again: $countdown is still more than 0, so off we go again. Eventually, $countdown is 1, we print our message, $countdown is decreased, and it's now 0. This time around, the test fails, and we exit the loop.

while (<STDIN>)

Recall that we talked about using <STDIN> to read from standard input (normally the keyboard). This statement reads the next line of standard input, up to and including the newline character:

```
$line_in = <STDIN>;
```

We can put this assignment within a while loop that will read from standard input until end of file (in Unix a ^D, or the Ctrl and D keys pressed at the same time, in Windows a ^Z<enter>). This loop reads a line at a time into $line_in and then prints the line read in:

```
while ($line_in = <STDIN>) {
    print $line_in;
}
```

This behavior, reading from standard input until end of file, is so common that if <STDIN> is by itself within the while loop parens (and only within the while loop parens), then the line of standard input is magically assigned to the special variable $_. This loop reads each line into $_, and then the line is printed:

```
while (<STDIN>) {
    print $_;
}
```

This is so common that print() defaults to printing $_:

```
while (<STDIN>) {
    print;
}
```

Let's look at an example of using this magic variable $_. This program will loop through standard input one line at a time until end of file, and for each line it will print a message followed by the line entered:

```
#!/usr/bin/perl -w
# while2.pl

use strict;
```

```
while (<STDIN>) {
    print "You entered: ";
    print;
}
```

Following is an example of running this program in Unix:

```
$ perl while2.pl
hello
You entered: hello
world
You entered: world
good
You entered: good
bye
You entered: bye
^D
$
```

The $_ variable is a useful variable—it is the default argument for many different functions. An example is the chomp() function. The statement

```
chomp $_;
```

could have been written as

```
chomp;
```

Many Perl programmers find it convenient and readable to write a loop like this one:

```
while ($line = <STDIN>) {
    chomp $line;
    ...
}
```

using the default nature of $_:

```
while (<STDIN>) {
    chomp;
    ...
}
```

Whether or not you write code to take advantage of the magic nature of $_ is a choice for you to make, but we suggest you practice with it enough to be able to read code that others have written where $_ is used.

Infinite Loops

The important but obvious point is that what we're testing gets changed inside the loop. If our condition is always going to give a true result, we have ourselves an infinite loop. Let's just remove the second of those two statements:

```
#!/usr/bin/perl -w
# while3.pl

use strict;

my $countdown = 5;

while ($countdown > 0) {
    print "Counting down: $countdown\n";
}
```

$countdown never changes. It's always going to be 5, and 5 is, we hope, always going to be more than 0. So this program will keep printing its message until you interrupt it by holding down Ctrl and C. Hopefully, you can see why you need to ensure that what you do in your loop affects your condition.

Should we actually want an infinite loop, there's a fairly standard way to do it. Just put a true value—typically 1—as the condition:

```
while (1) {
    print "Bored yet?\n";
}
```

The converse, of course, is to say while (0) in the loop's declaration, but nothing will ever happen because this condition is tested before any of the commands in the loop are executed. A bit silly really.

Looping Until

The opposite of if is unless, and the opposite of while is until. It's exactly the same as while (not *condition*) { ... }. Using the condition in the program while1.pl shown previously:

```
while ($countdown > 0) {
```

Its logical negation would be

```
until ($countdown <= 0) {
```

Therefore, we can write while1.pl as

```
#!/usr/bin/perl -w
# until.pl

use strict;

my $countdown = 5;

until ($countdown <= 0) {
    print "Counting down: $countdown\n";
    $countdown--;
}
```

And here's what it produces:

```
$ perl until.pl
Counting down: 5
Counting down: 4
Counting down: 3
Counting down: 2
Counting down: 1
$
```

The for Loop

Perl has a for loop, similar to the one found in C/C++/Java. Its syntax is

```
for (init_expr; test_expr; step_expr) {
    action
}
```

The *init_expr* is done first and once. Then the *test_expr* is tested to be true or false. If true, the *action* is executed, then the *step_expr* is executed. Then the *test_expr* is tested to be true or false, etc.

The most common use of a for loop is as an alternative way of writing a while loop that might resemble this one:

```
$i = 1;
while ($i <= 5) {
    # do something important
    $i++;
}
```

This can be written in a for loop as

```
for ($i = 1; $i <= 5; $i++) {
    # do something important
}
```

The foreach Loop

Perl has another loop called the foreach loop. It is used to loop through lists and arrays. We will talk about arrays in the next chapter, but since we have seen examples of a list, we can look at the foreach loop processing a list of numbers:

```
#!/usr/bin/perl -w
# foreach.pl

use strict;
```

```
my $number;

foreach $number (1 .. 10) {
    print "the number is: $number\n";
}
```

The foreach loop executes the body of the loop (the print() function in this example) for each number in the list. $number is called the *loop control variable*, and it takes on the values in the list, one at a time. Recall that (1 .. 10) is shorthand for (1, 2, 3, 4, 5, 6, 7, 8, 9, 10). This code produces this result:

```
$ perl foreach.pl
the number is: 1
the number is: 2
the number is: 3
the number is: 4
the number is: 5
the number is: 6
the number is: 7
the number is: 8
the number is: 9
the number is: 10
$
```

A note about the keywords for and foreach: they are synonyms for each other. In other words, we can say

```
foreach ($i = 1; $i <= 10; $i++)_ { .. }
```

and

```
for $number (1..10) { .. }
```

foreach is rarely used in place of for, but for is often used instead of foreach. In the spirit of minimal confusion, we will spell out foreach when we have a foreach loop.

We will talk more about foreach in the next chapter when we discuss the array data type.

do .. while and do .. until

When we were categorizing our lists, we divided indefinite loops into those that execute at least once and those that may execute zero times. The while loop we've seen so far tests the condition first, and so if the condition isn't true the first time around, the "body" of the loop never gets executed. There's two other ways to write our loop to ensure that the body is always executed at least once:

```
do { action } while ( condition );
do { action } until ( condition );
```

Now we do the test after the block. This is equivalent to moving the diamond in our flow chart from the top to the bottom.

Here is an example:

```perl
#!/usr/bin/perl -w
# dowhiledountil.pl

use strict;

my $i = 1;

print "starting do...while:\n";
do {
    print "    the value of \$i: $i\n";
    $i++;
} while ($i < 6);

$i = 1;

print "starting do...until\n";
do {
    print "    the value of \$i: $i\n";
    $i++;
} until ($i >= 6);
```

Executing this program produces the following:

```
$ perl dowhiledountil.pl
starting do...while:
    the value of $i: 1
    the value of $i: 2
    the value of $i: 3
    the value of $i: 4
    the value of $i: 5
starting do...until
    the value of $i: 1
    the value of $i: 2
    the value of $i: 3
    the value of $i: 4
    the value of $i: 5
$
```

The importance of the do..while and do..until loop is that the body of the loop is always executed at least once.

Expression Modifying

As before, you can use while as a statement modifier. Following the pattern for if, here's what you'd do with while:

```
while ( condition ) { statement }
```

becomes

```
statement while condition;
```

Similarly:

```
until ( condition ) { statement }
```

becomes

```
statement until condition;
```

Therefore, this loop:

```
while (<STDIN>) {
    print "You entered: $_";
}
```

can be written as

```
print "You entered: $_" while <STDIN>;
```

Loop Control Constructs

Perl provides constructs to allow us to control the flow of our loops. They allow us to break out of a loop, go to the next iteration of the loop, or reexecute the loop. We'll start with breaking out of a loop.

Breaking Out

The keyword last, in the body of a loop, will make Perl immediately exit, or "break out of" that loop. The remaining statements in the loop are not executed, and you end up right at the end. Here is an example of a program that breaks out of the loop when the user enters the text "done":

```
#!/usr/bin/perl -w
# last1.pl

use strict;

while (<STDIN>) {
    if ($_ eq "done\n") {
        last;
    }
    print "You entered: $_";
}

print "All done!\n";
```

```
$ perl last1.pl
Songs
You entered: Songs
from
You entered: from
the
You entered: the
Wood
You entered: Wood
done
All done!
$
```

You can use a last in any looping construct (while, until, for, and foreach). However, the last does not work with the do {} while or do {} until loops.

Note that last1.pl could have been written using an expression modifier. It can be argued that this code is a bit more readable:

```
#!/usr/bin/perl -w
# last2.pl

use strict;

while (<STDIN>) {
    last if $_ eq "done\n";
    print "You entered: $_";
}

print "All done!\n";
```

Going On to the Next

If you want to skip the rest of the processing of the body, but don't want to exit the loop, you can use next to immediately go execute the next iteration of the loop by testing the expression. Here is an example of a program that reads input from the user, and if the line of input is not blank, the line is printed. It the line is blank, then we immediately go back to read the next line:

```
#!/usr/bin/perl -w
# next1.pl

use strict;

print "Please enter some text:\n";
while (<STDIN>) {
    if ($_ eq "\n") {
        next;
    }
```

```
        chomp;
        print "You entered: [$_]\n";
    }
```

Here is an example of running this program in Windows:

```
$ perl next1.pl
Please enter some text:
testing
You entered: [testing]
one
You entered: [one]
two three
You entered: [two three]
^Z<enter>
$
```

Notice that when the user entered a blank line, then the program immediately read the next line of input.

This program could have be written with an expression modifier:

```
#!/usr/bin/perl -w
# next2.pl

use strict;

print "Please enter some text:\n";
while (<STDIN>) {
    next if $_ eq "\n";
    chomp;
    print "You entered: [$_]\n";
}
```

Reexecuting the Loop

On rare occasions, you'll want to go back to the top of the loop, but without testing the condition (in the case of a for or while loop) or getting the next element in the list (as in a for or while loop). If you feel you need to do this, the keyword to use is redo. This is illustrated in this example:

```
#!/usr/bin/perl -w
# redo.pl

use strict;

my $number = 10;

while (<STDIN>) {
    chomp;
    print "You entered: $_\n";
```

```perl
    if ($_ == $number) {
        $_++;
        redo;
    }
    print "Going to read the next number now...\n";
}
```

If the user enters the value 10, then the input is incremented to 11 and we jump to the beginning of the block, at which point the value will be chomped (which has no effect on the value since it does not end in newline) and then the value 11 is reported. Executing this program in Windows would look like the following:

```
$ perl redo.pl
5
You entered: 5
Going to read the next number now...
20
You entered: 20
Going to read the next number now...
10
You entered: 10
You entered: 11
Going to read the next number now...
^Z<enter>
$
```

Loop Labels

By default, last, next, and redo operate on the innermost looping construct only. For instance, in this code:

```perl
#!/usr/bin/perl -w
# looplabel1.pl

use strict;

my $i = 1;

while ($i <= 5) {
    my $j = 1;
    while ($j <= 5) {
        last if $j == 3;
        print "$i ** $j = ", $i ** $j, "\n";
        $j++;
    }
    $i++;
}
```

the last statement within the innermost loop construct (while ($j <= 5)) will last out of the innermost looping construct only. Therefore, each time $j reaches 3 within the inner loop, we last out of the inner loop and increment $i and go back up to test the expression for the outer while loop. This generates this output:

```
$ perl looplabel1.pl
1 ** 1 = 1
1 ** 2 = 1
2 ** 1 = 2
2 ** 2 = 4
3 ** 1 = 3
3 ** 2 = 9
4 ** 1 = 4
4 ** 2 = 16
5 ** 1 = 5
5 ** 2 = 25
$
```

To make the last statement last out of the outer looping construct, we must label the outer looping construct with a *loop label*. A loop label is a variable that the programmer creates (it is recommended that you use all uppercase names) followed by a colon, preceding the looping construct. This is illustrated in looplabel2.pl:

```perl
#!/usr/bin/perl -w
# looplabel2.pl

use strict;

my $i = 1;

OUTER: while ($i <= 5) {
    my $j = 1;
    while ($j <= 5) {
        last OUTER if $j == 3;
        print "$i ** $j = ", $i ** $j, "\n";
        $j++;
    }
    $i++;
}
```

Now, when the last statement is executed, the code jumps out of the outer loop named OUTER:

```
$ perl looplabel2.pl
1 ** 1 = 1
2 ** 1 = 2
$
```

goto

As a matter of fact, you can put a label before any statement whatsoever. If you want to really mess around with the structure of your programs, you can use goto `LABEL` to jump anywhere in your program. Whatever you do, don't do this. This is not to be used. Don't go that way.

We're telling you about it for the simple reason that if you see it in anyone else's Perl, you can laugh heartily at them. goto with a label is to be avoided like the plague.

Why? Because not only does it turn the clock back 30 years (the structured programming movement started with the publication of a paper called "Use of goto considered harmful"), but it tends to make your programs amazingly hard to follow. The flow of control can shoot off in any direction at any time, into any part of the file, maybe into a different file. You can even find yourself jumping into the middle of loops, which really doesn't bear thinking about. Don't use it unless you really, really, really understand why you shouldn't. And even then, don't use it. Larry Wall has never used goto with a label in Perl, and he created Perl.

Don't. (He's watching.—*Ed*)

Summary

Before this chapter, our programs plodded along in a straight line, following one statement with another.

We've now seen how we can react to different circumstances in our programs, which is the start of flexible and powerful programming. We can test whether something is true or false using if and unless, and take appropriate action. We've also examined how to test multiple related conditions using elsif.

We can repeat areas of a program, in several different ways, using while, until, for and foreach.

Finally, we've examined some ways to alter the flow of Perl's execution through these loops. We can break out of a loop with last, skip to the next element with next, and start processing the current element again with redo.

Exercises

1. Modify the number guessing program guessnum2.pl so that it loops until the correct answer is entered.

2. Write a program that prints the squares of the numbers between 1 and 10.

3. Write a program to print all the numbers between 1 and 50 that are evenly divisible by 5. Loop by 1, not by 5!

CHAPTER 4

■■■

Lists and Arrays

In Chapter 2 we introduced the idea of a scalar that is a single value—number or string. Having the ability to work with numbers and strings and having scalar variables into which we can store numbers and strings is nice—this allows us to write programs to manipulate data. However, scalars are somewhat limited since they can only contain a single value.

There are times when we'll want to group together information or express correspondences between information. Just like the ingredients in a recipe or the pieces in a jigsaw, some things belong together in a natural sequence: for example, individual lines in a file, or the names of players in a volleyball tournament. In Perl, we represent these relationships in *lists*—series of scalars. They can be stored in another type of variable called an *array*, and we call each piece of data in the list an *element*.

In this chapter, we'll see how we build up and work with lists. We'll also take another look at the foreach loop, which enables us to step through lists and arrays.

Lists

We're all familiar with lists from everyday life. Think about a shopping list: what properties does it have? First of all, it's a single thing, one piece of paper. Secondly, it's made up of a number of values. In the case of a shopping list, you might want to say that these values are actually strings—"potato chips", "Guinness", "cheese", and so on. Finally, it's also ordered, which means that there's a first item and a last item.

Lists in Perl aren't actually that much different; they're counted as a single thing, but they're made up of a number of values. In Perl, these values are scalars, rather than purely strings. They're also stored in the order they appear in the list.

We'll specify lists in our program code as literals, just like we did with strings and numbers. We'll also be able to perform certain operations on them. Let's begin by looking at a few simple lists and how we create them.

Simple Lists

The simplest shopping list is one where you have nothing to buy. Similarly, the simplest list in Perl has no elements in it, and it is called the *empty list*. Here's what it looks like:

```
()
```

A simple pair of parentheses—that's how we denote a list. However, it's not very interesting. Let's try putting in some values:

```
(42)
("cheese")
```

As you can see, we have created two lists, one containing a number, and one containing a string—so far so good. Remember the print() function? It treats its arguments as lists, and the magic about functions like print() that treat their arguments as lists is that you can omit the parentheses. Saying print "cheese" is just the same as saying print("cheese"). So now we know that what we give to print() is really a list. We're allowed to leave out the parentheses if we wish.

From this, we should be able to work out how to put multiple values into a list. When we said

```
print("Hello, ", "world", "\n");
```

we were actually passing the following list to the print() function:

```
("Hello ", "world", "\n")
```

As you can see, this is a three-element list, and the elements are separated with commas. Computers and computer people start counting from 0, so here's your chance to practice. The zeroth element is "Hello ", the first is "world", and the second is "\n". Now, let's do that again with numbers instead of strings:

```
(123, 456, 789)
```

This is exactly the same as before, and if we were to print this new list, this is what would happen:

```
#!/usr/bin/perl -w
# numberlist.pl

use strict;

print(123, 456, 789);
```

```
$ perl numberlist.pl
123456789$
```

As before, Perl doesn't automatically put spaces between list elements for us when it prints them out, it just prints them as it sees them. Similarly, it doesn't put a newline on the end for us. There's nothing special about lists from that point of view; if we want to add spaces and newlines, then we need to put them into the list ourselves.

Less Simple Lists

We can also mix strings, numbers, and variables in our lists. Let's see an example of a list with several different types of data. Although this isn't very different from what we were doing with print() in Chapter 2, this example reinforces the idea that lists can contain any scalar literals and scalar variables. So, type this in, and save it as mixedlist.pl:

```perl
#!/usr/bin/perl -w
# mixedlist.pl

use strict;

my $test = 30;

print
    "Here is a list containing strings, (this one) ",
    "numbers (",
    3.6,
    ") and variables: ",
    $test,
    "\n"
;
```

When you run that, here's what you should see:

```
$ perl mixedlist.pl
Here is a list containing strings, (this one) numbers (3.6) and variables: 30
$
```

Notice that the print() function prints a list of six elements, including literal strings, literal numbers, and a scalar variable for good measure.

```perl
print
    "Here is a list containing strings, (this one) ",
    "numbers (",
    3.6,
    ") and variables: ",
    $test,
    "\n"
;
```

Since variables interpolate in double-quoted strings inside lists just as well as at any other time, we could have done that all as one long single-element list:

```perl
print ("Here is a list containing strings, (this one) numbers (3.6) and
variables: $test\n");
```

There is a disadvantage of writing your code this way. Newlines in your string literals will turn into newlines in your output. So, if you keep the maximum length of the lines in your source code to about 80 columns (it's a good idea to keep your programs readable), one long string will wrap over and you'll see this sort of thing:

```
$ perl mixedlist.pl
Here is a list containing strings, (this one) numbers (3.6) and
variables: 30
$
```

So if you're ever printing long strings, consider splitting them up into a list of smaller strings on separate lines as we have done previously.

In the same way, single-quoted strings act no differently when they're list elements: ('A number:', '$test') will actually give you two strings, and if you print out that list, you will see this:

```
A number:$test
```

One last thing to note is that Perl automatically *flattens* lists. That is, if you try putting a list inside another list, the internal list loses its identity. In effect, Perl removes all the parentheses apart from the outermost pair. There's no difference at all between any of these three lists:

```
(3, 8, 5, 15)
((3, 8), (5, 15))
(3, (8, 5), 15)
```

Similarly, Perl sees each of these lists as exactly the same as the others:

```
('one', 'two', 'three', 'four')
(('one', 'two', 'three', 'four'))
('one', ('two', 'three'), 'four')
(('one','two'), ('three', 'four'))
```

So we can say in Perl that all lists (and all arrays) are *one dimensional*.

Creating Lists Easily with qw//

Perl provides a useful operator that allows a programmer the ability to easily create lists of one-word strings. The operator is qw//, which stands for *quote words*. It is related to the other "q" operators we saw in Chapter 2: q// and qq//. The operator takes all the things within the slashes that are separated by whitespace characters and creates a single-quoted list of them. For instance, this code:

```
qw/hello world good bye/
```

creates the following list:

```
('hello', 'world', 'good', 'bye')
```

The slashes that are part of qw// are called the *delimiters*, or the things that begin and end the operator. Any nonalphanumeric character can be used. So the preceding could have been written as either of these:

```
qw#hello world good bye#
qw|hello world good bye|
```

If the opening delimiter is either the open angle bracket, square bracket, parenthesis, or curly brace, the closing delimiter is the matching close character. Therefore, the preceding can be written as

```
qw<hello world good bye>
qw[hello world good bye]
qw(hello world good bye)
qw{hello world good bye}
```

Ranges

Often our lists will be a lot simpler than a group of different values. We'll want to talk about "the numbers 1 to 10" or "the letters a–z." Rather than write them out longhand, Perl gives us the ability to specify a range of numbers or letters. Suppose we say

```
(1 .. 6)
```

This will give us a list of six elements from 1 to 6, exactly the same as if we had said (1, 2, 3, 4, 5, 6). This can really save time when you're dealing with a few hundred elements, but note however that it only works for integers. Fractional values in the list are rounded towards 0.

```
(1.4 .. 6.9)
```

would produce (1, 2, 3, 4, 5, 6). There's no problem with using negative numbers in ranges. For example:

```
(-6 .. 3)
```

produces the list (-6, -5, -4, -3, -2, -1, 0, 1, 2, 3).

The right-hand number must, however, be higher than the left-hand one, so we can't use this technique to count down. Instead, you can reverse any list using the reverse() function, as we'll see very shortly.

We can do the same for letters as well:

```
('a'..'k')
```

This will give us an 11-element list, consisting of each letter from "a" to "k" inclusive. Note that we can't mix letters and numbers within a range. If we try, Perl will interpret the string as a number and treat it as 0.

Here's a demonstration of all the things we can do with ranges:

```
#!/usr/bin/perl -w
# ranges.pl

use strict;

print "Counting up: ", (1 .. 6), "\n";
print "Counting down: ", (6 .. 1), "\n";
print "Counting down  (properly this time) : ", reverse(1 .. 6), "\n";

print "Half the alphabet: ", ('a' .. 'm'), "\n";
print "The other half (backwards): ", reverse('n' .. 'z'), "\n";

print "Going from 3 to z: ", (3 .. 'z'), "\n";
```

```
print "Going from z to 3: ", ('z' .. 3), "\n";
```

Which of those will work and which won't? Let's find out . . .

```
$ perl ranges.pl
Argument "z" isn't numeric in range (or flop) at ranges.pl line 13.
Argument "z" isn't numeric in range (or flop) at ranges.pl line 14.
Counting up: 123456
Counting down:
Counting down  (properly this time): 654321
Half the alphabet: abcdefghijklm
The other half (backwards): zyxwvutsrqpon
Going from 3 to z::
Going from z to 3: :   0123
$
```

After the usual opening, we first count upwards with a range.

```
print "Counting up: ", (1 .. 6), "\n";
```

We've seen the range in action before, and we know this produces (1, 2, 3, 4, 5, 6). We pass print() a list containing the string "Counting up: ", the six elements, and a newline. Because a list inside a list gets flattened, we're actually just passing an eight-element list. It's the same as if we'd done the following:

```
print "Counting up: ", 1, 2, 3, 4, 5, 6, "\n";
```

And we get the expected result:

```
Counting up: 123456
```

Next, we try and count down:

```
print "Counting down: ", (6 .. 1), "\n";
```

This doesn't work because the right-hand side needs to be bigger than the left and all that's produced is the empty list, (). To count down properly, we need to make a list using (1 .. 6) as before, and turn it around. The reverse() function reverses a list. For example:

```
reverse (qw(The cat sat on the mat))
```

produces the same as

```
qw(mat the on sat cat The)
```

In this case, reverse(1..6) produces (1, 2, 3, 4, 5, 6) and then reverses it to become (6, 5, 4, 3, 2, 1), and we see the list appear in that order:

```
Counting down (properly this time) : 654321
```

Next we demonstrate a simple alphabetic range:

```
print "Half the alphabet: ", ('a' .. 'm'), "\n";
```

This range expands to the values "a", "b", "c", and so on all the way to "m". Doing that backwards is easy:

```
print "The other half (backwards): ", reverse('n' .. 'z'), "\n";
```

Now we come to the ones that don't work, and it's no surprise that Perl warns us against them:

```
Argument "z" isn't numeric in range (or flop) at ranges.pl line 13.
Argument "z" isn't numeric in range (or flop) at ranges.pl line 14.
```

The lines in question are

```
print "Going from 3 to z: ", (3 .. 'z'), "\n";
print "Going from z to 3: ", ('z' .. 3), "\n";
```

What does the error message mean? Pretty much what it says: we gave an argument of "z" to a range when it was expecting a number instead. The interpreter converted the "z" to a number as per the rules in Chapter 2, and got a 0. It's equivalent to this:

```
print "Going from 3 to z: ", (3 .. 0), "\n";
print "Going from z to 3: ", (0 .. 3), "\n";
```

The first one produces an empty list, and the second one counts up from 0 to 3.

Accessing List Values

We've now seen most of the ways of building up lists in Perl, and we can pass lists to functions like print(). But another thing we need to be able to do with lists is access a specific element or set of elements within them. The way to do this is to place the number of the elements we want in square brackets after a list, like this:

```
#!/usr/bin/perl -w
# access.pl

use strict;

print(('salt', 'vinegar', 'mustard', 'pepper')[2]);
print "\n";
```

Before you run this, though, see if you can work out which word will be printed.

```
$ perl access.pl
mustard
$
```

Did you think it was going to be "vinegar"? Don't forget that Perl starts counting things from 0!

You should also notice that we had to put parentheses around the arguments passed to print(); this is because the precedence of print() is extremely high. Without the parentheses, Perl groups the statement in two parts like this:

```
print('salt', 'vinegar', 'mustard', 'pepper')    [2];
```

This means the whole of the list is passed to print(), after which Perl attempts to retrieve the second element of print(). The problem is, you can only take an element from a list, and as we already know, print() isn't a list.

So, since print() needs to be passed a list, we make a list out of the element we want:

```
print (
    ('salt', 'vinegar', 'mustard', 'pepper')[2]
);
```

The element you want doesn't have to be given as a literal—variables work just as well. Here's an example of accessing an element of a list of months:

```
#!/usr/bin/perl -w
# months.pl

use strict;

my $month = 3;

print qw(
    January     February     March
    April       May          June
    July        August       September
    October     November     December
)[$month];
```

When this is run, you should now be expecting it to give you "April", and it does:

```
$ perl months.pl
April$
```

The key piece of code for this example is the last statement:

```
print qw(
    January     February     March
    April       May          June
    July        August       September
    October     November     December
)[$month];
```

We have $month as 3, and so we are telling Perl to print out the third element of the list, starting from 0. Because we're using qw//, we can use arbitrary whitespace, tabs, and newlines to separate each list element, which allows us to present the months in a neat table.

This is exactly the sort of situation for which `qw//` was created; we have a list comprised completely of single words, and we want to represent that to Perl in a readable way in our source code. It's far easier to read than spelling the list out longhand, even though the preceding `print()` statement is equivalent to

```
print (('January','February', 'March', 'April', 'May',
        'June', 'July', 'August', 'September', 'October',
        'November', 'December')[$month]);
```

What do you think would happen if we chose a noninteger value for our element? Let's use a value with a fractional part. Change the preceding file so that line 5 reads

```
my $month = 2.2;
```

Perl will round the number in this case, and you should get the answer "March". In fact, Perl always rounds towards 0, so anything between 2 and 3 will get you March.

What about negative numbers? Actually, something interesting happens here—Perl starts counting backwards from the end of the list. So element –1 is the last one, –2 the second to last one, and so on.

```
#!/usr/bin/perl -w
# backwards.pl

use strict;

print qw(
    January     February    March
    April       May         June
    July        August      September
    October     November    December
)[-1];
```

And, true to form, we'll get the last element of the array when we run the program.

```
$ perl backwards.pl
December$
```

List Slices

So much for getting a single element out of a list. What if we want to get several? Instead of putting a number or a scalar variable inside those square brackets, you can actually put a list. For example, this:

```
(19, 68, 47, 60, 53, 51, 58, 55, 47)[(4, 5, 6)]
```

returns another list consisting of the third, fourth, and fifth elements: (53, 51, 58). Actually, inside the square brackets we don't need the additional set of parentheses, so you might as well say

```
(19, 68, 47, 60, 53, 51, 58, 55, 47)[4, 5, 6]
```

We call this a *list slice,* and the same methods work with lists of strings, illustrated in the program multilist.pl. Just like the preceding examples, we're taking several elements from a list.

```
#!/usr/bin/perl -w
# multilist.pl

use strict;

my $mone;
my $mtwo;
($mone, $mtwo) = (1, 3);

print(("heads ", "shoulders ", "knees ", "toes ")[$mone, $mtwo]);
print "\n";
```

Try and think what it's going to produce before you run it. Here's what happens:

```
$ perl multilist.pl
shoulders toes
$
```

As you may have realized, we simply printed out the first and the third elements from the list, if you start counting from 0.

There are two key tricks in this example. The first is on line 7:

```
($mone, $mtwo) = (1, 3);
```

You might be able to see what this line does from how the rest of the program runs. The value of $mone is set to 1, and $mtwo to 3. But how does this work?

Perl allows lists on the left-hand side of an assignment operator. When we assign one list to another, the right-hand list is built up first, and then Perl assigns each element in turn from the right-hand side of the statement to the left. So 1 is assigned to $mone, and then 3 is assigned to $mtwo. This is called an *assignable list.*

If you're okay with that, then now's a good time for a quick quiz. Suppose we've done the preceding: $mone is 1 and $mtwo is 3. What do you think would happen if we said this?

```
($mone, $mtwo) = ($mtwo, $mone);
```

The right-hand list is built up first, so Perl looks at the values of the variables and constructs the list (3, 1). Then the 3 is assigned to $mone, and the 1 assigned to $mtwo. In effect, we've swapped the values of the variables around—a handy trick to learn and remember. Chances are that it's something you'll need to do again and again over time.

Back to our example! Once we've set $mone to 1 and $mtwo to 3, we can pick out these elements from a list. There's nothing that says that we have to use literals to pick out the elements we want. This:

```
print(("heads ", "shoulders ", "knees ", "toes ")[$mone, $mtwo]);
```

is interpreted by Perl just the same as this:

```
print(("heads ", "shoulders ", "knees ", "toes ")[1, 3]);
```

Indeed, both statements equate to the same thing—picking out a list consisting of the first and third elements of our original list and printing them. In effect, we call

```
print("shoulders ", "toes ");
```

which is indeed what happens.

Combining Ranges and Slices

We can, of course, use ranges in our list slices. This gets March through September:

```
(qw(Jan Feb Mar Apr May Jun Jul Aug Sep Oct Nov Dec)[2..8])
```

And this gets November through February via December and January (remember that –2 is the second to last element and –1 the last element):

```
(qw(Jan Feb Mar Apr May Jun Jul Aug Sep Oct Nov Dec)[-2..1])
```

We can also use a mixture of ranges and literals in our slice. This gives us January, April, and August to December:

```
(qw(Jan Feb Mar Apr May Jun Jul Aug Sep Oct Nov Dec)[0,3,7..11])
```

It may be a bit confusing, but have a go at slicing your own arrays and you'll get the hang of it in no time at all.

Arrays

Just as with scalar literals, there's only so much you can do with list literals. Literal lists get cumbersome to repeat, and don't allow us to manipulate them at all. If we wanted to say "the same list, but without the last element," we couldn't do it. As before, we need to find a way to store them in a variable.

The variable storage we use for lists is called an *array*. Whereas the name of a scalar variable started with a dollar sign, arrays start with an at sign (@). The same rules for naming your arrays apply as for any other variables: start with an alphabetic character or underscore, followed by zero or more alphabetic characters, underscores, or numbers.

Assigning Arrays

We store a list in an array just like we store a scalar literal into a scalar variable, by assigning it with =:

```
@array = (1,2,3);
```

Once we've assigned our array, we can use our array where we would use a list:

```
#!/usr/bin/perl -w
# dayarray.pl

use strict;
```

```
my @days;
@days = qw(Monday Tuesday Wednesday Thursday Friday Saturday Sunday);
print @days, "\n";
```

This prints

```
$ perl dayarray.pl
MondayTuesdayWednesdayThursdayFridaySaturdaySunday
$
```

Like scalars, arrays must be declared with my() if you use strict.

Note that $days is a completely different variable from @days—setting one does nothing to the other. In fact, if you were to do this:

```
#!/usr/bin/perl -w
# baddayarray1.pl

use strict;

my @days;
@days = qw(Monday Tuesday Wednesday Thursday Friday Saturday Sunday);
$days = 31;
```

you would get the following error:

```
Global symbol "$days" requires explicit package name at dayarray.pl line 8.
```

This is because you have declared @days to be a lexical variable, but not $days. Even when you declare them both, setting one has no effect on the other.

```
#!/usr/bin/perl -w
# baddayarray2.pl

use strict;

my @days;
my $days;
@days = qw(Monday Tuesday Wednesday Thursday Friday Saturday Sunday);
$days = 31;
print @days, "\n";
print $days, "\n";
```

prints

```
MondayTuesdayWednesdayThursdayFridaySaturdaySunday
31
```

What would happen if you assigned an array to a scalar variable? To find out, take a look at the following example of two arrays assigned to two different scalar variables:

```
#!/usr/bin/perl -w
# arraylen.pl

use strict;

my @array1;
my $scalar1;
@array1 = qw(Monday Tuesday Wednesday Thursday Friday Saturday Sunday);
$scalar1 = @array1;

print "Array 1 is @array1\nScalar 1 is $scalar1\n";

my @array2;
my $scalar2;
@array2 = qw(Winter Spring Summer Autumn);
$scalar2 = @array2;
print "Array 2 is @array2\nScalar 2 is $scalar2\n";
```

Executing this program gives this result:

```
$ perl arraylen.pl
Array 1 is Monday Tuesday Wednesday Thursday Friday Saturday Sunday
Scalar 1 is 7
Array 2 is Winter Spring Summer Autumn
Scalar 2 is 4
$
```

Hmm . . . the first array has seven elements, and the scalar value is 7. The second has four elements, and the scalar value is 4.

There are two things to note in this program. The first is how array variables interpolate in a double-quoted string. We've seen that if you put a scalar variable name inside a string, Perl will fill in the value of the variable. Now we've put an array variable in a string, and Perl has filled it in, but it has placed spaces between the elements. Look at the following two print() statements:

```
@array = (4, 6, 3, 9, 12, 10);
print @array, "\n";
print "@array\n";
```

The first one does exactly what we've seen with lists, printing all the elements next to each other. The second statement, however, inserts a space between each element:

```
46391210
4 6 3 9 12 10
```

This adding of spaces between elements is what happens when an array is interpolated in a double-quoted string. As with scalars, interpolation is not confined to print(). For example:

```
$scalar = "@array\n";
```

is the same as

```
$scalar = "4 6 3 9 12 10\n";
```

Forcing variables to make sense in a string is called *stringifying* them.

Scalar vs. List Context

What happens when we assign an array to a scalar variable? One key point to remember is that Perl knows exactly what type of value you want, whether a scalar or an array, at any stage in an operation, and will do its best to make sure you get it.

For example, if we're looking to assign to a scalar variable, we need to have a scalar value—the assignment is taking place in *scalar context*. On the other hand, for example, print() expects to see a list of arguments. Those arguments are in *list context*. However, some operations may return different values depending on which context they are called. That's what's happening in this case:

```
print @array1;
$scalar1 = @array1;
```

The first line is in list context. In list context, an array evaluates to the list of its elements. In the second line, however, the assignment wants to see a single result, or scalar value, and therefore we're in scalar context. In scalar context, an array evaluates to the number of its elements, in our case, seven for the days and four for the seasons.

If we were to do this:

```
@array2 = @array1;
```

we would be assigning to an array. So we're looking for a *list* of values to fill @array2. Here, we're back in list context, and so @array2 gets filled with all of the values of @array1.

We can force something to be in scalar context when it expects to be in list context by using the scalar() function. Compare these two statements:

```
print @array1;
print scalar @array1;
```

As we've explained before, print() usually wants a list, so Perl evaluates print()'s arguments in list context. In the preceding example, print() is looking to get a list from each of its arguments. That's why the first statement prints the contents of @array1. If we force @array1 into scalar context, then the number of elements in the array is passed to print(), and not the contents of the array.

■**Note** Perl distinguishes between operations that want a list and operations that want a scalar. Those that want a list, such as print() or assigning to an array, are said to be in list context. Those that want a scalar are said to be in scalar context. The value of an array in list context is the list of its elements—the value of an array in scalar context is the number of its elements.

Adding to an Array

How do we add elements to an array? One way to do it is by using the "list flattening" principle and treating our arrays as lists. This isn't a particularly good way to do it, but it works:

```
#!/usr/bin/perl -w
# addelem.pl

use strict;

my @array1 = (1, 2, 3);
my @array2;
@array2 = (@array1, 4, 5, 6);
print "@array2\n";

@array2 = (3, 5, 7, 9);
@array2 = (1, @array2, 11);
print "@array2\n";

$ perl addelem.pl
1 2 3 4 5 6
1 3 5 7 9 11
$
```

It's far better, however, to use the functions we're going to see later on—push(), pop(), shift(), and unshift().

Accessing an Array

Once we've got our list of scalars into an array, it would make sense to be able to get them back out again. We do this slightly differently to the way we get values out of lists.

Accessing Single Elements

We can now put elements into an array:

```
my @array = (10, 20, 30);
```

If we look at the array in scalar context, we get the number of elements in it. So

```
print scalar @array;
```

will print the value 3. But how do we get at one of those elements? We could use the list assignment we were looking at earlier:

```
#!/usr/bin/perl -w
# assignlist.pl

my $scalar0;
my $scalar1;
my $scalar2;
```

```perl
my @array = (10, 20, 30);

($scalar0, $scalar1, $scalar2) = @array;

print "Scalar zero is $scalar0\n";
print "Scalar one is $scalar1\n";
print "Scalar two is $scalar2\n";
```

This will print out each of the elements:

```
$ perl assignlist.pl
Scalar zero is 10
Scalar one is 20
Scalar two is 30
$
```

There is a better way to access a single element of an array using something quite similar to what we did with a list. To get a single element from a list, if you remember, we put the number we want in square brackets after it.

```perl
$a = (10, 20, 30)[0];
```

This will set $a to the zeroth element, 10. We could do this:

```perl
$a = (@array)[0];
```

in exactly the same way. However, it's more usual to write that as follows:

```perl
$a = $array[0];
```

Look carefully at that. Even though @array and $array are different variables, we use the $array[] form. Why?

Note The rule is this: the prefix represents what you want to get, not what you've got. So @ represents a list of values, and $ represents a single scalar. Hence, when we're getting a single scalar from an array, we never prefix the variable with @—that would mean a list. A single scalar is always prefixed with a $.

$array[0] can only refer to an element of the @array array. If you try and use the wrong prefix, Perl will complain with a warning.

```perl
#!/usr/bin/perl -w
# badprefix.pl

use strict;

my @array = (1, 3, 5, 7, 9);
print @array[1];
```

will print

```
$ perl badprefix.pl
Scalar value @array[1] better written as $array[1] at badprefix.pl line 7.
3$
```

We call the number in the square brackets the *array index* or *array subscript*. The array index is the number of the element that we want to get hold of.

Just like extracting elements from lists, we can use a scalar variable as our subscript:

```
#!/usr/bin/perl -w
# scalarsub.pl

use strict;

my @array = (1, 3, 5, 7, 9);
my $subscript = 3;
print $array[$subscript], "\n";
$array[$subscript] = 12;

print $array[$subscript], "\n";
```

This prints the third element from zero, which has the value 7. It then changes that 7 to a 12 and prints the value of that element. Negative subscripts work from the right-hand side; as before, $array[-1] will give you the last element in the array. Executing this program produces the following:

```
$ perl scalarsub.pl
7
12
$
```

Now let's look at a program to extract a given element from an array. We'll use arrays to write a program to tell us some (really bad) jokes. We actually set up two arrays—one containing the question, and one containing the answer.

```
#!/usr/bin/perl -w
# joke1.pl

use strict;

my @questions = qw(Java Python Perl C);
my @punchlines = (
    "None. Change it once, and it's the same everywhere.",
    "One. He just stands below the socket and the world revolves around him.",
    "A million. One to change it, the rest to try and do it in fewer lines.",
    '"CHANGE?!!"'
);
```

```
print "Please enter a number between 1 and 4: ";
my $selection = <STDIN>;
$selection -= 1;
print "How many $questions[$selection] ";
print "programmers does it take to change a lightbulb?\n\n";
sleep 2;
print $punchlines[$selection], "\n";
```

Here is an example of running this program:

```
$ perl joke1.pl
Please enter a number between 1 and 4: 3
How many Perl programmers does it take to change a lightbulb?

A million. One to change it, the rest to try and do it in fewer lines.
$
```

In this program, we first set up our arrays; one is a list of words, and so we can use qw// to specify it. The other is a list of strings containing whitespace characters, so we have to quote them using the ordinary list style.

```
my @questions = qw(Java Python Perl C);
my @punchlines = (
    "None. Change it once, and it's the same everywhere.",
    "One. He just stands below the socket and the world revolves around him.",
    "A million. One to change it, the rest to try and do it in fewer lines.",
    '"CHANGE?!!"'
);
```

We now ask the user to choose a joke:

```
print "Please enter a number between 1 and 4: ";
my $selection = <STDIN>;
$selection -= 1;
```

Why subtract 1 from $selection? We've asked for a number between 1 and 4, and our array subscripts go from 0 to 3.

Next we display the setup line:

```
print "How many $questions[$selection] ";
print "programmers does it take to change a lightbulb?\n\n";
```

From the first line we see that array elements stringify just like scalar variables. Next, this new function sleep():

```
sleep 2;
```

What sleep() does, as you'll know if you've run the program, is pause the program's operation for a number of seconds. In this case, we're telling it to sleep for two seconds.

After the user has had time to think about it, we display the punchline:

```
print $punchlines[$selection], "\n";
```

$#array

For any given array, for example @array, there is an easy way to obtain the value of its last index: $#array.

Therefore, for the array @a, its last index is $#a. For @b, its last index is $#b.

Note: this syntax gives us the last *index* of the array, not its last *value*. The last value of @a can be accessed by indexing with $#a into @a with the syntax $a[$#a] (looks a little weird, but it does work!). This is illustrated in the following example:

```
#!/usr/bin/perl -w
# lastindex.pl

use strict;

my @array = (2, 4, 6, 8);

print "the last index is:   ", $#array, "\n";
print "the last element is: ", $array[$#array], "\n";
```

Executing this code produces

```
$ perl lastindex.pl
the last index is:   3
the last element is: 8
$
```

The last index will assist us in looping through an array with indexes.

Looping Through an Array with Indexes

Since we can access an individual element of an array with the syntax

```
$array[$index]
```

and we know the first index of the array is 0 and the last index is $#array, we can loop through an array with a loop that resembles

```
my $i = 0;
while ($i <= $#array) {
    # process array element using the syntax $array[$i]
    $i++;
}
```

Most Perl programmers would implement this using a for loop:

```
for (my $i = 0; $i <= $#array; $i++) {
    # process array element using the syntax $array[$i]
}
```

Here is an example of using both the while loop and the for loop to process an array. It will loop left to right through an array named @names, accessing each element with $names[$i].

```perl
#!/usr/bin/perl -w
# whilefor.pl

use strict;

my @names = qw(John Joe Mary Sue);

print "processing using a while loop:\n";

my $i = 0;
while ($i <= $#names) {
    print "    Hello $names[$i]!\n";
    $i++;
}

print "processing using a for loop:\n";

for (my $i = 0; $i <= $#names; $i++) {
    print "    Hello $names[$i]!\n";
}
```

Executing this code results in the following:

```
$ perl whilefor.pl
processing using a while loop:
    Hello John!
    Hello Joe!
    Hello Mary!
    Hello Sue!
processing using a for loop:
    Hello John!
    Hello Joe!
    Hello Mary!
    Hello Sue!
$
```

Hopefully, you're starting to see alternative ways we can use arrays by now. Of course, we've only been pulling single values from arrays so far. The next logical step is to start working with multiple array elements.

Accessing Multiple Elements

If you'll recall, we created and used a list slice by putting ranges or several numbers in brackets to get multiple elements from a list. If we want to get multiple elements from an array, we can use the analogous concept, an *array slice*.

List slices, if you remember, looked like this:

```
(qw(Jan Feb Mar Apr May Jun Jul Aug Sep Oct Nov Dec))[3,5,7..9]
```

Can you work out which elements the preceding slice consists of? If not, write a short Perl program to print them out, and see if you can get it to separate them with spaces. (Hint: only arrays stringify with spaces, so you'll need to use one.)

Array slices look very similar. However, now that we are accessing multiple elements and expecting a list, we no longer want to use $ as the prefix—now we should be using @.

We can get the same list as the preceding one like this:

```
my @array = qw(Jan Feb Mar Apr May Jun Jul Aug Sep Oct Nov Dec);
print @array[3,5,7..9];
```

Array slices act like any normal list, and so can be assigned to. Here's a program that uses a bunch of slices, `aslice.pl`, implementing a year's sales results for a fictitious bathroom tile shop:

```
#!/usr/bin/perl -w
# aslice.pl

use strict;
```

```perl
my @sales = (69, 118, 97, 110, 103, 101, 108, 105, 76, 111, 118, 101);
my @months = qw(Jan Feb Mar Apr May Jun Jul Aug Sep Oct Nov Dec);

print "Second quarter sales:\n";
print "@months[3..5]\n@sales[3..5]\n";
my @q2 = @sales[3..5];

# Incorrect results in May, Aug, Oct, Nov and Dec!
@sales[4, 7, 9..11] = (68, 101, 114, 111, 117);

# Swap Apr and May
@months[3,4] = @months[4,3];
```

Most of the work is behind the scenes, but this is what you'd see if you run it:

```
$ perl aslice.pl
Second quarter sales:
Apr May Jun
110 103 101
```

Let's take a look at what's actually going on. We set up our two arrays, one holding our sales figures, and the other holding the names of the months:

```perl
my @sales = (69, 118, 97, 110, 103, 101, 108, 105, 76, 111, 118, 101);
my @months = qw(Jan Feb Mar Apr May Jun Jul Aug Sep Oct Nov Dec);
```

To extract the information about the second quarter, we use an array slice for the months in question:

```perl
print "Second quarter sales:\n";
print "@months[3..5]\n@sales[3..5]\n";
my @q2 = @sales[3..5];
```

As well as saving the relevant elements to another array, we can print out the slice and it will be stringified. We can also assign values to an array slice as well as getting data from it:

```perl
@sales[4, 7, 9..11] = (68, 101, 114, 111, 117);
```

This sets new values for $sales[4], $sales[7], $sales[9], $sales[10], and $sales[11].

Finally, we can use something similar to the ($a, $b) = ($b, $a) list trick to swap two array elements:

```perl
@months[3,4] = @months[4,3];
```

This is exactly the same as the following statement:

```perl
($months[3], $months[4]) = ($months[4], $months[3]);
```

As you can see, this isn't all that far from the list assignment to swap two variables:

```perl
($mone, $mtwo) = ($mtwo, $mone);
```

Processing Arrays with the foreach Loop

One thing we'll want to do quite often is run over each of the elements in an array or list in turn. If we want to double every value in an array, then *for each* element we come across, we multiply by 2. The keyword to use here is *foreach*. The foreach loop has the following syntax:

```
foreach scalar_variable ( list_or_array ) {
    body
}
```

The block must start with an opening brace and end with a closing brace, and the list or array that we're running over must be surrounded by parentheses.

This loop executes the body for each item in the list or array. As it passes through the list or array, the scalar variable (called the *control variable*, or *iterator variable*) is the element of the list or array. Here is a simple example:

```
#!/usr/bin/perl -w
# foreach1.pl

use strict;

my $element;

foreach $element ('zero', 'one', 'two') {
    print "the element is: $element\n";
}
```

This program first declares $element. This variable will be used to pass through the list. Then the body is executed three times—once for each element in the list. This produces the following output:

```
$ perl foreach1.pl
the element is: zero
the element is: one
the element is: two
$
```

The foreach loop can also process array variables. Here is an example that prints each element of an array followed by a newline:

```
#!/usr/bin/perl -w
# foreach2.pl

use strict;

my @array = qw(America Asia Europe Africa);
my $element;
```

```
foreach $element (@array) {
    print $element, "\n";
}
```

In this program we set up an array and we declare a scalar variable, $element. What we then say is "Set each element of @array to $element in turn, and then do all the statements in the following block." So, on our first iteration, $element is set to America, and then the print() statement is executed, then $element is set to Asia, and the print() statement runs again. This continues until the end of the array is reached.

This should print the following:

```
$ perl foreach2.pl
America
Asia
Europe
Africa
$
```

Choosing an Iterator

We can specify the iterator variable ourselves, as we did in the preceding examples, or we can use the default one, $_. Furthermore, if we're being good and using strict, we can make our iterator variable a lexical my variable as we go along. That is, we could write a program like this—note how $i is declared:

```
#!/usr/bin/perl -w
# foreach3.pl

use strict;

my @array = (1, 3, 5, 7, 9);
foreach my $i (@array) {
    print "This element: $i\n";
}
```

There's actually a very subtle difference between declaring your iterator inside and outside of the loop. If you declare your iterator outside the loop, any value it had then will be restored afterwards. We can check this out by setting the variable and testing it afterwards:

```
#!/usr/bin/perl -w
# foreach4.pl

use strict;

my @array = (1, 3, 5, 7, 9);
my $i = "Hello there";
foreach $i (@array) {
    print "This element: $i\n";
}
print "All done: $i\n";
```

This will produce the following output:

```
$ perl foreach4.pl
This element: 1
This element: 3
This element: 5
This element: 7
This element: 9
All done: Hello there
$
```

Declaring the iterator within the loop, as in foreach3.pl, will create a new variable $i each time, which will only exist for the duration of the loop.

As a matter of style, it's usual to keep the names of iterator variables very short; the traditional iterator is $i as we've used here. The length of a variable name should be related to the importance of the variable—iterators are usually throwaway variables that only exist for one block, so they shouldn't be prominently named.

Modifying the Value of an Iterator

When processing a foreach loop, Perl makes the iterator refer to each element of the list or array in turn, and then executes the block. If the block happens to change the value of the iterator, the corresponding array element changes as well. We can double each element of an array like this:

```
#!/usr/bin/perl -w
# foreach5.pl

use strict;

my @array = (10, 20, 30, 40);

print "Before: @array\n";

foreach (@array) {
    $_ *= 2;
}

print "After: @array\n";
```

This prints as follows:

```
$ perl foreach5.pl
Before: 10 20 30 40
After: 20 40 60 80
$
```

Notice that in the foreach loop in foreach5.pl there is no explicit control variable indicated:

```
foreach (@array) {
    $_ *= 2;
}
```

If the control variable is omitted, $_ is used by default.

If you need to know the number of the element you're currently processing, it's usually best to have the iterator as the range of numbers you're processing—from 0 up to the highest element number in the array. Let's rewrite the joke machine so that it tells *all* the bad jokes, without prompting:

```
#!/usr/bin/perl -w
# joke2.pl

use strict;

my @questions = qw(Java Python Perl C);
my @punchlines = (
    "None. Change it once, and it's the same everywhere.",
    "One. He just stands below the socket and the world revolves around him.",
    "A million. One to change it, the rest to try and do it in fewer lines.",
    '"CHANGE?!!"'
);

foreach (0..$#questions) {
    print "How many $questions[$_] ";
    print "programmers does it take to change a lightbulb?\n";
    sleep 2;
    print $punchlines[$_], "\n\n";
    sleep 1;
}
```

The changes to our old joke1.pl program produce this result:

```
$ perl joke2.pl
How many Java programmers does it take to change a lightbulb?
None. Change it once, and it's the same everywhere.

How many Python programmers does it take to change a lightbulb?
One. He just stands below the socket and the world revolves around him.

How many Perl programmers does it take to change a lightbulb?
A million. One to change it, the rest to try and do it in fewer lines.

How many C programmers does it take to change a lightbulb?
"CHANGE?!!"

$
```

In this version of the joke program, the foreach loop is now the main part of our program. Let's have a look at it again:

```
foreach (0..$#questions) {
    print "How many $questions[$_] ";
    print "programmers does it take to change a lightbulb?\n";
    sleep 2;
    print $punchlines[$_], "\n\n";
    sleep 1;
}
```

The key thing about this example is that we need to match the questions to the punchlines. This means we can't just go through one or the other of the arrays, but have to go through them both together. We do this by using a list, which counts up from 0 to the highest element of one of the arrays. Since the arrays are both the same size, it doesn't matter which one. The line that does this is

```
foreach (0..$#questions) {
```

$#questions is the index of the last element in the @questions array. That's different from the value we get when we look at @questions in a scalar context:

```
#!/usr/bin/perl -w
# elems.pl

use strict;

my @array = qw(alpha bravo charlie delta);

print "Scalar value : ", scalar(@array), "\n";
print "Highest index: ", $#array, "\n";
```

```
$ perl elems.pl
Scalar value : 4
Highest index: 3
$
```

Why? There are four elements in the array—so that's the scalar value. Their indices are 0, 1, 2, and 3. Since we're starting at 0, the highest index ($#array) will always be one less than the number of elements in the array.

So, we count up from 0 to the last index of @questions, which happens to be 3. We set the iterator to each number in turn. Where's the iterator? Since we didn't give one, Perl will use $_. Now we do the block four times, once when $_ is 0, once when it is 1, and so on.

```
print "How many $questions[$_] ";
```

This line prints the zeroth element of @questions the first time around, then the first, then the second, third, and fourth.

```
print $punchlines[$_], "\n\n";
```

And so it is with the punchlines. If we'd just said

```
foreach (@questions) {
```

$_ would have been set to each question in turn, but we would not have advanced our way through the answers.

A quick note: recall that the keywords for and foreach are synonyms for each other. We will stick to the style of calling a foreach a foreach, but some Perl programmers call the foreach a for. This also applies to the expression modifier form of the foreach.

Expression Modifier for the foreach Loop

Just as there was an expression modifier form of if, like this:

```
die "Something wicked happened" if $error;
```

there's also an **expression modifier** form of foreach. This means you can iterate an array, executing a single expression every time. Here, however, you don't get to choose your own iterator variable: it's always $_. It has this form:

statement foreach *list_or_array*;

Here is a quick example:

```
#!/usr/bin/perl -w
# foreach6.pl

use strict;

my @a = qw(hello world good bye);

print "[$_]\n" foreach @a;
```

Running this code produces the following:

```
$ perl foreach6.pl
[hello]
[world]
[good]
[bye]
$
```

Array Functions

It's time we met some more of the things we can do with arrays. These are called *array functions*. We've already met one of them: reverse(), which we used to count down ranges instead of counting up. We can use reverse() on arrays as well as lists:

```
#!/usr/bin/perl -w
# countdown.pl
```

```
use strict;

my @count = (1..5);

foreach (reverse(@count)) {
    print "$_...\n";
    sleep 1;
}

print "BLAST OFF!\n";
```

Hopefully, you should have a good idea of what this will print out before you run it.

```
$ perl countdown.pl
5...
4...
3...
2...
1...
BLAST OFF!
$
```

There are some very useful functions for adding elements to arrays. Here they are now along with a couple of other useful tips and tricks.

pop() and push()

We've already seen a simple way to add elements to an array: `@array = (@array, $scalar)`.

One of the original metaphors that computer programmers like to use to analyze arrays is a *stack* of spring-loaded plates in a cafeteria. You push down when you put another plate on the top, and the stack pops up when a plate is taken away:

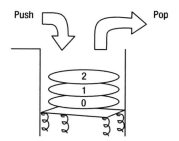

Following this metaphor, `push()` is the function that adds an element, or list of elements, to the end of an array. Similarly, to remove the top element—the element with the highest index—we use the `pop()` function. These are illustrated in the following example.

Stacks are all around us. Many times, they're all stacks of paper. We can manipulate arrays just as we can manipulate these stacks of paper:

```
#!/usr/bin/perl -w
# stacks.pl

use strict;

my $hand;
my @pileofpaper = ("letter", "newspaper", "gas bill", "notepad");

print "Here's what's on the desk: @pileofpaper\n";

print "You pick up something off the top of the pile.\n";
$hand = pop @pileofpaper;
print "You have now a $hand in your hand.\n";

print "You put the $hand away, and pick up something else.\n";
$hand = pop @pileofpaper;
print "You picked up a $hand.\n";

print "Left on the desk is: @pileofpaper\n";

print "You pick up the next thing, and throw it away.\n";
pop @pileofpaper;

print "You put the $hand back on the pile.\n";
push @pileofpaper, $hand;

print "You also put a leaflet and a bank statement on the pile.\n";
push @pileofpaper, "leaflet", "bank statement";

print "Left on the desk is: @pileofpaper\n";
```

Watch what happens:

```
$ perl stacks.pl
Here's what's on the desk: letter newspaper gas bill notepad
You pick up something off the top of the pile.
You have now a notepad in your hand.
You put the notepad away, and pick up something else.
You picked up a gas bill.
Left on the desk is: letter newspaper
You pick up the next thing, and throw it away.
You put the gas bill back on the pile.
You also put a leaflet and a bank statement on the pile.
Left on the desk is: letter gas bill leaflet bank statement
$
```

To see how this program works, let's talk about it line by line. First off, we initialize our $hand and our @pileofpaper. Since the pile of paper is a stack, the zeroth element (the letter) is at the bottom, and the notepad is at the top.

```
my $hand;
my @pileofpaper = ("letter", "newspaper", "gas bill", "notepad");
```

We use pop @pileofpaper to remove the top, or rightmost, element from the array and it returns that element, which we store in $hand. So, we take the notepad from the stack and put it into our hand. What's left? The letter at the bottom of the stack, then the newspaper and gas bill.

```
print "You pick up something off the top of the pile.\n";
$hand = pop @pileofpaper;
print "You have now a $hand in your hand.\n";
```

As we pop() again, we take the next element (the gas bill) off the top of the stack, or the right-hand side of the array, and store it again in $hand. Since we didn't save the notepad from last time, it's lost forever now.

```
print "You put the $hand away, and pick up something else.\n";
$hand = pop @pileofpaper;
print "You picked up a $hand.\n";
```

The next item is the newspaper. We pop() this as before, but we never store it anywhere.

```
print "You pick up the next thing, and throw it away.\n";
pop @pileofpaper;
```

We've still got the gas bill in $hand from previously. push @array, $scalar will add the scalar onto the top of the stack. In our case, we're putting the gas bill on top of the letter.

```
print "You put the $hand back on the pile.\n";
push @pileofpaper, $hand;
```

push() can also be used to add a list of scalars onto the stack—in this case, we've added two more strings. We could add the contents of an array to the top of the stack with push @array1, @array2. So we now know that we can replace a list with an array.

```
print "You also put a leaflet and a bank statement on the pile.\n";
push @pileofpaper, "leaflet", "bank statement";
```

As you might suspect, you can also push lists of lists onto an array—they simply get flattened first into a single list and then added.

shift() and unshift()

While the functions push() and pop() deal with the "top end," or right-hand side, of the stack, adding and taking away elements from the highest index of the array, the functions unshift() and shift() do the corresponding jobs for the bottom end, or left side, of the array:

```
#!/usr/bin/perl -w
# shift.pl

use strict;

my @array = ();
unshift @array, "first";
print "Array is now: @array\n";
unshift @array, "second", "third";
print "Array is now: @array\n";
shift @array ;
print "Array is now: @array\n";
```

```
$ perl shift.pl
Array is now: first
Array is now: second third first
Array is now: third first
$
```

First we unshift() an element onto the array, and the element appears at the beginning of the list. It's not easy to see this since there are no other elements, but it does. We then unshift() two more elements. Notice that the entire list is added to the beginning of the array all at once, and not one element at a time. We then use shift() to take off the first element, ignoring what it was.

sort()

One last thing you may want to do while processing data is put it in alphabetical or numeric order. The sort() function takes a list and returns a sorted version.

```
#!/usr/bin/perl -w
# sort1.pl

use strict;

my @unsorted = qw(Cohen Clapton Costello Cream Cocteau);
print "Unsorted: @unsorted\n";
my @sorted = sort @unsorted;
print "Sorted:   @sorted\n";
```

```
$ perl sort1.pl
Unsorted: Cohen Clapton Costello Cream Cocteau
Sorted:   Clapton Cocteau Cohen Costello Cream
$
```

This is **only good for strings and alphabetic sorting.** If you're sorting numbers, there is a problem. Can you guess what it is? This may help:

```perl
#!/usr/bin/perl -w
# sort2.pl

use strict;

my @unsorted = (1, 2, 11, 24, 3, 36, 40, 4);
my @sorted = sort @unsorted;
print "Sorted:   @sorted\n";
```

```
$ perl sort2.pl
Sorted:   1 11 2 24 3 36 4 40
$
```

What? 11 doesn't come between 1 and 2. What we need to do is compare the numeric values instead of the string ones. Cast your mind back to Chapter 2 and recall how to compare two numeric variables, $a and $b. Here, we're going to use the <=> operator. sort() allows us to give it a block to describe how two values should be ordered, and we do this by comparing $a and $b.These two variables are given to us by the sort() function:

```perl
#!/usr/bin/perl -w
# sort3.pl

use strict;

my @unsorted = (1, 2, 11, 24, 3, 36, 40, 4);

my @string = sort { $a cmp $b } @unsorted;
print "String sort:  @string\n";

my @number = sort { $a <=> $b } @unsorted;
print "Numeric sort:  @number\n";
```

```
$ perl sort3.pl
String sort:  1 11 2 24 3 36 4 40
Numeric sort:  1 2 3 4 11 24 36 40
$
```

Another good reason for using string comparison operators for strings and numeric comparison operators for numbers!

Summary

Lists are a series of scalars in order. Arrays are variable incarnations of lists. Both lists and arrays are flattened, so we cannot yet have a distinct list inside another list. We get at both lists and arrays with square-bracket subscripts; these can be single numbers or a list of elements. If we're looking up a single scalar in an array, we need to remember to use the form $array[$element] because the variable prefix always refers to what we want, not what we have got. We can also use ranges to save time and to specify list and array slices.

Perl differentiates between scalar and list context, and returns different values depending on what the statement is expecting to see. For instance, the scalar context value of an array is the number of elements in it, and the list context value is, of course, the list of the elements themselves.

Exercises

1. Write a program that assigns an array the value (2, 4, 6, 8) and uses two loops to output

   - 2 ** 2 = 4
   - 4 ** 2 = 16
   - 6 ** 2 = 36
   - 8 ** 2 = 64
   - 8 ** 2 = 64
   - 6 ** 2 = 36
   - 4 ** 2 = 16
   - 2 ** 2 = 4

2. When you assign to a list, the elements are copied over from the right to the left.

   ```
   ($a, $b) = ( 10, 20 );
   ```

   will make $a become 10 and $b become 20. Investigate what happens when

   - There are more elements on the right than on the left.
   - There are more elements on the left than on the right.
   - There is a list on the left but a single scalar on the right.
   - There is a single scalar on the left but a list on the right.

3. What elements make up the range ('aa' .. 'bb')? What about ('a0' .. 'b9')?

CHAPTER 5

■■■

Hashes

We have talked about two types of data: scalars and arrays. Scalars are single pieces of information, while arrays are single variables containing many different values.

Alternatively, some things are better expressed as a set of one-to-one correspondences. A phone book, for example, is a set of correspondences between addresses and phone numbers. In Perl, structures like the phone book are represented as a *hash*. Some people call them *associative arrays* because they look a bit like arrays where each element is associated with another value. Most Perl programmers find that a bit too long-winded, and end up just calling them *hashes*.

Comparing a hash to a phone book is helpful, but there is a slight difference in that a phone book is normally ordered—the names are sorted alphabetically. In a hash the data is totally unsorted and has no intrinsic order. In fact, it's more like directory enquiries than a phone book, in that you can easily find out what the number is if you have the name. Someone else keeps the order for you, and you needn't ask what the first entry is.

Here's where a diagram helps:

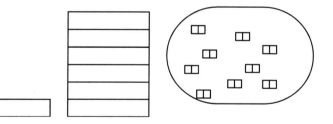

A scalar is one piece of data. It's like a single block. An array or a list is like a tower of blocks; it's kept in order, and it's kept together as a single unit. A hash, on the other hand, is more like the illustration above. It contains several pairs of data. The pairs are in no particular order, no pair is "first" or "top," and they're all scattered around the hash.

Creating a Hash

Just like scalar variables have a $ prefix, and arrays have a @ prefix, hashes have their own prefix—a percent sign. Again, the same naming rules apply, and the variables %hash, $hash, and @hash are all different.

One way of creating a hash variable is to assign it a list that is treated as a collection of key/value pairs:

```
%where = (
        "Gary"     , "Dallas",
        "Lucy"     , "Exeter",
        "Ian"      , "Reading",
        "Samantha" , "Oregon"
);
```

In this case, the hash could be saying that "Gary's whereabouts is Dallas," "Lucy lives in Exeter," and so on. All it really does is pair Gary and Dallas, Lucy and Exeter, and so on. How the pairing is interpreted is up to you.

If we want to make the relationship, and the fact that we're dealing with a hash, a little clearer, we can use the => operator. That's not >=, which is greater-than-or-equal-to; the => operator acts like a "quoting comma." That is, it's a comma, but whatever appears on the left-hand side of it—and only the left—is treated as a double-quoted string.

```
%where = (
        Gary     => "Dallas",
        Lucy     => "Exeter",
        Ian      => "Reading",
        Samantha => "Oregon"
);
```

The scalars on the left of the arrow are called the *hash keys*, the scalars on the right are the values. We use the keys to look up the values.

Note Hash keys must be unique. You cannot have more than one entry for the same name, and if you try to add a new entry with the same key as an existing entry, the old one will be overwritten. Hash values meanwhile need not be unique.

Key uniqueness is more of an advantage than a limitation. Every time the word "unique" comes into a problem, like counting the unique elements of an array, your mind should immediately echo "Use a hash!"

Because hashes and arrays are both built from structures that look like lists, you can convert between them, from array to hash, like this:

```
@array = qw(Gary Dallas Lucy Exeter Ian Reading Samantha Oregon);
%where = @array;
```

Assigning an array to a hash will work properly only when there are an even number of elements in the array.

The hash can then be assigned back to an array like so:

```
@array = %where;
```

However, you need to be careful when converting back from a hash to an array. Hashes do not have a guaranteed order; although values will always follow keys, you cannot tell what order the keys will come in. Since hash keys are unique, however, we can be sure that %hash1 = %hash2 is guaranteed to copy a hash accurately.

Working with Hash Values

To look up a value in a hash, we use something similar to the index notation for arrays. However, instead of locating elements by number, we're now locating them by name, and instead of using square brackets, we use curly braces.

Here's a simple example of looking up details in a hash:

```perl
#!/usr/bin/perl -w
# hash.pl

use strict;

my $who = "Ian";

my %where = (
        Gary     => "Dallas",
        Lucy     => "Exeter",
        Ian      => "Reading",
        Samantha => "Oregon"
);

print "Gary lives in ", $where{Gary}, "\n";
print "$who lives in $where{$who}\n";
```

```
$ perl hash.pl
Gary lives in Dallas
Ian lives in Reading
$
```

The first thing we do in this program is set up our main hash, which tells us where people live.

```perl
my %where = (
        Gary     => "Dallas",
        Lucy     => "Exeter",
        Ian      => "Reading",
        Samantha => "Oregon"
);
```

Like scalars and arrays, hash variables must be declared with my() when using strict. Now we can look up an entry in our hashes—we'll ask "Where does Gary live?"

```
print "Gary lives in ", $where{Gary}, "\n";
```

This is almost identical to looking up an array element, except for using curly braces instead of square brackets and the fact that we are now allowed to use strings to index our elements. Notice that the key Gary is not quoted within the curly braces. If the key contains no whitespace characters, it is assumed quoted within the curly braces. If the key does contain whitespace characters, then we will have to quote it.

The next line is

```
print "$who lives in $where{$who}\n";
```

Just as with array elements, we need not use a literal to index the element—we can look up using a variable as well.

Adding, Changing, and Removing Elements

Hash entries are very much like ordinary scalar variables, except that you need not declare an individual hash key before assigning to it or using it. We can add a new person to our hash just by assigning to their hash entry:

```
$where{Eva} = "Uxbridge";
print "Eva lives in $where{Eva}\n";
```

A new entry springs into existence, without any problems. We can also change the entries in a hash just by reassigning to them. Let's move people around a little:

```
$where{Eva}      = "Denver";
$where{Samantha} = "California";
$where{Lucy}     = "Tokyo";
$where{Gary}     = "Las Vegas";
$where{Ian}      = "Southampton";

print "Gary lives in $where{Gary}\n";
```

To remove an entry from a hash, you need to use the delete() function, as we do in this little variant on hash.pl:

```
#!/usr/bin/perl -w
# badhash.pl

use strict;

my %where = (
        Gary     => "Dallas",
        Lucy     => "Exeter",
        Ian      => "Reading",
        Samantha => "Oregon"
);
```

```
delete $where{Lucy};
print "Lucy lives in $where{Lucy}\n";
```

You can see that here we delete Lucy's entry in %where before we access it, so executing this program should produce an error. Sure enough, we get

```
$ perl badhash.pl
Use of uninitialized value in concatenation (.) at badhash.pl line 14
Lucy lives in
$
```

It's not that we haven't initialized poor Lucy, but rather that we've decided to get rid of her.

Hash in List Context

When we discussed lists and arrays, we spent a lot of time talking about the difference between list and scalar context. Let's look at what happens when we evaluate a hash in list context. This is demonstrated with the following program:

```perl
#!/usr/bin/perl -w
# listcontext.pl

use strict;

my %person = (
    name  => 'John Doe',
    age   => 39,
    phone => '555-1212',
    city  => 'Chicago'
);

my @data = %person;

print "list context: ", join("|", @data), "\n";
print "another way: ", %person, "\n";
```

This program takes the hash in list context in two ways. First, it assigns it to an array:

```perl
my @data = %person;
```

then the array is printed by joining its contents with the string "|" (more on the join() function in Chapter 7):

```perl
print "list context: ", join("|", @data), "\n";
```

The second way is to simply print it:

```perl
print "another way: ", %person, "\n";
```

Recall that all arguments to the print() function are treated in list context.

When executed, we can see that a hash variable in list context is a list of the key/value pairs in the order stored in memory (not necessarily in the order in which the hash was created):

```
$ perl listcontext.pl
list context: age|39|city|Chicago|phone|555-1212|name|John Doe
another way: phone555-1212age39cityChicagonameJohn Doe
$
```

We see a key (phone), followed by its value (555-1212), followed by a key (age), followed by its value (39), etc.

Hash in Scalar Context

A hash in scalar context is shown in this example:

```
#!/usr/bin/perl -w
# scalarcontext.pl

use strict;

my %person = (
    name  => 'John Doe',
    age   => 39,
    phone => '555-1212',
    city  => 'Chicago'
);

my $scalar = %person;

print "scalar context: $scalar\n";

if (%person) {
    print "%person has at least one key/value pair\n";
} else {
    print "%person is empty!\n";
}
```

Executing this program produces the following:

```
$ perl scalarcontext.pl
scalar context: 3/8
%person has at least one key/value pair
$
```

This code produces an unexpected result. The following code:

```
my $scalar = %person;

print "scalar context: $scalar\n";
```

prints the string "scalar context: 3/8". Therefore, this hash in scalar context is "3/8" which means that we are using three buckets, or memory locations, out of eight buckets allocated.

This string is not so interesting unless we notice that the string "3/8" is a true value in Perl. Also, if our hash was empty, its value in scalar context would be the empty string, "". So a hash in scalar context is normally treated as a true/false value—true if there is anything in it, false if empty:

```
if (%person) {
    print "%person has at least one key/value pair\n";
} else {
    print "%person is empty!\n";
}
```

Hash Functions

Since hashes in list context are apparently random collections of key/value pairs, we can't really use foreach loops on them directly. If we did, we would get both keys and values with no indication as to which was which. To help us, Perl provides three functions for iterating over hashes: keys(), values(), and each().

Also, Perl provides functions to remove elements (delete(), already seen previously), and to check to see if a key exists in the hash (exists()).

The keys() Function

First, there is keys(%hash). This gives us a list of the keys (all of the scalars on the left-hand side). This is usually what we want when we wish to visit each hash entry in turn as shown in this example:

```
#!/usr/bin/perl -w
# keys.pl

use strict;

my %where = (
        Gary     => "Dallas",
        Lucy     => "Exeter",
        Ian      => "Reading",
        Samantha => "Oregon"
);
```

```
foreach (keys %where) {
    print "$_ lives in $where{$_}\n";
}
```

Currently, this tells us

```
$ perl keys.pl
Lucy lives in Exeter
Samantha lives in Oregon
Gary lives in Dallas
Ian lives in Reading
$
```

You may find that the output appears in a different order on your machine.[1] Don't worry. As mentioned before, hashes are unordered, and there's no guarantee that the keys will come out in the same order each time. It really depends on the particular version of Perl that you are using.

Let's look at the part of the program that does all the work:

```
foreach (keys %where) {
    print "$_ lives in $where{$_}\n";
}
```

keys() is a function which, like sort() and reverse(), returns a list. The list in this case is qw(Lucy Samantha Gary Ian), and the foreach loop visited each of those values in turn. As $_ was set to each one, we could print the name and look up that entry in the hash.

The values() Function

The counterpart to keys() is values(), which returns a list of all of the values in the hash. This is somewhat less useful, since you can always find the value if you have the key, but you cannot easily find the key if you have the value. It's almost always advantageous to use keys() instead.

Here is an example using the values() function:

```
#!/usr/bin/perl -w
# values.pl

use strict;

my %where = (
        Gary      => "Dallas",
        Lucy      => "Exeter",
```

---

1. Or even different every time that you run it! Some 5.8.x Perl installations have hash order randomization turned on by default.

```
          Ian      => "Reading",
          Samantha => "Oregon"
);

foreach (values %where) {
    print "someone lives in $_\n";
}
```

Executing this program produces the following:

```
$ perl values.pl
someone lives in Exeter
someone lives in Oregon
someone lives in Dallas
someone lives in Reading
$
```

The each() Function

The next hash function is each(). It returns *each* hash entry as a key/value pair. Normally, the values returned are copied into an assignable list like this:

```
($k, $v) = each %where;
```

This is illustrated in each.pl:

```
#!/usr/bin/perl -w
# each.pl

use strict;

my %where = (
        Gary     => "Dallas",
        Lucy     => "Exeter",
        Ian      => "Reading",
        Samantha => "Oregon"
);

my($k, $v);
while (($k, $v) = each %where) {
    print "$k lives in $v\n";
}
```

Here is an example of this program executing:

```
$ perl each.pl
Lucy lives in Exeter
Samantha lives in Oregon
Gary lives in Dallas
Ian lives in Reading
$
```

The delete() Function

We have already seen the delete() function. It removes a key/value pair from a hash. This statement from badhash.pl removes the pair Lucy/Exeter from %where:

```
delete $where{Lucy};
```

Since we are on the subject, we should mention that the delete() function also deletes array elements. The following code would remove element 3 from the array @array. Note that the element returns to an uninitialized state:

```
delete $array[3];
```

The exists() Function

The last function we will look at is the exists() function. It returns true if the key exists in the hash, false if not. Here is an example:

```perl
#!/usr/bin/perl -w
# exists.pl

use strict;

my %where = (
        Gary      => "Dallas",
        Lucy      => "Exeter",
        Ian       => "Reading",
        Samantha => "Oregon"
);

print "Gary exists in the hash!\n"  if exists $where{Gary};
print "Larry exists in the hash!\n" if exists $where{Larry};
```

Running this program results in the following:

```
$ perl exists.pl
Gary exists in the hash!
$
```

Note exists() returns 1 when true, an empty string when false.

The exists() function also works for array elements. This code checks to see if element 3 exists in @array:

```perl
if (exists $array[3]) {
    print "element 3 exists!\n";
}
```

Hash Examples

Hashes are very useful variables and there are many uses for them. Here are a few examples of using hashes to solve common problems.

Creating Readable Variables

The most basic use of a hash is to be able to index into a variable to obtain information using a readable string which is far more user-friendly than using a numeric index as we would with an array. For instance, this program shows that we can create a record of strings representing RGB colors that one might find in an HTML page:

```perl
#!/usr/bin/perl -w
# colors.pl

use strict;

my %colors = (
    red    => '#FF0000',
    green  => '#00FF00',
    blue   => '#0000FF',
    white  => '#FFFFFF',
    black  => '#000000',
    purple => '#520063'
);

print "Red is:    $colors{red}\n";
print "Blue is:   $colors{blue}\n";
print "Purple is: $colors{purple}\n";
```

Notice how the information in the hash is laid out in such a way that it is readable by human beings. It is easy to see that the RGB string for "red" is "#FF0000" and indexing into the hash is the human-friendly $colors{red}.

Executing this code produces the following:

```
$ perl colors.pl
Red is:    #FF0000
Blue is:   #0000FF
Purple is: #520063
$
```

"Reversing" Information

Recall the hash we created earlier in this chapter that was a collection of people and where they lived:

```perl
%where = (
        Gary    => "Dallas",
        Lucy    => "Exeter",
```

```
    Ian       => "Reading",
    Samantha => "Oregon"
);
```

If you need to turn this hash around to look up people by where they live, you can use a hash in list context that produces a list of key/value pairs, reverse the list with the reverse() function, and then assign it to a new hash.

```
%who = reverse %where;
```

Be careful though—if you have two values that are the same, then converting them to keys means that one will be lost. Remember that keys must be unique.

Here is a program illustrating reversing a hash:

```
#!/usr/bin/perl -w
# reverse.pl

use strict;

my %where = (
    Gary      => "Dallas",
    Lucy      => "Exeter",
    Ian       => "Reading",
    Samantha => "Oregon"
);

my %who = reverse %where;

foreach (keys %who) {
    print "in $_ lives $who{$_}\n";
}
```

Executing this code produces the following:

```
$ perl reverse.pl
in Oregon lives Samantha
in Exeter lives Lucy
in Reading lives Ian
in Dallas lives Gary
$
```

After we assigned to %who, we created a hash indexed by the location producing the name that is the direct opposite of %where, which was indexed by name to produce the location.

Counting Things

A very common use of a hash variable is to count things. For instance, we can count the number of characters in a string or the items in an array. Let's look at counting items in an array.

We will create an array of names and then we will count the number of times each name occurs in the array. For instance, for this array:

```
my @names = qw(
    John    Sue     Larry
    Mary    John    Mary
    Larry   John    Joe
    Lisa    John    Mary
);
```

we see that @names is a collection of 12 names. Upon close inspection, we see that "John" occurs four times, "Sue" occurs once, and so on.

We can use a hash to keep a count of the number of times a name occurs in @names by creating a hash that will have the names as its keys, and the number of occurrences of the name as the value associated with the key. For instance, when all the names in @names are processed, we will end up with a hash that resembles

```
John  => 4,
Sue   => 1,
Larry => 2,
Mary  => 3,
Joe   => 1,
Lisa  => 1
```

Here is a program illustrating this concept:

```perl
#!/usr/bin/perl -w
# count.pl

use strict;

my @names = qw(
    John    Sue     Larry
    Mary    John    Mary
    Larry   John    Joe
    Lisa    John    Mary
);

my %count;

foreach (@names) {
    if (exists $count{$_}) {
        $count{$_}++;
    } else {
        $count{$_} = 1;
    }
}
```

```
foreach (keys %count) {
    print "$_ \toccurs $count{$_} time(s)\n";
}
```

Executing this code produces the following result:

```
$ perl count.pl
Joe     occurs 1 time(s)
Lisa    occurs 1 time(s)
John    occurs 4 time(s)
Mary    occurs 3 time(s)
Sue     occurs 1 time(s)
Larry   occurs 2 time(s)
$
```

The most important part of this program is when we loop through the array and keep count:

```
foreach (@names) {
    if (exists $count{$_}) {
        $count{$_}++;
    } else {
        $count{$_} = 1;
    }
}
```

This code implements the logic "For each name in the array, if the name already exists in the hash, then increment the value by 1 (incrementing the count); else if it does not exist in the hash, then add the name to the hash with the initial value of 1." After all the names are processed, then the hash will contain all the names and the number of times that each name is present in @names.

For minimalists, the if statement can be shortened because this logic:

```
if (exists $count{$_}) {
    $count{$_}++;
} else {
    $count{$_} = 1;
}
```

is built into the statement

```
$count{$_}++;
```

Therefore, our foreach loop could be changed to

```
foreach (@names) {
    $count{$_}++;
}
```

or more simply

```
$count{$_}++ foreach @names;
```

Summary

Hashes are unordered structures made up of pairs, each pair consisting of a key and a value, and given the key we can look up the value. Generally, $hash{$key} = $value. We can loop over all the elements of a hash by processing the keys using a foreach loop to go through the keys.

Hashes are very useful variables that allow us to create data that is human-readable, reversible, and often used for counting things.

Exercises

1. Create this hash variable:

   ```
   scalar => 'dollar sign',
   array  => 'at sign',
   hash   => 'percent sign'
   ```

   Process it with a foreach loop that prints the key/value pairs so that the keys are printed in sorted order:

   ```
   array: at sign
   hash: percent sign
   scalar: dollar sign
   ```

2. Store your important phone numbers in a hash. Write a program to look up numbers by the person's name.

3. Turn the joke machine program in Chapter 4 from two arrays into one hash. While doing so, write some better lightbulb jokes.

CHAPTER 6

■ ■ ■

Subroutines/Functions

When programming, there will naturally be activities we will want to do again and again: adding up the values in an array, stripping extraneous blank spaces from a string, getting information into a hash in a particular format, and so on. It would be tedious to write out the code for each of these little processes every time we need to use one, and maintaining each code segment would be horrific: if there's a bug in the way we've coded the activity, we'll have to go through and find each one of them and fix it. It would be better if we could define a particular process just once, and then be able to call on that just like we've been calling on Perl's built-in functions.

This is exactly what *subroutines* allow us to do. Subroutines (or *functions*, or simply *subs*) give us the ability to give a name to a section of code. Then when we need to use that code in our program, we just call it by name.

Functions help our programming for two main reasons: first, they let us reuse code, as described previously. This makes it easier to find and fix bugs, and makes it faster for us to write programs. The second reason is that they allow us to chunk our code into organizational sections. Each subroutine can, for example, be responsible for a particular task.

So, when is it appropriate to use subroutines in Perl? There are two cases when a piece of code should be put into a subroutine. First, you want to include code in a subroutine when you know it will be used to perform a calculation or action that's going to happen more than once. For instance, putting a string into a specific format, printing the header or footer of a report, turning an incoming data record into a hash, and so on.

Secondly, use subroutines if there are logical units of your program that you want to break up to make your program easier to understand. There is nothing worse than debugging several thousand lines of Perl that are not broken up in any way. Well, maybe one or two things. As an extreme example, sometimes—and only sometimes—it is desirable to have a "main program" that consists entirely of calls to subroutines, like this:

```
#!/usr/bin/perl -w

use strict;

setup();
get_input();
process_input();
output();
```

This immediately shows the structure of the program. Each of those four subroutines would, of course, have to be defined, and they'd probably call on other subroutines themselves. This allows us to partition up our programs, to change our single, monolithic piece of code into manageable chunks for ease of understanding, ease of debugging, and ease of maintaining the program.

One note about the term *subroutine*: in Perl, the words "subroutine" and "function" are synonyms—they both mean the same thing. We will use them interchangeably in this book.

Understanding Subroutines

Now that we know what subroutines are, it's time to look at how to define them and how to use them. First, let's see how to create subroutines.

Defining a Subroutine

We can give Perl some code, and we can give it a name, and that's our subroutine. Here's how we do it:

```
sub example_subroutine {
    ...
}
```

There are three sections to this declaration:

- The keyword sub.

- The name we're going to give it. The rules for naming a subroutine are exactly those for naming variables; names must begin with an alphabetic character or an underscore, to be followed by zero or more alphanumerics or underscores. Uppercase letters are allowed, but we tend to reserve all-uppercase names for special subroutines. And again, as for variables, you can have a scalar $fred, an array @fred, a hash %fred, and a subroutine fred(), and they'll all be distinct.

- A block of code delimited by curly braces, just as we saw when we were using while and if. Notice that we don't need a semicolon after the closing curly brace.

After we've done that, we can use our subroutine.

Before we go any further though, it's worth taking a quick time-out to ponder how we name our subroutines. You can convey a lot about a subroutine's purpose with its name, much like that of a variable. Here are some guidelines—not hard-and-fast rules—about how you should name subroutines:

- If they're primarily about doing something, name them with a verb—for example, summarize() or download().

- If they're primarily about returning something, name them after what they return—for example, greeting() or header().

- If they're about testing whether something is true or not, give them a name that makes sense in an if statement; starting with is_... or can_... helps, or if that isn't appropriate, name them with an adjective: for example, is_available(), valid(), or readable().

- Finally, if you're converting between one thing and another, try and convey both things—traditionally this is done with a 2 or _to_ in the middle: text2html(), meters_to_feet(). That way you can tell easily what's being expected and what's being produced.

Invoking a Subroutine

The conventional way to invoke a function is to follow the function name with parentheses. This invokes the example_subroutine() function:

```
example_subroutine();
```

If the function takes arguments (more on passing arguments later in this chapter), then drop them within the parentheses:

```
example_subroutine('Perl is', 'my favorite', $language);
```

Let's look at a complete example. It's traditional for programs to tell you their version and name either when they start up or when you ask them with a special option. It's also convenient to put the code that prints this information into a subroutine to get it out of the way. Let's take a recognizable program and update it for this traditional practice.

Here's what we started with, version 1:

```
#!/usr/bin/perl -w

print "Hello, world!\n";
```

And here it is with strict mode turned on and version information:

```
#!/usr/bin/perl -w
# hello2.pl

use strict;

sub version {
    print "Beginning Perl's \"Hello, world.\" version 2.0\n";
}

my $option = shift;    # defaults to shifting @ARGV

version() if $option eq "-v" or $option eq "--version";

print "Hello, world.\n";
```

Now, we're starting to look like a real utility:

```
$ perl hello2.pl -v
Beginning Perl's "Hello, world." version 2.0
Hello, world.
$
```

The first thing we see in `hello2.pl` is the definition of the `version()` function:

```
sub version {
    print "Beginning Perl's \"Hello, world.\" version 2.0\n";
}
```

It's a simple block of code that calls the `print()` function. It didn't have to—it could have done anything. Any code that's valid in the main program is valid inside a subroutine, including calling other functions.

We call this block the *body* of the subroutine, just like we had the body of a loop; similarly, it stretches from the open curly brace after the subroutine name to the matching closing curly brace.

Now that we've defined it, we can use it. We invoke the function with `version()`, and Perl runs that block of code, albeit with the proviso we've added the right flag on the command line.

```
version() if $option eq "-v" or $option eq "--version";
```

When it's finished executing `version()`, it comes back and carries on with the next statement:

```
print "Hello, world.\n";
```

No doubt version 3 will address the warnings that Perl gives if you call this program without appending -v or --version to its name.

Order of Declaration and Invoking Functions

Normally, functions are called using the parens as we did in the preceding program:

```
version()
```

We can also call them without the parentheses if the function is defined before it is invoked:

```
version
```

If we just call our subroutines by name without parentheses, as we just saw, we're forced to declare them before we use them. This may not sound like much of a limitation, but there are times when we'll want to declare our subroutines after the main part of the program; in fact, that's the usual way to structure a program. This is because when you open up the file in your editor, you can see what's going on right there at the top of the file, without having to scroll through a bunch of definitions first. Take the extreme example at the beginning of this chapter:

```
#!/usr/bin/perl -w

use strict;

setup();
get_input();
process_input();
output();
```

That would then be followed, presumably, by something like this:

```
sub setup {
    print "This is some program, version 0.1\n";
    print "Opening files...\n";
    open_files();
    print "Opening network connections...\n";
    open_network();
    print "Ready!\n";
}

sub open_files {
    ...
}
```

▓**Tip** That's far easier to understand than trawling through a pile of subroutines before getting to the four lines that constitute our main program.

In order to get this to work, we need to provide hints to Perl as to what we're doing: that's why the preceding calls to subroutines have a pair of parentheses: setup(), open_files(), and so on.

This helps to tell Perl that it should be looking for a subroutine somewhere instead of referring to another type of variable. What happens if we don't do this?

```
#!/usr/bin/perl -w
# subdecl.pl

use strict;

setup;

sub setup {
    print "This is some program, version 0.1\n";
}
```

```
$ perl subdec1.pl
Bareword "setup" not allowed while "strict subs" in use at subdecl.pl line 6.
Execution of subdecl.pl aborted due to compilation errors.
$
```

Perl didn't know what we meant at the time and complained. So, to tell it we're talking about a subroutine, we use parentheses, just like when we want to disambiguate the parameters to a function like print().

There's another way we can tell Perl that we're going to refer to a subroutine, and that's to provide a *forward definition*—also known as *predeclaring* the subroutine. This means "We're not going to define this right now, but look out for it later."

We do this by just saying sub NAME;, and note that this does require a semicolon at the end. Here's another way of writing the preceding example:

```
#!/usr/bin/perl -w

use strict;

sub setup;
sub get_input;
sub process_input;
sub output;
sub open_files;
sub open_network;
...
```

From now on, we can happily use the subroutines without the parentheses:

```
setup;
get_input;
process_input;
output;

sub setup {
    print "This is some program, version 0.1\n";
    print "Opening files...\n";
    open_files;
    print "Opening network connections...\n";
    open_network;
    print "Ready!\n";
}

sub open_files {
    ...
}
```

Alternatively, you can ask Perl to provide the forward declarations for you. If we say use subs (...), we can provide a list of subroutine names to be predeclared:

```
#!/usr/bin/perl -w

use strict;

use subs qw(setup get_input process_input output pen_files open_network);

...
```

You may also see yet another way of calling subroutines:

```
&setup;
&get_input;
&process_input;
&output;
```

This was popular in the days of Perl 4, and we'll see later why the ampersand is important. For the time being, think of the ampersand as being the "type symbol" for subroutines.

In this book we will stick to calling our functions with parentheses to clearly indicate that we are invoking a function. Sometimes, the more clarity the better.

Passing Arguments into Functions

As well as being set pieces of code to be executed whenever we need them, we can also use our user-defined functions just like Perl's built-in functions—we can pass *arguments* (aka *parameters*) to the subroutine and expect an answer back.

Just like with Perl's built-ins, we pass parameters by placing them between the parentheses:

```
my_sub(10,15);
```

What happens to them there? Well, they end up in one of Perl's special variables, the array @_, and from there we can get at them. We'll illustrate this with a subroutine that takes a list of values, adds them up, and prints the total. This example, total1.pl, contains a function named total() that loops through the argument list @_ and sums the arguments passed in:

```
#!/usr/bin/perl -w
# total1.pl

use strict;

total(111, 107, 105, 114, 69);
total(1...100);
```

```
sub total {
    my $total = 0;
    $total += $_ foreach @_;
    print "The total is $total\n";
}
```

And to see it in action:

```
$ perl total1.pl
The total is 506
The total is 5050
$
```

This program illustrates that we can pass any list to a subroutine, just like we can to print(). When we do so, the list ends up in @_, where it's up to us to do something with it. Here, we go through each element of it and add them up:

```
$total += $_ foreach @_;
```

This is a little cryptic, but it's how you're likely to see it done if written by an experienced Perl programmer. You could write this a little less tersely as follows:

```
my @args = @_;
foreach my $element (@args) {
    $total = $total + $element;
}
```

In the first example, @_ would contain (111, 107, 105, 114, 69), and we'd add each value to $total in turn.

Return Values

Sometimes we don't want to perform an action like printing out the total, but instead we want to return the total. We may also want to return a result to indicate whether what we were doing succeeded. This will allow us to say things like

```
$sum_of_100 = total(1..100);
```

There are two ways to do this: implicitly or explicitly. The implicit way is nice and easy—we just make the value we want to return the last thing in our subroutine:

```
#!/usr/bin/perl -w
# total2.pl

use strict;

my $total = total(111, 107, 105, 114, 69);
print "the total is: $total\n";
```

```perl
my $sum_of_100 = total(1..100);
print "the sum of 100 is: $sum_of_100\n";

sub total {
    my $total = 0;
    $total += $_ foreach @_;
    $total;
}
```

Running this code results in the following:

```
$ perl total2.pl
the total is: 506
the sum of 100 is: 5050
$
```

The last expression in the function doesn't need to be a variable: we could use any expression. We can also return a list instead of a single scalar.

Here is an example of returning a list from a function. Let's convert a number of seconds to hours, minutes, and seconds. We pass the time in seconds into the subroutine, and it returns a three-element list with the hours, minutes, and remaining seconds.

```perl
#!/usr/bin/perl -w
# seconds.pl

use strict;

my ($hours, $minutes, $seconds) = secs2hms(3723);
print "3723 seconds is $hours hours, $minutes minutes and $seconds seconds";
print "\n";

sub secs2hms {
    my ($h,$m);
    my $seconds = shift;      # defaults to shifting @_
    $h = int($seconds/(60*60));
    $seconds %= 60*60;
    $m = int($seconds/60);
    $seconds %= 60;
    ($h,$m,$seconds);
}
```

This tells us that

```
$ perl seconds.pl
3723 seconds is 1 hours, 2 minutes and 3 seconds
$
```

This program illustrates that just like a built-in function, when we're expecting a subroutine to return a list, we can use an array or list of variables to collect the return values:

```
my ($hours, $minutes, $seconds) = secs2hms(3723);
```

When secs2hms() returns, this will be equivalent to

```
my ($hours, $minutes, $seconds) = (1,2,3);
```

And now let's look at how the subroutine works. We start in the usual way: sub, the name, and a block.

```
sub secs2hms {
```

We have two variables to represent hours and minutes, and we read the parameters in from @_—if you don't tell shift() which array to take data from, it'll read from @_ if you're in a subroutine or @ARGV if you're not. Therefore, the first argument to secs2hms(), 3723, is shifted into $seconds:

```
my ($h,$m);
my $seconds = shift;
```

Then the actual conversion: there are 3600 (60*60) seconds in an hour, and so the number of hours is the number of seconds divided by 3600. However, that'll give us a floating point number—if we divided 3660 by 3600, we'd get 1.0341666. We'd rather have "one and a bit," so we use int() to get the integer value, the "1" part of the division, and use the modulus operator to get the remainder; having dealt with the first 3600 seconds, we want to carry on looking at the next 123.

```
$h = int($seconds/(60*60));
$seconds %= 60*60;
```

The second statement sets $seconds to $seconds % (60*60)—if it was 3723 before, it'll be 123 now.

The same goes for minutes: we divide to get "two and a bit," and getting the remainder tells us that there are 3 seconds outstanding. Hence, our values are 1 hour, 2 minutes, and 3 seconds.

```
$m = int($seconds/60);
$seconds %= 60;
```

We return this just by leaving a list of the values as the last thing in the subroutine.

```
($h,$m,$seconds);
```

The return Statement

The explicit method of returning something from a subroutine is to say return(...). The first return statement we come across will immediately return to the caller. For example:

```perl
sub secs2hms {
    my ($h,$m);
    my $seconds = shift;
    $h = int($seconds/(60*60));
    $seconds %= 60*60;
    $m = int($seconds/60);
    $seconds %= 60;
    return ($h,$m,$seconds);
    print "This statement is never reached.";
}
```

This also means we can have more than one `return` statement, and it's often useful to do so.

Understanding Scope

It's now time to have a look at what we're doing when we declare a variable with `my()`. The truth, as we've briefly glimpsed it, is that Perl has two types of variable. One type is the *global variable* (or *package variable*), which can be accessed anywhere in the program, and the second type is the *lexical variable* (or *local variable*), which we declare with `my()`.

Global Variables

All variables in the program are global by default. Consider this code:

```perl
#!/usr/bin/perl -w

$x = 10;
```

`$x` is a global variable. It is available in every subroutine in the program. For instance, here is a program that accesses a global variable:

```perl
#!/usr/bin/perl -w
# global1.pl

$x = 10;

access_global();

sub access_global {
    print "value of \$x: $x\n";
}
```

Executing this code shows that `$x` is accessible in `access_global()`:

```
$ perl global1.pl
value of $x: 10
$
```

Since variables within functions are global by default, functions can modify variables as shown in this program:

```
#!/usr/bin/perl -w
# global2.pl

$x = 10;

print "before: $x\n";
change_global();
print "after:  $x\n";

sub change_global {
    $x = 20;
    print "in change_global(): $x\n";
}
```

This program assigns the global variable $x the value 10 and then prints that value. Then, change_global() is invoked. It assigns $x the value 20—this accesses the global variable $x—and then prints its value. Then in the main part of the code, after the function is called, the global $x is printed with its new value—20. Here we see the proof:

```
$ perl global2.pl
before: 10
in change_global(): 20
after:  20
$
```

The fact that Perl function variables are global by default is itself not a bad thing, unless of course you are not expecting it. If you are not expecting it, then accidentally overwriting global variables can cause hard-to-find bugs. If you are expecting it, you will probably want to make function arguments local.

Introduction to Packages

When we start programming, we're in a *package* called main. A package is a collection of variables that is separate from another package. Let's say we have two packages: A and B. Each package can have its own variable named $x, and those two $x variables are completely distinct.

If we assign $x, as we did previously in global2.pl, then we create a package variable $x in package main (the main package is the default package). Perl knows it by its full name, $main::x—the variable $x in the main package—but because we're in the main package when we make the assignment, we can just call it by its short name, $x. It's like the phone system—you don't have to dial the area code when you call someone in the same area as you.[1]

---

1. Depending on your location, of course. Nowadays, with so many area codes in a metropolitan area, to call across the street often requires dialing 10 digits . . .

We can create a variable in another package by using a fully qualified name. Instead of the main package, we can have a package called Fred. Here we'll store all of Fred's variables and subroutines. So, to get at the $name variable in package Fred, we say $Fred::name, like this:

```
$x = 10;
$Fred::name = "Fred Flintstone";
```

The fact that it's in a different package doesn't mean we can't get at it. Remember that these are global variables, available from anywhere in our program. All packages do is give us a way of subdividing the namespace.

What do we mean by "subdividing the namespace"? Well, the namespace is the set of names we can give our variables. Without packages, we could only have one $name. What packages do is help us make $name in package Fred different to $name in package Barney and $name in package main.

```
#!/usr/bin/perl -w
# globals1.pl

$main::name   = "Your Name Here";
$Fred::name   = "Fred Flintstone";
$Barney::name = "Barney Rubble";

print "\$name in package main   is $name\n";
print "\$name in package Fred   is $Fred::name\n";
print "\$name in package Barney is $Barney::name\n";
```

```
$ perl globals1.pl
$name in package main   is Your Name Here
$name in package Fred   is Fred Flintstone
$name in package Barney is Barney Rubble
$
```

You can change what package you're currently working in with the aptly named package operator. We could write the preceding like this:

```
#!/usr/bin/perl -w
# globals2.pl

$main::name   = "Your Name Here";
$Fred::name   = "Fred Flintstone";
$Barney::name = "Barney Rubble";

print "\$name in package main   is $name\n";
package Fred;
print "\$name in package Fred   is $name\n";
package Barney;
print "\$name in package Barney is $name\n";
package main;
```

When use strict is in force, it makes us use the full names for our package variables. If we try and say this:

```
#!/usr/bin/perl -w
# strict1.pl

use strict;

$x = 10;
print $x;
```

Perl will give us an error—global symbol $x requires an explicit package name. The package name it's looking for is main, and it wants us to say $main::x.

```
#!/usr/bin/perl -w
# strict2.pl

use strict;

$main::x = 10;
print $main::x, "\n";
```

Global variables can be accessed and altered at any time by any subroutine or assignment that you care to apply to them. Of course, this is handy if you want to store a value—for instance, the user's name—and be able to get it anywhere.

It's also an absolute pain in the neck when it comes to subroutines. Here's why:

```
$a = 25;
$b = some_sub(10);
print $a;
```

Looks innocent, doesn't it? Looks like we should see the answer 25. But what happens if some_sub() uses and changes the global $a? Any variable anywhere in your program can be wiped out by another part of your program—we call this *action at a distance*, and it gets real spooky to debug. Packages alleviate the problem, but to make sure that we never get into this mess, we have to ensure that every variable in our program has a different name. In small programs, that's feasible, but in huge team efforts, it's a nightmare. It's far clearer to be able to restrict the possible effect of a variable to a certain area of code, and that's exactly what lexical variables do.

Lexical Variables (aka Local Variables)

The range of effect that a variable has is called its *scope*, and lexical variables declared with my() are said to have *lexical scope*. This is also known as *local scope*. That is, they exist from the point where they're declared until the end of the enclosing block. The name "lexical" comes from the fact that they're confined to a well-defined chunk of text.

```perl
my $x;
$x = 30;
{
    my $x;  # New $x
    $x = 50;
    # We can't see the old $x, even if we want to.
}
print $x;    # This $x is, and always has been, 30.
```

Great. We can now use variables in our subroutines in the knowledge that we're not going to upset any behavior outside them. Let's modify global2.pl by adding my() in the function (now called change_global_not()):

```perl
#!/usr/bin/perl -w
# my.pl

$x = 10;

print "before: $x\n";
change_global_not();
print "after:  $x\n";

sub change_global_not {
    my $x = 20;
    print "in change_global_not(): $x\n";
}
```

This gives us the output we expect:

```
$ perl my.pl
before: 10
in change_global_not(): 20
after:  10
$
```

Some Important Notes on Passing Arguments

Sometimes we want to pass things other than an ordinary list of scalars, so it's important to understand how passing arguments works.

Function Arguments Passed by Reference

An important thing to know about how Perl passes arguments into functions is that arguments are passed by reference, not by value. This is illustrated in the following example:

```perl
#!/usr/bin/perl -w
# byref1.pl
```

```perl
use strict;

my $var = 10;
print "before: $var\n";
change_var($var);
print "after:  $var\n";

sub change_var {
    print "in change_var() before: $_[0]\n";
    ++$_[0];
    print "in change_var() after:  $_[0]\n";
}
```

First, $var is assigned 10 and then printed. Then, $var is passed into the function change_var(). This function prints the value of $_[0], increments it, then prints it again. The important line of code in this function is

```perl
++$_[0];
```

Since the arguments to the function are passed in through the array @_, to access the zeroth argument of the array we use the syntax $_[0]—this function prints it, increments it, then prints it again. The important thing to note about this code is that since $var is passed into the function by reference, when $_[0] is incremented, Perl actually increments the argument passed in, $var, from 10 to 11. After the function call, the program then prints the resulting value of $var, which is now 11. Executing the code proves this:

```
$ perl byref1.pl
before: 10
in change_var() before: 10
in change_var() after:  11
after:  11
$
```

The fact that Perl passes arguments by reference is not in itself a bad thing, but it can be if you are not expecting it. Having functions modify arguments when we don't want them to can create hard-to-find bugs. There is a very simple way to ensure that our functions don't modify their arguments—simply copy them into my() variables as shown in this example:

```perl
#!/usr/bin/perl -w
# byref2.pl

use strict;

my $var = 10;
print "before: $var\n";
change_var($var);
print "after:  $var\n";
```

```perl
sub change_var {
    my($v) = @_;
    # or: my $v = shift;

    print "in change_var() before: $v\n";
    ++$v;
    print "in change_var() after:  $v\n";
}
```

The big change here is the first line of change_var():

```perl
my($v) = @_;
```

This copies the zeroth element of @_, or $_[0], into $v. As mentioned before and as indicated by the comment, we could have written this as

```perl
my $v = shift;
```

since the shift() function shifts @_ by default if invoked within a function (recall also that if shift() is invoked outside a function it shifts @ARGV by default). Now, since the argument is copied into $v, when we increment it with

```perl
++$v;
```

it increments the copy within the function; it does not increment $var. Executing the program proves this:

```
$ perl byref2.pl
before: 10
in change_var() before: 10
in change_var() after:  11
after:  10
$
```

Lists Are One Dimensional

Recall that all lists and all arrays are one dimensional. If we have this list:

```perl
(@a, @b)
```

it becomes a one-dimensional list containing the contents of @a followed by the contents of @b. This is an important rule when it comes to passing arrays into functions, since they will be passed in as a one-dimensional list. This is illustrated in the following example:

```perl
#!/usr/bin/perl -w
# passarrays.pl

use strict;

my(@nums1, @nums2);
```

```
@nums1 = (2, 4, 6);
@nums2 = (8, 10, 12);

process_arrays(@nums1, @nums2);

sub process_arrays {
    my(@a, @b) = @_;

    print "contents of \@a\n";
    print "[$_] " foreach @a;
    print "\n\n";

    print "contents of \@b\n";
    print "[$_] " foreach @b;
    print "\n";
}
```

This program creates two 3-element arrays, @nums1 and @nums2. These arrays are then passed into process_arrays() and are immediately copied into two arrays, @a and @b. We might think that @a receives the contents of @nums1 and @b receives the contents of @nums2, but that is not what happens. Since the arguments are passed in as

```
process_arrays(@nums1, @nums2);
```

the elements are flattened into this one-dimensional list:

```
(2, 4, 6, 8, 10, 12)
```

and this list is passed in and assigned to the assignable list:

```
my(@a, @b) = @_;
```

Since this assignable list contains an array, @a, it will consume all the elements that are assigned to it. Therefore, @b will be empty because there are no elements remaining to assign to it. So, when we execute this program, we will see that @a contains all the elements passed in and @b contains no elements:

```
$ perl passarrays.pl
contents of @a
[2] [4] [6] [8] [10] [12]

contents of @b

$
```

Later, when we discuss references in Chapter 11, we will see how to pass two arrays (or hashes) into a function and treat them as two separate variables.

Default Argument Values

One thing that's occasionally useful is the ability to give the arguments for your subroutine a default value. That is, give the argument a value to use in the subroutine if one is not specified when the subroutine is called. This is very easily done with the || operator (the logical *or* operator).

|| has a very special feature: it returns the last thing it evaluates. So, for instance, if we say $a = 3 || 5, then $a will be set to 3. Because 3 is a true value, the *or* operator has no need to examine anything else, and so 3 is the last thing the || evaluates. If, however, we say $a = 0 || 5, then $a will be set to 5; 0 is not a true value, so the operator looks at the next operand, 5, which is the last thing it evaluates. This behavior is called *short circuiting*.

Hence, anything we get from @_ that doesn't have a true value can be given a default with the || operator. We can create subroutines with a flexible number of parameters and have Perl fill in the blanks for us:

```perl
#!/usr/bin/perl -w
# defaults.pl

use strict;

log_warning("Klingons on the starboard bow", "Stardate 60030.2");
log_warning("/earth is 99% full, please delete more people");
log_warning();

sub log_warning {
   my $message = shift || "Something's wrong";
   my $time    = shift || localtime; # Default to now.
   print "[$time] $message\n";
}
```

```
$ perl defaults.pl
[Stardate 60030.2] Klingons on the starboard bow
[Wed May 5 04:07:50 2004] /earth is 99% full, please delete more people
[Wed May 5 04:07:51 2004] Something's wrong
$
```

One by-product of specifying defaults for parameters is the opportunity to use those parameters as flags. Your subroutine can then alter its functionality based on the number of arguments passed to it.

Named Parameters

One of the more irritating things about calling subroutines is that you have to remember the order of the parameters. Was it username first and then password, or host first and then username, or . . . ?

Named parameters are a neat way of solving this. What we'd rather say is something like this:

```
logon( username => $name, password => $pass, host => $hostname);
```

and then give the parameters in any order. Now, Perl makes this really, really easy because that set of parameters can be thought of as a hash:

```
sub logon {
    die "Parameters to logon should be even" if @_ % 2;
    my %args = @_;
    print "Logging on to host $args{hostname}\n";
    ...
}
```

Whether and how often you use named parameters is a matter of style; for subroutines that take lots of parameters, some of which may be optional, it's an excellent idea. For those that take two or three parameters, it's probably not worth the hassle.

Named parameters also help when we want to provide default values to our arguments. For instance, let's say we write a function named college_degree() and it expects three arguments: university, degree, year. We could call the function with all three arguments:

```
college_degree(
    university => 'Illinois',
    degree     => 'MSEE',
    year       => 2000
);
```

Since we are using named parameters, the order of those three argument pairs is not important—they could be in any order we want. We could also call the function with only two pairs as in

```
college_degree(
    degree     => 'MSEE',
    year       => 2000
);
```

provided our function defaults the arguments. This implementation of college_degree() ensures that the three arguments have default values:

```
sub college_degree {
    my %args = @_;

    $args{university} = 'Northwestern' unless exists $args{university};
    $args{degree}     = 'BSCS'         unless exists $args{degree};
    $args{year}       = 2004           unless exists $args{year};

    ...
}
```

Summary

Subroutines are a bit of code with a name, and they allow us to do two things: chunk our program into organizational units, and perform calculations and operations on pieces of data, possibly returning some more data. The basic format of a subroutine definition is

`sub name BLOCK`

We can call a subroutine by just saying `name` if we've had the definition beforehand. If the definition's lower down in the program, we can say `name()`, and you may see `&name` used in older programs. Otherwise, we can use a forward definition to tell Perl that `name` should be interpreted as the name of a subroutine. The conventional notation is `name()`.

When we pass arguments into a subroutine, they end up in the special array `@_`—this contains aliases of the data that was passed so data is passed in by reference. We discussed ways of passing variables in by value (copying the arguments into `my()` variables) and also how to implement default argument values with named parameters.

Exercises

1. Write a program that computes the factorial of a number. Just to remind you, the factorial of a number is that number times that number minus 1 and so on, stopping at 1. For instance, the factorial of 5 is

   `5! = 5 * 4 * 3 * 2 * 1`

   The factorial of 0 is 1.

2. Modify the `seconds.pl` program seen earlier in the chapter so that it contains a second subroutine that asks the user for a number, puts it into a global variable, and converts that into hours, minutes, and seconds.

## CHAPTER 7

Regular Expressions

11:15 Restate my assumptions:

1. *Mathematics is the language of nature.*

2. *Everything around us can be represented and understood through numbers.*

3. *If you graph these numbers, patterns emerge. Therefore: There are patterns everywhere in nature.*

—Max Cohen in π (Pi, 1998)

Whether or not you agree that Max's assumptions give rise to his conclusion is your own opinion, but his case is much easier to support in the field of computers—there are certainly patterns everywhere in programming.

Regular expressions allow us to look for patterns in our data. So far we've been limited to checking a single value against that of a scalar variable or the contents of an array or hash. By using the rules outlined in this chapter, we can use that one single value (or pattern) to describe what we're looking for in more general terms: we can check that every sentence in a file begins with a capital letter and ends with a period, find out how many times James Bond's name is mentioned in *Goldfinger* or even if there are any repeated sequences of numbers in the decimal representation of π greater than five in length.

However, regular expressions are a very big area—they're one of the most powerful features of Perl, and so our examination of them will be divided up into six sections:

- Basic patterns

- Special characters to use

- Quantifiers, anchors, and memorizing patterns

- Matching, substituting, and transforming text using patterns

- Backtracking

- A quick look at some simple pitfalls

Generally speaking, if you want to ask Perl something about a piece of text, regular expressions are going to be your first port of call—however, there's probably one simple question burning in your mind . . .

What Are They?

The term *regular expression* (now commonly abbreviated to *regex* or even *RE*) simply refers to a pattern that follows the rules of syntax outlined in the rest of this chapter. Regular expressions are not limited to Perl—Unix utilities such as sed and egrep use the same notation for finding patterns in text (well, not exactly the same since Perl regexes are an extension of egrep's regexes). So why aren't they just called "search patterns" or something less obscure?

The actual phrase itself originates from the mid-fifties when a mathematician named Stephen Kleene developed a notation for manipulating *regular sets*. Perl's regular expressions have grown and grown beyond the original notation and have significantly extended the original system, but some of Kleene's notation remains, and the name has stuck.

Patterns

History lessons aside, it's all about identifying patterns in text. So what constitutes a pattern? And how do you compare it against something?

The simplest pattern is a word—a simple sequence of characters—and we may, for example, want to ask Perl whether a certain string contains that word. We can split the string into separate words, and then test to see if each word is the one we're looking for. Here's how we might do that:

```perl
#!/usr/bin/perl -w
# match1.pl

use strict;

my $found = 0;
$_ = "Nobody wants to hurt you... 'cept, I do hurt people sometimes, Case.";

my $sought = "people";

foreach my $word (split) {
    if ($word eq $sought) {
        $found = 1;
        last;
    }
}

if ($found) {
    print "Hooray! Found the word 'people'\n";
}
```

Sure enough the program returns success . . .

```
$ perl match1.pl
Hooray! Found the word 'people'
$
```

But oh, that's messy! It's complicated, and it's slow to boot! Worse still, the split() function (which breaks each of our lines up into a list of "words"—we'll see more of this function later on in the chapter) actually *keeps* all the punctuation—the string "you" wouldn't be found in the preceding example, whereas "you . . ." would. This is looking like a hard problem, but it should be easy. Perl was designed to make easy things easy and hard things possible, so there should be a better way to do this. This is how it looks using a regular expression:

```
#!/usr/bin/perl -w
# match2.pl

use strict;

$_ = "Nobody wants to hurt you... 'cept, I do hurt people sometimes, Case.";

if ($_ =~ /people/) {
    print "Hooray! Found the word 'people'\n";
}
```

Much, much easier, and the same result. We place the text we want to find between forward slashes—that's the regular expression part—that's our pattern, what we're trying to match. We also need to tell Perl in which particular string we're looking for that pattern, and we do so with the =~ operator. This operator returns 1 if the pattern match was successful (in our case, whether the character sequence "people" was found in the string) and the empty string if it wasn't.

Before we get on to more complicated patterns, let's just have a quick look at that syntax. As we noted previously, a lot of Perl's operations take $_ as a default argument, and regular expressions are one such operation. Since we have the text we want to test in $_, we don't need to use the =~ operator to "bind" the pattern to another string. We could write the preceding even more simply:

```
$_ = "Nobody wants to hurt you... 'cept, I do hurt people sometimes, Case.";

if (/people/) {
    print "Hooray! Found the word 'people'\n";
}
```

Alternatively, we might want to test for the pattern not matching—the word not being found. Obviously, we could say unless (/people/), but if the text we're looking at isn't in $_, we may also use the negative form of that =~ operator, which is !~. For example:

```
#!/usr/bin/perl -w
# nomatch.pl

use strict;
```

```
my $gibson =
    "Nobody wants to hurt you... 'cept, I do hurt people sometimes, Case.";

if ($gibson !~ /fish/) {
    print "There are no fish in William Gibson.\n";
}
```

True to form, for cyberpunk books don't regularly involve fish, we get the result:

```
$ perl nomatch.pl
There are no fish in William Gibson.
$
```

Literal text is the simplest regular expression of all to look for, but we needn't look for just the one word—we could look for any particular phrase. However, we need to make sure that we exactly match *all* the characters—words (with correct capitalization), numbers, punctuation, and even whitespace.

```
#!/usr/bin/perl -w
# match3.pl

use strict;

$_ = "Nobody wants to hurt you... 'cept, I do hurt people sometimes, Case.";

if (/I do/) {
    print "'I do' is in that string.\n";
}

if (/sometimes Case/) {
    print "'sometimes Case' matched.\n";
}
```

Let's run this program and see what happens:

```
$ perl match3.pl
'I do' is in that string.
$
```

The other string didn't match, even though those two words are there. This is because everything in a regular expression has to match the string, from start to finish: first "sometimes", then a space, then "Case". In $_, there was a comma before the space, so it didn't match exactly. Similarly, spaces inside the pattern are significant:

```
#!/usr/bin/perl -w
# match4.pl

use strict;
```

```perl
my $test1 = "The dog is in the kennel";
my $test2 = "The sheepdog is in the field";

if ($test1 =~ / dog/) {
   print "This dog's at home.\n";
}

if ($test2 =~ / dog/) {
   print "This dog's at work.\n";
}
```

This will only find the first dog, as Perl was looking for a space followed by the three letters "dog":

```
$ perl match4.pl
This dog's at home.
$
```

So, for the moment, it looks like we shall have to specify our patterns with absolute precision. As another example, look at this:

```perl
#!/usr/bin/perl -w
# match5.pl

use strict;

$_ = "Nobody wants to hurt you... 'cept, I do hurt people sometimes, Case.";

if (/case/) {
   print "I guess it's just the way I'm made.\n";
} else {
   print "Case? Where are you, Case?\n";
}
```

```
$ perl match5.pl
Case? Where are you, Case?
$
```

Hmm, no match. Why not? Because we asked for a lowercase "c" when the string has an uppercase "C"—regexes are (if you'll pardon the pun) case sensitive. We can get around this by asking Perl to compare insensitively, and we do this by putting an "i" (for "insensitive") after the closing slash. If we alter the preceding code as follows:

```perl
if (/case/i) {
   print "I guess it's just the way I'm made.\n";
} else {
   print "Case? Where are you, Case?\n";
}
```

Then we find him:

```
$ perl match5.pl
I guess it's just the way I'm made.
$
```

This "i" is one of several *modifiers* that we can add to the end of the regular expression to change its behavior slightly. We'll see more of them later on.

Interpolation

Regular expressions work a little like double-quoted strings—variables and metacharacters are interpolated. This allows us to store patterns in variables, and determine what we are matching when we run the program—we don't need to have them hard-coded in.

This program illustrates this concept. It will ask the user for a pattern and then test to see if it matches our string. We can use this throughout the chapter to help us test the various styles of pattern we'll be looking at.

```
#!/usr/bin/perl -w
# matchtest.pl

use strict;

$_ = q("I wonder what the Entish is for 'yes' and 'no'," he thought.);
# Tolkien, Lord of the Rings

print "Enter some text to find: ";
my $pattern = <STDIN>;
chomp($pattern);

if (/$pattern/) {
    print "The text matches the pattern '$pattern'.\n";
} else {
    print "'$pattern' was not found.\n";
}
```

Now we can test out a few things:

```
$ perl matchtest.pl
Enter some text to find: wonder
The text matches the pattern 'wonder'.

$ perl matchtest.pl
Enter some text to find: entish
'entish' was not found.

$ perl matchtest.pl
Enter some text to find: hough
The text matches the pattern 'hough'.
```

```
$ perl matchtest.pl
Enter some text to find: and 'no',
The text matches the pattern 'and 'no''.
```

matchtest.pl has its basis in these three lines:

```
my $pattern = <STDIN>;
chomp($pattern);

if (/$pattern/) {
```

We're taking a line of text from the user. Then, since it will end in a newline and we don't necessarily want to find a newline in our pattern, we chomp() it off. Then we do our test.

Since we're not using the =~ operator, the test will be looking at the variable $_. The regular expression is /$pattern/, and just like the double-quoted string "$pattern", the variable $pattern is interpolated. Hence, the regular expression is purely and simply whatever the user typed in, once we have removed the newline.

Metacharacters and Escaping

Of course, regular expressions can be more than just words and spaces. The rest of this chapter is going to be about the various ways we can specify more advanced matches—where portions of the match are allowed to be one of a number of characters, for instance, or where the match must occur at a certain position in the string. To do this, we'll be describing the special meanings given to certain characters—called *metacharacters*—looking at what these meanings are and what sort of things we can express with them.

At this stage though, we might not want to use their special meanings—we may want to literally match the characters themselves. As you've already seen with double-quoted strings, we can use a backslash to escape these characters' special meanings. Hence, if you want to match ... in the preceding text, you need your pattern to say \.\.\.. For example:

```
$ perl matchtest.pl
Enter some text to find: Ent+
The text matches the pattern 'Ent+'.
```

```
$ perl matchtest.pl
Enter some text to find: Ent\+
'Ent\+' was not found.
```

We'll see later why the first one matched—due to the special meaning of +.

Note These are the characters that are given special meaning within a regular expression, which you will need to backslash if you want to use literally:

```
. * ? + [ ( ) { ^ $ | \
```

Any other characters automatically assume their literal meanings.

You can also turn off the special meanings using the escape sequence \Q. After Perl sees \Q, the 12 special characters shown in the preceding note will automatically assume their ordinary, literal meanings. This remains the case until Perl sees either \E or the end of the pattern.

For instance, if we wanted to adapt our matchtest.pl program just to look for literal strings instead of regular expressions, we could change it to look like this:

```
if (/\Q$pattern\E/) {
```

Now the meaning of + is turned off:

```
$ perl matchtest.pl
Enter some text to find: Ent+
'Ent+' was not found.
$
```

Note in particular that all \Q does is turn off the regular expression magic of those 12 characters shown earlier—it doesn't stop, for example, variable interpolation.

Tip Don't forget to change this back again: we'll be using matchtest.pl throughout the chapter to demonstrate the regular expressions we look at—we'll need that magic fully functional!

Anchors

So far, our patterns have all tried to find a match anywhere in the string. The first way we'll extend our regular expressions is by dictating to Perl where the match must occur—we can say "These characters must match the beginning of the string" or "This text must be at the end of the string." We do this by *anchoring* the match to either end.

The two anchors we have are ^, which appears at the beginning of the pattern, anchoring a match to the beginning of the string; and $, appearing at the end of the pattern, anchoring it to the end of the string. So, to see if our quotation ends in a period—and remember that the period is a special character—we say something like this:

```
$ perl matchtest.pl
Enter some text to find: \.$
The text matches the pattern '\.$'.
```

That's a period (which we've escaped to stop it being treated as a special character) and a dollar sign at the end of our pattern—to show that this must be the end of the string.

Note We suggest that you to get into the habit of reading out regular expressions in English—break them into pieces, and say what each piece does. Also remember to say that each piece must immediately follow the other in the string in order to match. For instance, the preceding regex could be read "Match a period immediately followed by the end of the string."

If you can get into this habit, you'll find that reading and understanding regular expressions becomes a lot easier, and that you'll be able to "translate" back into Perl more naturally as well.

Here's another example: do we have a capital "I" at the beginning of the string?

```
$ perl matchtest.pl
Enter some text to find: ^I
'^I' was not found.
$
```

We use ^ to mean "beginning of the string," followed by an "I". In our case, though, the character at the beginning of the string is a ", so our pattern does not match. If you know that what you're looking for can only occur at the beginning or the end of the string, it's extremely efficient to use anchors; instead of searching through the whole string to see whether the match succeeded, Perl only needs to look at a small portion, and can give up immediately if even the first character does not match.

Let's see one more example of this, where we'll combine looking for matches with looking through the lines in a file.

Imagine yourself as a poor poet. In fact, not just poor, but downright bad—so bad, you can't even think of a rhyme for "pink." So, what do you do? You do what every sensible poet does in this situation, and you write the following Perl program:

```
#!/usr/bin/perl -w
# rhyming.pl

use strict;

my $syllable = "ink";

while (<>) {
    print if /$syllable$/;
}
```

We can now feed it a file of words, and find those that end in "ink":

```
$ perl rhyming.pl wordlist.txt
blink
bobolink
brink
chink
clink
$
```

▓**Tip** For a really thorough result, you'll need to use a file containing every word in the dictionary—be prepared for a bit of a wait though if you do! For the sake of the example, however, any text-based file will do (though it will help if it is in English). A bobolink, in case you're wondering, is a migratory American song-bird, otherwise known as a ricebird or reedbird.

Let's look at this code in detail. First, we see the following:

```
while (<>) {
    print if /$syllable$/;
}
```

The first thing we see here is the <> within the while loop parentheses. We are going to talk about the <> in detail in the next chapter, but as a brief description, the <> reads from one of two places: either the file or files specified on the command line (here wordlist.txt) or from standard input if there are no files on the command line. The data is read into $_ by default until end of file(s).

Once each line of the file has been read into $_, we test to see if it matches the pattern, which is our syllable, "ink", anchored to the end of the line (with $). If so, we print it out. Recall that print() defaults to printing $_.

The important thing to note here is that Perl treats the "ink" as the last thing on the line, even though there is a newline at the end of $_. Regular expressions typically ignore the last newline in a string—we'll look at this behavior in more detail later.

Shortcuts and Options

This is all very well if we know exactly what it is we're trying to find, but finding patterns means more than just locating exact pieces of text—we may want to find a three-digit number, the first word on the line, four or more letters all in capitals, and so on.

We can begin to do this using *character classes*—these aren't just single characters, but something that signifies that any one of a *set* of characters is acceptable. To specify this, we put the characters we consider acceptable inside square brackets. Let's go back to our matchtest.pl program, using the same test string:

```
$_ = q("I wonder what the Entish is for 'yes' and 'no'," he thought.);
```

```
$ perl matchtest.pl
Enter some text to find: w[aoi]nder
The text matches the pattern 'w[aoi]nder'.
$
```

What have we done? We've tested whether the string contains a "w", followed by either an "a", an "o", or an "i", followed by "nder"; in effect, we're looking for either of "wander", "wonder", or "winder". Since the string contains "wonder", the pattern is matched.

Conversely, we can say that everything is acceptable *except* a given sequence of characters— we can "negate the character class." To do this, the character class should start with a ^, like so:

```
$ perl matchtest.pl
Enter some text to find: th[^eo]
'th[^eo]' was not found.
$
```

So, we're looking for "th" followed by something that is neither an "e" nor an "o". But all we have is "the" and "thought", so this pattern does not match.

If the characters you wish to match form a sequence in the character set you're using, you can use a hyphen to specify a range of characters rather than spelling out the entire range. For instance, the numerals can be represented by the character class [0-9]. A lowercase letter can be matched with [a-z]. Let's see if there are any numeric characters in our quote:

```
$ perl matchtest.pl
Enter some text to find: [0-9]
'[0-9]' was not found.
$
```

You can use one or more of these ranges alongside other characters in a character class, so long as they stay inside the brackets. If you wanted to match a digit and then a letter from "A" to "F", you would say [0-9][A-F]. However, to match a single hexadecimal digit you would write [0-9A-F], or [0-9A-Fa-f] if you wished to include lowercase letters.

Some character classes are going to come up again and again: digits, word characters, and the various types of whitespace. Perl provides us with some neat shortcuts for these. Table 7-1 lists the most common ones and what they represent.

Table 7-1. *Predefined Character Classes*

Shortcut	Expansion	Description
\d	[0-9]	Digits 0 to 9
\w	[0-9A-Za-z_]	A "word" character allowable in a Perl variable name
\s	[\t\n\r\f]	A whitespace character—that is, a space, tab, newline, return, or formfeed

The negative forms of the common shortcuts are listed in Table 7-2.

Table 7-2. *More Predefined Character Classes*

Shortcut	Expansion	Description
\D	[^0-9]	Any nondigit
\W	[^0-9A-Za-z_]	A non-"word" character
\S	[^ \t\n\r\f]	A non-whitespace character

So, if we wanted to see if there was a five-letter word in the sentence, you might think we could do this:

```
$ perl matchtest.pl
Enter some text to find: \w\w\w\w\w
The text matches the pattern '\w\w\w\w\w'.
$
```

But that's not right—there are no five-letter words in the sentence! The problem is that we've only asked for five letters in a row, and any word with *at least* five letters in a row will match that pattern. We actually matched "wonde", which was the first possible series of five letters in a row. To actually get a five-letter word, we might consider deciding that the word must appear in the middle of the sentence—that is, in between two spaces:

```
$ perl matchtest.pl
Enter some text to find: \s\w\w\w\w\w\s
'\s\w\w\w\w\w\s' was not found.
$
```

Word Boundaries

The problem with that is, when we're looking at text, words aren't always between two spaces. They can be followed by or preceded by punctuation, or appear at the beginning or end of a string, or otherwise next to nonword characters. To help us properly search for words in these cases, Perl provides the special \b metacharacter. The interesting thing about \b is that it doesn't actually match any character in particular—rather, it matches the point between something that isn't a word character (either \W or one of the ends of the string) and something that is (a word character)—hence \b for **b**oundary. So, for example, to look for one-letter words:

```
$ perl matchtest.pl
Enter some text to find: \s\w\s
'\s\w\s' was not found.
```

```
$ perl matchtest.pl
Enter some text to find: \b\w\b
The text matches the pattern '\b\w\b'.
```

As the "I" was preceded by a quotation mark, a space wouldn't match it—but a word boundary does the job. Later, we'll see how to tell Perl how many repetitions of a character or group of characters we want to match without spelling it out directly.

What, then, if we wanted to match anything at all? You might consider something like [\w\W] or [\s\S], for instance. Actually, matching any character is quite a common operation, so Perl provides an easy way of specifying it: the period, which matches any character except \n. What about an "r" followed by two characters—any two characters—and then an "h"?

```
$ perl matchtest.pl
Enter some text to find: r..h
The text matches the pattern 'r..h'.
$
```

Is there anything after the period?

```
$ perl matchtest.pl
Enter some text to find: \..
'\..' was not found.
$
```

What's that? One backslashed period to mean a period character, then an unescaped one to mean "any character but \n."

Alternatives

Instead of giving a series of acceptable characters, you may want to say "Match either this or that." The *either-or* operator in a regular expression is the same as the bitwise *or* operator, |. So, to match either "yes" or "maybe" in our example, we could say this:

```
$ perl matchtest.pl
Enter some text to find: yes|maybe
The text matches the pattern 'yes|maybe'.
$
```

That's either "yes" or "maybe"—but what if we wanted either "yes" or "yet"? To get alternatives on part of an expression, we need to group the options. In a regular expression, grouping is always done with parentheses:

```
$ perl matchtest.pl
Enter some text to find: ye(s|t)
The text matches the pattern 'ye(s|t)'.
$
```

If we had forgotten the parentheses, we would have tried to match either "yes" or "t". In this case, we'd still get a positive match, but it wouldn't be doing what we want—we'd get a match for any string with a "t" in it, whether the words "yes" or "yet" were there or not.

You can match either "this" or "that" or "the other" by adding more alternatives:

```
$ perl matchtest.pl
Enter some text to find: this|that|the other
'this|that|the other' was not found.
$
```

However, in this case, it's more efficient to separate out the common elements:

```
$ perl matchtest.pl
Enter some text to find: th(is|at|e other)
'th(is|at|e other)' was not found.
$
```

You can also nest alternatives—say you want to match one of these patterns:

- "the" followed by whitespace or a letter

- "or"

You might include something like this:

```
$ perl matchtest.pl
Enter some text to find: (the(\s|[a-z]))|or
The text matches the pattern '(the(\s|[a-z]))|or'.
$
```

It looks fearsome, but break it down into its components: our two alternatives are

- the(\s|[a-z])

- or

The second part is easy, while the first contains "the" followed by two alternatives: \s and [a-z]. Hence either "the" followed by either a whitespace or a lowercase letter, or "or". We can, in fact, tidy this up a little by replacing (\s|[a-z]) with the less cluttered [\sa-z].

```
$ perl matchtest.pl
Enter some text to find: (the[\sa-z])|or
The text matches the pattern '(the[\sa-z])|or'.
$
```

Repetition with Quantifiers

We've now moved from matching a specific character to matching a more general type of character—when we don't know (or don't care) exactly what the character will be. Now we're going to see what happens when we want to talk about a more general quantity of characters: more than three digits in a row, two to four capital letters, and so on. The metacharacters that we use to deal with a number of characters in a row are called *quantifiers*.

Indefinite Repetition

The easiest of these is the question mark. It should suggest uncertainty—something may be there, or it may not. That's exactly what it does: stating that the immediately preceding character(s)—or metacharacter(s)—may appear once, or not at all. It's a good way of saying that a particular character or group is optional. To match the words "he or she", you can do the following:

```
$ perl matchtest.pl
Enter some text to find: \bs?he\b
The text matches the pattern '\bs?he\b'.
$
```

▓Note Quantifiers operate on the thing immediately to their left. Therefore, in the preceding example, the ? operates only on "s".

To make a series of characters (or metacharacters) optional, group them in parentheses as before. Did he say "what the Entish is" or "what the Entish word is"? Either will do:

```
$ perl matchtest.pl
Enter some text to find: what the Entish (word )?is
The text matches the pattern 'what the Entish (word )?is'.
$
```

Notice that we had to put the space inside the group; otherwise we end up with two spaces between "Entish" and "is", whereas our text only has one:

```
$ perl matchtest.pl
Enter some text to find: what the Entish (word)? is
'what the Entish (word)? is' was not found.
$
```

As well as matching something one or zero times, you can match something one or more times. We do this with the plus sign—to match an entire word without specifying how long it should be, you can say:

```
$ perl matchtest.pl
Enter some text to find: \b\w+\b
The text matches the pattern '\b\w+\b'.
$
```

In this case, we match the first available word—"I".

If, on the other hand, you have something that may be there any number of times but might not be there at all—zero or one or many—you need what's called *Kleene's star*: the * quantifier. So, to find a capital letter after any—but possibly no—spaces at the start of the string, what would you do? The start of the string, then any number of whitespace characters, then a capital:

```
$ perl matchtest.pl
Enter some text to find: ^\s*[A-Z]
'^\s*[A-Z]' was not found.
$
```

Of course, our test string begins with a quote, so the preceding pattern won't match; but, sure enough, if you take away that first quote, the pattern will match fine.

Table 7-3 reviews the three quantifiers.

Table 7-3. *Quantifier Examples*

Quantifier	Description
/bea?t/	Matches either "beat" or "bet"
/bea+t/	Matches "beat", "beaat", "beaaat" . . .
/bea*t/	Matches "bet", "beat", "beaat" . . .

Novice Perl programmers tend to go to town on combinations of dot and star, and the results often surprise them, particularly when it comes to search-and-replace operations. We'll explain the rules of the regular expression engine shortly.

You should also consider the fact that .* and .+ in the middle of a regular expression will match as much of your string as they possibly can. We'll look more at this "greedy" behavior later on.

Well-Defined Repetition

If you want to be more precise about how many times a character or groups of characters might be repeated, you can specify the maximum and minimum number of repeats in curly braces. "2 or 3 spaces" can be written as follows:

```
$ perl matchtest.pl
Enter some text to find: \s{2,3}
'\s{2,3}' was not found.
$
```

So we have no doubled or tripled spaces in our string. Notice how we construct that—the minimum, a comma, and the maximum, all inside curly braces. Omitting the maximum signifies "or more." For example, {2,} denotes "2 or more." In these cases, the same warnings apply as for the star operator.

Finally, you can specify exactly how many things are to be in a row by simply putting that number inside the curly braces. Here's the five-letter-word example tidied up a little:

```
$ perl matchtest.pl
Enter some text to find: \b\w{5}\b
'\b\w{5}\b' was not found.
$
```

Summary Table

To refresh your memory, Table 7-4 lists the various metacharacters we've seen so far.

Table 7-4. *Metacharacter Summary*

Metacharacter	Meaning
[abc]	Any one of the characters a, b, or c
[^abc]	Any one character other than a, b, or c
[a-z]	Any one ASCII character between a and z
\d \D	A digit; a nondigit
\w \W	A "word" character; a non-"word" character
\s \S	A whitespace character; a non-whitespace character
\b	The boundary between a \w character and a \W character
.	Any character (except newline)
(abc)	The phrase abc as a group
?	Preceding character or group may be present 0 or 1 times.
+	Preceding character or group is present 1 or more times.
*	Preceding character or group may be present 0 or more times.
{x,y}	Preceding character or group is present between x and y times.
{x,}	Preceding character or group is present at least x times.
{x}	Preceding character or group is present x times.

Memory and Backreferences

What if we want to know what a certain regular expression matched? It was easy when we were matching literal strings: we knew that "Case" was going to match those four letters and nothing else—but now, what's matching? If we have /\w{3}/, which three word characters are getting matched?

Perl has a series of special variables in which it stores anything that's matched within a group in parentheses. Each time it sees a set of parentheses, it *triggers memory* and copies the matched text inside into a numbered variable—the first matched group goes in $1, the second group in $2, and so on. By looking at these variables, which we call the *backreference* variables, we can see what triggered various parts of our match, and we can also extract portions of the data for later use.

First, though, let's rewrite our test program so that we can see what's in those variables.

```
#!/usr/bin/perl -w
# matchtest2.pl

use strict;

$_ = '1: A silly sentence (495,a) *BUT* one which will be useful. (3)';

print "Enter a regular expression: ";
my $pattern = <STDIN>;
chomp($pattern);

if (/$pattern/) {
    print "The text matches the pattern '$pattern'.\n";
    print "\$1 is '$1'\n" if defined $1;
    print "\$2 is '$2'\n" if defined $2;
    print "\$3 is '$3'\n" if defined $3;
    print "\$4 is '$4'\n" if defined $4;
    print "\$5 is '$5'\n" if defined $5;
} else {
    print "'$pattern' was not found.\n";
}
```

Tip Note that we use a backslash to escape the first "dollar" symbol in each print() statement—thus displaying the actual symbol—while leaving the second in each to display the contents of the appropriate variable.

We have our special variables in place, and we have a new sentence on which we do our matching. Let's see what's been happening:

```
$ perl matchtest2.pl
Enter a regular expression: ([a-z]+)
The text matches the pattern '([a-z]+)'.
$1 is 'silly'
```

```
$ perl matchtest2.pl
Enter a regular expression: (\w+)
The text matches the pattern '(\w+)'.
$1 is '1'
```

```
$ perl matchtest2.pl
Enter a regular expression: ([a-z]+)(.*)([a-z]+)
The text matches the pattern '([a-z]+)(.*)([a-z]+)'.
$1 is 'silly'
$2 is ' sentence (495,a) *BUT* one which will be usefu'
$3 is 'l'
```

```
$ perl matchtest2.pl
Enter a regular expression: e(\w|n\w+)
The text matches the pattern 'e(\w|n\w+)'.
$1 is 'n'
```

By printing out what's in each of the groups, we can see exactly what caused Perl to start and stop matching, and when. If we look carefully at these results, we'll find that they can tell us a great deal about how Perl goes about handling regular expressions.

How the Regular Expression Engine Works

We've seen most of the syntax behind regular expression matching, and plenty of examples of it in action. The code that does all the regex work is called Perl's *regular expression engine*. You might be wondering about the exact rules applied by this engine when determining whether or not a piece of text matches, and how much of it matches. From what the examples have shown us, let us make some deductions about the engine's operation.

Our first expression, ([a-z]+), plucked out a set of one-or-more lowercase letters. The first such set that Perl came across was "silly". The next character after "y" was a space, and so no longer matched the expression.

- *Rule 1:* Once the engine starts matching, it will keep matching a character at a time for as long as it can. Once it sees something that doesn't match, however, it has to stop. In this example, it can never get beyond a character that is not a lowercase letter. It has to stop as soon as it encounters one.

Next, we looked for a series of word characters using (\w+). The engine started looking at the beginning of the string, and found one, "1". The next character was not a word character (it was a colon), and so the engine had to stop.

- *Rule 2:* The engine is *eager*. It's eager to start work and eager to finish, and it starts matching as soon as possible in the string; if the first character doesn't match, try and start matching from the second. Then take every opportunity to finish as quickly as possible.

Then we tried this: ([a-z]+)(.*)([a-z]+). The result we got with this was a little strange. Let's look at it again:

```
$ perl matchtest2.pl
Enter a regular expression: ([a-z]+)(.*)([a-z]+)
The text matches the pattern '([a-z]+)(.*)([a-z]+)'.
$1 is 'silly'
$2 is ' sentence (495,a) *BUT* one which will be usefu'
$3 is 'l'
$
```

Our first group was the same as what matched before—nothing new there. When we could no longer match lowercase letters, we switched to matching anything we could. Now, this *could* take up the rest of the string, but that wouldn't allow a match for the third group—we have to leave at least one lowercase letter.

So, the engine started to reverse back along the string, giving characters up one by one. It gave up the closing parenthesis, the 3, then the opening parenthesis, and so on, until we got to the first thing that would satisfy all the groups and let the match go ahead—namely a lowercase letter: the "l" at the end of "useful".

From this, we can draw up the third rule:

- *Rule 3:* The engine is *greedy*. If you use the +, *, or ? operators, they will try and consume as much of the string as possible. If the rest of the expression does not match, it grudgingly gives up a character at a time and tries to match again, in order to find the fullest possible match.

We can turn a greedy match into a nongreedy match by putting the ? operator after either the plus, star, or question mark. For instance, let's turn this example into a nongreedy version: ([a-z]+)(.*?)([a-z]+). This gives us an entirely different result:

```
$ perl matchtest2.pl
Enter a regular expression: ([a-z]+)(.*?)([a-z]+)
The text matches the pattern '([a-z]+)(.*?)([a-z]+)'.
$1 is 'silly'
$2 is ' '
$3 is 'sentence'
$
```

Now that we've shut off rule 3, rule 2 takes over: the smallest possible match for the second group was a single space. First, it tried to get nothing at all, but then the third group would be faced with a space—this wouldn't match. So, we grudgingly accept the space and try and finish again—this time the third group has some lowercase letters, and that can match as well.

What if we turn off greediness in all three groups, and say this: ([a-z]+?)(.*?)([a-z]+?):

```
$ perl matchtest2.pl
Enter a regular expression: ([a-z]+?)(.*?)([a-z]+?)
The text matches the pattern '([a-z]+?)(.*?)([a-z]+?)'.
$1 is 's'
$2 is ''
$3 is 'i'
$
```

What about this? The smallest possible match for the first group is the "s" of "silly"—we asked it to find one character or more, and so the smallest it could find was one. The second group actually matched no characters at all. This left the third group facing an "i", which it took to complete the match.

Our last example included an alternation:

```
$ perl matchtest2.pl
Enter a regular expression: e(\w|n\w+)
The text matches the pattern 'e(\w|n\w+)'.
$1 is 'n'
$
```

The engine took the first branch of the alternation and matched a single character, even though the second branch would actually satisfy greed. This leads us to the fourth rule:

- *Rule 4:* The regular expression engine *hates decisions*. If there are two branches, it will always choose the first one, even though the second one might allow it to gain a longer match.

To summarize: the regular expression engine starts as soon as it can, grabs as much as it can, then tries to finish as soon as it can, while taking the first decision available to it.

Working with Regexes

Now that we've matched a string, what do we do with it? Sometimes it's just useful to know whether or not a string contains a given pattern. However, a lot of the time we're going to be doing search-and-replace operations on text, and we'll explain how to do that here. We'll also cover some of the more advanced areas of dealing with regular expressions.

Substitution

Now that we know all about matching text, substitution is very easy. Why? Because all of the clever things are in the "search" part, rather than the "replace"—all the character classes, quantifiers, and so on only make sense when matching. You can't substitute, say, a word with any number of digits. So, all we need to do is take the "old" text—our match—and tell Perl the text that we want to replace it. This we do with the s/// operator.

The s is for "substitute"—between the first two slashes, we put our regular expression as before. Before the final slash, we put our text to replace. Just as with matching, we can use the =~ operator to apply the substitution to a certain string. If this is not given, it applies to the default variable $_.

```
#!/usr/bin/perl -w
# subst1.pl

use strict;

$_ = "Awake! Awake! Fear, Fire, Foes! Awake! Fire, Foes! Awake!";
# Tolkien, Lord of the Rings
```

```
s/Foes/Flee/;
print $_,"\n";
```

```
$ perl subst1.pl
Awake! Awake! Fear, Fire, Flee! Awake! Fire, Foes! Awake!
$
```

Here we have substituted the first occurrence of "Foes" with the word "Flee". Had we wanted to change every occurrence, we would have needed to use another modifier—just as the /i modifier matches case insensitively, the /g modifier on a substitution acts globally:

```
#!/usr/bin/perl -w
# subst2.pl

use strict;

$_ = "Awake! Awake! Fear, Fire, Foes! Awake! Fire, Foes! Awake!";
# Tolkien, Lord of the Rings

s/Foes/Flee/g;
print $_,"\n";
```

```
$ perl subst2.pl
Awake! Awake! Fear, Fire, Flee! Awake! Fire, Flee! Awake!
$
```

Like the left-hand side of the substitution, the right-hand side also works like a double-quoted string and is thus subject to variable interpolation. One useful thing, though, is that we can use the backreference variables we collected during the match on the right-hand side. So, for instance, to swap the first two words in a string, we would say something like this:

```
#!/usr/bin/perl -w
# subst3.pl

use strict;

$_ = "there are two major products that come out of Berkeley: LSD and UNIX";
# Jeremy Anderson

s/(\w+)\s+(\w+)/$2 $1/;
print $_, "?\n";
```

```
$ perl subst3.pl
are there two major products that come out of Berkeley: LSD and UNIX?
$
```

What would happen if we tried doing that globally? Let's do it and see:

```
#!/usr/bin/perl -w
# subst4.pl

use strict;

$_ = "there are two major products that come out of Berkeley: LSD and UNIX";
# Jeremy Anderson

s/(\w+)\s+(\w+)/$2 $1/g;
print $_, "?\n";

$ perl subst4.pl
are there major two that products out come Berkeley of: and LSD UNIX?
$
```

Here, every word in a pair is swapped with its neighbor—when processing a global match, Perl always starts where the previous match left off.

Changing Delimiters

You may have noticed that // and s/// resemble the operators q// and qq//. Just like q// and qq//, we can change the delimiters when matching and substituting to increase the readability of our regular expressions. The same rules apply: any nonword character can be the delimiter, and paired delimiters such as <>, (), {}, and [] may be used—with two provisos.

First, if you change the delimiters on //, you must put an m in front of it ("m" for "match"). This is so that Perl can still recognize it as a regular expression, rather than a block or comment or anything else.

```
m/^\s*[A-Z]/;
```

can be written as

```
m#^\s*[A-Z]#;
```

Secondly, if you use paired delimiters with the substitution operator, you must use two pairs.

```
s/old text/new text/g;
```

becomes

```
s{old text}{new text}g;
```

You may, however, leave spaces or newlines between the pairs for the sake of clarity:

```
s{old text}
 {new text}g;
```

Also, they can be different pairs:

```
s{old text}(new text)g;
```

The prime example of when you would want to do this is when you are dealing with file paths, which contain a lot of slashes. For instance, if you are moving files on your Unix system from /usr/local/share/ to /usr/share/, you may want to munge[1] the filenames like this:

```
s/\/usr\/local\/share\//\/usr\/share\//g;
```

However, it's far easier to read if alternative delimiters are used in this case:

```
s#/usr/local/share/#/usr/share/#g;
```

Modifiers

We've already seen the /i modifier being used to indicate that the match should be case insensitive. We've also seen the /g modifier to apply a substitution. What other modifiers are there?

- /m: Treat the string as multiple lines. Normally, ^ and $ match the very start and very end of the string. If the /m modifier is used, then ^ and $ will match the starts and ends of individual lines in the string (separated by \n). For example, given the string "one\ntwo", the pattern /^two$/ will not match, but /^two$/m will.

- /s: Treat the string as a single line. Normally, . does not match a newline character; when /s is given, then it will.

- /g: As well as globally replacing in a substitution, this allows us to match multiple times. When using this modifier, placing the \G anchor at the beginning of the regex will anchor it to the end point of the last match.

- /x: Allow the use of whitespace and comments inside a match.

Regular expressions can get quite difficult to read at times. The /x modifier helps make the regex more readable. For instance, if you're matching a string in a log file that contains a time followed by a computer name in square brackets and then a message, the expression you'll create to extract the information may easily end up looking like this:

```
# Time in $1, machine name in $2, text in $3
/^([0-2]\d:[0-5]\d:[0-5]\d)\s+\[([^\]]+)\]\s+(.*)$/
```

However, if you use the /x modifier, you can stretch it out as follows:

---

1. Most dictionaries define *munge* to be a derogatory term for imperfectly transforming data. But in the Perl culture, munge is not derogatory—being able to transform data, even if imperfectly, is one thing that Perl programmers aspire to.

```
/
^               # Match at the beginning of the string
(               # First group: time
   [0-2]\d
   :
   [0-5]\d
   :
   [0-5]\d
)
\s+
\[              # Square bracket
   (           # Second group: machine name
   [^\]]+      # Anything that isn't a square bracket
   )
\]              # End square bracket

\s+
   (           # Third group: everything else
   .*
   )
$               # Finally, match the end of the string
/x
```

Another way to tidy this up is to put each of the groups into variables and interpolate them:

```
my $time_re = '([0-2]\d:[0-5]\d:[0-5]\d)';
my $host_re = '\[[^\]]+)\]';
my $mess_re = '(.*)';

/^$time_re\s+$host_re\s+$mess_re$/;
```

The split() Function

We briefly saw split() earlier on in the chapter where we used it to break up a string into a list of words. In fact, we only saw it in a very simple form, and strictly speaking, it was a bit of a cheat to use it at all—we didn't see it then, but split() was actually using a regular expression to do its work.

Using split() on its own is equivalent to saying

```
split /\s+/, $_
```

which breaks the default string $_ into a list of substrings using one or more whitespace characters as a delimiter. However, we can also specify our own regular expression: Perl goes through the string, breaking it whenever the regex matches. The delimiter itself is thrown away.

For instance, on the Unix operating system, configuration files are sometimes a list of fields separated by colons. A sample line from the password file looks like this:

```
kake:x:10018:10020::/home/kake:/bin/bash
```

To get at each field, we can split when we see a colon:

```perl
#!/usr/bin/perl -w
# split.pl

use strict;

my $passwd = "kake:x:10018:10020::/home/kake:/bin/bash";
my @fields = split /:/, $passwd;
print "Login name : $fields[0]\n";
print "User ID : $fields[2]\n";
print "Home directory : $fields[5]\n";
```

```
$ perl split.pl
Login name : kake
User ID : 10018
Home directory : /home/kake
$
```

Note that the fourth field (0-based) stored in $fields[4] is the empty string because Perl recognized that there were two colons next to one another. The field was empty so the array element is the empty string. Therefore, $fields[5] contains /home/kake. Be careful though—if the line you are splitting contains empty fields at the *end*, they will get dropped.

The join() Function

To do the exact opposite, we can use the join() function. This takes a specified delimiter and glues it between the elements of a list. For example:

```perl
#!/usr/bin/perl -w
# join.pl

use strict;

my $passwd = "kake:x:10018:10020::/home/kake:/bin/bash";
my @fields = split /:/, $passwd;
print "Login name : $fields[0]\n";
print "User ID : $fields[2]\n";
print "Home directory : $fields[5]\n";

my $passwd2 = join "#", @fields;
print "Original password : $passwd\n";
print "New password :      $passwd2\n";
```

```
$ perl join.pl
Login name : kake
User ID : 10018
Home directory : /home/kake
```

```
Original password : kake:x:10018:10020::/home/kake:/bin/bash
New password :       kake#x#10018#10020##/home/kake#/bin/bash
$
```

Common Blunders

There are a few common mistakes people tend to make when writing regexes—we've already seen that /a*b*c*/ will happily match any string at all, since it matches each letter zero times. What else can go wrong?

- *Forgetting to group:*

  /Bam{2}/ will match "Bamm", while /(Bam){2}/ will match "BamBam", so be careful when choosing which one to use. The same goes for alternation: /Simple|on/ will match "Simple" and "on", while /Sim(ple|on)/ will match both "Simple" and "Simon"—group each option separately.

- *Getting the anchors wrong:*

  ^ goes at the beginning, $ goes at the end. A dollar anywhere else in the string makes Perl try and interpolate a variable.

- *Forgetting to escape special characters:*

  Do you want them to have a special meaning? These are the characters to be careful of: . * ? + [( ) { ^ $ | and, of course, \ itself.

- *Not counting from 0:*

  The first entry in an array is given the index 0.

- *Counting from 0:*

  Yes, all along we've been telling you that computers start counting from 0. Nevertheless, there's always the odd exception—the first backreference is $1. $0 has another special use—a string containing the way in which the program was executed.

Backreferences (Again)

Finally, in our tour of regular expressions, let's look again at backreferences. Suppose you want to find any repeated words in a string—how would you do it? You might think about doing this:

```
if (/\b(\w+) $1\b/) {
   print "Repeated word: $1\n";
}
```

Except this doesn't work, because $1 is only set when the match is complete. In fact, if you have warnings turned on, you'll be alerted to the fact the $1 is undefined every time. In order to match while still inside the regular expression, you need to use the following syntax:

```
if (/\b(\w+) \1\b/) {
   print "Repeated word: $1\n";
}
```

However, when you're replacing, you'll get a warning if you try and use the \<number> syntax on the wrong side. It will work, but you'll be told \1 better written as $1.

Summary

Regular expressions are quite possibly the most powerful means at your disposal of looking for patterns in text, extracting subpatterns, and replacing portions of text. They're the basis of any text shuffling you do in Perl, and they should be your first port of call when you need to do some string manipulation.

In this chapter, we've seen how to match simple text, different classes of text, and then different amounts of text. We've also seen how to provide alternative matches, how to refer back to portions of the match, and how to substitute text.

The key to learning and understanding regular expressions is to be able to break them down into their component parts and unravel the language, translating it piecewise into English. Once you can fluently read out the intention of a complex regular expression, you're well on your way to creating powerful matches of your own.

We only scratched the surface of regular expressions in this chapter. There are so many features and so much power in regular expressions that an entire book could be written on the subject. As a matter of fact, that has already happened—the book is entitled *Mastering Regular Expressions, Second Edition* by Jeffrey Friedl (O'Reilly & Associates, 2002). We suggest you check out this book for everything you need to know about regular expressions, and then some.

Exercises

1. Translate each of the following regular expressions into English:

    - /hello.*world/

    - /^\d+\s\w*$/

    - /\b[A-Z][a-z]*\b/

    - /(.).*\1/

2. Translate each of the following English statements into regular expressions:

    - A digit at the beginning of the string and a digit at the end of the string

    - A string that contains only whitespace characters or word characters

    - A string with no whitespace characters

3. Write a program that loops through lines of a file or standard input, each line containing a single word, and prints out words that have two vowels next to one another.

4. Modify the preceding to match words with exactly two vowels occurring anywhere in the word.

CHAPTER 8

■ ■ ■

Files and Data

We're starting to write real programs now, and real programs need to be able to read and write files from and to your hard drive. At the moment, all we can do is ask the user for input using <STDIN> and print data on the screen using print(). Pretty simple stuff, yes—but these two ideas actually form the basis of a great deal of the file handling you'll be doing in Perl.

What we want to do in this chapter is extend these techniques into reading from and writing to files using *filehandles*, and we'll also look at the other techniques we have for handling files and data including the very useful diamond (<>).

Filehandles

A *filehandle* is a variable that we associate with a file. After this association, we can either read from the file or write to the file (depending on how the file was opened).

We've already seen a filehandle: the STDIN of <STDIN>. This is a filehandle for the special input stream *standard input*, and whenever we've used the idiom <STDIN> to read a line, we've been reading from standard input. Standard input is the input provided by a user either directly, as we've seen, by typing on the keyboard; or indirectly, through the use of a "pipe" that, as we'll see later, pumps input into the program.

As a counterpart to standard input, there's also standard output: STDOUT. This is the exact opposite—it's the output we provide to a user, which at the moment we're doing by writing on the screen; every time we've used the print() function so far, we've been implicitly using STDOUT.

```
print STDOUT "Hello, world!\n";
```

is just the same as our original example in Chapter 1. There's one more "standard" filehandle: standard error, or STDERR, which is where we write the error messages when we die().

The open() Function

The open() function opens files. The preferred way of executing open() is with three arguments: the filehandle that we choose to associate with the file, the mode in which we are opening the file, and the filename:

```
open(filehandle, mode, filename)
```

An example would be:

```
open(FH, '<', 'input.txt')
```

The left angle bracket indicates *read mode*. More on all the modes later. It is also common to call the function with two arguments by combining the mode in the string that contains the filename:

```
open(filehandle, filename_with_mode)
```

Opening input.txt in this form would look like the following:

```
open(FH, '< input.txt')
```

This function returns true on success, false on failure. We should always handle the failure of opening a file—if we fail to open a file we expect to open, it is usually considered a severe error. We handle such errors by die()ing when the open fails—recall from Chapter 2 that die() sends its argument standard error and then exits the program. Here is an example:

```
open(FH, $mode, $filename) or die $!;
```

What's $!? This is one of Perl's *special variables*, variables that have a special use or meaning within Perl. In the case of $!, Perl is passing on an error message from the system, and this error message should tell you why the open() failed: it's usually something like "No such file or directory" or "Permission denied." See perldoc perlvar for a complete list of all the special variables.

Filehandles are slightly different from the other variables that we have seen, and they do not need to be declared with my(), even if you're using strict as you should. It's traditional to use all capitals for a filehandle to distinguish them from keywords.

The second and third arguments can be provided as variables or as a string literal, like this:

```
open(FH, $mode, $file)    or die $!;
open(FH, '<', 'output.log') or die $!;
```

You may specify a full path to a file, but don't forget that if you're on Windows, a backslash in a double-quoted string introduces an escape character. So, for instance, you should say this:

```
open(FH, '<', 'c:\test\news.txt') or die $!;
```

rather than

```
open(FH, '<', "c:\test\news.txt") or die $!;
```

as \t in a double-quoted string is a tab, and \n is a newline. You could also say "c:\\test\\news.txt", but that's a little hard to read. Recall that Windows allows forward slashes internally, and forward slashes do not need to be escaped: "c:/test/news.txt" should work perfectly fine.

We will look at three different ways to open a file in just a few pages.

The close() Function

When we are finished reading from or writing to a file, the filehandle should be closed. This is done with the close() function:

close(*filehandle*)

If you don't explicitly close a filehandle, it is not the end of the world—Perl will autoclose it for you. But it is considered good programming style to close files when you are finished with them.

Here is an example of opening and closing a file successfully:

```perl
#!/usr/bin/perl -w
# goodopen.pl

use strict;

open(FH, '<', 'goodopen.dat') or die $!;

print "goodopen.dat opened successfully\n";

close FH;
```

This example assumes, of course, that the file goodopen.dat exists in the current directory. If that is the case, here is the output of this program:

```
$ perl goodopen.pl
goodopen.dat opened successfully
$
```

Here is an example of opening a file that does not exist (assuming, of course, that badopen.dat does not exist). Note the value of $!.

```perl
#!/usr/bin/perl -w
# badopen.pl

use strict;

open(FH, '<', 'badopen.dat') or die "We have a problem: $!";

print "Did we make it here?  Nope...\n";

close FH;
```

Here is what happens when we attempt to execute this program:

```
$ perl badopen.pl
We have a problem: No such file or directory at badopen.pl line 6.
$
```

Recall that if the argument you give to die() does not end with a newline, Perl automatically adds the name of the program and the line number that had the problem. If you want to avoid this, always remember to put newlines on the end of the string you pass to the die() function.

Three Ways to Open a File

We will discuss three ways of opening a file: read mode, write mode, and append mode. If the file is opened in read mode, we can only read from the file. If opened in write mode, the file is opened, truncated (that means it is emptied out), and we can only write into it. Append mode means that the file is opened, the contents persevered (not overwritten), and then we can write to the end of the file.

Read Mode

We often write programs that read input data from an external place such as a file on disk. This data can be any data that our program needs, for example, a list of addresses or information to send out in an email. When it comes time to read that input in from a file, the file must first be opened, and we must open the file in *read mode*. Read mode means we can only read in from the file; we cannot modify the contents of the file. In Perl, read mode is the default mode for opening a file.

If we attempt to open a file in read mode, the open() function will fail if the file does not exist or if we do not have permission to read it. This is the default mode, so this example opens as read only:

```
open(FH, 'data.txt') or die $!;
```

We can explicitly open in read mode by using the left angle bracket (<) as the first character in the string that contains the filename:

```
open(FH, '<data.txt') or die $!;
```

Or better yet, use the preferred three-argument syntax:

```
open(FH, '<', 'data.txt') or die $!;
```

Write Mode

Up to this point, our programs have printed text to standard output or the user's terminal. This is fine for some programs, but the data that is printed out is lost as soon as it is printed. Sometimes we will want our program to generate some output that can exist beyond the execution of the program. If we want the output data to be accessible later on, we can write the data out to a file that will be saved on disk. To do this, we open the file in *write mode.*

An important note: write mode will overwrite the file if it already exists. That means that all the contents of the file will be lost, and the file will start as empty. If you want to keep the contents of the file intact and add to them, then the file should be opened in *append mode,* discussed in the next section.

We can open a file in write mode by using the right angle bracket (>) as the second argument to open() (or as the first character of the string that contains the filename if we are using two-argument invocation). As mentioned in the preceding paragraph, if we attempt to open a file in write mode and the file exists, the file will be overwritten—the contents will be lost. If we attempt to open a file in write mode and the file does not exist, it will be created. The open() function will fail if we open in write mode and we do not have permission to create the file or write to the file. Here is an example:

```
open(FH, '>', 'data.txt') or die $!;
```

Here is the same example using the two-argument version:

```
open(FH, '>data.txt') or die $!;
```

Append Mode

To write to the file and keep its current content intact, open it in *append mode*. In append mode, the file is opened and *not* overwritten, and any output that we write into the file will be added to the bottom of the file.

A file can be opened in append mode by using two right angle brackets (>>) as the second argument (or in the string that contains the filename if we use the two-argument invocation). If we attempt to open a file in append mode and the file exists, we will add to the bottom of the file. If the file does not exist, it will be created. The open() function will fail if we do not have permission to create the file or if we do not have write permission to the file. Here is an example:

```
open(FH, '>>', 'data.txt') or die $!;
```

Or, using the two-argument version:

```
open(FH, '>>data.txt') or die $!;
```

Reading in Scalar Context

To read from a file opened in read mode, simply wrap the filehandle in angle brackets:

```
<FH>
```

We did this before when we read from standard input: <STDIN>. Just like reading from standard input, there are two ways to read from any filehandle: scalar context and list context.

Scalar context reads the next line of the file, newline included:

```
$line = <FH>;
```

Here is an example of reading line by line through a file until end of file. Notice that <FH> is not assigned to a variable within the while loop parentheses—like <STDIN>, it is automatically assigned to $_:

```
while (<FH>) {
    # process the line
}
```

Here is an example of reading through a file and printing each line of the file with the line number prepended:

```
#!/usr/bin/perl -w
# nl1.pl

use strict;

open(FILE, '<', 'nlexample.txt') or die $!;
my $lineno = 1;
```

```perl
while (<FILE>) {
    print $lineno++;
    print ": $_";
}

close FILE;
```

Next, create the file `nlexample.txt` with the following contents:

```
One day you're going to have to face
    A deep dark truthful mirror,
And it's gonna tell you things that I still
    Love you too much to say.
####### Elvis Costello, Spike, 1988 #######
```

This is what you should see when you run the program:

```
$ perl nl1.pl
1: One day you're going to have to face
2:     A deep dark truthful mirror,
3: And it's gonna tell you things that I still
4:     Love you too much to say.
5. ####### Elvis Costello, Spike, 1988 #######
$
```

Looking at this program in detail, we begin by opening our file and making sure it was opened correctly.

```perl
open(FILE, '<', 'nlexample.txt') or die $!;
```

Since we're expecting our line numbers to start at 1, we'll initialize our counter as follows:

```perl
my $lineno = 1;
```

Now we read each line from the file in turn:

```perl
while (<FILE>) {
```

Recall that this syntax is actually equivalent to the following:

```perl
while (defined ($_ = <FILE>)) {
```

That is, we read a line from a file and assign it to $_, and we see whether it is defined. If it is, we do whatever's in the loop—if not, we are at the end of the file so we fall out of the loop. This gives us a nice, easy way of setting $_ to each line in turn.

As we have a newline, we print out its line number and advance the counter.

```perl
print $lineno++;
```

Finally, we print out the line in question:

```
print ": $_";
```

There's no need to add a newline since we didn't bother chomp()ing the incoming line. Of course, using a statement modifier, we can make this program even more concise:

```
open(FILE, '<', 'nlexample.txt') or die $!;
my $lineno = 1;

print $lineno++, ": $_" while <FILE>;

close FILE;
```

But since we're going to want to expand the capabilities of our program—adding more operations to the body of the loop—we're probably better off with the original format.

Reading with the Diamond

We who come from the Unix world have used the sort command (some of us in the Windows world have used its version of sort as well). If invoked with a command line argument, sort treats the argument as a filename and reads from that file, sorting the content and printing the sorted content to standard output:

```
$ sort nlexample.txt
    A deep dark truthful mirror,
    Love you too much to say.
####### Elvis Costello, Spike, 1988 #######
And it's gonna tell you things that I still
One day you're going to have to face
$
```

The reason the first two lines are printed first is that they begin with a space character which is a string less than "#", which in turn is a string less than "A" and "O".

Ever wonder what happens if sort is invoked with no command line arguments? It reads from standard input until end of file (^D is end-of-file for Unix standard input and ^Z<enter> is end-of-file in Windows):

```
$ sort
the
power
to
believe
^D
believe
power
the
to
$
```

This important behavior is evident in many different Unix (and Windows) commands:

- If the program is invoked with command line arguments, treat the arguments as filenames and read from them.

- If the program is invoked with no command line arguments, read from standard input.

If Perl is to be indeed practical, there should be a way to perform this behavior, and it should be easy to do. It is easy—with the *diamond*.

The diamond (<>) checks to see if the program was invoked with command line arguments. If so, it reads from them in scalar context one file at a time, one line at a time. If it is invoked with no command line arguments, it reads from standard input just like <STDIN>.

Here is an example called diamond1.pl:

```
#!/usr/bin/perl -w
# diamond1.pl

use strict;

while (<>) {
    print "text read: $_"
}
```

Here is an example of invoking this program with command line arguments. Given the file file1.dat:

```
this is file1.dat
it is not too exciting...
```

and file2.dat:

```
this is file2.dat
equally unexciting...
```

Here is what the program generates when executed with these two filenames:

```
$ perl diamond1.pl file1.dat file2.dat
text read: this is file1.dat
text read: it is not too exciting...
text read: this is file2.dat
text read: equally unexciting...
$
```

As can be seen from this example, the file file1.dat is opened and read first. The first line is read and processed, then the second line. When the entire content of file1.dat is read, then the program opens file2.dat and reads each line until end of file.

Now let's run the same program with no command line arguments. Notice it reads from standard input.

```
$ perl diamond1.pl
I
text read: I
Don't
text read: Don't
Want
text read: Want
to
text read: to
Be
text read: Be
a
text read: a
Star
text read: Star
^D
$
```

Here we see the practical nature of Perl showing itself—being able to mimic this important behavior and able to do so easily.

Let's modify nl1.pl to read from the file on the command line. Notice we now do not need to explicitly open and close the file.

```perl
#!/usr/bin/perl -w
# nl2.pl

use strict;

my $lineno = 1;

while (<>) {
    print $lineno++;
    print ": $_";
}
```

When we execute the program, we provide the data file on the command line. This invocation produces the same output as nl1.pl:

```
$ perl nl2.pl nlexample.txt
1: One day you're going to have to face
2:     A deep dark truthful mirror,
3: And it's gonna tell you things that I still
4:     Love you too much to say.
5: ####### Elvis Costello, Spike, 1988 #######
$
```

@ARGV: The Command Line Arguments

There is some behind-the-scenes work that is going on with the diamond. When a program is invoked, all the command line arguments—the text after the program name—are stored in the special array variable @ARGV. Let's write a program that will display this array's contents:

```
#!/usr/bin/perl -w
# argv1.pl

use strict;

print "[$_]\n" foreach @ARGV;
```

This program simply loops through all the elements of @ARGV, printing them to standard output. Note that since @ARGV is a special array variable, it does not need to be declared with my() even though we are using strict. As a matter of fact, don't declare it with my()—if we do we will break its magic.

If the program is invoked with no arguments after the program name, @ARGV is empty:

```
$ perl argv1.pl
$
```

If invoked with arguments it is a bit more interesting:

```
$ perl argv1.pl king crimson rocks
[king]
[crimson]
[rocks]
$
```

Notice that text after the program name is treated as a whitespace-separated list of terms, and each is its own element of @ARGV. One more invocation shows that the contents of @ARGV is entirely dependent on the command line arguments:

```
$ perl argv1.pl It was the best of times,
[It]
[was]
[the]
[best]
[of]
[times,]
$
```

The command line arguments can be stored into variables for later use by simply accessing the elements of @ARGV.

```
my $zeroth_arg = $ARGV[0];
my $first_arg  = $ARGV[1];
```

It is common to do this in a different way (TIMTOWDI) by shifting @ARGV.

```perl
my $zeroth_arg = shift @ARGV;
my $first_arg  = shift @ARGV;
```

And because we can, we might want to shorten this code a bit by taking advantage of the fact that the shift() function, outside the body of a function definition, shifts @ARGV by default. So this code is produces the same result as the preceding code:

```perl
my $zeroth_arg = shift;
my $first_arg  = shift;
```

@ARGV and <>

The diamond and @ARGV have a functional relationship (as opposed to a dysfunctional one). Here is how <> really works:

- If there are any elements in @ARGV, shift out the first one, treat it as a file, and read from it; repeat for each element in @ARGV until @ARGV is empty.

- If @ARGV is empty, read from standard input.

Here is a program that illustrates this relationship. In argv2.pl, @ARGV is assigned the value of three files. Then, when the <> is read from within the while loop parentheses, it will read from the files that were assigned to @ARGV.

```perl
#!/usr/bin/perl -w
# argv2.pl

use strict;

@ARGV = qw(file1.dat file2.dat file3.dat);

while (<>) {
    print "text read: $_";
}
```

Executing this program produces the following:

```
$ perl argv2.pl
text read: this is file1.dat
text read: it is not too exciting...
text read: this is file2.dat
text read: equally unexciting...
text read: this is file3.dat
text read: yep, you guessed it, not too exciting...
$
```

Note: in this program we assign to @ARGV, which overwrites its value. If this program were executed with command line arguments, they would be immediately overwritten and lost. We could easily change the code to add the three files to the command line arguments by using the push() function:

```
push @ARGV, qw(file1.dat file2.dat file3.dat);
```

$ARGV

As the <> reads through the files on the command line, the file that it is reading is stored in the special variable $ARGV. This variable can be used if the name of the file being read from is desired. Here is a program that prints its value as it is reading:

```
#!/usr/bin/perl -w
# argv3.pl

use strict;

@ARGV = qw(file1.dat file2.dat file3.dat);

while (<>) {
    print "text read from $ARGV: $_";
}
```

Executing this code produces the following:

```
$ perl argv3.pl
text read from file1.dat: this is file1.dat
text read from file1.dat: it is not too exciting...
text read from file2.dat: this is file2.dat
text read from file2.dat: equally unexciting...
text read from file3.dat: this is file3.dat
text read from file3.dat: yep, you guessed it, not too exciting...
$
```

Like @ARGV, $ARGV does not need to be declared with my(). Moreover, it should not be declared or its magic will be broken.

Reading in List Context

Sometimes we'll want to read more than just one line at a time. When you read from a filehandle in a scalar context, as we've been doing so far, it will give you the next line. However, in list context, it will return all of the remaining lines (newlines included). This is known as a *file slurp*. For instance, you can read in an entire file like this:

```
open(INPUT, '<', 'somefile.dat') or die $!;
my @data;
@data = <INPUT>;
close INPUT;
```

This can be memory-intensive however—Perl has to store every single line of the file into the array, whereas you may only want to be dealing with one or two of them. Usually, you'll want to step through a file with a `while` loop as before. However, for some things, an array is the easiest way of processing data. For example, how do you print the last five lines in a file?

The problem with reading a line at a time is that you don't know how much left you've got to read—you can only tell when you run out of data, so you'd have to keep an array of the last five lines read, and drop an old line when a new one comes in. You'd do it something like this:

```
#!/usr/bin/perl -w
# tail1.pl

use strict;

open(FILE, '<', 'gettysburg.txt') or die $!;
my @last5;

while (<FILE>) {
    push @last5, $_;            # add to the end
    shift @last5 if @last5 > 5; # take from the beginning
}

close FILE;

print "Last five lines:\n", @last5;
```

And that's exactly how you'd do it if you were concerned about memory use on big files—given a suitably primed gettysburg.txt, this is what you'd get:

```
$ perl tail1.pl
Last five lines:
gave the last full measure of devotion--that we here highly
resolve that these dead shall not have died in vain, that
this nation shall have a new birth of freedom, and that
government of the people, by the people, for the people
shall not perish from the earth.
$
```

However, if memory wasn't a problem or you knew you were going to be primarily dealing with small to medium-size files, this would be perfectly sufficient:

```
#!/usr/bin/perl -w
# tail2.pl

use strict;
```

```
open(FILE, '<', 'gettysburg.txt') or die $!;
my @speech = <FILE>;   # slurp the whole file into memory
close FILE;

print "Last five lines:\n", @speech[-5 .. -1];
```

Writing to Files

We're now ready to write to a file, which we'll do by using a form of the print() function.
Normally, to print things out on standard output, we say this:

```
print list;
```

When we want to write to a file associated with the filehandle FH, we'll use this instead:

```
print FH list;
```

Yes, that's print(), followed by a space, followed by a filehandle, followed by a space (*not*
a comma), followed by the stuff to print.

So, for instance, here's a program that demonstrates one way of copying a file. This program
takes two command line arguments—the first is the file to read, the second is the file to write.

```
#!/usr/bin/perl -w
# copy.pl

use strict;

my $source      = shift @ARGV;
my $destination = shift @ARGV;

open(IN, '<', $source)       or die "Can't read source file $source: $!\n";
open(OUT, '>', $destination) or die "Can't write to file $destination: $!\n";

print "Copying $source to $destination\n";

while (<IN>) {
   print OUT $_;
}

close IN;
close OUT;
```

Now there isn't much to see when we run this program, but let's run it anyway:

```
$ perl copy.pl gettysburg.txt speech.txt
Copying gettysburg.txt to speech.txt
$
```

Let's look at this program in detail. First, we get the name of the file to copy and the name of the destination file from the command line:

```
my $source      = shift @ARGV;
my $destination = shift @ARGV;
```

The command line arguments to our program are in the @ARGV array, and we use shift() (which removes and returns the left-most element of an array) to get an element out—we could quite easily have said this:

```
my $source      = $ARGV[0];
my $destination = $ARGV[1];
```

However, shift() is a slightly more common way of grabbing the command line argument. Next, we open our two files:

```
open(IN, '>', $source)       or die "Can't read source file $source: $!\n";
open(OUT, '>', $destination) or die "Can't write to file $destination: $!\n";
```

The first open() opens the source file in read mode and the second open() opens the destination file in write mode. Notice that we're taking care to check the files can be opened for reading and writing—it is essential to let the user know if, for example, they do not have permission to access a certain file, or the file does not exist. There is rarely a really good reason not to do this.

The copying procedure is simple enough: read a line from the source file, and then write it to the destination.

```
while (<IN>) {
    print OUT $_;
}
```

The while loop is reading from <IN> in scalar context—one line at a time—until end of file. In list context <IN> returns a list of all the remaining lines in the file. So why don't we just say

```
print OUT <IN>;
```

The trouble is, that's not very memory conscious—Perl would have to read in the *whole* file at once in order to construct the list, and only then pass it out to print(). For small files, this is fine. For large files, it is usually better to read line by line in scalar context.

Let's see another example. This time, instead of immediately writing the file, we'll first sort the lines. In this case, we can't avoid reading in every line into memory—we need to have all the lines in an array or something similar. Let's see how we'd go about doing this. This program will take two arguments—the input file to sort and the output file that will contain the sorted content.

If you've ever needed to sort the lines in a file, this is for you. The program works in three stages:

• First, open the input file and the output file that the user specifies.

• Then read in the input file and sort its content.

• Finally, write out the sorted content.

Here's the full listing:

```perl
#!/usr/bin/perl -w
# sort1.pl

use strict;

my $input  = shift;
my $output = shift;
open(INPUT, '<', $input)   or die "Couldn't open file $input: $!\n";
open(OUTPUT, '>', $output) or die "Couldn't open file $output: $!\n";

my @file = <INPUT>;
@file = sort @file;

print OUTPUT @file;

close INPUT;
close OUTPUT;
```

If we have the following file, `sortme.txt`:

```
Well, I finally found someone to turn me upside-down
And nail my feet up where my head should be
If they had a king of fools then I could wear that crown
And you can all die laughing, because I'd wear it proudly
```

We can run our program like this:

```
$ perl sort1.pl sortme.txt sorted.txt
$
```

And we'll end up with a file, `sorted.txt`:

```
And nail my feet up where my head should be
And you can all die laughing, because I'd wear it proudly
If they had a king of fools then I could wear that crown
Well, I finally found someone to turn me upside-down
```

The first stage of this program—that of opening the files—is very similar to what we did before, with one small change:

```perl
my $input  = shift;
my $output = shift;
open(INPUT, '<', $input)   or die "Couldn't open file $input: $!\n";
open(OUTPUT, '>', $output) or die "Couldn't open file $output: $!\n";
```

We don't tell Perl which array to shift()—so it assumes we want @ARGV, which is just as well, because in this case, we do!

Getting the file sorted is a simple matter of reading it into an array and calling sort(), passing in the array.

```
my @file = <INPUT>;
@file = sort @file;
```

In fact, we could just say my @file = sort <INPUT>; and that would be slightly more efficient—Perl would only have to store the lines of text in memory once.

Finally, we write out the sorted array:

```
print OUTPUT @file;
```

We could even do all this in one line, without using an array:

```
print OUTPUT sort <INPUT>;
```

This is arguably the most efficient solution, and you might think it's relatively easy to understand. What are we doing after all? Printing to the output file the sorted input file. But it's the least extensible way of writing it. We can't change any of the stages when it's written like that.

Buffering

Try this little program:

```
#!/usr/bin/perl -w
# time1.pl

use strict;

foreach (1..20) {
   print ".";
   sleep 1;
}
print "\n";
```

You'd probably expect it to print 20 dots, leaving a second's gap between each one—on Windows with ActiveState Perl, that's exactly what it does. However, this is something of an exception: on most other operating systems, you'll have to wait for 20 seconds first, before it prints all 20 dots at once.

So what's going on? Operating systems often won't actually write something to (or read something from) a filehandle until the end of the line character—this is to save doing a lot of short, repetitive read/write operations. Instead, they keep everything you've written queued up in a buffer and access the filehandle once only. This is called *buffering*.

However, you can tell Perl to stop the OS doing this by modifying the special variable $|. If this is set to 0, which it usually is, Perl will tell the operating system to use standard output buffering if possible. If it's set to 1, Perl turns off standard output buffering.

So, to make our program steadily print out dots—as you might do to show progress on a long operation—we just need to set $| to 1 before we do our printing:

```
#!/usr/bin/perl -w
# time2.pl

use strict;

$| = 1;
foreach (1..20) {
    print ".";
    sleep 1;
}
print "\n";
```

Opening Pipes

The open() function can be used for more than just plain old files—you can read data from and send data to programs as well. Anything that can read from standard input or write to standard output can talk directly to Perl via a *pipe*.

Pipes were invented by Doug MacIlroy for the Unix operating system, and were soon carried over to other operating systems. They're one of those things that sound amazingly obvious once someone else has thought of it.

Note A pipe is something that connects two filehandles together.

That's it. Usually, you'll be connecting the standard output of one program to the standard input of another. Unix users are probably quite familiar with pipes. Here is a command that will list all the nonhidden files in a directory (ls) and then page through the output (more):

```
$ ls | more
```

The vertical bar character (|) connects the standard output of the ls command to the standard input of the more command. This causes the file listing output to be sent into the more command, whose job it is to page through it.

The Windows version of this command is

```
$ dir | more
```

We can write Perl programs that pipe into programs (our Perl program will write into the pipe) or pipe from programs (our Perl program will read from the pipe).

Piping In from a Process

To read the output of a program, simply use open() using the two-argument form and the name of the program (with any command line arguments you want to give it) and put a pipe at the end. For instance, let's write a program to sort either the file on the command line or standard input (sort2.pl):

```
#!/usr/bin/perl -w
# sort2.pl

use strict;

my @text = <>;

print sort @text;
```

Recall that the <> reads from either the file or files on the command line, or standard input if there are no command line arguments. Reading from <> into @text will read in list context, slurping the contents into the array. We then print the array sorted.

Here is an example of executing this program:

$ perl sort2.pl gettysburg.txt

This invocation would produce the content of gettysburg.txt in sorted order.

Let's write a program that will execute this program and print every third line of the output. We'll call it sortslash3.pl.

```
#!/usr/bin/perl -w
# sortslash3.pl

use strict;

open(FH, 'perl sort2.pl gettysburg.txt |');

my $i = 1;

while (<FH>) {
    if ($i % 3 == 0) {
        print;
    }
    $i++;
}

close FH;
```

The important line in this program is

```
open(FH, 'perl sort2.pl gettysburg.txt |');
```

This line starts a process that executes the sort2.pl program, passing the argument gettysburg.txt. The vertical bar as the last character in the string means "Pipe from this program's standard output into our program." Since this standard output is coming into our program, we can read from the pipe by wrapping the filehandle variable in angle brackets.

```
<FH>
```

Opening a pipe to read from can also be done using the three-argument form of the open() function.

```perl
open(FH, '-|', 'perl sort2.pl gettysburg.txt');
```

In the while loop, we are reading from the filehandle in scalar context, one line of output at a time. We then keep count of what line we are processing and if that line is divisible by 3 (we determine that by using the modulus operator %), we print that line to standard output.

Running this program produces the following:

```
$ perl sortslash3.pl
```

```
Nov. 19, 1863
This we may, in all propriety do. But in a larger sense, we
dedicated to the proposition that all men are created equal.
great task remaining before us--that from these honored dead
here, but it can never forget what they did here.
resolve that these dead shall not have died in vain, that
this continent a new nation, conceived in liberty and
$
```

Piping Out to Processes

As well as reading data in from external programs, we can write out to the standard input of another program. For instance, we could send mail out by writing to a program like sendmail,[1] or we could be generating output that we'd like to have sorted before it gets to the user. We'll deal with the second example because, while it's easy enough to collect the data into an array and sort it ourselves before writing it out, we know we have a sorting program handy—since we wrote one a few pages ago. It is called sort2.pl.

Here is a program that will count things and then open a pipe into our sort2.pl program, displaying those things and their counts in sorted order. This program will also illustrate a very common use of a hash variable—counting (we talked about using a hash to count things at the end of Chapter 5).

Things hide in the kitchen cabinet. Tins of tomatoes can lurk unseen for weeks and months, springing only to vision after another can has been purchased. Every so often, then, we need to investigate the cabinets and take inventory to enumerate our baked beans and root out reticent ravioli. The following program can help us do that:

```perl
#!/usr/bin/perl -w
# inventory.pl

use strict;

my %inventory;
print "Enter individual items, followed by a new line.\n";
```

---

1.   sendmail is arguably the most ubiquitous Mail Transfer Agent (MTA) used on the Internet. See www.sendmail.org for more information.

```perl
print "Enter a blank line to finish.\n";
while (<STDIN>) {
    chomp;
    last if $_ eq "";
    $inventory{lc $_}++;
}

open(SORT, "| perl sort2.pl");

while (my ($item, $quantity) = each %inventory) {
    if ($quantity > 1) {
        $item =~ s/^(\w+)\b/$1s/ unless $item =~ /^\w+s\b/;
    }
    print SORT "$item: $quantity\n";
}

close SORT;
```

Now let's take stock:

```
$ perl inventory.pl
Enter individual items, followed by a new line.
Enter a blank line to finish.
jar of jam
loaf of bread
can of tuna
packet of pancake mix
can of tomatoes
can of tuna
packet of pasta
clove of garlic
packet of pasta

can of tomatoes: 1
cans of tuna: 2
clove of garlic: 1
jar of jam: 1
loaf of bread: 1
packet of pancake mix: 1
packets of pasta: 2
```

As you can see, we get a sorted list of totals back. Let's look at this code in more detail.

Whenever you're counting how many of each thing you have in a list, you should immediately think about hashes. Here we use a hash to key each item to the quantity—each time we see another one of those items, we add to the quantity in the hash:

```
while (<STDIN>) {
    chomp;
    last unless $_ eq "";
    $inventory{lc $_}++;
}
```

This loop will end when we reach end of file or if $item contains nothing after having been chomped—it was nothing more than a newline.

To ensure that the capitalization of our item is not significant, we use the lc() function to return a lowercase version of the item. Otherwise, "Can of beans", "CAN OF BEANS", and "can of beans" would be treated as three totally separate items, instead of three examples of the same thing. By forcing them into lowercase, we remove the difference.

Tip The lc() function returns the string it was given, but with uppercase characters turned into lower-case, so print lc("FuNnY StRiNg"); should give you the output "funny string". There's also a uc() function which returns an uppercased version of the string, so print uc("FuNnY StRiNg"); will output "FUNNY STRING".

Next, we open our pipe. We're going to pass data from our program to another, external program:

```
open(SORT, "| perl sort2.pl");
```

We could have used the three-argument form of open() as in

```
open(SORT, "|-", "perl sort2.pl");
```

Now we can print the data out:

```
while (my ($item, $quantity) = each %inventory) {
```

We use each() to get each key/value pair from the hash, as explained in Chapter 5.

```
if ($quantity > 1) {
    $item =~ s/(\w+)/$1s/ unless $item =~ /\w+s\b/;
}
```

This will make the output a little more presentable—if there is more than one of the current item, the name should be pluralized, unless it already ends in an "s". \w+ will get the first word in the string, the parentheses will store that word in $1, and we then add an "s" after it.

Last of all, we print this out by printing to the SORT filehandle. That filehandle is in turn connected to the standard input of the sort2.pl program so the output is in sorted order.

Bidirectional Pipes

A common mistake is to attempt to pipe into a process, and then pipe out of the same process. Speaking in code, this would look like the following:

```
open(P, '| some_program |');
```

This doesn't work—you can't pipe into and then out of the same process. However, this behavior is very common—sometimes we want to be able to do this. The syntax to accomplish this is a bit beyond the scope of this book, but you can quench your curiosity by checking out `perldoc IPC::Open2`.

File Tests

So far, we've just been reading and writing files, and `die()`ing if anything bad happens. For small programs, this is usually adequate; but if we want to use files in the context of a larger application, we should really check their status before we try and open them and, if necessary, take preventative measures. For instance, we may want to warn the user if a file we wish to overwrite already exists, giving them a chance to specify a different file. We'll also want to ensure that, for instance, we're not trying to read a directory as if it were a file.

■**Tip** This sort of programming—anticipating the consequences of future actions—is called *defensive programming*. Just like defensive driving, you assume that everything is out to get you. Just because this is paranoid behavior does not mean they are not out to get you—files will not exist or not be writable when you need them, users will specify things inaccurately, and so on. Properly anticipating, diagnosing, and working around these areas is the mark of a top-class programmer.

Perl provides us with *file tests*, which allow us to check various characteristics of files. Most of these act as logical operators and return a true or false value. For instance, to check if a file exists, we write this:

```
if (-e "somefile.dat") {...}
```

The test is `-e` and it takes a filename (or filehandle) as its argument. Just like `open()`, this filename can also be specified from a variable—you can just as validly say

```
if (-e $filename) {...}
```

where `$filename` contains the name of the file you want to check.

For a complete list of file tests, see `perldoc perlfunc`—Table 8-1 shows the most common ones.

Table 8-1. *File Test Operators*

Test	Meaning
-e	True if the file exists
-f	True if the file is a plain file—not a directory
-d	True if the file is a directory
-z	True if the file has zero size
-s	True if the file has nonzero size—returns size of file in bytes
-r	True if the file is readable by you
-w	True if the file is writable by you
-x	True if the file is executable by you
-o	True if the file is owned by you

The last four tests will only make complete sense on operating systems for which files have meaningful permissions, such as Unix and Windows NT. If this isn't the case, they'll frequently *all* return true (assuming the file or directory exists)—so, for instance, if we're going to write to a file, we should check to see whether the file already exists, and if so, what we should do about it.

Tip Note that on systems that don't use permissions comprehensively, -w is the most likely of the last four tests to have any significance, testing for read-only status.

This program does all it can to find a safe place to write a file:

```perl
#!/usr/bin/perl -w
# filetest.pl

use strict;

my $target;
while (1) {
    print "What file should I write to? ";
    $target = <STDIN>;
    chomp $target;
    if (-d $target) {
        print "No, $target is a directory.\n";
        next;
    }
    if (-e $target) {
        print "File already exists. What should I do?\n";
        print "(Enter 'r' to write to a different name, ";
        print "'o' to overwrite or\n";
        print "'b' to back up to $target.old)\n";
        my $choice = <STDIN>;
        chomp $choice;
        if ($choice eq "r") {
            next;
        } elsif ($choice eq "o") {
            unless (-o $target) {
                print "Can't overwrite $target, it's not yours.\n";
                next;
            }
            unless (-w $target) {
                print "Can't overwrite $target: $!\n";
                next;
            }
```

```
        } elsif ($choice eq "b") {
            if ( rename($target, $target.".old") ) {
                print "OK, moved $target to $target.old\n";
            } else {
                print "Couldn't rename file: $!\n";
                next;
            }
        } else {
            print "I didn't understand that answer.\n";
            next;
        }
    }
    last if open(OUTPUT, '>', $target);
    print "I couldn't write to $target: $!\n";
    # and round we go again.
}
print OUTPUT "Congratulations.\n";
print "Wrote to file $target\n";

close OUTPUT;
```

So, after all that, let's see how it handles our input. First of all with a text file that doesn't exist:

```
$ perl filetest.pl
What file should I write to? test.txt
Wrote to file test.txt
$
```

Seems OK. What about if we "accidentally" give it the name of a directory? Or give it a file that already exists? Or give it a response it's not prepared for?

```
$ perl filetest.pl
What file should I write to? work
No, work is a directory.
What file should I write to? filetest.pl
File already exists. What should I do?
(Enter 'r' to write to a different name, 'o' to overwrite or
'b' to back up to filetest.pl.old)
r
What file should I write to? test.txt
File already exists. What should I do?
(Enter 'r' to write to a different name, 'o' to overwrite or
'b' to back up to test.txt.old)
```

```
g
I didn't understand that answer.
What file should I write to? test.txt
File already exists. What should I do?
(Enter 'r' to write to a different name, 'o' to overwrite or
'b' to back up to test.txt.old)
b
OK, moved test.txt to test.txt.old
Wrote to file test.txt
$
```

There is a lot going on with this program. Let's look at it in detail.

The main program takes place inside an infinite loop—the only way we can exit the loop is via the last statement at the bottom:

```
last if open(OUTPUT, '>', $target);
```

That last will only happen if we're happy with the filename and we can successfully open the file. In order to be happy with the filename, though, we have a gauntlet of tests to run:

```
if (-d $target) {
```

We need to first see whether or not what has been specified is actually a directory. If it is, we don't want to go any further, so we go back and get another filename from the user:

```
    print "No, $target is a directory.\n";
    next;
```

We print a message and then use next to take us back to the top of the loop.

Next, we check to see whether or not the file already exists. If so, we ask the user what we should do about this.

```
if (-e $target) {
    print "File already exists. What should I do?\n";
    print "(Enter 'r' to write to a different name, ";
    print "'o' to overwrite or\n";
    print "'b' to back up to $target.old\n";
    my $choice = <STDIN>;
    chomp $choice;
```

If they want a different file, we merely go back to the top of the loop:

```
if ($choice eq "r") {
    next;
```

If they want us to overwrite the file, we see if this is likely to be possible:

```
} elsif ($choice eq "o") {
```

First, we see if they actually own the file: it's unlikely they'll be allowed to overwrite a file that they do not own.

```
unless (-o $target) {
    print "Can't overwrite $target, it's not yours.\n";
    next;
}
```

Next we check to see if there are any other reasons why we can't write to the file, and if there are, we report them and go around for another filename:

```
unless (-w $target) {
    print "Can't overwrite $target: $!\n";
    next;
}
```

If they want to back up the file—that is, rename the existing file to a new name, we see if this is possible:

```
} elsif ($choice eq "b") {
```

The rename() function renames a file; it takes two arguments: the current filename, and the new name.

```
if ( rename($target, $target.".old") ) {
    print "OK, moved $target to $target.old\n";
} else {
```

If we couldn't rename the file, we explain why and start from the beginning again:

```
    print "Couldn't rename file: $!\n";
    next;
}
```

Otherwise, they said something we weren't prepared for:

```
} else {
    print "I didn't understand that answer.\n";
    next;
}
```

You may think this program is excessively paranoid—after all, it's 50 lines just to print a message to a file. In fact, it isn't paranoid enough: it doesn't check to see whether the backup file already exists before renaming the currently existing file. This just goes to show you can never be too careful when dealing with the operating system. Later, we'll see how to turn big blocks of code like this into reusable elements so we don't have to reinvent the wheel every time we want to safely write to a file.

Summary

Files give our data permanence by allowing us to store it on the disk—it's no good having the best accounting program in the world, say, if it loses all your accounts every time the computer is switched off. What we've seen here are the fundamentals of getting data in and out of Perl.

Files are accessed through filehandles. Perl gives us three filehandles when our program executes: standard input (STDIN), standard output (STDOUT), and standard error (STDERR). We can open other filehandles, either for reading or for writing, with the open() function, and we must always remember to check the return value of the open() function.

Wrapping the filehandle in angle brackets—<FILEHANDLE>—reads from the specified filehandle. We can read in scalar context (one line at a time) or list context (all remaining lines until end of file).

Writing to a file is done with the print() function. By default, this writes to standard output, so the filehandle must be specified.

The diamond, <>, allows us to write programs that read from the files provided on the command line, or STDIN if no files are given.

Pipes can be used to talk to programs outside of Perl. We can read in and write out data to them as if we were looking at the screen or typing on the keyboard. We can also use them as filters to modify our data on the way in or out of a program.

File test operators can be used to check the status of a file in various ways, and we've seen an example of using file test operators to ensure that there are no surprises when we're reading or writing a file.

Exercises

1. Read each line of gettysburg.txt. Ignore all blank lines of the file. For all other lines, break the line into all the text separated by whitespace (keep all punctuation) and write each piece of text to the output file ex1out.txt on its own line.

2. Write a program that when given command line arguments displays their contents. For instance, if the program is invoked as

   ```
   $ perl ex2.pl file1.dat
   ```

   it would display the contents of file1.dat. If invoked as

   ```
   $ perl ex2.pl file2.dat file3.dat
   ```

   it would display the contents of file2.dat followed by file3.dat. However, if invoked with no arguments like so:

   ```
   $ perl ex2.pl
   ```

   it always displays the contents of file1.dat followed by file2.dat followed by file3.dat.

3. Modify the file backup facility in filetest1.pl so that it checks to see if a backup already exists before renaming the currently existing file. When a backup does exist, the user should be asked to confirm that they want to overwrite it—if not, they should be returned to the original query.

CHAPTER 9

■ ■ ■

String Processing

Perl was created to be a text processing language, and it is arguably the most powerful text processing language around. One way that Perl displays its power in processing text is through its built-in regular expression support that we discussed in Chapter 7. Perl also has many built-in string operators (such as the string concatenation operator . and the string replication operator x) and string functions. In this chapter we will explore several string functions and one very helpful string operator.

Character Position

Before we get started with some of Perl's built-in functions, we should talk about the ability to access characters in a string by *indexing* into the string. The numeric position of a character in a string is known as its *index*. Recall that Perl is 0-based—it starts counting things from 0, and this applies to character indexing as will. So, for this string:

```
"Wish You Were Here"
```

here are the characters of the string and their indexes:

```
character 0:  W
character 1:  i
character 2:  s
character 3:  h
character 4:  <space>
character 5:  Y
...
character 17: e
```

We can also index characters by starting at the right-most character and counting down starting from –1 (much like accessing an array). Therefore, the characters in the preceding string are also known by these indices:

```
character -1:  e
character -2:  r
character -3:  e
```

```
character -4:   H
character -5:   <space>
character -6:   e
...
character -18: W
```

String Functions

Perl has many string functions built into the language. We will now discuss several of the most common functions used to process text.

The length() Function

To determine the length of a string, we can use the length() function.

```
length(string)
```

This function returns the number of characters of its argument. If no argument is given, length() returns the number of characters of $_. Here is an example:

```
#!/usr/bin/perl -w
# length.pl

use strict;

my $song = 'The Great Gig in the Sky';
print 'length of $song: ', length($song), "\n";
# the *real* length is 4:44

$_ = 'Us and Them';
print 'length of $_: ', length, "\n";
# this one is 7:40
```

Running this code produces the following:

```
$ perl length.pl
length of $song: 24
length of $_: 11
$
```

The index() Function

The index() function locates substrings in strings. Its syntax is

```
index(string, substring)
```

It returns the starting index (0-based) of where the substring is located in the string. If the substring is not found, it returns –1. This invocation:

```
index('Larry Wall', 'Wall')
```

would return 6 since the substring "Wall" is contained within the string "Larry Wall" starting at position 6 (0-based, remember?). This invocation:

```
index('Pink Floyd', 'ink');
```

would return 1.

The index() function has an optional third argument that indicates the starting position from which it should start looking. For instance, this invocation:

```
index('Roger Waters', 'er', 0)
```

tells index() to try to locate the substring "er" in "Roger Waters" (www.roger-waters.com) and to start looking from position 0. Position 0 is the default, so it is not necessary to include it, but it is OK if you do. This function returns 3. If we provide another starting position as in

```
index('Roger Waters', 'er', 5)
```

it tells index() to search for the substring "er" in "Roger Waters" but start searching from index 5. This returns 9 because it finds the "er" in "Waters".

Here is an example illustrating the use of the index() function. It prompts the user for a string and then a substring and determines if the substring is in the string. If so, index() returns something other than –1, so we print that result to the user. Otherwise we inform the user that the substring was not found.

```
#! /usr/bin/perl -w
# index.pl

use strict;

print "Enter a string:    ";
chomp(my $string = <STDIN>);

print "Enter a substring: ";
chomp(my $substring = <STDIN>);

my $result = index($string, $substring);

if ($result != -1) {
    print "the substring was found at index: $result\n";
} else {
    print "the substring was not found\n";
}
```

Here is an example of running this program:

```
$ perl index.pl
Enter a string:    Perl is cool!
Enter a substring: cool
the substring was found at index: 8
```

```
$ perl index.pl
Enter a string:    hello, world!
Enter a substring: cool
the substring was not found
$
```

The rindex() Function

The rindex() function is similar to index() except that it searches the string from right to left (instead of left to right). The syntax is similar:

```
rindex(string, substring)
```

This function searches right-to-left through the string searching for the substring. It returns the 0-based index of where the substring is in the string, or –1 if the substring is not found.

An important note: even though this function searches through the string from right to left, the 0th character of the string is still the left-most character.

This invocation:

```
rindex('David Gilmour', 'i')
```

searches from the right-hand side of "David Gilmour" looking for the substring "i". It finds it at position 7 (the "i" in "Gilmour").

This function also has an optional third argument that is the character position from which it begins looking for the substring. This invocation:

```
rindex('David Gilmour', 'i', 6)
```

starts at position 6 (the "G" in "Gilmour") and looks right to left for an "i" and finds it at position 3.

The substr() Function

When processing text, we often have the situation where a string follows a specific column layout. For example, a string that contains a customer's last name in columns 1–20, the last name in columns 21–40, and address in columns 40–70. We can use the substr() function to extract these fields out of the string. Its syntax is

```
substr(string, starting_index, length)
```

It returns *length* number of characters starting from *starting_index* in *string*. If the number of characters extends beyond the length of the string, then it returns all the characters of the string from *starting_index* to the end. For example, let's say we have read a fixed-length record in from a file, and we know that from column 24 (0-based) to column 53 is the job title for that record. Here is an example line from the file:

```
'John A.    Smith        Perl programmer'
```

If this record was read into the variable $record, this invocation would access John's job:

```
$s = substr($record, 24, 30);
```

Since there is more than one way to do it in Perl (TMTOWTDI), this invocation of substr() can be performed with a regular expression:

```
($s) = $record =~ /^.{24}(.{1,30})/;
```

This statement matches the string literal $record against a regex that translates to "Match 24 of any character but '\n' at the beginning of the string followed between 1 and 30 of any character but '\n'". The parentheses around .{1,30} store those characters in $1. Then an assignment is made to the list ($s) that copies over $1 and stores it into $s. As a result, $s is the string "Perl programmer".

An interesting feature of the substr() function is that it can be on the left-hand side of an assignment. For instance, this code:

```
substr($record, 24, 30) = 'Technical manager';
```

would overwrite the substring of $record starting from position 24 length 30 (John's job, "Perl programmer") with the string "Technical manager". This results in $record being modified to be

```
'John A.     Smith        Technical manager'
```

Is this a promotion or a demotion?

Here is an example of using substr(). It prompts the user for a string, a starting index, and a length and then prints the substring to the user. It then overwrites the first five characters of the string the user enters with the string "hello, world!" and prints the result:

```perl
#!/usr/bin/perl -w
# substr.pl

use strict;

print "Enter a string:      ";
chomp(my $string = <STDIN>);

print "Enter starting index: ";
chomp(my $index = <STDIN>);

print "Enter length:        ";
chomp(my $length = <STDIN>);

my $s = substr($string, $index, $length);

print "result: $s\n";

# now, overwrite $string
substr($string, 0, 5) = 'hello, world!';

print "string is now: $string\n";
```

Here is an example of executing this code:

```
$ perl substr.pl
Enter a string:        practical extraction and report language
Enter starting index: 10
Enter length:          8
result: extracti
string is now: hello, world!ical extraction and report language
$
```

Transliteration

Now let's look at another text processing operator—the transliteration operator. Its syntax is

```
tr/old/new/
```

This operator resembles the substitute operator, s///, that we saw in Chapter 7 when we discussed regular expressions. While the tr/// operator resembles s///, the only thing it has in common with the substitute is that both operators operate on $_ by default. The tr/// operator has nothing to do with regular expressions.

What this operator does is to correlate the characters in its two arguments, one by one, and use these pairings to substitute individual characters in the referenced string. The code tr/one/two/ replaces all instances of "o" in the referenced string with "t", all instances of "n" with "w", and all instances of "e" with "o".

This operator translates the characters in $_ by default. To translate a string other than $_, use the =~ operator as in

```
$string =~ tr/old/new/;
```

Let's say you wanted to replace, for some reason, all the numbers in a string with letters. You might say something like this:

```
$string =~ tr/0123456789/abcdefghij/;
```

This would turn, say, "2011064" into "cabbage". You can use ranges in transliteration, but not any of the character classes. We could write the preceding as

```
$string =~ tr/0-9/a-j/;
```

The return value of this operator is, by default, the number of characters transliterated. You can therefore use the transliteration operator to count the number of occurrences of certain characters. For example, to count the number of vowels in a string, you can use

```
my $vowels = $string =~ tr/aeiou//;
```

Note that this will not actually change any of the vowels in the variable $string—as the second group is blank, it is exactly the same as the first group. However, the transliteration operator can take the /d modifier, which *will* delete occurrences on the left that do not have a correlating character on the right. So, to get rid of all spaces in a string quickly, you could use this line:

```
$string =~ tr/ //d;
```

Here is an example program that loops through the diamond operator, reading line by line through either the file or files on the command line or standard input. For each line, the tr/// operator is used to uppercase the lowercase letters in $_:

```perl
#!/usr/bin/perl -w
# tr.pl

while (<>) {
    tr/a-z/A-Z/;
    print;
}
```

Here is an example of executing this program. We invoke it with no command line arguments so it reads though our standard input until end of file (^D in Unix, ^Z<enter> in Windows):

```
$ perl tr.pl
And
AND
she's
SHE'S
buying
BUYING
a
A
stairway
STAIRWAY
^D
$
```

Summary

In this chapter we have discussed some very useful functions and operators to help us process text files. We determined the length of a string with length(). We worked with string indices and substrings with the functions index(), rindex(), and substr(). Finally, we looked at the transliteration operator, tr///, which translates characters in a string.

Exercises

1. Open ex1.dat in read mode. Each line of the file is a string with customer information. The information in the line is based on these character positions:

1–24	Customer name
25–52	Address
53–72	City
73–74	State
76–80	Zip code

Print the information for each line so that it resembles

```
Record:
name     : John Q Public
address  : 23 Main St.
city     : Des Moines
state    : IA
zip      : 50309
```

2. Write a program to perform the rot13 encoding algorithm. Rot13 is a simple encoding algorithm with the purpose of making text temporarily unreadable. It is called rot13 because it rotates alpha characters 13 positions in the alphabet. For instance, "a" is the first character of the alphabet and it is rotated 13 positions to the 14th character, "n". The second character, "b", is rotated to the 15th character "o" and so on through "m", the 13th character rotated to "z", the 26th character. When the 14th character, "n", is rotated 13 positions, it rotates back around to "a", "o" to "b", and so on through "z" to "m":

```
a -> n       A -> N
b -> o       B -> O
...          ...
m -> z       M -> Z
n -> a       N -> A
o -> b       O -> B
...          ...
z -> m       Z -> M
```

This program will read with the diamond. Execute the program like this:

```
$ perl ex2.pl ex2.dat
```

To double-check your work, take the standard output from the program and pipe it back into the standard input of the same program:

```
$ perl ex2.pl ex2.dat | perl ex2.pl
```

CHAPTER 10

■ ■ ■

Interfacing to the Operating System

Perl is a popular language for system administrators and programmers who have to work with files and directories due to the fact that there are many built-in functions to perform sys admin activities. These activities include creating directories, changing the names of files, creating links, and executing programs in the operating system.

In this chapter we will look at several functions that make working with files and directories easy. Also, we will look at two ways of executing operating system commands or other applications: system() and backquotes.

The %ENV Hash

When a Perl program starts executing, it inherits from the shell all of the shell's exported environment variables. If you are curious about what environment variables are defined in your shell, try this command in Unix:

```
$ env
```

Depending on what shell you are using, you might need to execute

```
$ printenv
```

In Windows try

```
c:> set
```

All of the environment variables that the Perl program inherits are stored in the special hash %ENV. Here are a few possible examples:

```
$ENV{HOME}
$ENV{PATH}
$ENV{USER}
```

These environment variables can be assigned. If you want to change the path for the current execution of the program, simply assign to $ENV{PATH} (note that this will not change the path for the shell that is invoking this program).

```
$ENV{PATH} = '/bin:/usr/bin:/usr/local/bin';
```

The following program whereis.pl, is an example of reading from %ENV. It will implement the whereis command, a useful program found in Unix that reports to the user the location of a program within the PATH environment variable. Here is the code:

```perl
#!/usr/bin/perl -w
# whereis.pl

use strict;

my $prog = shift @ARGV;
die "usage: perl whereis.pl <file>" unless defined $prog;

my $found = 0;

foreach my $dir (split /:/, $ENV{PATH}) {
    if (-x "$dir/$prog") {
        print "$dir/$prog\n";
        $found = 1;
        last;
    }
}

print "$prog not found in PATH\n" unless $found;
```

First, we grab the command line argument and place it in $prog. This argument is the program that we are trying to locate. If the argument is not provided, we complain:

```perl
my $prog = shift @ARGV;
die "usage: perl whereis.pl <file>" unless defined $prog;
```

Then we see the following:

```perl
my $found = 0;

foreach my $dir (split /:/, $ENV{PATH}) {
    if (-x "$dir/$prog") {
        print "$dir/$prog\n";
        $found = 1;
        last;
    }
}
```

First, we assume we won't find the program and we assign $found the value 0, or false. We'll check this variable at the end of the program and print a message, if necessary. The foreach loop loops through each directory listed in $ENV{PATH}, a colon-separated list of filenames.

For each of these directories, we test to see if the program we are looking for is an executable file in that directory:

```
if (-x "$dir/$prog") {
```

If so, we print the directory/filename, set $found to true since we found the program, and then last out of the outer loop.

Finally, if we did not find the program, the program says so:

```
print "$prog not found in PATH\n" unless $found;
```

Executing this code produces the following:

```
$ perl whereis.pl sort
/usr/bin/sort
$ perl whereis.pl noprogram
noprogram not found in PATH
$
```

Working with Files and Directories

Perl provides several mechanisms to work with files and directories. In this section we will explore the concept of file globbing, directory streams, and several built-in functions that allow us to perform operating system actions. First, file globbing.

File Globbing

Those of us who are Unix users know that this command lists all the files in the current directory that end with the .pl extension:

```
$ ls *.pl
```

A similar command in Windows would be

```
c:> dir *.pl
```

The part of these commands that indicates which files we want to list is *.pl. This is known as a *file glob*—it globs, or collects together, all the filenames that end in .pl. Those filenames are then listed.

We can perform a similar action in Perl by taking the glob pattern and, like reading from a filehandle, wrap it in angle brackets:

```
<*.pl>
```

There are two ways of reading from a file glob—scalar context or list context. In scalar context, it returns back the next filename that ends in .pl:

```
$nextperlfilename = <*.pl>;
```

In list context, it returns back all the filenames that end in `.pl`:

```
@alltheperlfilenames = <*.pl>;
```

Like using the `ls` or `dir` commands, we can indicate more than one pattern to glob. These patterns can be absolute or relative paths. For instance, this example globs all the filenames in the current directory that end in `.pl` and all the filenames that end in `.dat`:

```
<*.pl *.dat>
```

This example lists all the `.c` and `.h` files in specific directories:

```
</usr/src/*.c /usr/include/*.h>
```

Like reading from a filehandle, if we read from a glob within a `while` loop, and the glob is not explicitly assigned to a variable, it is assigned to `$_` by default:

```
while (<*.dat>) {
    print "found a data file: $_\n";
}
```

This program lists the contents of the current directory and uses file tests to examine each file:

```
#!/usr/bin/perl
# directory-glob.pl

use strict;

print "Contents of the current directory:\n";
foreach (<*>) {
    next if $_ eq "." or $_ eq "..";
    print $_, " " x (30 - length($_));
    print "d" if -d $_;
    print "r" if -r _;
    print "w" if -w _;
    print "x" if -x _;
    print "o" if -o _;
    print "\t";
    print -s _ if -r _ and -f _;
    print "\n";
}
```

The first thing we see after a friendly `print()` is

```
foreach (<*>) {
```

This loops `foreach` filename returned by `<*>`, or all files in the current directory. The filename is read into `$_`. Then we check to see if it is either `.` or `..`, special directories in DOS and

Unix that refer to the current and parent directories respectively. We skip these in our program:

```
next if $_ eq "." or $_ eq "..";
```

We then print out the name of each file, followed by some spaces. The length of the filename plus the number of spaces will always add up to 30, so we have nicely arranged columns.

```
print $_, " " x (30 - length($_));
```

First we test to see if the file is a directory using the file tests we saw in Chapter 8:

```
print "d" if -d $_;
```

Then we test to see if the file is readable, writable, executable, and owned by us:

```
print "r" if -r _;
print "w" if -w _;
print "x" if -x _;
print "o" if -o _;
```

No, this isn't a typo: we do mean _ and not $_ here. Just as $_ is the default value for some operations, such as print(), _ is the default filehandle for file tests. It actually refers to the last file explicitly tested. Since we tested $_ previously, we can use _ for as long as we're referring to the same file.

▓**Note** When Perl does a file test, it actually looks up all the data at once—ownership, readability, writability, and so on; this is called a *stat* of the file. _ tells Perl not to do another stat, but to use the data from the previous one. As such, it's more efficient than stat-ing the file each time.

Finally, we print out the file's size—this is only possible if we can read the file, and only useful if it is a regular file:

```
print -s _ if -r _ and -f _;
```

Executing this code produces the following:

```
$ perl directory-glob.pl
Contents of the current directory:
a.dat                         rwo        20
addsizes.pl                   rwo        242
b.dat                         rwo        20
```

```
backquote.pl                rwo        297
dir1                        drwxo
directory-dir.pl            rwo        460
directory-glob.pl           rwo        371
links.pl                    rwo        316
os.pl                       rwo        1049
system.pl                   rwo        132
whereis.pl                  rwo        334
$
```

The number at the end of the line is the size of the file in bytes; as for the letters, "d" shows that this is a directory, "r" stands for readable, "w" for writable, "x" for executable, and "o" shows that the user that is running the program is the owner.

Reading Directories

Directories can be treated kind of like files—we can open them and read from them. Instead of using open() and a filehandle, which are used with files, we use opendir() and a *directory handle*:

```
opendir DH, "." or die "Couldn't open the current directory: $!";
```

To read each file in the directory, we use readdir() on the directory handle.

Previously, we saw directory-glob.pl, a program to perform file tests on files that we obtained from a glob. In the spirit of TMTOWTDI, let's do the same action using a directory handle instead of a file glob:

```
#!/usr/bin/perl
# directory-dir.pl

use strict;

print "Contents of the current directory:\n";
opendir DH, "." or die "Couldn't open the current directory: $!";
while ($_ = readdir(DH)) {
    next if $_ eq "." or $_ eq "..";
    print $_, " " x (30 - length($_));
    print "d" if -d $_;
    print "r" if -r _;
    print "w" if -w _;
    print "x" if -x _;
    print "o" if -o _;
    print "\t";
    print -s _ if -r _ and -f _;
    print "\n";
}
closedir DH;
```

The only changes from the previous program are these two lines:

```
opendir DH, "." or die "Couldn't open the current directory: $!";
while ($_ = readdir(DH)) {
```

and this line:

```
closedir DH;
```

The current directory, ., is opened. Then we read from the directory with readdir(), and as long as we have a filename, we perform the same tests as before. After we are all finished with the files, we close the directory handle. This program produces the same result as directory-glob.pl:

```
$ perl directory-dir.pl
Contents of the current directory:
a.dat                    rwo        20
addsizes.pl              rwo        242
b.dat                    rwo        20
backquote.pl             rwo        297
dir1                     drwxo
directory-dir.pl         rwo        460
directory-glob.pl        rwo        371
links.pl                 rwo        316
os.pl                    rwo        1049
system.pl                rwo        132
whereis.pl               rwo        334
$
```

Functions to Work with Files and Directories

Perl provides many built-in functions to perform operating system actions on files and directories. Let's look at a few of them.

The chdir() Function

To change directories within a Perl script, use the chdir() function. Its syntax is

```
chdir(directory)
```

This function attempts to change directories to the directory passed as its argument (defaulting to $ENV{HOME}). If it successfully changed directories, it returns true, otherwise false.

■**Note** chdir() changes the working directory in the script. This has no effect on the shell in which the script is invoked—when the script exits the user will be in whatever directory they were in when they executed the program.

The fact that this function returns true on success or false on failure can be very helpful to us. We should always check the return value and respond appropriately if the directory change failed. For instance, this code attempts to change directory and die()s if we couldn't make the change:

```
chdir '/usr/local/src' or die "Can't change directory to /usr/local/src: $!";
```

Recall that $! is a variable that contains the error string of whatever just went wrong.

The unlink() Function

The unlink() function deletes files from disk. Its syntax is

```
unlink(list_of_files)
```

This function removes the files from disk. It returns true if successful, false if not. This function acts like the Unix rm command and the Windows del command. Here is an example:

```
unlink 'file1.txt', 'file2.txt' or warn "Can't remove files: $!";
```

The rename() Function

The rename() function renames one file to a new name. Its syntax is

```
rename(old_file_name, new_file_name)
```

This function renames the old file to the new name. It returns true if successful, false if not. This function acts like the Unix mv command and the Windows ren command. Here is an example:

```
rename 'old.txt', 'new.txt' or warn "Can't rename file: $!";
```

Note that you can also move a file with this function (like the mv command in Unix and move command in Windows):

```
rename 'oldir/old.txt', 'newdir/new.txt' or warn "Can't move file: $!";
```

The link(), symlink(), and readlink() Functions

These functions allow us to work with hard and soft links. These functions are Unix-centric—they don't function the same in the Windows world, so it is suggested you avoid using them there.

The link() function creates a hard link. Its syntax is

```
link(file_to_link_to, link_name)
```

The symlink() function creates a symbolic link. Its syntax is

```
symlink(file_to_link_to, sym_link_name)
```

To find out what file a symbolic link points to, use the readlink() function:

```
readlink(sym_link_name)
```

Here is an example of creating a soft link in Perl and finding out the name of the file to which it links:

```
#!/usr/bin/perl -w
# links.pl

use strict;

my $filetolink = 'links.pl';
my $linkname   = 'linktolinks.pl';

symlink($filetolink, $linkname) or die "link creation failed: $!";

print "link created ok!\n";

my $readlinkresult = readlink($linkname);
print "$linkname is a sym link to $readlinkresult\n";
```

Here is an example of executing this code. Note that the link doesn't exist before the code is executed:

```
$ ls -l link*
-rw-r--r--  1 jdoe    users   349 22 Apr 14:05 links.pl
$ perl links.pl
link created ok!
linktolinks.pl is a sym link to links.pl
$ ls -l link*
-rw-r--r--  1 jdoe    users   349 22 Apr 14:05 links.pl
lrwxr-xr-x  1 jdoe    users     8 22 Apr 14:06 linktolinks.pl -> links.pl
$
```

The mkdir() and rmdir() Functions

The mkdir() function makes a directory. Its syntax is

```
mkdir(directory_name, mode)
```

This function creates *directory_name*. It returns true on success, false on failure. The *mode*, or permissions, are applied to the directory (possibly modified by the umask). Note that the *mode* should be represented as an octal number by preceding it with a 0 since Unix interprets the number representation of the mode as an octal value.

Here is an example of mkdir() that creates the directory newdir in the current directory with the permissions of 751 (in the Unix world, this looks like rwxr-x--x):

```
mkdir('newdir', 0751) or die $!;
```

As usual, we are handling the failure of this function—in this case we are die()ing.

The rmdir() removes an empty directory. It returns true on success, false on failure. Its syntax is

```
rmdir(directory_name)
```

The chmod() Function

Speaking of permissions, the chmod() function changes the mode, or permissions, on a file or directory. Its syntax is

```
chmod(file_or_directory_name, mode)
```

Again, the *mode* should be represented as an octal number since that is how Unix interprets it. This changes the mode of the file resume.txt to be readable only by the owner of the file, die()ing if the chmod fails:

```
chmod('resume.txt', 0600) or die $!;
```

An Example

Here is an example program using a bunch of these functions. The comments describe what is going on:

```
#!/usr/bin/perl -w
# os.pl

use strict;

# first prompt the user for a directory name and attempt
# to create the directory in the current directory
print "please enter a directory name: ";
chomp(my $dir = <STDIN>);

mkdir $dir, 0777 or die "failed to make directory $dir: $!\n";
print "made the directory $dir ok!\n";

# so far so good - now, change directory into the
# directory
chdir $dir or die "failed to change into $dir: $!\n";
print "changed into $dir ok!\n";

# ok, now move the file ../a.dat into this new directory
# giving it a new name
print "enter new file name: ";
chomp(my $newname = <STDIN>);
rename "../a.dat", $newname or die "rename failed: $!\n";
print "file moved successfully!\n";
```

```
# list the contents of the directory
# using a directory handle
print "contents of the new directory:\n";
opendir DH, '.' or die "opendir failed: $!";
my $filename;
while ($filename = readdir(DH)) {
    print "    $filename\n";
}
close DH;

# that's it, say goodbye
print "we are all done... goodbye!\n";
```

Here is what happens when it is executed on a Unix system:

```
$ perl os.pl
please enter a directory name: newdir
made the directory newdir ok!
changed into newdir ok!
enter new file name: new.dat
file moved successfully!
contents of the new directory:
    .
    ..
    new.dat
we are all done... goodbye!
$
```

Executing External Programs

There are times when we want our Perl program to execute external programs such as another Perl script, shell commands (like ls and dir), or other programs or applications.

There are several ways to execute other programs from within a Perl script. We have already seen one way: opening pipes with the open() function discussed in Chapter 8. In this chapter we will discuss two other ways: the system() function and backquotes.

The system() Function

The system() function takes an argument and executes that argument as if it were entered into a shell. If the command produces any standard output, system() allows it to go to standard output. Its syntax is

system(*command*)

It returns the error status of *command*. In Unix and Windows, the error status is a way for a program to report back to whoever invoked it, informing the calling program or shell whether or not the program executed correctly. By convention, when all is well, the error status is 0. If there was a problem, the program will return a non-0 value (such as 1 or 255).

THINK TWICE BEFORE YOU USE SYSTEM()

The system() function can perform all sorts of operating system commands such as making directories, copying files, moving files, etc. For instance, in Unix we could execute

```
system "rm a.dat";   # delete the file a.dat in Unix
```

instead of

```
unlink 'a.dat';
```

There are two main reasons not to use the system() function instead of the unlink() function to remove a file. First, passing "rm a.dat" to the system() function as shown previously works fine in Unix, but not in Windows (in Windows we would use the del command). Therefore, in many cases, the system() function is not portable between operating systems, while the unlink() function is portable.

Second, the unlink() function is named unlink() because it calls the low-level operating system library function named unlink(), immediately removing the file. The system() function, on the other hand, creates a shell. The shell is a big program that must start up, reading various configuration files. The shell is then passed the argument to the system() function as if a user typed it into the shell. The shell then parses the string, determines that the user wants to remove a file, and calls the low-level operating system function named unlink(). So, you can call the unlink() function yourself using the Perl function named unlink(), or you can start up a big program that does a lot of work before finally calling the low-level operating system unlink() function.

A shell is also created when using one of these two methods of executing an external program: backquotes, and opening pipes with open(), so keep this in mind when deciding between built-in functions such as unlink() and rename() and using another Perl mechanism to perform operating system actions.

Another important note: the program system.pl displayed the current date using the system() function:

```
my $error_status = system 'date';
```

This created a shell, which is an inefficient way of determining the date on the machine. A better way is to use the localtime() function in scalar context:

```
print scalar(localtime), "\n";
```

A rule of thumb is this: most actions that you want to take in Perl are implemented in the language in a way that does not require launching a shell. Mentioning every feature of Perl is not the intent of this book, so we will not discuss all the different ways of doing the same thing.[1] But a little bit of searching on your part may uncover an efficient, cool way of taking action in Perl without going out to the shell, so get in the habit of looking deeper into this language when you are trying to do something new.[2]

---

1. Remember TMTOWTDI? Divining how many is left as an exercise to the reader.
2. www.perl.com, www.perlmonks.org, www.google.com, and perdoc are our friends.

Here is an example program that executes the date command—its job is to print to standard output the date in a readable format. The return from system() is stored in a variable and then printed to standard output.

```
#!/usr/bin/perl -w
# system.pl

use strict;

my $error_status = system 'date';

print "system() returned: $error_status\n";
```

Executing this program might produce the following:

```
$ perl system.pl
Fri Apr 23 07:17:31 CDT 2004
system() returned: 0
$
```

Backquotes

The system() function prints the output of its argument to the screen. Sometimes, however, we want to capture the output and bring it into our program. The backquotes allow us to do just that. Here is the syntax:

`command`

That is the backquote (aka the grave character), not the single quote character.

The backquotes execute the operating system command, capturing and returning its standard output, if any. The error status is available in the special variable $?. The backquotes can be read in either scalar context or in list context:

```
$output = `$command`;
@output = `$command`;
```

In scalar context, the entire output including newline characters is returned as a single string (here stored in $output). In list context, the entire output is returned as a list, newlines included; each line of output is a single element in the list (here stored in @output).

Here is an example that executes the program directory-dir.pl that we discussed previously in this chapter and adds up all the sizes of the files:

```
#!/usr/bin/perl -w
# addsizes.pl

use strict;

my @result = `perl directory-dir.pl`;
```

```perl
my $size = 0;

foreach (@result) {
    if (/^.{30}[drwox]*\t(\d+)$/) {
        $size += $1;
    }
}

print "The total size of all files: $size\n";
```

First, we execute the script `directory-dir.pl` and capture the output of the backquotes in list context. This means that `@result` will be an array and each element is an individual line of output from the script:

```perl
my @result = `perl directory-dir.pl`;
```

Then, the size is initialized to 0:

```perl
my $size = 0;
```

Now it is time to examine the output:

```perl
foreach (@result) {
    if (/^.{30}[drwox]*\t(\d+)$/) {
        $size += $1;
    }
}
```

The `foreach` is looping though each line of output. If the line matches the pattern that includes a size (that is, the `\d+`), then we use the parentheses to extract the size into `$1`. The size is added to `$size`.

Executing this program produces the following:

```
$ perl addsizes.pl
The total size of all files: 3241
$
```

There's More

There are many other ways that Perl interfaces to the operating system—we've only covered the basics here. There are dozens of built-in functions available to do all sorts of system administration stuff (see `perldoc perlfunc` for a list). Other operating system things that Perl can do include create child processes (with `fork()`), send processes signals (with `kill()`), low-level file i/o (with `sysread()` and `syswrite()`), read password information (with `getpwent()` and others), and many more . . .

Summary

In this chapter, we have discussed several ways of performing operating system actions from within a Perl script. These include file globs, executing built-in functions such as `mkdir()` and `rename()`, and executing operating system commands with `system()` and backquotes.

Exercises

1. Write a program that takes two arguments: a directory and an integer. Change into the directory that is the first argument and list all the files that have a size greater than or equal to the second argument. First use a glob and then use a filehandle.

2. Automate a task that you perform on a regular basis.

CHAPTER 11

◼ ◼ ◼

References

When we discussed lists and arrays in Chapter 4, we learned that all lists and all arrays are one-dimensional collections of scalars. Similarly, when we discussed hashes in Chapter 5, we learned that hash values are scalars. Therefore, up to this point in our discussion of Perl, we have not been able to create arrays of arrays (also known as multidimensional arrays) or other more complex data types.

However, being able to create more complex data types is something we will want to do from time to time. For instance, we might want to represent a chessboard as eight arrays of eight squares so that we can address each square by row and column (an array of arrays). We might also want to store a bunch of information about someone—their address, phone number, and occupation—and key it to their name (a hash of hashes).

In this chapter, we will look at another scalar data that will allow us to create these and other more complex data types—*references*.

What Is a Reference?

Put at its very simplest, a reference is a piece of data that tells us the location of another piece of data—if we told you to "See the first paragraph on page 130," we'd effectively be giving you a reference to the text in that paragraph. It wouldn't be the text itself, but it would tell you where to find it. This would also let us talk about (refer to) the text right away, despite the fact that it's somewhere else in the book. That's why references are so useful—we can specify data once, and they let us access it from wherever else we are.

In Perl, a reference is always a scalar, although the data it refers to may not be: our cross-reference in the previous paragraph wasn't even a sentence, but referred to an entire paragraph. Likewise, a reference, even though it's only a scalar, can talk about the data stored in an array or hash.

Languages like C and C++ have a feature that's similar to references, called *pointers*. They are similar to Perl references in that both point us to locations in the computer's memory—however, C's pointers tend to leave interpretation of what's there for the programmer to disentangle. Perl's references, on the other hand, only store memory locations for specific, clearly defined data structures—maybe not *pre*defined, but defined nevertheless. They allow you to leave the arrangement of computer memory to the computer itself—this can be a huge relief for us mere mortal programmers, as the machine is far better at that sort of thing than we are.

The main use we have for references is the one we previously discussed—being able to treat arrays and hashes as single things. We can now refer *unambiguously* to the contents of an array or a hash using a single scalar—so we're now in a position to do things like putting hashes inside hashes, arrays inside arrays, even hashes in arrays and vice-versa. But that's not all . . .

Anonymity

We can also use references to create *anonymous data*. Anonymous data, as you might have guessed, is data that doesn't have a variable name attached to it. Instead, it's placed at a certain memory location, and we're given a simple reference to that location—our array (or hash or whatever) has no name to speak of, but we know exactly where to find it, should we need to use it.

For example, instead of creating an array (1,2,3) called @array and then creating a reference to @array, we can cut out the middleman by referencing (1,2,3) directly.

This allows us to create real scalars, arrays, and hashes containing data that we can refer to and modify just as if it was a normal variable. This doesn't mean that we leave arrays and hashes floating about randomly in our program to be plucked out of the air whenever we need them—we know where to find this anonymous data (we have a reference that's telling us just this), and it only exists for as long as part of our program is using it.

The Life Cycle of a Reference

To understand how we deal with references, let's look at the three areas of a reference's life cycle—creation, use, and destruction. After that, we'll see how we can practically use references to create more complicated data structures than simple arrays and hashes.

Reference Creation

There are two ways to create a reference, one for each of the following situations:

- You already have the data in an existing variable.

- You want to use anonymous data to go straight to a reference.

The simple rule for the first situation where the variable is already defined is as follows:

> You create a reference by putting a backslash in front of the variable.

That's it. Let's see some examples:

```
my @array   = (2, 4, 6, 8, 10);
my $array_r = \@array;
```

We create a perfectly normal array variable, and then take a reference to it by putting a backslash before the variable's name—that's literally all there is to it. In the same way, we can create a reference to a hash:

```
my %hash   = ( apple => "pomme", pear => "poire" );
my $hash_r = \%hash;
```

or a scalar:

```
my $scalar   = 42;
my $scalar_r = \$scalar;
```

We can treat our references just like ordinary scalars—so we can put them in an array:

```
my $a = 3;
my $b = 4;
my $c = 5;
my @refs = (\$a, \$b, \$c);
```

We can also put references in a hash, but only as values—Perl keys are simple strings. You can certainly do this, though:

```
my @english = qw(January February March April May June);
my @french  = qw(Janvier Fevrier  Mars  Avril Mai Juin);
my %months  = ( english => \@english, french => \@french );
```

So what does this give us? We have a hash with two keys, english and french. The english key contains a reference to an array of English month names, while the french key contains a reference to an array of French month names. With these references, we can access and modify the original data, which means that, in effect, we've stored two arrays inside a single hash.

We can use the same trick to store arrays inside arrays:

```
my @array1 = (10, 20, 30, 40, 50);
my @array2 = ( 1, 2, \@array1, 3, 4);
```

Now @array2 is made up of five scalars, and the middle one is a reference to another array. We can do this over and over again, if we want to:

```
my @array3 = (2, 4, \@array2, 6, 8);
my @array4 = (100, 200, \@array3, 300, 400);
```

This gives us a very versatile way to store complex data structures; what we've just done is to store a structure that looks like this:

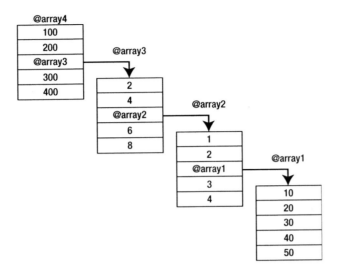

Anonymous Arrays and Anonymous Hashes

Our next step is to do all this without having to go through the interim stages of creating the variables. Anonymous variables will let us go straight from our raw data to a reference, and the rules here are just as simple:

- To get a reference to an anonymous array, use square brackets ([ ]) instead of parentheses.

- To get a reference to an anonymous hash, use curly braces ({ }) instead of parentheses.

So, referring to our previous examples, instead of doing this:

```
my @array   = (1, 2, 3, 4, 5);
my $array_r = \@array;
```

we can create a reference to an anonymous array like this:

```
my $array_r = [1, 2, 3, 4, 5];
```

Likewise, to get a hash reference, instead of doing this:

```
my %hash   = ( apple => "pomme", pear => "poire" );
my $hash_r = \%hash;
```

we say

```
my $hash_r = { apple => "pomme", pear => "poire" };
```

Now we have two variables—the array with no name referred to only by $array_r and the hash with no name referred to by $hash_r.[1]

We can put anonymous variables inside hashes and arrays, just like references created from variables:

```
my %months   = (
    english => ["January", "February", "March", "April", ",May", ",June"],
    french  => ["Janvier", "Fevrier", "Mars", "Avril", "Mai", "Juin"]
);
```

And we can put anonymous variables inside anonymous variables:

```
my @array = ( 100,200,[ 2,4,[ 1,2,[ 10,20,30,40,50 ],3,4 ],6,8 ],300,400 );
```

That's exactly the same structure as shown in the preceding picture. Here it is again, with a lot more spacing added:

```
my @array = ( 100, 200,
            [ 2, 4,
              [ 1, 2,
                [ 10, 20, 30, 40, 50 ],
              3, 4 ],
            6, 8 ],
          300, 400 );
```

Using References

Once we've created our references (whether to real variables or anonymous data), we're going to want to use them—so how do we access the data? The operation we use to get data back from a reference is called *dereferencing*, and once again, the rule is very simple.

> To dereference data, put the reference in curly braces wherever you would normally use a variable's name.

First, we'll see how to do this with arrays—say we've got an array and a reference:

```
my @array   = (1, 2, 3, 4, 5);
my $array_r = \@array;
```

We can get at the array like this:

```
my @array2  = @{$array_r};
```

---

1. Hmmm, variables with no names—now you see why they are called anonymous variables.

We put the reference, $array_r, inside curly braces, and use that instead of our original array variable name array. We can use this dereferenced array, @{$array_r}, anywhere we might otherwise use an array.

Let's start with a simple example. We'll just create a reference to an array, and then use it as we'd normally use an array.

```
#!/usr/bin/perl -w
# deref1.pl

use strict;

my @array   = (2, 4, 6, 8, 10);
my $array_r = \@array;

print "This is our dereferenced array: @{$array_r}\n";
foreach (@{$array_r}) {
    print "An element: $_\n";
}
print "The highest index is $#{$array_r}\n";
print "This is what our reference looks like: $array_r\n";
```

Let's run this:

```
$ perl deref1.pl
This is our dereferenced array: 2 4 6 8 10
An element: 2
An element: 4
An element: 6
An element: 8
An element: 10
The highest index is 4
This is what our reference looks like: ARRAY(0x806eb8)
$
```

Looking at this program in more detail, we first define an array variable and its contents, and then backslash it to create a reference to it.

```
my @array   = (2, 4, 6, 8, 10);
my $array_r = \@array;
```

Now we can use @{$array_r} instead of @array—both refer to exactly the same data, and both do exactly the same things. For instance, @{$array_r} will interpolate inside double quotes:

```
print "This is our dereferenced array: @{$array_r}\n";
```

Just as if we'd used the original @array, our dereferenced array prints out the contents of the array, separated by spaces:

```
This is our dereferenced array: 2 4 6 8 10
```

In the same way, we can use the array in a foreach loop, with no surprises:

```
foreach (@{$array_r}) {
    print "An element: $_\n";
}
```

Finally, we can also get the highest element number in the array, just as if we'd said $#array, like this:

```
print "The highest index is $#{$array_r}\n";
```

Now, we take a look at what our reference actually looks like itself. After all, it's a scalar, so it must have a value that we can print out and look at. It does, and this is what we get if we print out the reference:

```
This is what our reference looks like: ARRAY(0x806eb8)
```

The ARRAY part obviously tells us that we have an array reference, but what about the part in parentheses? We know that a reference is a memory location, telling us where the data is stored in Perl's virtual memory. We generally don't need to worry about this actual value, as we can't do that much with it. Note also that it's unlikely that you'll get exactly the same value as this example. It will simply depend on what hardware your system has, what other software you're running, and what Perl is doing.

Tip There is one way you might want to make use of this value directly: to see if two references refer to the same piece of data, you can compare them as numbers using ==.

If we try and manipulate it, it ceases to be a reference and becomes an ordinary number—the value of the hexadecimal shown earlier. We can see that if we run the following program:

```
#!/usr/bin/perl -w
# noref.pl

use strict;

my $ref = [1, 2, 3];
print "Before: $ref\n";
print "@{$ref}\n";
$ref++;
print "After: $ref\n";
print "@{$ref}\n";
```

it will give us something like this:

```
$ perl noref.pl
Before: ARRAY(0x800368)
1 2 3
```

```
After: 8389481
Can't use string ("8389481") as an ARRAY ref while "strict refs" in use at noref.pl
  line 11.
$
```

When we tried to modify our reference, it degenerated to the ordinary number 8389480, which is the equivalent of the hexadecimal number 0x800368 shown previously. Adding 1 to that number gave us the 8389481, which is an ordinary string, rather than a reference—Perl then complains if we try and use it as a reference.

This is why we can't use references as hash keys—hash keys can only be strings, so our references will get stringified to something like the preceding form. Once that happens, we're not able to use them as references again.

Array Elements

What about the individual elements in an array—how do we access these? The rule is pretty much the same as for the array as a whole—just use the reference in curly braces in the same way you would the array name:

```
#!/usr/bin/perl -w
# deref2.pl

use strict;

my @band = qw(Crosby Stills Nash Young);
my $ref  = \@band;
foreach (0..$#band) {
    print "Array    : ", $band[$_]  , "\n";
    print "Reference: ", ${$ref}[$_], "\n";
}
```

As you can see, $band[$_] and ${$ref}[$_] refer to the same thing:

```
$ perl deref2.pl
Array    : Crosby
Reference: Crosby
Array    : Stills
Reference: Stills
Array    : Nash
Reference: Nash
Array    : Young
Reference: Young
$
```

The important thing to note here is that these are not two different arrays—they are two ways of referring to the *same* piece of data—this is very important to remember when we start modifying references.

As we saw earlier, the last index of @band is $#band. We could have used the reference to obtain that value: $#{$ref}.

Reference Modification

If we want to modify the data referred to by a reference, the same rule applies as before—replace the name of the array with the reference in curly braces. However, when we do this, the data in the original array will change too.

```perl
#!/usr/bin/perl -w
# modify1.pl

use strict;

my @band = qw(Crosby Stills Nash Young);
my $ref  = \@band;
print "Band members before: @band\n";
pop @{$ref};
print "Band members after: @band\n";
```

```
$ perl modify1.pl
Band members before: Crosby Stills Nash Young
Band members after: Crosby Stills Nash
$
```

Now CSN&Y has changed forever.[2]

We can still use push(), pop(), shift(), unshift() (and so on) to manipulate the array using its reference. However, in doing so, we'll also be changing what's stored in @band.

It's quite possible to have multiple references to the same data—just as before, if you use one to change the data, you change it for the others too. This will give the same results as before:

```perl
my @band = qw(Crosby Stills Nash Young);
my $ref1 = \@band;
my $ref2 = \@band;
print "Band members before: @band\n";
pop @{$ref1};
print "Band members after: @{$ref2}\n";
```

and the same goes for anonymous arrays:

```perl
my $ref1 = [qw(Crosby Stills Nash Young)];
my $ref2 = $ref1;
print "Band members before: @{$ref2}\n";
```

---

2. For the worse?

```
pop @{$ref1};
print "Band members after: @{$ref2}\n";
```

Notice here that we're using [qw(...)], which is the same as saying

```
[('Crosby', 'Stills', 'Nash', 'Young')]
```

and the parentheses inside the square brackets get removed, just like when we said ((1,2,3)) back in Chapter 4.

You can also modify individual elements, using the syntax ${$reference}[$element]:

```
#!/usr/bin/perl -w
# modelem.pl

use strict;

my @array = (68, 101, 114, 111, 117);
my $ref = \@array;
${$ref}[0] = 100;
print "Array is now : @array\n";
```

```
$ perl modelem.pl
Array is now 100 101 114 111 117
$
```

and again, you can do the same with anonymous data:

```
my $ref = [68, 101, 114, 111, 117];
${$ref}[0] = 100;
print "Array is now : @{$ref}\n";
```

Hash References

For references to hashes, the rule is exactly the same—replace the hash's name with the reference in curly braces. So, to access the hash pointed to by a reference, you use %{$hash_r}. If you want to get at a hash entry $hash{green}, you say ${$hash_r}{green}.

```
#!/usr/bin/perl -w
# hashref.pl

use strict;

my %hash = (
    1 => "January",    2 => "February", 3 => "March",     4 => "April",
    5 => "May",        6 => "June",     7 => "July",      8 => "August",
    9 => "September", 10 => "October", 11 => "November", 12 => "December"
);

my $href = \%hash;
foreach (keys %{$href}) {
```

```
    print "Key: ", $_, "\t";
    print "Hash: ", $hash{$_}, "\t";
    print "Ref: ", ${$href}{$_}, "\n";
}
```

As expected, we get the same data when using the hash as when using the reference:

```
$ perl hashref.pl
Key: 6  Hash: June       Ref: June
Key: 11 Hash: November   Ref: November
Key: 3  Hash: March      Ref: March
Key: 7  Hash: July       Ref: July
Key: 9  Hash: September  Ref: September
Key: 12 Hash: December   Ref: December
Key: 2  Hash: February   Ref: February
Key: 8  Hash: August     Ref: August
Key: 1  Hash: January    Ref: January
Key: 4  Hash: April      Ref: April
Key: 10 Hash: October    Ref: October
Key: 5  Hash: May        Ref: May
$
```

This should also help to remind you that Perl's hashes aren't ordered as you might expect!

Notation Shorthand Using ->

You can run into problems when you have one reference stored inside another. If we have the following array reference:

```
$ref = [ 1, 2, [ 10, 20 ] ];
```

we can get at the internal array reference by saying ${$ref[2]}. But say we want to get at the first element (0-based) of that array—the one containing the value 20? We could store the reference inside another scalar and then dereference it, like this:

```
$inside  = ${$ref}[2];
$element = ${$inside}[1];
```

Or we could get the element directly, by repeatedly substituting references for array names:

```
$element = ${${ref}[2]}[1];
```

This gets very ugly very quickly, especially if you're dealing with hash references where it becomes hard to tell if the curly braces surround a reference or a hash key.

So, to help us clear it up again, we introduce this rule:

- Instead of ${$ref}, we can say $ref->.

Let's demonstrate this by taking one of our previous examples, modelem.pl, and incorporating this into the code. Here's the relevant piece of the original:

```perl
my @array = (68, 101, 114, 111, 117);
my $ref = \@array;
${$ref}[0] = 100;
print "Array is now : @array\n";
```

and here it is rewritten:

```perl
my @array = (68, 101, 114, 111, 117);
my $ref = \@array;
$ref->[0] = 100;
print "Array is now : @array\n";
```

Likewise for hashes: we can use this arrow notation to make things a bit clearer for ourselves. Recall hashref.pl from a little while ago:

```perl
foreach (keys %{$href}) {
    print "Key: ", $_, "\t";
    print "Hash: ", $hash{$_}, "\t";
    print "Ref: ", ${$href}{$_}, "\n";
}
```

Instead of that, we can write the following:

```perl
foreach (keys %{$href}) {
    print "Key: ", $_, "\t";
    print "Hash: ", $hash{$_}, "\t";
    print "Ref: ", $href->{$_}, "\n";
}
```

Now we can get at our array-in-an-array like this:

```perl
$ref = [ 1, 2, [ 10, 20 ] ];
$element = ${$ref->[2]}[1];
```

or more simply:

```perl
$element = $ref->[2]->[1];
```

However, we've got one more subrule that can simplify this even further:

- Between sets of square brackets, the arrow is optional.

We can therefore rewrite the preceding as

```perl
$element = $ref->[2][1];
```

Reference Counting and Destruction

We've now seen all the ways you can create and use references. It is time to discuss how references are destroyed. Every piece of data in Perl has something called a *reference count* attached to it. This keeps track of the number of references that refer to that exact chunk of data.

When we create a reference to some data, the data's reference count goes up by 1. When we stop referring to it—we reassign the reference variable, or "break" it (as we saw previously, when we tried to modify its value)—the reference count goes down. When nobody's using the data and the reference count gets down to 0, the data is removed. Consider the following example:

```
#!/usr/bin/perl -w
# refcount.pl

use strict;

my $ref;
{
    my @array = (1, 2, 3);
    $ref = \@array;
    my $ref2 = \@array;
    $ref2 = "Hello!";
}
undef $ref;
```

Now, let's look at the references to the array (1, 2, 3) as we go through the program. To start with:

```
my $ref;
{
    my @array = (1, 2, 3);
```

the array is created, and the data (1, 2, 3) has one reference—it's in use by the array @array. Next we create another reference to it:

```
    $ref = \@array;
```

and the reference count increases to 2. Once again we create a reference:

```
    my $ref2 = \@array;
```

and the count goes up to 3. Next, we change that reference to be an ordinary string:

```
    $ref2 = "Hello!";
```

$ref2 is not pointing at our array any more, so the reference count on (1, 2, 3) goes back down to 2. Note that changing $ref2 doesn't affect the original array—that only happens when we dereference. Now a block ends, and all the lexical variables—the my() variables—inside that block go out of scope:

```
}
```

That means that $ref2 and @array are destroyed. The reference count of the data (1, 2, 3) goes down again because @array is not referring to it. However, $ref still has a reference to it, so the reference count is still 1, and the data itself is not removed from memory. $ref still refers to (1, 2, 3) and can access and change this data as before. That is, of course, until we get rid of it:

```
undef $ref;
```

Now the final reference to the data (1, 2, 3) is removed and the memory for the array is finally freed.

Counting Anonymous References

Anonymous data works in the same way—however, it doesn't get its initial reference count from being attached to a variable, but rather from when its first explicit reference is created:

```
my $ref = [1, 2, 3];
```

This data therefore has a reference count of 1, rather than

```
my @array = (1, 2, 3);
my $ref = \@array;
```

which has a count of 2.

Using References for Complex Data Structures

Now that we've looked at what references are, you might be asking, "Why on earth would we want to use them?" As mentioned in the introduction, we often want to create data structures that are more complex than simple arrays or hashes. We may need to store arrays inside arrays, or hashes inside hashes, and references help us do this.

So let's now take a look at a few of the complex data structures we can create with references—it won't be exhaustive by any means, but it should serve to give you ideas as to how complex data structures look and work in Perl, and it should help you to understand the most common data structures.

Matrices

What is a matrix? No, not the thing that Neo wants out of. A *matrix* is simply an array of arrays—you can refer to any single element with a combination of two subscripts, which you might want to think of as a row number and a column number; it's harking back to the chessboard example we mentioned in the introduction.

If you use the arrow syntax, matrices are very easy to use—you get at an element by saying

```
$array[$row]->[$column]
```

which can be written as

`$array[$row][$column]`

`$array[$row]` is an array reference, and we're dereferencing the `$column`'th element in it. With a chessboard example, it would look like this:

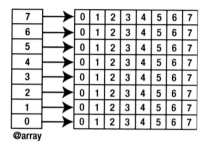

So, `$array[0][0]` would be the bottom left-hand corner of our chessboard, and `$array[7][7]` would be the top right.

Autovivification

There's one last thing we need to know about references before we go on—if we assign values to a reference, Perl will automatically create all the appropriate references necessary to make it work. So, if we say this:

```
my $ref;
$ref->{UK}->{England}->{Oxford}->[1999]->{Population} = 500000;
```

Perl will automatically know that we need `$ref` to be a hash reference. So, it'll make us a nice new anonymous hash:

`$ref = {};`

Then we need `$ref->{UK}` to be a hash reference because we're looking for the hash key England—that hash entry needs to be an array reference, and so on. Perl effectively does this:

```
$ref = {};
$ref->{UK} = {};
$ref->{UK}->{England} = {};
$ref->{UK}->{England}->{Oxford} = [];
$ref->{UK}->{England}->{Oxford}->[1999] = {};
$ref->{UK}->{England}->{Oxford}->[1999]->{Population} = 500000;
```

What this means is that we don't have to worry about creating all the entries ourselves. So we can just go ahead and write

```
my @chessboard;
$chessboard[0]->[0] = "WR";
```

This is called *autovivification*—things springing into existence. We can use it to greatly
simplify the way we use references.

Now that we can represent our chessboard, let's set up a chess game. This will consist of
two stages: setting up the board, and making moves. The computer will have no idea of the
rules, but will simply function as a board, allowing us to move pieces around. Here's our
program:

```
#!/usr/bin/perl -w
# chess.pl

use strict;

my @chessboard;
my @back = qw(R N B Q K N B R);
foreach (0..7) {
    $chessboard[0]->[$_] = "W" . $back[$_]; # White Back Row
    $chessboard[1]->[$_] = "WP";            # White Pawns
    $chessboard[6]->[$_] = "BP";            # Black Pawns
    $chessboard[7]->[$_] = "B" . $back[$_]; # Black Back Row
}

while (1) {
    # Print board
    foreach my $i (reverse (0..7)) { # Row
        foreach my $j (0..7) {       # Column
            if (defined $chessboard[$i]->[$j]) {
                print $chessboard[$i]->[$j];
            } elsif ( ($i % 2) == ($j % 2) ) {
                print "..";
            } else {
                print "  ";
            }
            print " ";  # End of cell
        }
        print "\n";     # End of row
    }

    print "\nStarting square [x,y]: ";
    my $move = <>;
    last unless ($move =~ /^\s*([1-8]),([1-8])/);
    my $startx = $1-1; my $starty = $2-1;

    unless (defined $chessboard[$starty]->[$startx]) {
        print "There's nothing on that square!\n";
```

```perl
        next;
    }
    print "\nEnding square [x,y]: ";
    $move = <>;
    last unless ($move =~ /([1-8]),([1-8])/);
    my $endx = $1-1; my $endy = $2-1;

    # Put starting square on ending square.
    $chessboard[$endy]->[$endx] = $chessboard[$starty]->[$startx];
    # Remove from old square
    undef $chessboard[$starty]->[$startx];
}
```

Now let's see the first part of a game in progress:

```
$ perl chess.pl
BR BN BB BQ BK BN BB BR
BP BP BP BP BP BP BP BP
   ..    ..    ..    ..
..    ..    ..    ..
   ..    ..    ..    ..
..    ..    ..    ..
WP WP WP WP WP WP WP WP
WR WN WB WQ WK WN WB WR

Starting square [x,y]: 4,2

Ending square [x,y]: 4,4
BR BN BB BQ BK BN BB BR
BP BP BP BP BP BP BP BP
   ..    ..    ..    ..
..    ..    ..    ..
   ..    WP    ..    ..
..    ..    ..    ..
WP WP WP .. WP WP WP WP
WR WN WB WQ WK WN WB WR

Starting square [x,y]: 4,7

Ending square [x,y]: 4,5
BR BN BB BQ BK BN BB BR
BP BP BP BP BP BP BP
   ..    ..    ..    ..
..    ..    BP    ..    ..
   ..    WP    ..    ..
..    ..    ..    ..
WP WP WP .. WP WP WP WP
WR WN WB WQ WK WN WB WR
```

Let's look at this program in detail. Our first task is to set up the chessboard, with the pieces in their initial positions. Remember that we're assigning $chessboard[$row][$column] = $thing. First, we set up an array of pieces on the "back row." We'll use this to make it easier to put each piece in its appropriate column.

```
my @back = qw(R N B Q K N B R);
```

Now we'll go over each column.

```
foreach (0..7) {
```

In row 0, the back row for white, we want to place the appropriate piece from the array in each square.

```
$chessboard[0]->[$_] = "W" . $back[$_]; # White Back Row
```

In row 1 of each column, we want a white pawn, WP.

```
$chessboard[1]->[$_] = "WP";             # White Pawns
```

Now we do the same again for black's pieces on rows 6 and 7.

```
$chessboard[6]->[$_] = "BP";             # Black Pawns
$chessboard[7]->[$_] = "B" . $back[$_]; # Black Back Row
}
```

What about the rest of the squares on board? Well, they don't exist right now, but will spring into existence when we try and read from them.

Next we go into our main loop, printing out the board and moving the pieces. To print the board, we obviously want to look at each piece—so we loop through each row and each column:

```
foreach my $i (reverse (0..7)) { # Row
    foreach my $j (0..7) {        # Column
```

If the element is defined, it's because we've put a piece there, so we print it out.

```
        if (defined $chessboard[$i]->[$j]) {
            print $chessboard[$i]->[$j];
```

Note that at this point, we're accessing all 64 squares, so any square that didn't exist before will exist from now on. This next piece of prettiness prints out the "checkered" effect. On a checkerboard, dark squares come on odd rows in odd columns and even rows in even columns. $x % 2 tests whether $x divides equally by 2—whether it is odd or even. If the "oddness" (or "evenness") of the row and column is the same, we print a dark square.

```
        } elsif ( ($i % 2) == ($j % 2) ) {
            print "..";
```

Otherwise, we print a blank square consisting of two spaces:

```
        } else {
            print "  ";
        }
```

To separate the cells, we use a single space.

```
    print " ";  # End of cell
}
```

And at the end of each row, we print a new line.

```
  print "\n";      # End of row
}
```

Now we ask for a square to move from:

```
print "\nStarting square [x,y]: ";
my $move = <>;
```

We're looking for two digits with a comma in the middle:

```
last unless ($move =~ /([1-8]),([1-8])/);
```

Now we convert human-style coordinates (1 to 8) into computer-style coordinates (0 to 7):

```
my $startx = $1-1; my $starty = $2-1;
```

Next, check if there's actually a chess piece there. Note that a y coordinate is a row, so it goes first—look back at the diagram if you're not sure how this works.

```
unless (defined $chessboard[$starty]->[$startx]) {
   print "There's nothing on that square!\n";
   next;
}
```

We do the same for the ending square, and then move the piece. We copy the piece to the new square:

```
$chessboard[$endy]->[$endx] = $chessboard[$starty]->[$startx];
```

And then we delete the old square:

```
undef $chessboard[$starty]->[$startx];
```

We've now used a matrix, a two-dimensional array. The nice thing about Perl's autovivification is that we didn't need to say explicitly that we were dealing with references—Perl takes care of all that behind the scenes, and we just assigned the relevant values to the right places. However, if we were to look at the contents of the @chessboard array, we'd see eight array references.

Trees

We're now going to build on the principle of matrices, by introducing *tree*-like data structures, in which we use hashes as well as arrays. The classic example of one of these structures is an address book—suppose we want to keep someone's address and phone number in a hash. We could say this:

```
%paddy = (
    address => "23, Blue Jay Way",
    phone   => "404-6599"
);
```

That's all very well, and it makes sense—the only problem is, you have to create a separate hash for each person in your address book, and put each one in a separate variable. This isn't easy at all at run time, and is very messy to write—so instead, you use references.

What we do is create a main "address book" hash, referenced as $addressbook, with everyone else's hashes as values off that:

```
$addressbook{"Paddy Malone"} = {
    address => "23, Blue Jay Way",
    phone   => "404-6599"
};
```

Note Note that if you've included the use strict; pragma, you'll have to declare this hash explicitly as my %addressbook; before using it.

It's now very easy to take new entries from the user, and add them to our address book:

```
print "Give me a name:";  chomp($name    = <>);
print "Address:";         chomp($address= <>);
print "Phone number:";    chomp($phone   = <>);
$addressbook{$name} = {
    address => $address,
    phone   => $phone
};
```

To print out a single person, we'd use this:

```
if (exists $addressbook{$who}) {
    print "$who\n";
    print "Address:  ", $addressbook{$who}{address}, "\n";
    print "Phone no: ", $addressbook{$who}{phone},   "\n";
}
```

And to print every address:

```
foreach $who (keys %addressbook) {
    print "$who\n";
    print "Address:  ", $addressbook{$who}{address}, "\n";
    print "Phone no: ", $addressbook{$who}{phone},   "\n";
}
```

Deleting an address is very simple:

```
delete $addressbook{$who};
```

How about adding another level to our tree? Can we have an array of "friends" for each person? No problem—we just use an anonymous array:

```
$addressbook{"Paddy Malone"} = {
   address => "23, Blue Jay Way",
   phone   => "404-6599",
   friends => [ "Baba O'Reilly", "Mick Flaherty" ]
};
```

We can get at each person's friends by saying $addressbook{$who}{friends}, and that'll give us an anonymous array. We can then dereference that to a real array and print it out:

```
foreach $who (keys %addressbook) {
   print "$who\n";
   print "Address:  ", $addressbook{$who}{address}, "\n";
   print "Phone no: ", $addressbook{$who}{phone},   "\n";
   my @friends = @{$addressbook{$who}{friends}};
   print "Friends:\n";
   foreach (@friends) {
      print "\t$_\n";
   }
}
```

This would now give us something like the following:

```
Paddy Malone
Address:  23, Blue Jay Way
Phone no: 404-6599
Friends:
        Baba O'Reilly
        Mick Flaherty
```

What we now have is one hash (address book), containing another hash (peoples' details), in turn containing an array (each person's friends).

We can quite easily *traverse* the tree structure—that is, move from person to person—by following links. We do this by visiting a link, and then adding all of that person's friends onto a "to do" array. We must be very careful here not to get stuck in a loop—if one person links to another, and the other links back again, we need to avoid bouncing about between them indefinitely. One simple way to keep track of the links we've already processed is to use a hash. Here's how we can do it:

```
$, = "\t"                 # Set output field separator for tabulated display
my @todo = ("Paddy Malone"); # Start point
my %seen;
```

```
while (@todo) {
    my $who = shift @todo; # Get person from the end
    $seen{$who}++;          # Mark them as seen.
    my @friends = @{$addressbook{$who}{friends}};
    print "$who has friends: ", @friends, "\n";
    foreach (@friends) {
        # Visit unless they're already visited
        push @todo, $_ unless exists $seen{$_};
    }
}
```

The hash %seen is used to build up a table of everyone whose name has been held in the variable $who. The foreach loop at the bottom only adds names to the @todo list if they're not defined in that hash—that is, if they've not been displayed already. Given a fairly closed community, we could see something like this:

```
Paddy Malone has friends Baba O'Reilly Mick Flaherty
Baba O'Reilly has friends Bob McDowell Mick Flaherty Andy Donahue
Mick Flaherty has friends Paddy Malone Timothy O'Leary
Bob McDowell has friends Andy Donahue Baba O'Reilly
Andy Donahue has friends Jimmy Callahan Mick Flaherty
Timothy O'Leary has friends Bob McDowell Mick Flaherty Paddy Malone
Jimmy Callahan has friends Andy Donahue Baba O'Reilly Mick Flaherty
```

Summary

We've looked at references, a way to put one type of data structure inside another. References work because they allow us to use a scalar to refer to another piece of data. They tell us where Perl stores it, and give us a way to get at it with a scalar.

We can create a reference explicitly by putting a backslash in front of a variable's name: \%hash or \@array, for example. Alternatively, we can create an anonymous reference by using {} instead of () for a hash, and [] instead of () for an array. Finally, we can create a reference by creating a need for one—if a reference needs to exist for what we're doing, Perl will spring one into existence by autovivification.

We can use a reference by placing it in curly braces where a variable name should go. @{$array_r} can replace @array everywhere. We can then access elements of array or hash references using the arrow notation: $array_ref->[$element] for an array, and $hash_ref->{$key} for a hash.

We've also seen a few complex data structures: matrices, which are arrays of arrays; and trees, which may contain hashes or arrays. For more information on these kinds of data structure, consult the Perl "Data Structures Cookbook" documentation (perldoc perldsc) or the Perl "List of Lists" documentation (perldoc perllol).

If you're really interested in data structures from a computer science point of view, *Mastering Algorithms in Perl* by Orwant et al. (O'Reilly & Associates, 1999) has some chapters on these kinds of structure: primarily trees and tree traversal. The ultimate guide to data structures is still *The Art Of Computer Programming, Volume 1*, by Donald Knuth (Addison Wesley, 1997)—affectionately known as "The Bible."

Exercises

1. Modify the chessboard example to detect when a piece is taken. This occurs when a piece is sitting in a square that another piece moves into. The piece that was originally in the square is taken by the new piece and removed from the board.

2. Without being concerned with checks, checkmates, and castling, check to ensure that a move is valid. If you don't know the rules of chess, just check the following things: no player may take either king (K), and no player may take their own pieces.

3. Turn the snippets of address book code into an address book management program. Allow the user to add, search for, and delete entries. See if you can think of a way to save the hash to disk and load it again.

CHAPTER 12

■ ■ ■

Object-Oriented Perl

There are two main schools of thought when approaching a solution to a problem in the programming world. The first school of thought is one that we have used in this book up to this point: *procedural programming*. This approach is based on what actions to take— *procedures*—and developing subroutines that carry out those actions. In procedural programming, we take the overall system and break it up into smaller and smaller pieces, code the steps for the individual pieces into functions, and then put the functions together to form the entire system.

The other school of thought is an approach that has been quite popular for the last 10 or 15 years: *object-oriented programming* (OOP, or simply OO for short). In the OO approach, we take a step back from what the program needs to do and instead look at the nature of the things with which we are working.

In this chapter, we'll learn how to start thinking in OO terms. OO involves a lot of jargon, so the first thing we'll do is look in some detail at all the new terms associated with OO and what they mean to a Perl programmer. After that, we'll see how we go about approaching a problem using this style of programming. We'll use a Perl module that involves creating an object, and we'll also construct some object-oriented modules of our own.

This chapter is meant only as a beginning in OO in Perl. For more details, we recommend the excellent book *Object Oriented Perl* by Damian Conway (Manning Publications, 1999).

Improving Your Vocabulary

Object-oriented programming wouldn't be a good buzz phrase if it didn't use a lot of familiar words in unfamiliar contexts. Before we go any further, let's investigate the jargon that we'll need in order to understand object-oriented Perl programming.

The first thing to note is that object-oriented programming is a concept, rather than a standard—there are a few things that object-oriented languages should do, a lot they can do, but nothing that they absolutely *have* to do. Other languages may implement more or less of these ideas than Perl does, and may well do so in a completely different way. We'll explain here the terms that are most commonly used by object-oriented programmers.

Objects

What is an object, anyway? Previously, we mentioned briefly that an object is a chunk of data that has behaviors, but that's not all. To be honest, an object can be anything—it really depends on what your application is. For instance, if you're writing a contact management database, a single contact might be an object. If you're communicating with a remote computer via FTP, you could make each connection to the remote server an object.

An object can always be described in terms of two things:

- What it can do (*actions* or *methods*)

- What we know about it (*information* or *attributes*)

With a "contact record" object, we'd probably know the contact's name, date of birth, address, and so on—these are the object's *attributes*. We might also be able to ask it to do certain things: print an address label for this contact; work out how old they are; or send them an email—these are the object's *methods*.

In Perl, what we see as an object is simply a reference—in fact, you can convert any ordinary reference *into* an object simply by using the bless() function. We'll see later on how that happens. Typically, however, objects are represented as references to a hash, and that's the model we'll use in this chapter.

Attributes

An *attribute* is something we know about an object. A contact database object will possess attributes such as date of birth, address, and name. An FTP session will possess attributes such as the name of the remote server we're connected to, the current directory, and so on. Two contacts will have different values for their name attribute, unless we have duplicates in the database, but they will both have the name attribute.

If we're using a reference to a hash, it's natural to have the attributes as hash entries. Our person object then becomes a blessed version of the following:

```
my $person = {
    lastname    => "Galilei",
    firstname   => "Galileo",
    address     => "9.81 Pisa Apts.",
    occupation  => "bombadier"
};
```

We can get to (and change) our attributes simply by accessing these hash values directly (that is, by saying something like $person->{address}—remember that we use this syntax because we're dealing with a reference), but this is generally regarded as a bad idea. For starters, it requires us to know the internal structure of the object and where and how the attributes are stored, which, as end users, we should have no need or desire to fiddle with. Secondly, it doesn't give the object a chance to examine the data you're giving it to make sure it makes sense. Instead, access to an attribute usually goes through a *method*.

Methods

A *method* is anything you can tell the object to do. It could be something complicated, such as printing out address labels and reports, or something simple such as accessing an attribute. Those methods directly related to attributes are called *get-set* methods, as they'll typically either *get* the current value of the attribute or *set* a new one.

The fact that methods are all about instructions for doing things may give you a clue as to how we represent them in Perl—methods in Perl are just subroutines. However, there is a special syntax called the *arrow operator* (->), which we use to call methods. So instead of getting the address attribute directly, as in the preceding example, we're more likely to say something like this:

```
print "Address: ", $person->address(), "\n";
```

We're also able to set an attribute (change its value) like this:

```
$person->address("Campus Mirabilis, Pisa, Italy");
```

Alternatively, we can call a method to produce an envelope for this object:

```
$person->print_envelope();
```

This syntax $object->method(@arguments) "invokes" the method, which just means that it calls the given subroutine—in our examples this is either address() or print_envelope(). We'll see how it's done shortly.

Classes

Our contact object and FTP session object are very different things—they have different methods and attributes. While $person->date_of_birth() may make sense, you wouldn't expect $ftp_session->date_of_birth() to do anything sensible.

A *class* is the formal term for a *type* of object—it is a general description of a group of things. Classes define the methods an object can have and how those methods work. All objects in the Person class will have the same set of methods and possess the same attributes, and these will be different from the FTP class. An object is sometimes referred to as an *instance* of a class; this just means that it's a specific thing created from a general category.

In Perl's object-oriented philosophy, a class is an ordinary package. Let's start piecing this together:

- A method is a subroutine in a package. For instance, the date_of_birth() method in the Person class is merely the subroutine date_of_birth() in the Person package.

- Blessing a scalar just means telling it from what package to take its methods. At that point, it's more than just a complex data structure, or scalar reference. It has attributes—the data we've stored in the hash reference or elsewhere; and it has methods—the subroutines in its package; therefore it can be considered a full-fledged object.

Classes can also have what are known as *class methods* (some programming languages call these *static methods*). These are methods that do things relevant to the whole class rather than individual objects. Instead of acting on an object, as you would by saying $object->method(), you act on the class: Person->method(). An important thing to note is that Perl doesn't necessarily know whether a given subroutine is a class method, an object method, or just an ordinary subroutine, so programmers have to do the checking themselves.

Similarly, classes can have attributes that refer to the whole class—in Perl these are just package variables (some programming languages call these *static data*). For instance, we might have a `population` attribute in our `Person` class, which tells us how many `Person` objects are currently in existence.

One final note—you'll probably have noticed that we capitalized `Person`. The Perl convention is to capitalize all class names, so as to help distinguish them from object names.

Polymorphism

The word *polymorphism* comes from the Greek πολυ μορφου, meaning "many forms." What it means in object-oriented programming is that a single method can do different things depending on the class of the object that calls it. For instance, `$person->address()` would return the person's address, but `$ftp_session->address()` might return the IP address of the remote server. On the other hand, `$object->address()` would *have* to do the right thing according to which class `$object` was in.

When we invoke `$person->address()`, we are calling the subroutine `Person::address()`, and when we invoke `$ftp_session->address()`, we are calling the subroutine `FTP::address()`. They're defined completely separately, in different packages, probably even in different files. Since Perl already knows what class each object belongs to, neither you nor Perl need to do anything special to make the distinction. Perl looks at the object, finds the class it is in, and calls the subroutine in the appropriate package. This brings us to . . .

Encapsulation

One of the nice things about object-oriented programming is that it hides complexity from the user—this is known as *encapsulation* (or *abstraction*). This means that users of the object need not care how the class is structured or how the attributes are represented in the object. Nor do users have to care how the methods work or where they come from—they can just use them.

This also means that the author of the class has complete freedom to change its internal workings at any time. As long as the methods have the same names and take the same arguments, all programs using the class should continue to work and produce the same results. That is as long as they use the method *interface*, or way of invoking the method, as they should, rather than trying to access or modify the data directly.

In this sense, working with objects is a little like driving a car. Our object, the car, has a set of attributes, such as the model, current speed, and amount of fuel in the tank. We can't get at these directly, but some read-only methods like the speedometer and the fuel gauge expose them to us. It also provides us with some more methods and a well-defined interface to get it to do things.

We have a pedal to make it accelerate and one to make it brake, a stick to change gear, a hole to put fuel into the tank, and so on. We don't actually need to know how the engine works if we're prepared to stick to using these methods; of course, we do need to know what each of them does. We don't even need to know the whereabouts of the fuel tank, we just put fuel in the appropriate place. If we really want to, we can lift the hood, look inside it, and fiddle with it—but then we only have ourselves to blame if it breaks!

Inheritance

Another property that makes object-oriented programming easy to use is its support for *inheritance*. Classes can be built quickly by specifying how they differ from other classes. For example, humans inherit attributes from their parents, such as hair color and height, while

Perl's classes inherit methods. If a class inherits from another class, it receives the ability to call every method defined by the class from which it inherits. If the new class wants to implement a method differently, it defines the method in its own class. If it doesn't want its own version of the method, it will automatically get the method from the parent class. The parent class, which provides the new class with the methods, is called the *superclass* or *base class*, and the class which inherits from the superclass is known as a *subclass* or *derived class*.

The relationship between the classes can be described as an *IS-A* relationship. If we have a superclass Animal, we may create a subclass Vertebrate. We could then say that a Vertebrate IS-A Animal. In fact, the classification system for animals can be thought of as a series of IS-A relationships, with more specific subclasses inheriting properties of their superclasses:

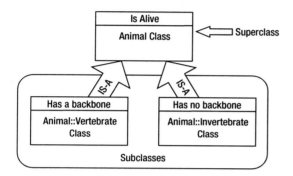

Here we see that vertebrates and invertebrates are both subclasses of a general animal class. They both inherit the fact that they are alive, and so we need not specify this in the subclass. Next we could create an Animal::Vertebrate::Mammal class, which would be a subclass of Animal::Vertebrate. We wouldn't need to specify that the mammal had a backbone or was alive, because these characteristics would be inherited from the superclass.

We won't talk much about inheritance in this book. This topic is perhaps the most difficult topic in OO and deserves a chapter, if not several chapters, of its own. Once you grasp the basic concepts of OO, we recommend that you check out the book *Object Oriented Perl* for an excellent discussion of inheritance.

Constructors

Objects have to come from somewhere, and in keeping with the principles of encapsulation, users of a class shouldn't be expected to put together an object themselves. This would require knowledge of how the object is represented and what initialization is required. To take this responsibility away from the user, there's a class method that all classes should possess—it's called the *constructor*.

As the name implies, this constructs and returns a new object. For this reason, it's usually called new().[1] We may pass arguments to the constructor, which it can then use to do the initial setup of the object. Sometimes these arguments are in the form of a hash, allowing us to create an object like this:

---

1. It is also called new() so that our C++ brethren will feel a sense of familiarity when they create objects in Perl.

```
my $galileo = Person->new(
    lastname    => "Galilei",
    firstname   => "Galileo",
    address     => "9.81 Pisa Apts.",
    occupation  => "bombadier",
);
```

There's also another syntax for calling methods, which you'll particularly see used with the constructor:

```
my $galileo = new Person (...);
```

The constructor will now check that the arguments are acceptable, do any conversion it requires, and create a hash reference, bless() it, and return it to us. More on this later in this chapter.

Destructors

When the object is no longer in use—when it's a lexical variable that goes out of scope—Perl automatically destroys it. However, before doing so, Perl will attempt to call a method named DESTROY(). If the class provides this method, it should be responsible for any tasks that need to be performed before the object is disposed of. For instance, our FTP session object will want to ensure that it has closed the connection to the remote server.

An Example

It is now time for an example. Let's start off by using a class that is already created for us: Net::FTP.[2] This class (also known as a *module*) allows us to create objects that transfer files to and from an FTP server. The following example will connect to a famous website in the Perl world—the CPAN[3] (more on CPAN in Chapter 13)—and download the README.html file. This example will illustrate some of the buzz words mentioned previously.

We'll now use the Net::FTP module to create an object that will let us get files from an FTP site. In our case, we'll connect to CPAN and download the README.html file.

```
#!/usr/bin/perl -w
# ftp.pl

use strict;
use Net::FTP;

my $ftp = Net::FTP->new("ftp.cpan.org")
    or die "Couldn't connect: $@\n";
```

---

2. Written by Graham Barr. Thanks, Graham!
3. The Comprehensive Perl Archive Network—CPAN. Don't confuse this with CSPAN—that is something completely different.

```
$ftp->login("anonymous");
$ftp->cwd("/pub/CPAN");
$ftp->get("README.html");
$ftp->close();
```

Network and firewalls permitting, this should retrieve the file—although it may take some time. Here is the proof on a Windows machine:

```
$ perl ftp.pl
$ dir README.html
README~1 HTM          2,902          ...    ...         README.html
$
```

The first line of interest in this program is

```
use Net::FTP;
```

This line finds the file that contains the definition of the Net::FTP class (its name happens to be FTP.pm and it is located in a directory named Net) and compiles it for use with our program. More on this in the next section.

After loading the Net::FTP module, we create ourselves an object:

```
my $ftp = Net::FTP->new("ftp.cpan.org")
    or die "Couldn't connect: $@\n";
```

Our class is called Net::FTP, the same as the module—this is because, as mentioned previously, a class is just an ordinary package.

We create the object by calling the constructor, which is the class method new(). This takes a number of arguments: a remote machine to which we want to connect and a hash specifying things like whether we have a firewall, which port to connect to, whether we want debugging information, and so on. These arguments will become the attributes of the object. If we don't specify them, the constructor comes up with some sensible defaults for us. In our case, the defaults are fine, so we just need to supply a remote machine—we'll use the CPAN server, ftp.cpan.org.

When we call the constructor, it takes our argument (the remote host), and stashes it away internally in the object—encapsulation means we don't need to know how or where. Then it takes a reference to that hash, blesses the reference, and returns it to us. That blessed reference is our new object (our FTP session), and we're now ready to do things with it (more on bless() later in this chapter).

Then we see a call to the login() method:

```
$ftp->login("anonymous");
```

First of all, we have to log in to the server. The usual way of getting things from an FTP server is by logging in with a username of "anonymous" and your email address as the password. The login() method tells the object to issue the appropriate login commands.

How did Perl know that it should use Net::FTP::login() rather than any other login()? When our constructor blessed the reference, it gave the reference knowledge of where to find the methods. To quote from the perlobj documentation, "an object is just a reference that happens to know which class it belongs to."

Since Perl takes care of passing the object to the subroutine as the first parameter, the method automatically receives all the data it needs. This means we can easily have multiple objects doing different things.

```perl
my $ftp1 = Net::FTP->new("ftp.cpan.org");
my $ftp2 = Net::FTP->new("ftp.apress.com");
$ftp1->login("anonymous");
```

The object $ftp1 is just a blessed reference to a hash, and that hash contains all the data about the connection to CPAN, like the settings, the filehandles, and anything else that Net::FTP needs to store. These are the object's attributes. Everything we know about the connection is bundled into that object. The important thing to note is that it's completely independent from $ftp2, which is another object containing another set of data about a different connection. Hence, the method call $ftp1->login() has no impact on the other connection at all.

After logging in, we change the working directory on the target machine and get the file.

```perl
$ftp->cwd("/pub/CPAN");
$ftp->get("README.html");
```

cwd() and get() are two more methods our object supplies. The object has a huge number of methods, due to the fact that it has a long chain of inheritance. However, there are some methods Net::FTP defines directly that you should know about. They mainly relate directly to FTP commands—Table 12-1 presents an incomplete list of them.

Table 12-1. *Net::FTP Methods*

Method Name	Behavior
$ftp->login($login,$passwd)	Log into the server with the given username and password.

$ ftp->type($type)
$ ftp->ascii()
$ ftp->binary()
	Set the transfer type to ASCII or binary; this is quite similar to Perl's binmode operator.

$ ftp->rename($old,$new)	Rename a file.
$ ftp->delete($file)	Delete a file.
$ ftp->cwd($directory)	Change directory on the FTP server.
$ ftp->pwd()	Give the name of the current directory.
$ ftp->ls()	List the current directory on the FTP server.
$ ftp->get($remote, $local, $offset)	Get a file from the remote server.
$ ftp->put($local, $remote)	Put a file to the remote server.

There are also some get-set methods that will affect the object's attributes—for instance, the $ftp->hash() method controls an attribute that determines whether or not to print a # character after every 1024 bytes transferred.

After we've called the get() method to get our file, we'll call the close() method to shut down the connection to the server.

```
$ftp->close();
```

So, we've used our first class. Hopefully, you can see that using objects and classes in Perl is just as easy as calling functions. In fact, it's easier—Perl not only takes care of finding out where to find the subroutine you're trying to call, but it also takes care of passing a whole bunch of data to the subroutine for you.

Because this all goes on behind the scenes, we can happily pretend that an object contains a bunch of methods that act on it, and it alone. In fact, it doesn't—it only contains information regarding where to find methods that can act on any object in that class.

Including Other Files with use

In ftp.pl we saw this statement:

```
use Net::FTP;
```

As mentioned previously, this statement attempts to locate a file named FTP.pm in a directory named Net. The .pm filename extension means that this is a "Perl module," or a collection of data and functions in its own package (more on this later in this chapter).

What we want to do is get Perl to read the .pm file and use it as part of our own program. We have three ways of doing this: do, require, and use.

do

This is the most difficult of the three to understand—the others are just slightly varied forms of do.

do will look for a file by searching the @INC path (more on that later). If the file can't be found, it will silently move on. If it is found, it will run the file just as if it was placed in a block within our main program—but with one slight difference: we won't be able to see lexical variables from the main program once we're inside the additional code. So if we have a file dothis.pl:

```
#!/usr/bin/perl -w
# dothis.pl

use strict;

my $a = "Been there, done that, got the T-shirt";
do "printit.pl";
```

and a file printit.pl:

```
print $a;
print "this should go to standard output...\n";
```

dothis.pl will do, or execute, the file printit.pl. This means that the contents of printit.pl are compiled and executed. Executing this code produces the following:

```
$ perl dothis.pl
Use of uninitialized value in print at printit.pl line 1.
this should go to standard output...
$
```

The first line of output is a warning that $a is undefined. The second line of output is a result of executing the second print() function.

This program shows that do can execute arbitrary code in another file. On the other hand, we can have subroutines in our included file and call them from the main file.

require

require is like do, but it'll only do it once. It'll record the fact that a file has been loaded, and will henceforth ignore further requests to require it again. It also fails with an error if it can't find the file you're loading.

```
#!/usr/bin/perl -w
# cantload.pl

use strict;

require "not_there.pl";
```

will die() with an error like this:

```
$ perl cantload.pl
Can't locate not_there.pl in @INC (@INC contains:
/usr/local/lib/perl5/5.8.3/cygwin /usr/local/lib/perl5/5.8.3
/usr/local/lib/perl5/site_perl/5.8.3/cygwin
/usr/local/lib/perl5/site_perl/5.8.3 /usr/local/lib/perl5/site_perl .)
at cantload.pl line 6.
$
```

This is the @INC array, which contains a list of paths in which Perl looks for modules and other additional files. The first two paths are where Perl keeps the standard library. The first includes the word cygwin, which is the operating system this example is running on and that contains the parts of the library specific to this operating system. The second is the part of the standard library, which does not depend on the operating system. In Windows, these two libraries are C:/Perl/lib and C:/Perl/site/lib by default.

The next two paths are the local "site" modules, which are third-party modules that we'll install from CPAN or create ourselves. They've got the version (5.8.3) in there to remind us that these are modules specific to that version—the next path doesn't have a Perl version number in it, and that's for site modules which do not need a particular version of Perl. Finally, the . represents the current directory.

You can also use `require` like this:

```
require Wibble;
```

Using a bareword tells Perl to look for a file called `Wibble.pm` in the `@INC` path. It also converts any instance of `::` into a directory separator. For instance:

```
require Monty::Python;
```

will send Perl looking for `Python.pm` in a directory called `Monty`, which is itself in one of the directories given in `@INC`.

use

The way we normally use modules is, logically enough, with the `use` statement. This is like `require`, except that Perl applies it *before* anything else in the program starts—if Perl sees a `use` statement *anywhere* in your program, it'll include that module. So, for instance, you can't say this:

```
if ($graphical) {
    use MyProgram::Graphical;
} else {
    use MyProgram::Text;
}
```

because when Perl's reading your program, it will include *both* modules—the use takes place way before the value of `$graphical` is decided. We say that use takes place at compile time and not at run time.

Changing @INC

The default contents of the search path `@INC` are decided when Perl is compiled—if we move those directories elsewhere, we'll have to recompile Perl to get it working again. However, we can tell it to search in directories other than these—`@INC` is an ordinary array, so you might expect us to be able to say

```
unshift @INC, "my/module/directory";
use Wibble;
```

However, this isn't going to work. Why not? Remember that the preceding statement will execute at run time. Unfortunately the `use` statement takes place at compile time, well before that. No problem! There's a special subroutine called `BEGIN` that is guaranteed execution at compile time, so we can put it there:

```
sub BEGIN {
    unshift @INC, "my/module/directory";
}
use Wibble;
```

Now that'll work just fine—however, it's a little messy, and what's more, there's an easier way to do it. We can use the `lib` pragma to add our directory to @INC before anything else gets a chance to look at it:

```
use lib "my/module/directory";
use Wibble;
```

The directory that is indicated is inserted into the front of @INC so that it is the first directory searched when Perl is looking for the module.

Rolling Your Own Classes

We've seen how to use a class and an object. Let's now see how to make our own classes. As an example, we'll implement the `Person` class we used in our definitions.

As we mentioned previously, a class is just a package—nothing more, nothing less. So the simplest class looks like this:

```
package Person;
```

That's it. However, this class has nothing—no methods, no attributes, no constructor, nothing. It's a totally empty class. We will eventually want to add more stuff (attributes and methods) to this class.[4]

Usually, you'll want to put your class into its own file. It's not necessary by any means, but it gets the implementation out of the way. So, let's create a module by putting the following in the file `Person1.pm`. The file must end in the `.pm` file extension because when we use this class we will say

```
use Person1;
```

and this looks for the file named `Person1.pm`. Here is its content:

```
package Person1;
# Person1.pm

# Class for storing data about a person

use strict;

1;
```

Normally, the name of the package is the same as the name of file (minus the `.pm` extension). So if the package name is `Person1`, the filename is `Person1.pm`. Likewise, if the filename is `Person1.pm`, the package name is `Person1`.

As we discuss the various features of OO in this chapter, we will develop a class that represents a person. We will start with package `Person1`, then enhance that package to be `Person2`, and so on. Keep in mind that these packages are representing an evolution of a definition.

---

4. Because, let's face it, there are already enough empty `Person`s in the world.

That 1; at the end of the file looks weird, but it is necessary because Perl expects to see a true value as the last thing in the package; this tells Perl that everything went OK when loading the file. Now in a separate program, we can say use Person1; and start using the class, like this:

```
#!/usr/bin/perl -w
# person1.pl

use strict;
use Person1;
```

This program doesn't do anything except read in and compile the class we created, because we can't yet create any objects as we do not yet have a constructor. Therefore, the next step is to write a constructor.

What does our constructor create? It creates an object, which is a blessed reference. Before we go any further, then, let's have a look at what bless() is and what it does.

Bless You, My Reference

The bless() function takes a reference and turns it into an object. The way it does that is simple: it changes the type of the reference. Instead of being an array reference or a hash reference, Perl now thinks of it as a Person1 reference (or whatever other class we bless() the reference into).

We can use the ref() function to tell us what type of reference we have:

```
#!/usr/bin/perl -w
# reftypes.pl

use strict;

my $a = [];
my $b = {};
my $c = \1;
my $d = \$c;
print '$a is a ', ref($a), " reference\n";
print '$b is a ', ref($b), " reference\n";
print '$c is a ', ref($c), " reference\n";
print '$d is a ', ref($d), " reference\n";
```

```
$ perl reftypes.pl
$a is a ARRAY reference
$b is a HASH reference
$c is a SCALAR reference
$d is a REF reference
$
```

The syntax of bless() is

```
bless(reference, package);
```

If the package isn't given, the reference is blessed into the current package. Let's bless() a reference into the Person1 package.

```
#!/usr/bin/perl -w
# bless1.pl

use strict;

my $a = {};

print '$a is a ', ref($a), " reference\n";

bless($a, "Person1");

print '$a is a ', ref($a), " reference\n";
```

```
$ perl bless1.pl
$a is a HASH reference
$a is a Person1 reference
$
```

Okay, so we've changed $a into a Person1 reference. So what just happened?

Actually, nothing changed in the structure of $a at all. It's still a hash reference, and we can still dereference it—or add, access, and delete entries in the hash, and so on. It still has the same keys and values. Nothing magical has happened.

But $a is now a reference with knowledge of which package it belongs to, and if we try and call a method with it, Perl now knows that it should look in the Person1 package for a definition of that method. It has become an object.

What if we bless() it again? What happens then? Let's try it.

```
#!/usr/bin/perl -w
# bless2.pl

use strict;

my $a = {};

print '$a is a ', ref($a), " reference\n";

bless($a, "Person1");
print '$a is a ', ref($a), " reference\n";

bless($a, "Animal::Vertebrate::Mammal");
print '$a is a ', ref($a), " reference\n";
```

```
$ perl bless2.pl
$a is a HASH reference
$a is a Person1 reference
$a is a Animal::Vertebrate::Mammal reference
$
```

All that's happened is we've once again changed what type of reference it is. We've changed where Perl should look if any methods are called by the reference. Note that at this stage we haven't even *defined* an `Animal::Vertebrate::Mammal` package, but that's OK because we're not going to call any methods yet—if we did, they would surely fail.

Again, the internal structure of that reference hasn't changed. It's still a hash reference with the same keys and values. You usually don't want to `bless()` an object that's already been `blessed`. This is because something that was originally a `Person1` may have different attributes to what the new class expects it to have when methods are called. Worse still, the program using the object could well try and call a method that was fine in the old class but doesn't exist in the new one—attempting to magically turn a person into an FTP session can only have undesirable (and pretty weird) results.

Storing Attributes

Before we look at methods, let's examine attributes. An attribute is, as defined at the start of this chapter, something we know about the object. In other words, it's a piece of data that belongs to this particular object. How do we store this data, then?

This is what the reference is for; if we store our data in the reference, our object carries around both a set of data unique to it and knowledge of where to find methods to act on that data. If we know that our object is only going to contain one attribute, one piece of data, we could conceivably use a scalar reference, like this:

```
my $attribute = "green";
my $object = \$attribute;
bless $object, "Simple";
```

Now we have a nice simple object that stores a single attribute contained in the `Simple` class. We can access and change the attribute just as we'd work with an ordinary scalar reference:

```
$var      = ${$object};
${$object} = "red";
```

This is nice and simple, but it's not very flexible. Similarly, we could have an array reference and `bless()` that to turn it into an object, which is slightly more flexible. We can access attributes as elements in the array, and we can add and delete attributes by using array operations. If we are storing a set of unnamed data, this is perfectly adequate.

However, for maximum flexibility, we can use a hash to give names to our attributes. Here is an example of creating a reference to an anonymous hash and then `blessing` it as an object of our class:

```
my $object = {
    lastname    => "Galilei",
    firstname   => "Galileo",
    address     => "9.81 Pisa Apts.",
    occupation  => "bombadier",
};
bless $object, "Person1";
```

This allows us easy access to the individual attributes, as if we were carrying a bunch of variables around with us. Therefore, we generally use an anonymous hash reference for any nontrivial class.

The Constructor

We're now ready to create objects. Let's put this knowledge into a constructor, and put a constructor into our currently empty Person1 class. As mentioned previously, our definition of a person is a work in progress, so we will call the next version Person2 and store it in Person2.pm.

To construct an object, we make a hash reference, and bless() it as an object of the class.

```perl
package Person2;
# Person2.pm

# Class for storing data about a person

use strict;

sub new {
   my $self = {};
   bless $self, "Person2";
   return $self;
}

1;
```

Now we can use our Person2 class to create an object:

```perl
#!/usr/bin/perl -w
# persontest.pl

use strict;
use Person2;

my $person = Person2->new();
```

which should execute without any errors.

Our constructor does a simple job, and does it well. First, we create our hash reference:

```perl
my $self = {};
```

$self is the traditional name for an object when it's being manipulated by methods inside the class. Now we'll turn it into an object by telling it which class it belongs to:

```perl
bless $self, "Person2";
```

Finally, we return the object:

```
return $self;
```

Excellent. Now let's see how we can improve this.

Considering Inheritance

It's possible that someone someday will want to inherit from this class, and we won't necessarily be told about it. If they don't provide their own constructor, they'll get ours, and as things stand, that'll produce an object blessed into our class—not theirs.

We really need to remove the hard-wired "Person2" in our constructor and replace it with the called class. How do we know what the called class is though? Perl translates Class->new() into new("Class"). In other words, the class name is magically passed into the constructor as its first argument. Therefore, we know what class the user wants because it's the first argument to the constructor. All we need to do is take that argument and use that as the class to bless() into (the second argument to the bless() function). So here's a more general constructor that takes inheritance into account:

```
sub new {
    my $class = shift;
    my $self = {};
    bless $self, $class;
    return $self;
}
```

As usual, shift() without any arguments means shift @_—it takes the first element of the argument array. This gives us the first thing we were passed, the class name. We can therefore use this to bless our reference without needing to hard-code the name.

Providing Attributes

Now let's make one more enhancement. At the moment, we can create a completely anonymous Person2 with no attributes at all. We want to be able to give the end user of the class the opportunity to specify some attributes when the object is created. So let's take the next step in our evolution and define class Person3.

As before, we're going to store the data in a hash reference. The object's data will be provided to the constructor through its argument list. Ideally, we'll want the constructor to be called something along these lines:

```
my $object = Person3->new(
    lastname   => "Galii",
    firstname  => "Galileo",
    address    => "9.81 Pisa Apts.",
    occupation => "bombardier"
);
```

This is the easiest syntax for the user, because it allows them to specify the attributes in any order, and give as many or as few as they want. It's also a lot easier to use and remember than if we make them use a list like this:

```perl
my $object = Person3->new ("Galilei","Galileo","9.81 Pisa Apts.","bombardier");
```

In fact, it's the easiest syntax for us too. Since we want our attributes stored in a hash, and the key-value syntax we proposed previously *is* a hash, all we've got to do is place the arguments straight into our hash reference:

```perl
my $self = {@_};
```

Let's plug this into our package:

```perl
package Person3;
# Person3.pm

# Class for storing data about a person

use strict;

sub new {
    my $class = shift;
    my $self = {@_};
    bless $self, $class;
    return $self;
}

1;
```

What have we done? Since Perl magically passes in the class name as the first argument to the function, Perl sees something like this when we call the constructor:

```perl
@_ = (
    "Person3",
    "lastname",   "Galilei",
    "firstname",  "Galileo",
    "address",    "9.81 Pisa Apts.",
    "occupation", "bombardier"
);
```

The first line of the constructor grabs the class name as before.

```perl
my $class = shift;
```

Now what's left in the argument array @_ is

```perl
@_ = (
    "lastname",   "Galilei",
```

CHAPTER 12 ▓ OBJECT-ORIENTED PERL   271

```
    "firstname",  "Galileo",
    "address",    "9.81 Pisa Apts.",
    "occupation", "bombardier"
);
```

This is what we put verbatim into our hash reference:

```
my $self = {@_};
```

Our hash now contains all the attributes we provided. As usual, it's blessed and returned to the caller.

We now have a full-featured constructor. We've taken some initial data and constructed an object out of it, storing the data as attributes in the object. Now it's time to add some methods so we can actually do something with it!

Creating Methods

Our constructor was a class method; creating an object method will be very similar. In the same way that a class method magically gets passed the name of the class as the first argument, an object method is just a subroutine that magically gets passed the object as the first argument.

Let's create a method to return the last name of the person. This directly accesses an attribute—sometimes called an *accessor method*. Remember that the lastname attribute is just an entry in the hash, referenced by the object. So what does this involve? We'll need to

- Receive the object being passed to us.

- Extract the lastname entry from the hash.

- Pass it back to the caller.

Using the techniques we learned in Chapter 11 for directly accessing values in a hash reference, we can code the accessor and add it into our class creating the next iteration, Person4.

```
package Person4;
# Person4.pm

# Class for storing data about a person

use strict;

sub new {
    my $class = shift;
    my $self = {@_};
    bless $self, $class;
    return $self;
}
```

```perl
sub lastname {
   my $self = shift;
   return $self->{lastname};
}

1;
```

Now we can create an object with some attributes, and retrieve the attributes again.

```perl
#!/usr/bin/perl -w
# accessor1.pl

use strict;
use Person4;

my $object = Person4->new(
   lastname    => "Galilei",
   firstname   => "Galileo",
   address     => "9.81 Pisa Apts.",
   occupation  => "bombadier"
);

print "This person's last name: ", $object->lastname(), "\n";
```

If all is well, we should be told the last name.

```
$ perl accessor1.pl
This person's last name: Galilei
$
```

Our accessor method is a very simple one—it takes an object, and extracts an attribute from it. First, we use shift() to get the object passed to us.

```perl
my $self = shift;
```

Then we take out the relevant hash entry and pass it back.

```perl
return $self->{lastname};
```

Don't confuse the arrow used here for accessing parts of a reference with the arrow used as a method call. When accessing a reference, there will be either a curly brace or a square bracket at the end of the arrow.

```perl
$reference->{lastname}; # Accesses a hash reference
$reference->[3];        # Accesses an array reference
```

When calling a method, there will be a name following the arrow.

```perl
$reference->lastname();
```

So while our method is called with $object->lastname(), the last name entry in the hash is accessed with $self->{lastname}.

Get-Set Methods

As well as getting the value of an attribute, we may well want to set or change it. The syntax we'll use is as follows:

```
print "Old address: ", $object->address(), "\n";
$object->address("Campus Mirabilis, Pisa, Italy");
print "New address: ", $object->address(), "\n";
```

This kind of accessor is called a *get-set method* because we can use it to both get and set the attribute. Turning our current read-only accessors into accessors that can also set the value is simple. Let's create a get-set method for address():

```
sub address {
    my $self = shift;

    # Receive more data
    my $data = shift;

    # Set the address if there's any data there.
    $self->{address} = $data if defined $data;

    return $self->{address};
}
```

If we don't particularly want to trap calling the method as a class method (since it'll generate an error when we try to access the hash entry anyway), we can write really miniature get-set methods like this:

```
sub address   { $_[0]->{address } = $_[1] if defined $_[1]; $_[0]->{address  } }
sub lastname  { $_[0]->{lastname } = $_[1] if defined $_[1]; $_[0]->{lastname } }
sub firstname { $_[0]->{firstname} = $_[1] if defined $_[1]; $_[0]->{firstname} }
```

While that's fine for getting classes up and running quickly, writing out the get-set method in full as shown previously allows us to easily extend it in various ways, like testing the validity of the data, doing any notification we need to when the data changes, and so on.

Class Attributes

Classes can have attributes, too—instead of being entries in a hash, they're variables in a package. Just like object attributes, it's a really good idea to access them through get-set methods, but since they're ordinary variables, our methods are a lot simpler. Let's use a class attribute to keep score of how many times we've created a Person5 object (Person5 is our next step in creating our definition of a person). We'll call our attribute $Person5::Population, and we'll get the current value of it via the method headcount().

A class attribute is a package variable, and an accessor method just returns or sets the value of that variable. Here, we make our accessor method read-only to stop the end user changing it and confusing their own code:

```
package Person5;
# Person5.pm

# Class for storing data about a person

use strict;

my $Population = 0;

sub new {
   my $class = shift;
   my $self = {@_};
   bless $self, $class;
   $Population++;
   return $self;
}

# Object accessor methods
sub address   { $_[0]->{address  } = $_[1] if defined $_[1]; $_[0]->{address  } }
sub lastname  { $_[0]->{lastname } = $_[1] if defined $_[1]; $_[0]->{lastname } }
sub firstname { $_[0]->{firstname} = $_[1] if defined $_[1]; $_[0]->{firstname} }
sub phone_no  { $_[0]->{phone_no } = $_[1] if defined $_[1]; $_[0]->{phone_no } }
sub occupation {
   $_[0]->{occupation}=$_[1] if defined $_[1]; $_[0]->{occupation}
}

# Class accessor methods
sub headcount { return $Population; }

1;
```

Now as we create new objects, the population increases:

```
#!/usr/bin/perl -w
# classatr1.pl

use strict;
use Person5;

print "In the beginning: ", Person5->headcount(), "\n";
my $object = Person5->new(
   lastname   => "Galilei",
   firstname  => "Galileo",
```

```
    address    => "9.81 Pisa Apts.",
    occupation => "bombadier"
);
print "Population now: ", Person5->headcount(), "\n";

my $object2 = Person5->new(
    lastname   => "Einstein",
    firstname  => "Albert",
    address    => "9E16, Relativity Drive",
    occupation => "Plumber"
);
print "Population now: ", Person5->headcount(), "\n";
```

```
$ perl classatr1.pl
In the beginning: 0
Population now: 1
Population now: 2
$
```

There's actually nothing object-oriented-specific about this example. All we're doing is taking advantage of the way Perl's scoping works. A lexical variable can be seen and used by anything in the current scope and inside any curly braces. So, naturally enough, with

```
Package Person5;

my $Population;

sub headcount { return $Population; }
```

the package variable $Population is declared at the top of the package, and is therefore visible everywhere in the package. Even though we call headcount() from another package, it accesses a variable in its own package.

Similarly, when we increment its value as part of new(), we're accessing a variable in the same package. Since it's a package variable, it stays around for as long as the package does, which is why it doesn't lose its value when we do things in our main program.

Let's make one more addition and create the Person6 class: we'll allow our main program to process all of the names of people in our contacts database, and we'll have a class method to return to us an array of the objects created. Instead of keeping a separate variable for the population, we'll reimplement $Population in terms of the scalar value of that array.

```
package Person6;
# Person6.pm

# Class for storing data about a person

use strict;

my @Everyone;
```

```perl
sub new {
    my $class = shift;
    my $self = {@_};
    bless $self, $class ;
    push @Everyone, $self;
    return $self;
}

# Object accessor methods
sub address   { $_[0]->{address  } = $_[1] if defined $_[1]; $_[0]->{address  } }
sub lastname  { $_[0]->{lastname } = $_[1] if defined $_[1]; $_[0]->{lastname } }
sub firstname { $_[0]->{firstname} = $_[1] if defined $_[1]; $_[0]->{firstname} }
sub phone_no  { $_[0]->{phone_no } = $_[1] if defined $_[1]; $_[0]->{phone_no } }
sub occupation {
    $_[0]->{occupation}=$_[1] if defined $_[1]; $_[0]->{occupation}
}

# Class accessor methods
sub headcount { return scalar @Everyone; }
sub everyone  { return @Everyone;        }

1;
```

Note that we're pushing one reference to the data onto the array, and we return another reference. There are now two references to the same data, rather than two copies of the data. This becomes important when it comes to destruction. Anyway, this time we can construct our objects and loop through them.

```perl
#!/usr/bin/perl -w
# classatr2.pl

use strict;
use Person6;

print "In the beginning: ", Person6->headcount(), "\n";
my $object = Person6->new(
    lastname    => "Galilei",
    firstname   => "Galileo",
    address     => "9.81 Pisa Apts.",
    occupation  => "bombadier"
);
print "Population now: ", Person6->headcount(), "\n";

my $object2 = Person6->new(
    lastname    => "Einstein",
    firstname   => "Albert",
```

```
    address     => "9E16, Relativity Drive",
    occupation  => "Plumber"
);
print "Population now: ", Person6->headcount(), "\n";

print "\nPeople we know:\n";
foreach my $person(Person6->everyone()) {
    print $person->firstname(), " ", $person->lastname(), "\n";
}
```

```
$ perl classatr2.pl
In the beginning: 0
Population now: 1
Population now: 2

People we know:
Galileo Galilei
Albert Einstein
$
```

Normally, you won't want to do something like this. It's not the class's business to know what's being done with the objects it creates. Since we know that in these examples we'll be putting all the Person6 objects into a database, it's reasonable to get the whole database with a single method. However, this isn't a general solution—people may not use the objects they create, or may use them in multiple databases, or in other ways you haven't thought of. Let the user keep copies of the object themselves.

Privatizing Your Methods

The things we did with our class attributes in new( ) in the two preceding examples were a bit naughty. We directly accessed the class variables, instead of going through an accessor method. If another class wants to inherit from this class, it has to make sure it too carries a package variable of the same name in the same way.

What we usually do in these situations is to put all the class-specific parts into a separate method, and use that method internally in the class. Inheriting classes can then replace these *private methods* with their own implementations. To mark a method as private, for use only inside the class, it's customary to begin the method's name with an underscore. Perl doesn't treat these methods any differently—the underscore means nothing significant to Perl but is purely for human consumption. Think of it as a "keep out" sign to mark the method as for use by authorized personnel only!

Typically, the constructor is one place where we'll want to do a private setup, so let's convert the code for adding to the @Everyone array into a private method in the class Person7:

```
package Person7;
# Person7.pm

# Class for storing data about a person
```

```perl
use strict;

my @Everyone;

# Constructor and initialization
sub new {
    my $class = shift;
    my $self = {@_};
    bless $self, $class;
    $self->_init();
    return $self;
}

sub _init {
    my $self = shift;
    push @Everyone, $self;
}

# Object accessor methods
sub address   { $_[0]->{address  } = $_[1] if defined $_[1]; $_[0]->{address  } }
sub lastname  { $_[0]->{lastname } = $_[1] if defined $_[1]; $_[0]->{lastname } }
sub firstname { $_[0]->{firstname} = $_[1] if defined $_[1]; $_[0]->{firstname} }
sub phone_no  { $_[0]->{phone_no } = $_[1] if defined $_[1]; $_[0]->{phone_no } }
sub occupation {
    $_[0]->{occupation}=$_[1] if defined $_[1]; $_[0]->{occupation}
}

# Class accessor methods
sub headcount { return scalar @Everyone; }
sub everyone  { return @Everyone;        }

1;
```

What we have now is pretty much the standard constructor. Let's go over it again:

```perl
sub new {
```

First, we retrieve our class name, which will be passed to us automatically when we do `Class->new()`, by using `shift` as a shorthand for `shift @_`.

```perl
my $class = shift;
```

Then we put the rest of the arguments, which should be a hash with which to initialize the attributes, into a new hash reference.

```perl
my $self = {@_};
```

Now we `bless()` the reference to tell it which class it belongs to, making it an object.

```perl
bless $self, $class;
```

Do any further initialization we need to do by calling the object's private _init() method. Note that due to inheritance, this private method may be provided by a subclass.

```
$self->_init();
```

Finally, return the constructed object.

```
    return $self;
}
```

Utility Methods

Our methods have mainly been accessors so far, but that's by no means all we can do with objects. Since methods are essentially subroutines, we can do almost anything we want inside them. Let's now add some methods that do things—*utility methods*:

```perl
package Person8;
# Person8.pm

# Class for storing data about a person

use strict;

my @Everyone;

# Constructor and initialization
#...

# Object accessor methods
#...

# Class accessor methods
#...

# Utility methods
sub fullname {
    my $self = shift;
    return $self->firstname() . " " . $self->lastname();
}

sub printletter {
    my $self      = shift;
    my $name      = $self->fullname();
    my $address   = $self->address();
    my $firstname = $self->firstname();
    my $body      = shift;
    my @date      = (localtime)[3,4,5];
    $date[1]++;       # Months start at 0! Add one to humanize!
```

```perl
    $date[2]+=1900;   # Add 1900 to get current year.
    my $date    = join "/", @date;

    print <<EOF;
$name
$address

$date

Dear $firstname,

$body

Yours faithfully,
EOF
    return $self;
}

1;
```

This adds two methods, fullname() and printletter(). fullname() returns the full name of the person the object describes. printletter() prints out a letter with a body supplied by the user. Notice that to print the name in the text of the letter, printletter() itself calls fullname(). It's good practice for utility methods to return the object if they have nothing else to return. This allows you to string together calls by using the returned object as the object for the next method call, like this: $object->one()->two()->three();.

Here's an example of those utility methods in use:

```perl
#!/usr/bin/perl -w
# utility1.pl

use strict;
use Person8;

my $object = Person8->new(
    lastname    => "Galilei",
    firstname   => "Galileo",
    address     => "9.81 Pisa Apts.",
    occupation  => "bombadier"
);
$object->printletter("You owe me money. Please pay it.");
```

This produces our friendly demand:

```
$ perl utility1.pl
Galileo Galilei
9.81 Pisa Apts.
```

4/5/2004

Dear Galileo,

You owe me money. Please pay it.

Yours faithfully,
$

Death of an Object

We've seen how we construct an object, and we've made ourselves a constructor method that returns a blessed reference. What happens at the end of the story, when an object needs to be destructed? Object destruction happens in two possible cases, either implicitly or explicitly:

- Explicit destruction happens when no reference to the object remains. Just like when dealing with ordinary references, you may have more than one reference to the data in existence. As we saw in Chapter 11, some of these references may be lexical variables, which go out of scope. As they do, the reference count of the data is decreased. Once it falls to zero, the data is removed from the system.

- Implicit destruction happens at the end of your program. At that point, all the data in your program is released.

When Perl needs to release data and destroy an object, whether implicitly or explicitly, it calls the method DESTROY() on the object. Unlike other utility methods, this doesn't mean Perl is telling you what to do. Perl will destroy the data for you, but this is your chance to clean up anything else you have used, close any files you opened, shut down any network sockets, and so on. (Larry Wall joked that it should have been called something like YOU_ARE_ABOUT_TO_BE_SHOT_DO_YOU_HAVE_ANY_LAST_REQUESTS() instead.)

If Perl doesn't find a method called DESTROY(), it won't complain but will silently release the object's data.

Our Finished Class

Let's put all the pieces of our class together and examine the class all the way through:

```
package Person8;
```

First of all, let's reiterate that a class is nothing more than a package. We start off our class by starting a new package. As usual, we want to make sure this package is at least as pedantic as the one that called it, so we turn on strictness:

```
# Class for storing data about a person

use strict;
```

Next we declare our class attributes. These are ordinary package variables.

```
# Class attributes
my @Everyone;
```

We provide a nice and general constructor, which calls a private method to do its private initialization. We take the class name, create a reference, and bless() it:

```
# Constructor and initialization
sub new {
    my $class = shift;
    my $self = {@_};
    bless $self, $class;
    $self->_init();
    return $self;
}
```

Our private method just adds a copy of the current object to a general pool. In more elaborate classes, we'd want to check that the user's input makes sense and get it into the format we want, open any external files we need, and so on.

```
sub _init {
    my $self = shift;
    push @Everyone, $self;
}
```

Next we provide very simple object accessor methods to allow us to get at the keys of the hash reference where our data is stored. These are the only interfaces we provide to the data inside the object, and everything goes through them:

```
# Object accessor methods
sub address   { $_[0]->{address  } = $_[1] if defined $_[1]; $_[0]->{address  } }
sub lastname  { $_[0]->{lastname } = $_[1] if defined $_[1]; $_[0]->{lastname } }
sub firstname { $_[0]->{firstname} = $_[1] if defined $_[1]; $_[0]->{firstname} }
sub phone_no  { $_[0]->{phone_no } = $_[1] if defined $_[1]; $_[0]->{phone_no } }
sub occupation {
    $_[0]->{occupation}=$_[1] if defined $_[1]; $_[0]->{occupation}
}
```

Accessing class attributes is even easier, since these are simple variables.

```
# Class accessor methods
sub headcount { return scalar @Everyone; }
sub everyone  { return @Everyone;         }
```

Finally, we have a couple of utility methods, which perform actions on the data in the object. The fullname() method uses accessors to get at the first name and last name stored in the object, and returns a string with them separated by a space.

```
# Utility methods
sub fullname {
   my $self = shift;
   return $self->firstname() . " " . $self->lastname();
}
```

Second, `printletter()` is a slightly more elaborate method that prints out a letter to the referenced person. It uses the address and first name accessors plus the `fullname()` method to get the object's details. Notice that in both methods we're using `my $self = shift` to grab the object as it was passed to us.

```
sub printletter {
   my $self      = shift;
   my $name      = $self->fullname();
   my $address   = $self->address();
   my $firstname = $self->firstname();
   my $body      = shift;
   my @date      = (localtime)[3,4,5];
   $date[1]++;       # Months start at 0! Add one to humanize!
   $date[2]+=1900;   # Add 1900 to get current year.
   my $date      = join "/", @date;

   print <<EOF;
$name
$address

$date

Dear $firstname,

$body

Yours faithfully,
EOF
}

1;
```

Do You Need OO?

Now that we have discussed the basics of OO in Perl, how do you decide whether or not you should be using a procedural or an OO style in your programs? Here are five guidelines to help you decide.

Are Your Subroutines Tasks?

If your program naturally involves a series of unconnected tasks, you probably want to be using a procedural style. If your application is *data-driven*, then you're dealing primarily with data structures rather than tasks, so consider using an OO style instead.

Do You Need Persistence?

After your task is completed, do you need somewhere to store data that you want to receive next time you process that data? If so, you may find it easier to use an OO interface. If each call to a subroutine is completely independent of the others, you can use a procedural interface.

For instance, if you're producing a cross-reference table, your cross-reference subroutine will need to know whether or not the thing it's processing has turned up before or not. Since an object packages up everything we know about a piece of data, it's easy to deal with that directly.

Do You Need Sessions?

Do you want to process several different chunks of data with the same subroutines? For instance, if you have two different "sessions" that signify database connections or network connections, you may find it easier to package up each session into an object.

Do You Need Speed?

Object-oriented programs generally run slower than equally well-written procedural programs that do the same job, because packaging things into objects and passing objects around is expensive both in terms of time spent and resources used. If you can get away with not using object orientation, you probably should.

Do You Want the User to Be Unaware of the Object?

If you want to hide the details of how a thing behaves, OO is a good approach. You can design the object to store the data in any way that you choose, then provide the user with an easy-to-use interface. The user can then use the object without having to know how the information about the object is implemented.

Are You Still Unsure?

Unless you know you need an OO model, it's probably better to use a procedural model to help maintenance and readability. If you're still unsure, go with an ordinary procedural model.

Summary

Object-oriented programming is another way of thinking about programming. You approach it in terms of data and the relationships between pieces of data, which we call *objects*. These objects belong to divisions called *classes*—these have properties (*attributes*) and can perform actions (*methods*).

Perl makes object-oriented programming neat and simple:

- An *object* is a reference that has been blessed into a class.

- A *class* is an ordinary Perl package.

- A *method* is an ordinary Perl subroutine that has the class name or object reference magically passed in.

From these three basic principles, we can start to build data-driven applications.

Exercises

1. Using Person8.pm, write a program to do the following:

    - Create three different Person8 objects.

    - Print the number of Person8 objects.

    - Loop through the Person8 objects and print a letter to each one.

CHAPTER 13

■ ■ ■

Modules

In Chapter 12 we discussed Perl's object-oriented programming features. In describing Perl's OO capabilities, we created packages and placed those packages into .pm files, then used the packages in our programs. These packages are also known as *modules*.

Very simply, a module is a package within a file—a collection of subroutines (methods) and variables that all work together to perform some set of tasks that we can use to solve our programming problems.

There exists a large collection of prewritten Perl modules—we programmers can use these modules, free of charge, to solve our problems. The modules are available at CPAN, the Comprehensive Perl Archive Network (www.cpan.org and mirrors all over the world). There are modules available at CPAN that are easy-to-use solutions to many different problems—for example, modules to simplify network programming, process XML files, create web programs (CGI and others), connect to SQL databases, and do complex mathematics. This list could go on and on, but we suggest you visit http://search.cpan.org/, which offers both browsing and searching of the CPAN.

In this chapter we will be looking at several of these very useful modules. This discussion is only meant to be a sample of what is available at CPAN; we suggest that you point your browser at CPAN and start installing and using modules—they will almost certainly make your programming life easier.

We will also show how to create a module. You may be wondering, didn't we do that in Chapter 12? In that chapter we created OO modules—in this chapter we will create a module that is not OO in nature, but rather is a collection of useful subroutines that can be used within any Perl program that uses the module.

Why Do We Need Them?

Why should you use modules? The simple answer is that it saves time—if you need that program written yesterday, it's exceptionally handy to be able to download a bunch of modules that you know will do the job, and then simply glue them together.

The second answer is because most of us programmers are lazy—that's just a fact of life. Programmers are, on the whole, naturally lazy people and don't like reinventing the wheel. Now, don't get us wrong—there's good laziness and there's bad laziness. Bad laziness says "I should get someone else to do this for me," whereas good laziness says "Maybe someone's already done this." The good kind pays off. Most of the programming you'll be doing will, at some level, have been done before.

Modules that have been around on CPAN for a while will have been used by thousands of individuals, many of whom will have spent time fixing bugs and returning the results to the maintainer. Most of the borderline cases will have been worked out by now, and you can be pretty confident that the modules will do things right. When it comes to things like parsing HTML or processing CGI form data, we're perfectly willing to admit that the people who wrote HTML::Parser and the CGI modules have done more work on the subject than we have—so we use their code, instead of trying to work out our own.

In short: don't reinvent the wheel—use modules.

Package Hierarchies

We've already seen how packages can help us break up a namespace: $Fred::name isn't the same variable as $Barney::name. When modules come into play, packages are used to identify the module. Now our variables have a nice namespace, but our modules have to identify themselves by a single word. With several thousand modules out there, it gets hard to find the one we want. So the librarians at CPAN have come up with a solution: we split up the module package names into hierarchies. Instead of having dozens of modules about sorting, we now have Sort::Fields, Sort::Versions, and so on.

Note This hierarchy is only a naming scheme. It doesn't mean that Sort::Fields and Sort::Versions are somehow related to a bigger package called Sort—it's simply a way of making it easier to categorize modules.

So how do we store these in files? Some operating systems won't let us have colons inside filenames, so Sort::Versions.pm won't be legal. However, since these names represent a consistent hierarchy, there's a natural way we can organize them on the disk: as mentioned in Chapter 12, require and use translate colons into directory separators, so Sort::Versions will actually be stored in a file called Versions.pm in a directory called Sort somewhere off one of the site paths in @INC.

Exporters

Since modules are usually packages stored in a file, a subroutine in the Text::Wrap module, for example, would normally be tucked away in the Text::Wrap package. However, let's say it would be more convenient for us to have this as a subroutine in the package we're currently in—usually the main package. To do this, Perl uses a module called Exporter, which provides it with a way of importing subroutines from the module into the caller's package. Here's how it works.

When you use a module, as well as reading and executing the code, Perl will try and run a subroutine called import inside the module's package. If that's not found, nothing happens, and there's no error. If it is found, though, it's called with all the parameters given on the use line. So, for instance:

```
use Wibble ("wobble", "bounce", "boing");
```

loads the Wibble module and then runs the following:

```
Wibble::import("wobble", "bounce", "boing");
```

Note Theoretically, this import() subroutine could do anything. In fact, a few modules use it to let you pass parameters to set up the module. However, you'll usually want to use it to import subroutines and variables.

Exporter lets the modules that use it borrow a standard import() subroutine. This subroutine checks a number of variables inside the module as well as the parameters that we give it. If we give an empty list, like this:

```
use Wibble ();
```

then nothing will be imported. If there's a particular subroutine we want to use—wobble() for example—then we could call it as Wibble::wobble(), and we'll get it imported into our current package. We can only import subroutines that the module is prepared to export, and it'll detail those in a package variable called @EXPORT_OK. So if, for instance, we wanted to make a Wibble module from which we could import wobble(), bounce(), and boing(), we'd say this:

```
package Wibble;

use strict;

use Exporter;
our @ISA = qw(Exporter);
our @EXPORT_OK = qw(wobble bounce boing);

sub wobble { print "wobble\n" }
sub bounce { warn  "bounce\n" }
sub boing  { die   "boing!\n" }

1;
```

Recall from Chapter 12 that all files that we use must end with a true value, normally 1;.

If we don't pass any parameters at all, we get the default subroutines, which are defined in @EXPORT. So if our module looked like this:

```
package Wibble;

use strict;

use Exporter;
our @ISA = qw(Exporter);
our @EXPORT_OK = qw(wobble bounce boing);
our @EXPORT      = qw(bounce);

sub wobble { print "wobble\n" }
sub bounce { warn  "bounce\n" }
sub boing  { die   "boing!\n" }

1;
```

and we ran use Wibble; in our main program, we'd be able to call bounce() from the main program, but not wobble() or boing()—we would have to call these as Wibble::wobble() and Wibble::boing().

We can also define tags with the %EXPORT_TAGS hash. This allows us to group together a bunch of subroutines or variables under a group name. For instance, the CGI module (which we'll be using in Chapter 14) allows us to say

```
use CGI qw(:standard);
```

which will import all its most useful subroutines.

Online Documentation

The perldoc program is a simple way to view the online documentation for a module. Simply provide the module name as its argument:

```
$ perldoc Data::Dumper
```

You can also check out www.perldoc.com and www.cpan.org for module documentation.

Creating a Non-OO Module

Creating a module is a good thing. It allows you to reuse useful functions across multiple programs by simply using them. Now we will look at creating a module in a different way than we did in Chapter 12—we will create a module that is not object oriented in nature, but rather a collection of useful functions.

Let's say we are working on a team that is developing software for the Acme webserver.[1] We have been assigned the role of developing an easy-to-use logging interface. It will utilize

---

1. This is probably not a good idea, since there is already a really good webserver available for free—www.apache.org.

the idea of *log levels*, or logging at varying degrees of detail. Level 1 is the least detail, and higher values indicate more details.

We want to make our module easy to use and functional. What we need the module to do is to open and close the log file, write into the log file, and set the log level (which has the default value of 1, or the least level of detail).

First we need to create a name for our logging interface. Since we work for the Acme company and are creating a logging system for a webserver, let's call the module Acme::Webserver::Logger. Recall that this name means that somewhere under @INC will be a directory named Acme, and under that directory will be a directory named Webserver, and in that directory is the file Logger.pm. To declare its name, we say this at the top of the file:

```
package Acme::Webserver::Logger;
```

We want to provide the user a function to open the file. A good name for the function is open_log(), since it is opening the log file, and it might look like this:

```
sub open_log {
    my $filename = shift;
    open(LOGFILE, '>>', $filename) or die "can't open $filename: $!";
    print LOGFILE "Log started: ", scalar(localtime), "\n";
}
```

This function grabs the first argument, which is the filename to open. Then, the log file is opened in append mode and a message is printed to the log file stating that the logging has begun. We also need a function to close the log file:

```
sub close_log {
    close LOGFILE;
}
```

Next, we need a function to write into the log file:

```
sub write_log {
    my($level, $message) = @_;
    print LOGFILE "$message\n" if $level <= $LEVEL;
}
```

This function is expecting two arguments: the log message level and the message. The message is then printed if the level of the message is less than or equal to the level that is set for this logger.

Finally, we need a way to set the log level in case we want more (or less) detail. Here it is:

```
sub log_level {
    my $level = shift;
    $LEVEL = $level if $level =~ /^\d+$/;
}
```

The argument is assigned to $LEVEL if the argument is a positive integer.

> **Note** A note about these functions: we should probably add a lot more error checking to these functions to make them a bit harder to break. For instance, what if write_log() was called with no log level and message? The function would work (printing an empty string to the log file since it would treat the level as 0, less than our minimum level, and the message would be undef), but it would be polite to instead report to the user that they are using the function incorrectly. Also, any real logging module would lock the file with flock(). But if error checking and file locking were added to this example, it would be way too long and complicated for our purpose here.

Here is the whole module, including the initial value assigned to $LEVEL:

```
package Acme::Webserver::Logger;
# Acme/Webserver/Logger.pm

# always a good idea to turn these on
# use warnings is needed because there is
# no -w in modules
use strict;
use warnings;

my $LEVEL = 1;  # default level is 1

sub open_log {
    my $filename = shift;
    open(LOGFILE, '>>', $filename) or die "can't open $filename: $!";
    print LOGFILE "Log started: ", scalar(localtime), "\n";
}

sub close_log {
    close LOGFILE;
}

sub write_log {
    my($level, $message) = @_;
    print LOGFILE "$message\n" if $level <= $LEVEL;
}

sub log_level {
    my $level = shift;
    $LEVEL = $level if $level =~ /^\d+$/;
}

1;
```

Here is a program that uses the module. Notice how the functions are invoked with the package name preceding the function names.

```perl
#!/usr/bin/perl -w
# logtest1.pl

use strict;
use Acme::Webserver::Logger;

Acme::Webserver::Logger::open_log("webserver.log");

# this will go to the log file
Acme::Webserver::Logger::write_log(1, "A basic message");

# this won't - the level is too high
Acme::Webserver::Logger::write_log(10, "A debugging message");

# set the level so the debugging message will end up
# in the log file
Acme::Webserver::Logger::log_level(10);
Acme::Webserver::Logger::write_log(10, "Another debugging message");

Acme::Webserver::Logger::close_log();
```

When executed, this program creates and adds text to the log file webserver.log.

$ **perl logtest1.pl**

Here is the content of the log file:

```
Log started: Fri Jul  2 11:42:12 2004
A basic message
Another debugging message
```

The syntax for calling the functions in the module is way too long! We can shorten these lines by exporting the function names in the module. We discussed how to do this previously in this chapter—by becoming an Exporter. So let's modify the module a bit to look like this:

```perl
package Acme::Webserver::Logger;
# Acme/Webserver/Logger.pm

# always a good idea to turn these on
# use warnings is needed because there is
# no -w in modules
use strict;
use warnings;

# become an exporter and export the functions
use Exporter;
our @ISA = qw(Exporter);
our @EXPORT = qw(open_log close_log write_log log_level);
```

```perl
my $LEVEL = 1;  # default level is 1

sub open_log {
    my $filename = shift;
    open(LOGFILE, '>>', $filename) or die "can't open $filename: $!";
    print LOGFILE "Log started: ", scalar(localtime), "\n";
}

sub close_log {
    close LOGFILE;
}

sub write_log {
    my($level, $message) = @_;
    print LOGFILE "$message\n" if $level <= $LEVEL;
}

sub log_level {
    my $level = shift;
    $LEVEL = $level if $level =~ /^\d+$/;
}

1;
```

Now we can modify the program that calls these functions to be

```perl
#!/usr/bin/perl -w
# logtest2.pl

use strict;
use Acme::Webserver::Logger;

open_log("webserver.log");

# this will go to the log file
write_log(1, "A basic message");

# this won't - the level is too high
write_log(10, "A debugging message");

# set the level so the debugging message will end up
# in the log file
log_level(10);
write_log(10, "Another debugging message");

close_log();
```

Ah, much better! Executing this program will add to the log file:

```
$ perl logtest2.pl
```

so that its content is

```
Log started: Fri Jul  2 11:42:12 2004
A basic message
Another debugging message
Log started: Fri Jul  2 11:50:41 2004
A basic message
Another debugging message
```

The Perl Standard Modules

Not only can we create our own modules, we can also use modules that others have created and made available to us at CPAN (more on using CPAN later in this chapter). When Perl is installed, there are many modules automatically installed. These are called the *standard modules*. We will look at a few of the more interesting ones here. For a complete list of all the modules in the Perl distribution, execute `perldoc perlmodlib` at a shell prompt.

Data::Dumper

`Data::Dumper` stringifies data types in Perl syntax so a programmer can see a visual representation of the data structure. Here is a simple example:

```perl
#!/usr/bin/perl -w
# data1.pl

use strict;
use Data::Dumper qw(Dumper);  # import the Dumper() function

# create a complex data type

my @a = (
    'hello, world',
    1234.56,
    [ 2, 4, 6 ],
    { one => 'first', two => 'second' }
);

# create a reference to it

my $r = \@a;

# dump it out
print Dumper($r);
```

This program first uses Data::Dumper, importing the Dumper() function. It then creates a complex data type: an array that contains a string, a float, an anonymous array, and an anonymous hash. Then, a reference to the array is created. Finally, that reference is dumped out. This code produces

```
$ perl data1.pl
$VAR1 = [
          'hello, world',
          '1234.56',
          [
            2,
            4,
            6
          ],
          {
            'one' => 'first',
            'two' => 'second'
          }
        ];
```

This displays the complex data type so we programmers can read it and understand it. It appears that $VAR1 (a name chosen for us by Data::Dumper) is a reference to an array that contains a string, a float, an anonymous array, and an anonymous hash. Being able to view this output can assist in debugging our program.[2]

Data::Dumper chooses the variable name $VAR1 for us. Perhaps we want to name the variable ourselves. A small change to data1.pl will do the trick:

```
#!/usr/bin/perl -w
# data2.pl

use strict;
use Data::Dumper;

# create a complex data type

my @a = (
    'hello, world',
    1234.56,
    [ 2, 4, 6 ],
    { one => 'first', two => 'second' }
);
```

_____

2. This output can also be stored for later use. If we store this output into a scalar variable, we can eval() that variable, which will reconstruct the data structure (for information on eval(), check out perldoc -f eval).

```
# create a reference to it

my $r = \@a;

# dump it out
print Data::Dumper->Dump([$r], ['myvarname']);
```

This code produces the following:

```
$ perl data2.pl
$myvarname = [
                'hello, world',
                '1234.56',
                [
                  2,
                  4,
                  6
                ],
                {
                  'one' => 'first',
                  'two' => 'second'
                }
              ];
```

File::Find

File::Find is a module for traversing directory trees, visiting each file in turn and running a subroutine (the callback) on them. This module has a very useful method: find(). It does a depth-first search, visiting directories only after their files have been processed. This is useful if, for example, you want to delete entire directory trees, since you're not usually permitted to delete a directory until you've deleted all the files in it.

We call the subroutine with two parameters: the callback subroutine reference, and the directory (or a list of directories) from which to start:

```
find(\&wanted, "/home/simon/");
```

The subroutine wanted() is executed for every file that it finds in the directory. For each of the files, the following is true:

- You are moved into the same directory as the file under consideration.

- The current directory, relative to the top of the tree, is held in $File::Find::dir.

- $_ contains the name of the current file.

- $File::Find::name is the name including the directory.

With that, we can do anything we want to do. Here is a program to delete useless files:

```perl
#!/usr/bin/perl -w
# hoover.pl

use strict;
use File::Find;

find(\&cleanup, "/");

sub cleanup {
    # Not been accessed in six months?
    if (-A > 180) {
        print "Deleting old file $_\n";
        unlink $_ or print "oops, couldn't delete $_: $!\n";
        return;
    }
    open (FH, $_) or die "Couldn't open $_: $!\n";
    foreach (1..5) { # You've got five chances.
        my $line = <FH>;
        if ($line =~ /Perl|Camel|important/i) {
            # Spare it.
            return;
        }
    }
    print "Deleting unimportant file $_\n";
    unlink $_ or print "oops, couldn't delete $_: $!\n";
}
```

This code assumes, of course, that any file that contains "Perl," "Camel," or "important" in the first five lines is, well, important. You can alter this so it doesn't look for the words "Perl," "Camel," or "important" in the first five lines and indeed so it doesn't look through and delete files from your entire directory structure.

Getopt::Std

The Getopt::Long and Getopt::Std modules provide a flexible way to use command line arguments in our programs. Getopt::Std is the simpler of the two, providing us with a way to get single-letter switches with values and support for clustered flags (-a -l written as -al)—we can also arrange to have the flags placed in a hash. For instance, to provide our wonderful "Hello World" program (from Chapter 1) with help, a version identifier, and internationalization, we could do this:

```perl
#!/usr/bin/perl -w
# hello3.pl
# Hello World (Deluxe)
```

```perl
use strict;
use Getopt::Std;

my %options;
getopts("vhl:", \%options);

if ($options{v}) {
    print "Hello World, version 3.\n";
    exit;
} elsif ($options{h}) {
    print <<EOF;

$0: Typical Hello World program

Syntax: $0 [-h|-v|-l <language>]

    -h : This help message
    -v : Print version on standard output and exit
    -l : Turn on international language support.
EOF
    exit;
} elsif ($options{l}) {
    if ($options{l} eq "french") {
        print "Bonjour, tout le monde.\n";
    } else {
        die "$0: unsupported language\n";
    }
} else {
    print "Hello, world.\n";
}
```

getopts() takes the following as its arguments: a specification (the letters for which we provide options) and a hash reference. If we follow a letter with a colon, we expect that a value will be stored in the hash. If we don't use a colon, then the hash value stored is just true or false depending on whether or not the option was given. We can now get output like this:

```
$ perl hello3.pl -l french
Bonjour, tout le monde.
$
```

Getopt::Std also produces a warning if it sees options it's not prepared for:

```
$ perl hello3.pl -f
Unknown option: f
Hello, world.
$
```

Getopt::Long

The Free Software Foundation, when they were developing the GNU project, decided
that single-letter flags weren't friendly enough, so they invented "long" flags. These use
a double minus sign followed by a word. To give a value for the option, you'd say something like --language=french.

The module Getopt::Long handles this style of option. Its documentation is extremely
informative (perldoc Getopt::Long), but it's still useful to see an example. Let's convert the
preceding program to GNU options:

```perl
#!/usr/bin/perl -w
# hellolong.pl
# Hello World (Deluxe) - with long flags

use strict;
use Getopt::Long;

my %options;
GetOptions(\%options, "language:s", "help", "version");

if ($options{version}) {
    print "Hello World, version 3.\n";
    exit;
} elsif ($options{help}) {
    print <<EOF;

$0: Typical Hello World program

Syntax: $0 [--help|--version|--language=<language>]

    --help    : This help message
    --version : Print version on standard output and exit
    --language : Turn on international language support.
EOF
    exit;
} elsif ($options{language}) {
    if ($options{language} eq "french") {
        print "Bonjour, tout le monde.\n";
    } else {
        die "$0: unsupported language\n";
    }
} else {
    print "Hello, world.\n";
}
```

We can still use the previous syntax, but now we can also say

```
$ perl hellolong.pl --language=french
Bonjour, tout le monde.
$
```

File::Spec

If we want to write really portable programs in Perl, we have to be careful when doing things like dealing with filenames. File::Spec is a module for handling, constructing, and breaking apart filenames.

Normally it has an object-oriented interface, but it's much easier to use the subroutine interface, File::Spec::Functions. Here are some of the subroutines it provides:

Function and Syntax	Description
canonpath(*$path*)	Cleans up *$path* to its simplest form
catdir(*$directory1, $directory2*)	Concatenates the two directories together to form a new path to a directory, ensuring an appropriate separator in the middle, and removing the separator from the end
catfile(*$directory, $file*)	Like catdir(), but the path will end with a filename
tmpdir()	Finds a writable directory for temporary files (See the File::Temp module before working with temporary files!)
splitpath(*$path*)	Splits up a path into volume (drive on Windows, nothing on Unix), directories, and filename
splitdir(*$path*)	Splits a path into its constituent directories: the opposite of catdir()
path()	Returns the search path for executable files

Here is an example of locating a copy of the sort program:

```perl
#!/usr/bin/perl -w
# whereisit.pl

use strict;
use File::Spec::Functions;

foreach my $path (path()) {
    my $test = catfile($path, "sort");
    if (-e $test) {
        print "Yes, sort is in the $_ directory.\n";
        exit;
    }
}
print "sort was not found here.\n";
```

Executing this code might produce the following:

```
$ perl whereisit.pl
Yes, sort is in the /usr/bin directory.
$
```

Note To read all the documentation for File::Spec, be sure to check out File::Spec::Unix or File::Spec:Win32, depending on your operating system.

Benchmark

There's More Than One Way To Do It—that's our motto (TMTOWTDI). However, some ways are always going to be faster than others. How can you tell? You could analyze each of the statements for efficiency, or you could simply roll up your sleeves and try it out.

Our next module is for testing and timing code. Benchmark provides two methods: timethis() and timethese(). The first of these, timethis(), is quite easy to use:

```
#!/usr/bin/perl -w
# benchtest1.pl

use strict;
use Benchmark;

my $howmany = 10000;
my $what    = q/my $j=1; foreach (1..100) {$j *= $_}/;

timethis($howmany, $what);
```

This program provides timethis() some code and a number of times to run it. Make sure the code is in single quotes so that Perl doesn't attempt to interpolate it. You should, after a little while, see some output. This will, of course, vary depending on the speed of your CPU and how busy your computer is, but here is an example:

```
$ perl benchtest1.pl
timethis 10000:  3 wallclock secs ( 2.58 usr +  0.00 sys =  2.58 CPU) @
3871.47/s (n=10000)
$
```

This tells us we ran something 10,000 times, and it took 3 seconds of real time. These seconds were 2.58 spent in calculating ("usr" time) and 0 seconds interacting with the disk (or other noncalculating time). It also tells us that we ran through 3871.47 iterations of the test code each second.

To test several things and compare them, we can use timethese(). This method takes as its second argument an anonymous hash. The values of the hash are strings (single quoted again) that will be executed $howmany number of times.

To check the fastest way to read a file from the disk, we could do this:

```
#!/usr/bin/perl -w
# benchtest2.pl

use strict;
use Benchmark;

my $howmany = 100;

timethese($howmany, {
    line => q{
        my $file;
        open TEST, "words" or die $!;
        while (<TEST>) { $file .= $_ }
        close TEST;
    },
    slurp => q{
        my $file;
        local undef $/;
        open TEST, "words" or die $!;
        $file = <TEST>;
        close TEST;
    },
    join => q{
        my $file;
        open TEST, "words" or die $!;
        $file = join "", <TEST>;
        close TEST;
    }
});
```

One way reads the file in a line at a time, one slurps the whole file in at once, and one joins the lines together. As you might expect, the slurp method is considerably faster:

```
$ perl benchtest2.pl
Benchmark: timing 100 iterations of join, line, slurp...
    join: 42 wallclock secs (35.64 usr +  3.78 sys = 39.43 CPU) @  2.54/s (n=100)
    line: 37 wallclock secs (29.77 usr +  3.17 sys = 32.94 CPU) @  3.04/s (n=100)
    slurp:  6 wallclock secs ( 2.87 usr +  2.65 sys =  5.53 CPU) @ 18.09/s (n=100)
$
```

Also bear in mind that each benchmark will not only time differently between each machine and the next, but often between times you run the test—so *don't* base your life around benchmark tests. If a pretty way to do it is a thousandth of a second slower than an ugly way to do it, choose the pretty one.

Win32

Those familiar with Windows' labyrinthine Win32 APIs will probably want to examine the libwin32 modules. These all live in the Win32:: hierarchy and come as standard with Active-State Perl. If you've compiled another Perl yourself on Windows, you can get a copy of the modules from CPAN—we'll see how later in this chapter.

These modules, which give you access to such things as Semaphores, Services, OLE, the Clipboard, and a whole bunch of other things besides, will probably be of most interest to existing Windows programmers. For the rest of us though, there are two modules that will be of particular use:

Win32::Sound

The first, Win32::Sound, lets us play with the sound subsystem—we can play .wav files, set the speaker volume, and so on. We can also use it to play the standard system sounds.

The following program will play all the .wav files in the current directory:

```
#!/usr/bin/perl -w
# wavplay.pl

use strict;
use Win32::Sound;

Win32::Sound::Volume(65535);
while (<*.wav>) {
   Win32::Sound::Play($_);
}
```

You won't see any output, but if you're in a directory containing .wav files, you should certainly be able to hear some!

The Win32::Sound module provides us with a number of subroutines.

Function	Description
Win32::Sound::Volume($left, $right)	Sets the left and right speaker volumes to the requested amount. If only $left is given, both speakers are set to that volume. If neither is given, the current volume is returned. You can give the volume either as a percentage or a number from 0 to 65535.
Win32::Sound::Play($name)	Plays the named sound file, or the named system sound (for example, SystemStart).
Win32::Sound::Format($filename)	Returns information about the format of the given sound file.
Win32::Sound::Devices()	Lists all the available sound-related devices on the system.
Win32::Sound::DeviceInfo($device)	Provides information on the given sound device.

You can get a full list of the subroutines from the Win32::Sound documentation page if you have the module installed (perldoc Win32::Sound).

Win32::TieRegistry

Windows uses a centralized system database to store information about applications, users, and its own state. This is called the *registry*, and we can get at it by using Perl's Win32::TieRegistry module. This just provides a convenient layer around the Win32::Registry module, which is rather more technical in nature. Win32::TieRegistry transforms the Windows registry into a Perl hash.

The registry is a complicated beast, and revolves around a hierarchical tree structure—like a hash of hashes or a directory. For instance, information about users' software is stored under HKEY_CURRENT_USER\Microsoft\Windows\CurrentVersion\. Now we can get to this particular part of the hash by saying the following:

```
#!/usr/bin/perl -w
# registry.pl

use strict;
use Win32::TieRegistry (Delimiter => "/") ;
```

We load the module, and change the delimiter from a backslash to a forward slash so we don't end up drowning in a sea of backslashes.

```
my $users = $Registry->
  {HKEY_CURRENT_USER/Software/Microsoft/Windows/CurrentVersion/};
```

Now that we've got that key, we can dig further into the depths of the registry. This is where the Windows Explorer tips are stored:

```
my $tips = $users->{Explorer/Tips};
```

and from there we can add our own tips:

```
$tips->{/186} = "It's easy to use Perl as a Registry editor with the " .
                "Win32::TieRegistry module.";
```

We can always delete them again, using ordinary hash techniques.

```
delete $tips->{/186};
```

Again, if you're after more information, it's available in the Win32::TieRegistry documentation.

CPAN

So far we've been looking at standard modules provided with most Perl distributions. However, as we mentioned in the introduction, there's also a central repository for Perl modules—collections of code that will do virtually any kind of job: the Comprehensive Perl Archive Network, or CPAN, which you can find on the web at www.cpan.org. You can also find the standard Perl modules on CPAN and can read their documentation in web browser–friendly HTML by surfing http://search.cpan.org/.

So before you ask "How do I do . . . ?" or start plugging away at any long task, it's always worth taking a quick look here to see if it's already been done. CPAN is searchable in plenty of different ways—the most common are by keyword, by topic, or by module name. There are also a few CPAN search engines, but the easiest for browsing is probably the web-based CPAN search engine at http://search.cpan.org/.

This lets us look up modules by category, as well as searching for words in the modules' documentation. Once we've found a module that might do what we want, we follow a link to get further information on it and get ourselves a download. For example, this is what we get for the Archive::Tar module:

Now that we've seen how to find the modules we want, we're ready to look at the various ways in which we can install them.

Installing Modules with PPM

If you're using ActivePerl, module installation is made very simple by the Perl Package Manager (PPM). This is a useful little tool that's provided along with installations of ActivePerl, which allows us to install modules from the command line with the minimum of effort.

Note It is important to mention that PPM is not an interface to CPAN; it is a convenient program that allows us to install copies from CPAN, many of which are in some stage of being out-of-date. There is no guarantee that what is available on CPAN will be available with PPM. The rule of thumb is for the latest and greatest, visit CPAN.

So without further ado, let's install Net::Telnet—a module that allows us to automate a telnet session.

1. Type **ppm** at the command line; this will give you the PPM prompt: PPM>.

2. Now type **install Net::Telnet**—you may be asked to confirm your request, if so type **y**.

3. Exit the PPM prompt by typing **quit**, and now you have Net::Telnet installed.

Installing a Module Manually

We'll now take a look at what's involved in installing a module using CPAN. If you search CPAN for the module Net::Telnet, you should find yourself looking at the file libnet-1.18.tar.gz (unless there's a newer version out by the time you read this . . .) Download and unpack this file. On Unix systems, gzip -dc libnet-1.18.tar.gz | tar -xvf (or tar xzvf libnet-1.18.tar.gz if your version of tar also unzips) should do the trick, while you can use WinZip to extract these files on Windows.

Every module should contain a Makefile.PL, which can be used to generate the instructions to install the module. Let's run that file first:

```
$ perl Makefile.PL
```

If you can't install in Perl's site directories because you don't have the appropriate permissions, run

```
$ perl Makefile.PL PREFIX=/my/module/path
```

Makefile.PL first checks that we have all the modules it requires, and then that we've got everything we should have in the module archive itself—a file called MANIFEST contains a list of what should be in the archive.

Now we're ready to type make—assuming, of course, we have make on our system:

```
$ make
```

Once that's done, we check to see if our module's working:

```
$ make test
```

Finally, we actually install it, moving the files to the correct location:

```
$ make install
```

Hooray! The module's now installed.
However, there's a much, much easier way of doing it.

The CPAN Module

Another easy way to navigate and install modules from CPAN is to use the standard module called CPAN. The "CPAN Shell" is an extremely powerful tool for finding, downloading, building, and installing modules.

To get into the CPAN shell, type

```
$ perl -MCPAN -e shell
```

This is actually just the same as saying

```
#!/usr/bin/perl
use CPAN;
shell();
```

The whole shell is actually a function in the (massively complex) CPAN module. The first time we run it, we'll see something like this:

```
/usr/local/lib/perl5/5.8.3/CPAN/Config.pm initialized.

CPAN is the world-wide archive of perl resources. It consists of about
100 sites that all replicate the same contents all around the globe.
Many countries have at least one CPAN site already. The resources
found on CPAN are easily accessible with the CPAN.pm module. If you
want to use CPAN.pm, you have to configure it properly.

If you do not want to enter a dialog now, you can answer 'no' to this
question and I'll try to autoconfigure. (Note: you can revisit this
dialog anytime later by typing 'o conf init' at the cpan prompt.)

Are you ready for manual configuration? [yes]
```

Press the Enter key, and you'll be asked a series of questions about your computer and the nearest CPAN server—if you don't know, just keep hitting Enter through the answers. Eventually, you'll end up at a prompt like this:

```
cpan shell -- CPAN exploration and modules installation (v1.7601)
ReadLine support available (try "install Bundle::CPAN")

cpan>
```

Now we're ready to issue commands. The install command, as shown in the prompt, will download and install a module. For example, we could install the DBD::mysql module by simply saying

```
cpan>install DBD::mysql
```

Alternatively, we could get information on a module with the i command. Let's get some information on the MLDBM module:

```
cpan>i MLDBM
Module id = MLDBM
    DESCRIPTION  Transparently store multi-level data in DBM
    CPAN_USERID  GSAR (Gurusamy Sarathy <gsar@ActiveState.com>)
```

```
CPAN_VERSION  2.01
CPAN_FILE     C/CH/CHAMAS/MLDBM-2.01.tar.gz
DSLI_STATUS   RdpO (released,developer,perl,object-oriented)
INST_FILE     (not installed)
```

This tells us the module is called MLDBM, and there's a description of it. It was written by the CPAN author GSAR, which translates to Gurusamy Sarathy in the real world. It's at version 2.01, and it's stored on CPAN in the directory C/CH/CHAMAS/MLDBM-2.01.tar.gz.

The funny little code thing is the CPAN classification. It tells us this module has been released (the implication being that it's been released for a while), that you should contact the developer if you need any support on it, that it's written purely in Perl without any extensions in C, and that it's object oriented—and finally, that we don't have it installed. So let's install it:

```
cpan> install MLDBM
```

■**Note** In fact, you don't even have to go into the shell to install a module. As well as exporting the `shell` subroutine, CPAN provides us with `install`, with which we can simply say `perl -MCPAN -e 'install "MLDBM"'` to produce the same results.

You'll then see a few lines that will be specific to your computer—different systems have different ways of downloading files, and depend on whether or not you have the external programs `lynx`, `ftp`, or `ncftp`, or the Perl `Net::FTP` module installed.

The CPAN module will download the file, and then, if you've got the `Digest::MD5` module installed, download a special file called a *checksum*—it's like a summary of that file so we make sure that what we've downloaded is what's on the server.

```
Checksum for /home/simon/.cpan/sources/authors/id/ C/CH/CHAMAS/MLDBM-2.01.tar.gz ok
```

You should then see tons of output: the tar file is unpacked, a Makefile is generated and executed, the module is tested, and then installed. Once all this takes place, you will see the CPAN prompt again:

```
cpan>
```

Successfully installed, and with the minimum of effort!

How about if we don't actually know the name of the module we're looking for? CPAN lets us use a regular expression match to locate modules. For instance, if we're about to do some work involving MIDI electronic music files, we could search for "MIDI." Here is a portion of what we might see:

```
cpan>i /MIDI/
Author        MIDI ("Michael Diekmann" <michael.diekmann@undef.de>)
Distribution  B/BM/BMAMES/MIDI-XML-0.02.tar.gz
Distribution  C/CH/CHURCH/MIDI-Trans-0.15.zip
Module        MIDI           (S/SB/SBURKE/MIDI-Perl-0.8.tar.gz)
```

```
Module        MIDI::Event     (S/SB/SBURKE/MIDI-Perl-0.8.tar.gz)
Module        MIDI::Music     (S/SE/SETHJ/MIDI-Music-0.01.tar.gz)
Module        MIDI::Opus      (S/SB/SBURKE/MIDI-Perl-0.8.tar.gz)
Module        MIDI::Realtime  (F/FO/FOOCHRE/MIDI-Realtime-0.01.tar.gz)
Module        MIDI::Score     (S/SB/SBURKE/MIDI-Perl-0.8.tar.gz)
Module        MIDI::Simple    (S/SB/SBURKE/MIDI-Perl-0.8.tar.gz)
Module        MIDI::Tab       (R/RS/RSYMES/MIDI-Tab-0.01.tar.gz)
Module        MIDI::Tools     (C/CR/CRENZ/MIDI-Tools-0.01.tar.gz)
Module        MIDI::Track     (S/SB/SBURKE/MIDI-Perl-0.8.tar.gz)
Module        MIDI::Trans     (C/CH/CHURCH/MIDI-Trans-0.15.zip)
```

"Distributions" are archive files: zips or tar.gz files containing one or more Perl modules. We see that MIDI-Realtime contains just the MIDI::Realtime module.

Bundles

Some modules depend on other modules being installed. For instance, the Win32::TieRegistry module needs Win32::Registry to do the hard work of getting at the registry. If you're downloading packages from CPAN manually, you'll have to try each package, find out what's missing, and download another repeatedly until you've got everything you need. The CPAN module does a lot of this work for you—it can detect dependencies in packages and download and install everything that's missing.

This is fine for making sure that things work, but as well as *needing* other modules, some merely *suggest* other modules. For instance, the CPAN module itself works fine with nothing other than what's in the core, but if you have Term::Readline installed, it gives you a much more flexible prompt, with tab completion, a command history (meaning you can use the up and down arrows to scroll through previous commands), and other niceties.

Enter bundles—collections of packages that go well together. The CPAN bundle, Bundle::CPAN, for instance, contains various modules that make the CPAN shell easier to use: Term::ReadLine as mentioned previously, Digest::MD5 for security checking the files downloaded, some Net:: modules to make network communication with the CPAN servers nicer, and so on.

We'll now look here at two particularly useful bundles, which contain modules that we personally wouldn't go *anywhere* without.

Bundle::LWP

Bundle::LWP contains modules for *everything* to do with the Web. It has modules for dealing with HTML, HTTP, MIME types, handling URLs, downloading and mirroring remote web sites, creating web spiders and robots, and so on.

The main chunk of the bundle is the LWP (libwww-perl) distribution, containing the modules for visiting remote web sites. Let's have a look at what it gives us.

This module will export five methods to our current package.

- The get() method fetches a web site and returns the underlying HTML. This subroutine knows all about proxies, error codes, and other things:

```
$file = get("http://www.perl.com/");
```

- The head() method fetches the header of the site and returns a few headers: what type of document the page is (such as text/html), how big it is in bytes, when it was last modified, when it should be regarded as old (these are both Unix times suitable for feeding to localtime()), and what the server has to say about itself. Some servers may not return all these headers.

```
($content_type, $document_length, $modified_time, $expires, $server) =
    head("http://www.perl.com/");
```

The next three methods are all quite similar in that they all involve retrieving an HTML page.

- The first, getprint(), retrieves the HTML file and then prints it out to standard output—useful if you're redirecting to a file or using a filter as some sort of HTML formatter. You can copy a web page to a local file like this:

```
getprint("http://www.perl.com/");
```

- Alternatively, you can use the getstore() subroutine to store it to a file.

```
perl -MLWP::Simple -e
    'getstore("http://www.perl.com/", "perlpage.html")'
```

- Finally, mirror() is like getstore(), except it checks to see if the remote site's page is newer than the one we've already got.

```
perl -MLWP::Simple -e
    'mirror("http://www.perl.com/","perlpage.html")'
```

Be sure to read the main LWP documentation and the lwpcook page, which contains a few ideas for things to do with LWP.

Bundle::libnet

Similarly, Bundle::libnet contains a bunch of stuff for dealing with the network, although it's not nearly as big as LWP. The modules in Bundle::libnet and its dependencies allow you to use FTP, telnet, SMTP mail, and other network protocols.

Submitting Your Own Module to CPAN

CPAN contains almost everything you'll ever need. Almost. There'll surely come a day when you're faced with a problem where no known module can help you. If you think it's a sufficiently general problem that other people are going to come across, why not consider making your solution into a module and submitting it to CPAN? Think of it as a way of giving something back to the community that gave you all this . . .

Seriously, if you do have something you think would be useful to others, there are a few things you need to do to get it to CPAN:

- Check to make sure it has not already been written. Search CPAN at http://search.cpan.org/.

- Read the `perlmod` and `perlmodlib` documentation pages until you really understand them.

- Learn about the `Carp` module, and use `carp()` and `croak()` instead of `warn()` and `die()`.

- Learn about the `Test` module and how to produce test suites for modules.

- Learn about documenting your modules in POD, Plain Old Documentation.

- Look at the source to a few simple modules like `Text::Wrap` and `Text::Tabs` to get a feel of how modules are written.

- Take a deep breath, and issue the following command:

```
$ h2xs -AXn Your::Module::Name
```

- Edit the files produced, remembering to create a test suite and provide really good documentation.

- Run `perl Makefile.PL` and then `make`.

Your module's now ready to ship!

For more information, check out the excellent book *Writing Perl Modules for CPAN* by Sam Tregar (Apress, 2002). Also, be sure to read `perldoc perlnewmod`, written by one of your humble authors.

Summary

Modules save you time. In essence, a module is just a package stored in a file, which we load with the `use` statement.

Perl provides a number of standard modules. You can get documentation on each and every one by running `perldoc`. We looked briefly at `Data::Dumper` (to print out data structures), `File::Find` (for examining files in directory trees), the `Getopt` modules (for reading options from the command line), the `File::Spec::Functions` module (for portable filename handling), the `Benchmark` module (for timing and testing code), and the `Win32` modules (for access to the Windows system and registry).

CPAN is the Comprehensive Perl Archive Network. It's a repository of free Perl code. You can search it from http://search.cpan.org/, or use the Perl module `CPAN` for easy searching and installation. The `CPAN` module has the advantage of knowing about file dependencies and can therefore download and install files in the correct order.

Bundles provide sets of related modules. We looked at `LWP::Simple` (from the `libwww` bundle) and the `libnet` bundle. Finally, we looked at some of what's involved in abstracting your code and putting it into a module.

CHAPTER 14

■■■

Introduction to CGI

The Common Gateway Interface (CGI) is a method used by webservers to run external programs (known as *CGI scripts*), most often to generate web content dynamically. Whenever a web page queries a database, or a user submits a form, a CGI script is usually called upon to do the work.

CGI is simply a specification, which defines a standard way for webservers to run CGI scripts and for those programs to send their results back to the server. The job of the CGI script is to read information that the browser has sent (via the server), and to generate some form of valid response, usually (but not always) visible content. Once it has completed its task, the CGI script finishes and exits.

Perl is a very popular language for CGI scripting thanks to its unrivalled text-handling abilities, easy scripting, and relative speed. It is probably true to say that a large part of Perl's current popularity is due to its success in dynamic web page generation. Also, there is an excellent module available for Perl that makes writing CGI scripts easy—CGI.pm.

■**Note** Usually, when we refer to Perl modules we do not include the ".pm". For instance, when we talk about the DBI module, we never call it "the DBI.pm module." However, with the CGI module, we call it "the CGI.pm module." We are not sure why this is, perhaps it is historical—once upon a time we CGI programmers used a set of functions in a file called cgi.pl. Since that file was named cgi.pl, we suppose everyone called the new object-oriented version CGI.pm. Another reason may be an effort to distinguish the CGI.pm module from the CGI protocol. Whatever the reason, we will continue the tradition of calling it CGI.pm.

In this chapter we will discuss the basics of CGI, how data is sent to CGI scripts, how the server responds back to the client, and how to make all this simple with the use of CGI.pm.

This chapter is not meant to be an exhaustive study of writing CGI scripts with Perl, but rather an introduction with enough information for you to get started and with pointers to where to look for more information. The best place to find out all you need to know is by picking up a copy of the book entitled *Official Guide to Programming with CGI.pm* written by Lincoln Stein (Wiley & Sons, 1998). Of course, the online documentation for CGI.pm is available by executing perldoc CGI. The most important thing to remember about CGI with Perl—it's fun! So let's get started.

We Need a Webserver

The first step in writing CGI programs is to obtain access to a webserver. While we have several options (including obtaining an account with an ISP that provides a webserver or convincing a friend with a computer that has a webserver and Internet connection to give us access—taking them out for a nice meal is good way to convince them), we will briefly discuss installing a webserver on our machine and working locally.

The webserver that we are going to suggest is the most popular server used on the Internet: Apache. As this chapter is being written (May 2004), Apache has more than 67% of the webserver market (you can see a comparison of all the different servers at http://news.netcraft.com/archives/web_server_survey.html)—more than twice the number of all the other servers *combined*. Apache is popular because it is a solid program, extensible, highly securable, and open source (meaning free!).

The Apache webserver can be found at http://httpd.apache.org/. To download a version for your machine, visit http://httpd.apache.org/ and click the download link. The latest version as of May 2004 is version 2.0.49, but version 1.3.x is suggested for beginners because it is very stable and is much easier to use than version 2.0.x. As of May 2004, 1.3.31 is the latest and greatest. Follow the installation directions found at http://httpd.apache.org/docs/install.html to install it on your machine. Or, better yet, go out and get a copy of *Apache Essentials: Install, Configure, Maintain* by Darren James Harkness (friends of ED, 2004) for a simple and concise guide to Apache. This book will help you get Apache up and running in no time.

A note to Unix users: chances are, Apache is installed and is running on your machine—yet another reason to like Unix! To verify if your machine is ready to serve a web client, point your browser to http://127.0.0.1/.

127.0.0.1 is a special address that points to the machine that you are sitting in front of. This address is also known as *localhost*. If you see a response page that tells you Apache is up and running, you are ready to go! 127.0.0.1 can be replaced by localhost, as you can see in the examples in this chapter, which all use http://localhost/. But beware—if your machine does not have a webserver running, you are likely to end up at http://www.localhost.com/.

Creating a CGI Directory

Once Apache is installed, a CGI directory must be created and configured. To learn how to do this, see http://httpd.apache.org/docs-2.0/howto/cgi.html. The location of this directory will vary from machine to machine, but common Unix locations are /usr/local/apache/cgi-bin/ and /home/httpd/cgi-bin/. Your mileage may vary on this location, however.

Writing CGI Programs

Now that Apache is installed and the CGI directory is configured, it is time to write some CGI scripts. We often say that writing CGI in Perl is so easy—if you can print "hello, world!" you are halfway there! We will illustrate this with our first example.

All the examples in this chapter will be placed in the directory that /cgi-bin/ points to. So, for instance, if we write a program named foo.pl and place it in our CGI bin directory, we can execute the program by loading this URL in our browser:

```
http://localhost/cgi-bin/foo.pl
```

"hello, world!" in CGI

Our first example will be a program that sends "hello, world!", our zen-like greeting, to the browser:

```perl
#!/usr/bin/perl -w
# hello.pl

use strict;

print "Content-Type: text/plain\n";
print "\n";
print "hello, world!\n";
```

If this program were located in the CGI directory and had the proper executable permissions (755 in the Unix world), we could view the result by loading http://localhost/cgi-bin/hello.pl in our browser. It would produce this response:

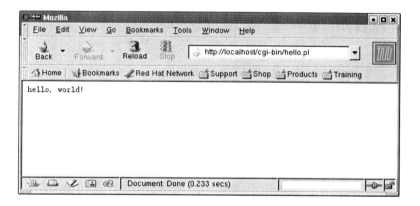

The first few lines of this program are familiar. Then we see the statement

```perl
print "Content-Type: text/plain\n";
```

This print is very important—it prints the content type of the information that follows. This is sent to the client in what is known as the *HTTP header*. The header is the mechanism the server uses to inform the client what kind of information it is sending. One piece of information in the header is the type of content—here we are telling the client that what follows is to be treated as plain text, and to deal with it appropriately which is normally by displaying it in fixed width font.

After we print the content type, we see this line:

```perl
print "\n";
```

This prints a blank line. Printing a blank line is very important! The header must be followed by a blank line so that the client knows that the header is complete and the following information is the body, or the main part of the information that is sent. If we forget to print the blank line, we will normally get a "Server Error" message on the browser.

Then we print the message that we want the world to see:

```
print "hello, world!\n";
```

What to Do If Things Go Wrong

If you don't see the warm, friendly greeting in your browser, then you might suspect something is not working correctly. There are many things that can go wrong with CGI scripts; here are some things you can do to troubleshoot the problem:

- The file must be located in the directory in which Apache is looking. Double-check that it is, and if not, move it over to the appropriate place and try again.

- Make sure the permissions on the file are set so that the server can execute the program. In Unix, the permissions are usually set to 755, so chmod the file and test it again.

- The script might have a syntax error (hey, it happens!). An easy way to check this is to execute the program on the command line using the -c option:

```
$ perl -c hello.pl
hello.pl syntax OK
```

This should tell you that the syntax is OK. If not, fix the problem and try again.

- That blank line is really important—if you forgot to print it a server error is the normal result. A simple way to make sure there is the all-important-gotta-have-it blank line, simply execute the program from the command line:

```
$ perl hello.pl
Content-Type: text/plain

hello, world!
```

Do you see the blank line? If not, print that extra \n.

- Make sure that content type is something expected. For this program, it should be text/plain.

- It is possible that Apache is not configured properly. This is harder to fix—you will have to read through the Apache configuration documents to troubleshoot this problem.

- When all else fails, have a look in Apache's error log file (normally found in a directory named logs in the file named error_log). Apache reports errors to this file—it might tell you why the script failed.

If there is still a problem that you can't figure out, head over to www.perlmonks.org. This is a great website created as a place where Perl programmers can ask other Perl programmers questions and expect polite, useful answers. Emphasis on polite! There are many places on the web where a question can result in a fiery response—Perl Monks is not one of them.

The CGI Environment

When the webserver executes a CGI program, it makes available to that program a considerable amount of information through exported environment variables. To grab the environment variables in a Perl program, we look in %ENV. Here is a program showing several important things that the program knows about the client requesting the CGI program:

```perl
#!/usr/bin/perl -w
# env1.pl

use strict;

print "Content-Type: text/plain\n";
print "\n";

print "your hostname is:      $ENV{REMOTE_ADDR}\n";
print "your outbound port is: $ENV{REMOTE_PORT}\n";
print "your browser is:       $ENV{HTTP_USER_AGENT}\n";
```

If we point our browser to http://localhost/cgi-bin/env1.pl, we would see

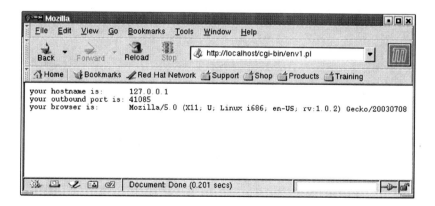

As this program shows, the server knows the Internet address of the client, the port number that the client is coming from on their machine, and the web browser they are using.

You may be wondering what other environment variables that the server has available. This program will display them to you:

```perl
#!/usr/bin/perl -w
# env2.pl
```

```
use strict;

print "Content-Type: text/plain\n";
print "\n";

foreach (sort keys %ENV) {
    print "$_ = $ENV{$_}\n";
}
```

Loading http://localhost/cgi-bin/env2.pl will display all our environment variables as shown in this example:

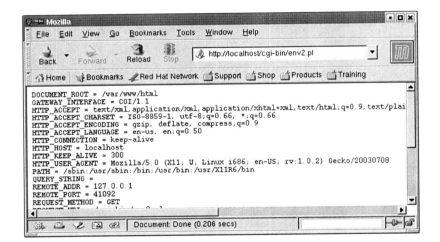

Generating HTML

Our CGI programs will not normally print plain text. Instead, they will print HTML to the client and the browser will render that text appropriately. To tell the client that our CGI program is generating HTML is as simple as changing the Content-Type:

```
#!/usr/bin/perl -w
# env3.pl

use strict;

print "Content-Type: text/html\n";
print "\n";

foreach (sort keys %ENV) {
    print "$_ = $ENV{$_}";
    print "<br />";
}
```

Changing the content type to text/html tells the browser that what follows is HTML and to handle the text as it would any other HTML. Note that while we are printing the environment variables and their values, we don't need to print newline characters since the browser treats those characters in HTML as simple whitespace characters. To get the line break we want we must print the break tag <br />.

If we look at http://localhost/cgi-bin/env3.pl, we might see

Since we can generate arbitrary HTML, let's make this output a bit more readable by putting it in a table:

```perl
#!/usr/bin/perl -w
# env4.pl

use strict;

print "Content-Type: text/html\n";
print "\n";

print "<table border=\"1\">";
foreach (sort keys %ENV) {
    print "<tr><th>$_</th><td>$ENV{$_}</td>";
}
print "</table>";
```

Ah, that's better (http://localhost/cgi-bin/env4.pl):

Take a moment to view the output from the program that the browser sees and renders by viewing the source: select the View menu on the browser and pull down to Source (it might be Page Source or View Source, depending on your browser). This pops up a window that contains the HTML source code, which is the output from the CGI script. Handy tool, this View ➤ Source—the web is what it is in large part due to the fact that you can see the HTML that others create. This is an excellent way to learn what it takes to code good web pages.

Introducing CGI.pm

As we can see from these examples, writing CGI programs is straightforward: generate standard output with print() function calls, remembering to start the output with the Content-Type line followed by a blank line (don't forget the blank line!). That blank line is followed by whatever we want to display on the browser: text, HTML, etc.

We will now introduce one of the most popular Perl modules (perhaps the most popular module): CGI.pm. This module, written by Lincoln Stein, makes it easy for us to generate HTML and process form data (we'll talk about form data a little later in this chapter) by providing some helpful methods.

Let's jump right into this module by looking at an example. First, we will present a program to generate a web page by printing plain HTML without the use of CGI.pm, then we'll see exactly the same web page generated by a program using CGI.pm.

Here is the non-CGI.pm version:

```perl
#!/usr/bin/perl -w
# html1.pl

# this program generates HTML without the use
# of CGI.pm

use strict;
```

```
print "Content-Type: text/html\n";
print "\n";
print "<html>\n";
print "<head>\n";
print "<title>Generating HTML</title>\n";
print "</head>\n";
print "<body>\n";
print "<h1>Now Is:</h1>\n";
print "<p>\n";
print "The current date and time is: ";

print scalar(localtime);

print "</p>\n";
print "<hr />\n";
print "<h1>Our CGI Scripts</h1>\n";
print "<p>\n";
print "By the time this chapter is over, you will write all of \n";
print "these scripts:\n";

print "<br />$_\n" foreach <*.pl>;

print "</p>\n";
print "<h1>Go Here For Excellent Books!</h1>\n";
print "<p>\n";
print "Check out the \n";
print "<a href=\"http://www.apress.com/\">Apress Home Page</a>.\n";
print "</p>\n";
print "</body>\n";
print "</html>\n";
```

Most of this code is simply printing HTML. Let's look at two lines of this program in detail. First:

```
print scalar(localtime);
```

The localtime() function called in scalar context returns a nice readable string showing the current date/time stamp on the computer.[1] This program prints that string to standard output, which will be displayed in the body of the browser. The next line of interest is

```
print "<br />$_\n" foreach <*.pl>;
```

This code uses the expression modifier form of the foreach loop, looping through all files that match the glob pattern *.pl. Each of the files is printed with a preceding <br /> tag.

---

1. In list context, localtime() returns something similar but different. See perldoc -f localtime for all the useful information that localtime() returns.

Loading this page (http://localhost/cgi-bin/html1.pl) into your browser should display something that resembles the following:

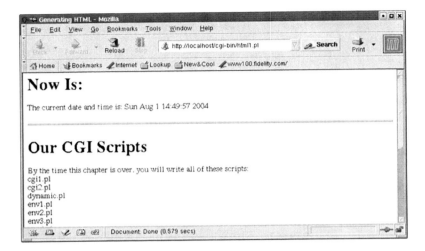

As you can see, all those print() functions with the double quotes, newlines, and semicolons make the code a bit hard to read. This program might be better written with a here-document as shown in this example (html2.pl):

```perl
#!/usr/bin/perl -w
# html2.pl

# this program generates HTML without the use
# of CGI.pm - this time with a here document

use strict;

print "Content-Type: text/html\n";
print "\n";

print <<EOHTML;
<html>
<head>
<title>Generating HTML</title>
</head>
<body>
<h1>Now Is:</h1>
<p>
The current date and time is:
EOHTML

print scalar(localtime);
```

```
print <<EOHTML;
</p>
<hr />
<h1>Our CGI Scripts</h1>
<p>
By the time this chapter is over, you will write all of
these scripts:
EOHTML

print "<br />$_\n" foreach <*.pl>;

print <<EOHTML;
</p>
<h1>Go Here For Excellent Books!</h1>
<p>
Check out the
<a href="http://www.apress.com/">Apress Home Page</a>.
</p>
</body>
</html>
EOHTML
```

Notice that the here-documents are useful when printing static text. However, when we print scalar(localtime) and loop through all the .pl files, we need to make sure those executable statements are outside of a here-document.

This content can be generated by using CGI.pm and its methods. First, let's look at the program (cgi1.pl) and then we'll step through the code line by line:

```
#!/usr/bin/perl -w
# cgi1.pl

# this program generates HTML with the use
# of CGI.pm

use strict;
use CGI ':standard';

print header();
print start_html('Generating HTML');
print h1('Now Is:');
print p('The current date and time is:', scalar(localtime));
print hr();
print h1('Our CGI Scripts');

my $file_listing = '';
$file_listing .= "<br />$_" foreach <*.pl>;
```

```
print p('By the time this chapter is over, you will write all of',
        'these scripts:', $file_listing);
print h1('Go Here For Excellent Books!');
print p('Check out the',
        a({ href => 'http://www.apress.com/' }, 'Apress Home Page'));
print end_html();
```

The first part of this program is like any other Perl program: the shebang followed by optional comments followed by use strict;. Then we see the line that makes the use of CGI.pm possible:

```
use CGI ':standard';
```

This statement looks slightly different than other use statements we have seen since there is the additional ':standard'. This string tells CGI.pm that we want to use the methods in the module without having to call them using an object. In other words, if we use the :standard mode, we can call the header() method like this:

```
print header();
```

instead of like this:

```
my $q = new CGI;
print $q->header();
```

The header() method is very convenient—it prints the header (clever name, eh?). In other words, in generates the text

```
Content-Type: text/html
```

Yep, there is a blank line after the Content-Type line, so the header() generates that all-important, gotta-have-it blank line for us, so we don't have to remember to do it ourselves. Then we see a method that generates the start of the HTML:

```
print start_html('Generating HTML');
```

This invocation of the start_html() method generates this HTML:

```
<html><head><title>Generating HTML</title>
</head><body>
```

Notice that the argument to start_html() is placed between the <title>...</title> tags for us.

Next up is

```
print h1('Now Is:');
```

This method generates the <h1>...</h1> tags with the argument to the method placed between the open and close tags.

```
<h1>Now Is:</h1>
```

Then we see

```
print p('The current date and time is:', scalar(localtime));
```

Like h1(), p() generates <p>...</p> with the argument(s) between the tags. This method has two arguments—a string and a function call comma separated. CGI.pm is smart enough to take these two arguments and concatenate the string and the function return value together with a space automatically added to separate them. Therefore, this method generates something that resembles

```
<p>The current date and time is: Fri Jun 18 19:02:48 2004</p>
```

The next method:

```
print hr();
```

generates <hr />. This is similar to h1() and p().

A couple of lines later we see this code:

```
my $file_listing = '';
$file_listing .= "<br />$_" foreach <*.pl>;

print p('By the time this chapter is over, you will write all of',
        'these scripts:', $file_listing);
```

This creates a variable $file_listing that will be all the Perl scripts in the current directory. For each Perl file, we append a <br /> tag along with the file's name to $file_listing. That variable is then included as an argument to p(). This generates the text:

```
<p>By the time this chapter is over, you will write all of  these scripts:
<br />cgi1.pl<br />cgi2.pl<br />dynamic.pl<br />env1.pl<br />env4.pl<br />
form.pl<br />html1.pl<br />html2.pl<br />widgets.pl</p>
```

Next is a call to p() that includes a call to a():

```
print p('Check out the',
        a({ href => 'http://www.apress.com/' }, 'Apress Home Page'));
```

This method generates

```
<p>Check out the <a href="http://www.apress.com/">Apress Home Page</a></p>
```

We will discuss the first argument to the a() method in detail a little later in this chapter. Finally, we see

```
print end_html();
```

This generates the ending HTML tags:

```
</body></html>
```

Conventional Style of Calling Methods

The `cgi1.pl` program has several different `print()` function calls—one for each method that produces HTML. This is way too many `print()` function calls. The conventional style of using `CGI.pm` is to combine all the prints into one as shown in `cgi2.pl`:

```perl
#!/usr/bin/perl -w
# cgi2.pl

# this program generates HTML with the use
# of CGI.pm using the conventional style

use strict;
use CGI ':standard';

print
    header(),
    start_html('Generating HTML'),
    h1('Now Is:'),
    p('The current date and time is:', scalar(localtime)),
    hr(),
    h1('Our CGI Scripts');

my $file_listing = '';
$file_listing .= "<br />$_" foreach <*.pl>;

print
    p('By the time this chapter is over, you will write all of',
        'these scripts:', $file_listing),
    h1('Go Here For Excellent Books!'),
    p('Check out the',
      a({ href => 'http://www.apress.com/' }, 'Apress Home Page')),
    end_html();
```

This generates exactly the output as the other examples we have seen before. Note how all the methods are arguments to a single `print()` function call. This is considered by many to be more readable than having a separate `print()` for each method call—if you agree then feel free to use this style.

> ▓**Note** A word of caution: if the `h1()` method, for instance, were followed by a semicolon instead of
> a comma (a very common mistake!):
>
> `h1('Here Is An Example Web Page');`
>
> that semicolon would terminate the `print()`, so the following methods (`p()`, `hr()`, etc.) would not be
> printed. It is our experience that if only a portion of the web page is displayed, it is often the result of
> a misplaced semicolon.

CGI.pm Methods

There are basically two types of `CGI.pm` methods: those that generate only one tag, and those
that generate more than one tag.

Methods That Generate More Than One Tag

We have seen a couple of examples of methods that generate more than one tag. One was
`start_html()`, which generates `<html><head><title>...</title></head><body>`. This method
is used to generate all the HTML that is at the top of the HTML content. The way we invoked
the method was with one argument, and that argument was understood by the method to be
the title of the web page and was placed between the `<title>...</title>` tags.

Named Parameters

There is another way to invoke the method: using *named parameters*. Since `start_html()`
generates the `<body>` tag, we would like to be able to easily set certain attributes of that tag
when we invoke the method. Here is an example of giving our web page a title, background
color, and text color:

```
start_html(
    -title   => 'Generating HTML',
    -bgcolor => '#cccccc',
    -text    => '#520063'
),
```

This sets the title to "Generating HTML", the background color to a nice gray, "#cccccc",
and the text color to an excellent shade of purple, "#520063."[2]

There are many different named parameters available to `start_html()`—check out
`perldoc CGI` for a complete list.

---

2.   How excellent? Go to www.nwu.edu for a demonstration.

Methods That Generate One Tag

We saw several examples of methods that generate one tag including h1(), p(), and hr(). These methods generate the tags that share their name: h1() produces <h1>...</h1>, p() produces <p>...</p>, and hr() generates <hr />.

There are many other examples of these methods—more-or-less one for each tag available in HTML. Examples include i() (<i>...</i>), b() (...), li() (<li>...</li>), and many others.

Providing Attributes

Many of these tags have optional attributes. Providing attributes to these methods involves passing an anonymous hash containing the attributes and their values as the first argument to the method. For instance, let's say we want the <h1> tag to be aligned in the center of the page; we would call the h1() method in this fashion:

```
h1({ align => 'center'}, 'Here Is An Example Web Page'),
```

which generates

```
<h1 align="center">Here Is An Example Web Page</h1>
```

Providing more than one attribute is simply a matter of specifying more than one key/value pair to the anonymous hash. This method invocation generates an <hr /> tag with a pixel size of 10 and no shading set:

```
hr({ size => 10, noshade => 1 }),
```

which generates

```
<hr size="10" noshade="1" />
```

Now we see the magic involved in the a() method that we have seen before.

```
a({ href => 'http://www.apress.com/' }, 'Apress Home Page'),
```

generates

```
<a href="http://www.apress.com/">Apress Home Page</a>
```

Processing Form Data

CGI scripts don't merely generate HTML—they usually do some back-end, server-side processing. One major category of such processing is to gather information from the user by grabbing the data posted from a *form*. A form is a collection of *widgets* that allow the user to input data, select some options, click buttons, etc.

Most of us have filled out forms on the web: when we have purchased books from an online store, filled out a survey, or created an account at www.slashdot.org.

Forms are created by using `<form>` through `</form>` surrounding one or more widgets. The most important attribute to the `<form>` tag is the *action*, or CGI script, that is to be invoked when the user submits the form by clicking the submit button.

Here is an example of a simple form that will allow the user to enter their name and age (form.html):

```
<html>
  <head>
    <title>A Simple Form</title>
  </head>
  <body>
    <h1>Please Enter Your Name</h1>
    <form action="http://localhost/cgi-bin/form.pl">
      First name: <input type="text" name="firstname">
      <br>
      Last name: <input type="text" name="lastname">
      <br>
      <input type="submit">
    </form>
  </body>
</html>
```

This generates the form shown here (after a user enters some text):

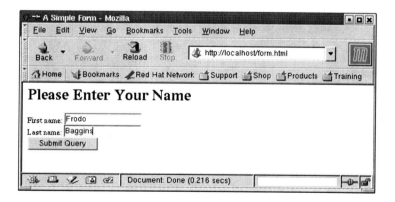

The CGI program associated with this form, as indicated by the action= attribute, is http://localhost/cgi-bin/form.pl. This program will obtain the information entered by the user into the form and process it. The key to this program will be the important param() method.

The param() Method

The param() method is invoked in one of two ways: with no arguments and with one argument.

When invoked with no argument, the param() method returns back a list of all the *parameters* in the form. A parameter is simply the name of the widget indicated by the name= attribute. In the form.html example previously, we see that there are two named widgets: firstname and lastname. The param() method invoked with no arguments would produce the list

```
('firstname', 'lastname')
```

When invoked with one argument, the param() method returns back the value of that parameter. Therefore, if the user enters their first name as "Frodo", then param('firstname') returns "Frodo". If they enter their first name as "Bilbo", the method returns back "Bilbo". Likewise, param('lastname') returns back the last name entered by the user into the form.

And now the code to process the form (form.pl):

```perl
#!/usr/bin/perl -w
# form.pl

use strict;
use CGI ':standard';

my @params     = param();
my $firstname = param('firstname') || 'you have no first name!';
my $lasthame  = param('lastname')  || 'you have no last name!';

print
    header(),
    start_html(
        -title   => 'Welcome!',
        -text    => '#520063'
    ),
    h1("Hello, $firstname $lastname!"),
    end_html();
```

This program produces this result (assuming the user enters "Frodo" for the first name and "Baggins" for the last name):

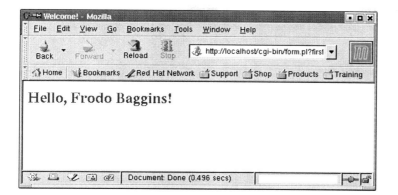

The important lines in this program are

```
my @params    = param();
my $firstname = param('firstname') || 'you have no first name!';
my $lastname  = param('lastname')  || 'you have no last name!';
```

The first statement assigns @params a list of all the parameters, or widget names, in the form that was posted. In our example, they are 'firstname' and 'lastname'. This line is followed by two assignments that are very similar. The first assigns $firstname the value that was entered into the name field in the form. The || operator ensures that the variable $firstname has a meaningful value—if the user does not enter a name, param('firstname') will be the empty string, which is false, so the || will evaluate the operand on the right and assign 'you have no first name!' to $firstname. A similar assignment is made to $lastname.

Then we see the two variables printed in the print() function.

Dynamic CGI Program

The example we just looked at had an HTML file that was separate from the CGI program. The HTML was stored in form.html and the CGI program was stored in form.pl. This is known as a *static* CGI program—loading in a static HTML file that has as its action a separate CGI program.

Sometimes keeping the HTML and CGI program in separate files creates a situation that is more difficult to manage. Perhaps it is better to have the HTML generated by the same program that processes the posted data. Enter a *dynamic* CGI program.

A dynamic CGI program does one of two things:

- If there is posted data, process the data.

- If there is no posted data, build the form.

Recall that the param() method returns a list of all the parameters posted by the form. If this list is empty, then the CGI program was invoked with no parameters. Therefore, a dynamic CGI program has this general form:

```perl
if (param()) {
    # the program was invoked with parameters,
    # process the posted data
} else {
    # the program was invoked with no parameters,
    # build the form
}
```

Here is an example of a dynamic CGI program that implements the scenario we saw previously: it either builds a form that accepts a user's name and age, or it processes the form data (dynamic.pl):

```perl
#!/usr/bin/perl -w
# dynamic.pl

use strict;
use CGI ':standard';

if (param()) {
    # we have parameters, so process the form data

    my @params    = param();
    my $firstname = param('firstname') || 'you have no first name!';
    my $lastname  = param('lastname')  || 'you have no last name!';

    print
        header(),
        start_html(
            -title   => 'Welcome!',
            -text    => '#520063'
        ),
        h1("Hello, $firstname $lastname!"),
        end_html();

} else {
    # no parameters, so build the form

    print
        header(),
        start_html('A Simple Form'),
        h1('Please Enter Your Name'),
        start_form(),
        'First name: ',
        textfield(-name => 'firstname'),
        br(),
        'Last name: ',
        textfield(-name => 'lastname'),
```

```
    br(),
    submit(),
    end_form(),
    end_html();

}
```

This program generates the same form as `form.html` and it processes the form the same as `form.pl`. Note that it builds the form using `CGI.pm` methods. There are a few methods used that are worth noting. First:

```
start_form(),
```

The `start_form()` method builds the beginning `<form>` tag. The action can be specified with `{ -action => '/cgi-bin/whatever.pl' }`, but we are using the default action, which is the same CGI program that built the form. The form is eventually closed with

```
end_form(),
```

The text form widget is created with

```
textfield(-name => 'lastname'),
```

The `textfield()` method is one of many methods that are used to create form widgets. This chapter is not meant to be an exhaustive study of forms and form widgets, but there is a method for each different type of widget available. For a complete list, see `perldoc CGI`.

Let's Play Chess!

It's time to roll all the topics we have discussed into a single example. This CGI script will be a web implementation of the chess program, `chess.pl`, that we discussed in Chapter 11. Since we are playing chess on the web, we'll call this CGI script `webchess.pl`. This program will illustrate that with just a little bit of additional code we can web-enable a program that we wrote for the shell.

Before we look at the program, we need to talk about an important concept when it comes to CGI. A CGI script is *stateless*. That means the CGI script in and of itself cannot remember anything about the most recent execution, or state, of the script. As a result, we will somehow have to remember the recent state of the chessboard so that we can pick up the game from the last move the user made. This is different than the `chess.pl` program—each move was made within the same execution of the program, so `chess.pl` always knew the state from move to move.

We will keep track of the state of the chessboard in a file named `webchess.dat`. This file will be an eight-line file, with each line being one row on the board. Each row will have its eight pieces, colon separated. Here is the initial state of the chessboard:

```
BR:BN:BB:BQ:BK:BN:BB:BR
BP:BP:BP:BP:BP:BP:BP:BP
:::::::
```

```
:::::::
:::::::
:::::::
WP:WP:WP:WP:WP:WP:WP:WP
WR:WN:WB:WQ:WK:WN:WB:WR
```

We can see that the first, second, seventh, and eighth rows have pieces. The middle four rows are empty—if two colons are right next to one another that means that square does not have a piece on it.

If webchess.pl is going to keep its state in webchess.dat, we will need some code to read from the data file and to write to the data file. These operations are placed within two functions: read_in_chessboard(), which will, you guessed it, read in the chessboard. The equally well-named function write_out_chessboard() will write it out.

It's time to jump into the code:

```perl
#!/usr/bin/perl -w
# webchess.pl

use strict;
use CGI ':standard';

my @chessboard = read_in_chessboard();

# grab the posted data, if any:
my $start = param('start') || '';
my $end   = param('end')   || '';

my $startx = '';
my $starty = '';
my $endx   = '';
my $endy   = '';

# time to make our move!
if ($start and $end) {
    if ($start =~ /^\s*([1-8]),([1-8])/) {
        $startx = $1 - 1;
        $starty = $2 - 1;
    }
    if ($end =~ /^\s*([1-8]),([1-8])/) {
        $endx = $1 - 1;
        $endy = $2 - 1;
    }
    if ($startx ne '' and $starty ne '' and
        $endx ne ''   and $endy ne '' ) {
        # put starting square on ending square
        $chessboard[$endy]->[$endx] = $chessboard[$starty]->[$startx];
        # remove from old square
        undef $chessboard[$starty]->[$startx];
```

```perl
            # we have changed the chessboard, so write
            # back out
            write_out_chessboard(@chessboard);
        }
}

# time to print to the browser
print
    header(),
    start_html('Web Chess'),
    h1('Web Chess');

# start the table that will contain the board
print '<table>';

# loop, printing each piece
foreach my $i (reverse (0..7)) { # row
    print '<tr>';
    foreach my $j (0..7) {          # column
        print '<td>';
        if (defined $chessboard[$i]->[$j]) {
            print $chessboard[$i]->[$j];
        } elsif ( ($i % 2) == ($j % 2) ) {
            print "..";
        }
        print '</td>';
    }
    print "</tr>";      # end of row
}

# we are done with our table
print '</table>';

# print a form for the next move
# and end the html
print
    hr(),
    start_form(),
    'Starting square [x,y]:',
    textfield(-name => 'start'),
    br(),
    'Ending square [x,y]:',
    textfield(-name => 'end'),
    br(),
    submit(),
    end_form(),
    end_html();
```

```perl
### function definitions ###

sub read_in_chessboard {
    # this function opens webchess.dat and builds
    # the chessboard
    # an example line from webchess.dat is:
    # BR:BN:BB:BQ:BK:BN:BB:BR

    # this is our local copy of the chessboard,
    # we'll return this later
    my @cb;
    open FH, '<', 'webchess.dat';

    foreach my $i (0..7) {
        my $line = <FH>;
        # split the line on a : or any whitespace
        # which will take care of the \n at the
        # end of the line
        my @linearray = split /[:\s]/, $line;
        # $#linearray should be 7!
        foreach my $j (0..$#linearray) {
            # if the text between the colons is
            # not the empty string, we have a piece,
            # so assign it to our chessboard
            if ($linearray[$j]) {
                $cb[$i]->[$j] = $linearray[$j];
            }
        }
    }
    close FH;

    # time to return back the chessboard
    return @cb;
}

sub write_out_chessboard {
    # the chessboard is passed in as our
    # argument
    my @cb = @_;

    # write the chessboard to webchess.dat
    # so that each piece on a row is colon separated
    open FH, '>', 'webchess.dat';
    foreach my $i (0..7) {
        foreach my $j (0..7) {
            if (defined $chessboard[$i]->[$j]) {
                print FH $chessboard[$i]->[$j];
            }
```

```
            if ($j < 7) {
                print FH ':';
            }
        }
        print FH "\n";
    }
}
```

Wow, that's a lot of code. Let's look at it a chunk at a time. We'll start at the bottom of the program with the functions to read from and write to the input data file. First, the relevant code in read_in_chessboard():

```
# this is our local copy of the chessboard,
# we'll return this later
my @cb;
open FH, '<', 'webchess.dat';

foreach my $i (0..7) {
    my $line = <FH>;
    # split the line on a : or any whitespace
    # which will take care of the \n at the
    # end of the line
    my @linearray = split /[:\s]/, $line;
    # $#linearray should be 7!
    foreach my $j (0..$#linearray) {
        # if the text between the colons is
        # not the empty string, we have a piece,
        # so assign it to our chessboard
        if ($linearray[$j]) {
            $cb[$i]->[$j] = $linearray[$j];
        }
    }
}
close FH;

# time to return back the chessboard
return @cb;
```

This function creates a my() variable @cb that will hold a local copy of the chessboard. The input data file is opened in read mode. Then, for the eight rows on the board, a line of text is read from the input file and split on either the colon or whitespace character. This split() will break the line into eight parts—the pieces for that row. Then we loop for each square on the row— if there is a piece in the square (no piece will be represented by the empty string, which is false, so any true value indicates a piece is present), the square on the chessboard is assigned the piece. After each square in each row is assigned, the input file is closed and the chessboard is returned to whoever called it.

Then we see the function to write the chessboard back out to the file:

```perl
sub write_out_chessboard {
    # the chessboard is passed in as our
    # argument
    my @cb = @_;

    # write the chessboard to webchess.dat
    # so that each piece on a row is colon separated
    open FH, '>', 'webchess.dat';
    foreach my $i (0..7) {
        foreach my $j (0..7) {
            if (defined $chessboard[$i]->[$j]) {
                print FH $chessboard[$i]->[$j];
            }
            if ($j < 7) {
                print FH ':';
            }
        }
        print FH "\n";
    }
}
```

This function opens the data file in write mode. It then loops eight times, once for each row. For each row, it loops eight times, once for each square in the row. If there is a defined value, it is printed (it will either be the piece such as "WB" or the empty string). Then a colon is printed after all but the last square on the row. After the row is printed, we end the line with \n. After all rows are printed, the output file is closed.

Now, on to the main code in the program. First, we create a variable to hold the chessboard by calling the function that reads from the data file:

```perl
my @chessboard = read_in_chessboard();
```

Then, we read in the posted data, if there is any. This data will be the starting and ending coordinates (such as 4,2). Note that if there is no posted data for either the start or end square, the variable will be assigned the empty string:

```perl
# grab the posted data, if any:
my $start = param('start') || '';
my $end   = param('end')   || '';
```

Now that $start and $end have the starting and ending square if they were entered, let's break those up into the X and Y coordinates. Note that we first check to make sure we have both a starting and ending pair, otherwise there is no reason to do this work:

```perl
my $startx = '';
my $starty = '';
my $endx   = '';
my $endy   = '';
```

```
# time to make our move!
if ($start and $end) {
    if ($start =~ /^\s*([1-8]),([1-8])/) {
        $startx = $1 - 1;
        $starty = $2 - 1;
    }
    if ($end =~ /^\s*([1-8]),([1-8])/) {
        $endx = $1 - 1;
        $endy = $2 - 1;
    }
    if ($startx ne '' and $starty ne '' and
        $endx ne ''    and $endy ne '' ) {
        # put starting square on ending square
        $chessboard[$endy]->[$endx] = $chessboard[$starty]->[$startx];
        # remove from old square
        undef $chessboard[$starty]->[$startx];

        # we have changed the chessboard, so write
        # back out
        write_out_chessboard(@chessboard);
    }
}
```

It is important to note that we are doing several checks here. First, we check to see if the user entered any coordinates. Then, we make sure that we have good values for the X and Y values for both the starting and ending square. Only when we determine that we have to make a move do we modify the chessboard. And only when the chessboard has been modified do we write the chessboard back out to the data file.

Next, we start printing to the browser. First, the beginning HTML stuff:

```
# time to print to the browser
print
    header(),
    start_html('Web Chess'),
    h1('Web Chess');
```

Then we print the chessboard. It is almost identical to the code that prints the chessboard in chess.pl except that we are going to put this into an HTML table, so we have to print the necessary table tags:

```
# start the table that will contain the board
print '<table>';

# loop, printing each piece
foreach my $i (reverse (0..7)) { # row
    print '<tr>';
    foreach my $j (0..7) {        # column
        print '<td>';
```

```perl
            if (defined $chessboard[$i]->[$j]) {
                print $chessboard[$i]->[$j];
            } elsif ( ($i % 2) == ($j % 2) ) {
                print "..";
            }
            print '</td>';
        }
        print "</tr>";      # end of row
    }

    # we are done with out table
    print '</table>';
```

First, we start the table. Then, for each row, we print `<tr>` to start the row. Then for each column in the row we wrap either the chessboard piece, "..", or nothing at all inside `<td>..</td>`. Then we end the row with `</tr>`. Finally, the table is finalized with `</table>`.

Next we see the code to print the form to read in the user's move:

```perl
# print a form for the next move
# and end the html
print
    hr(),
    start_form(),
    'Starting square [x,y]:',
    textfield(-name => 'start'),
    br(),
    'Ending square [x,y]:',
    textfield(-name => 'end'),
    br(),
    submit(),
    end_form(),
    end_html();
```

Whew! That was a long program. Enough talk—now it is time to play chess. Load http://localhost/cgi-bin/webchess.pl into your browser and you will see

Let's make an opening move: the white pawn from 4,2 to 4,4:

Improvements We Can Make

There are many enhancements we can make to this script beyond the fact that there are no built-in chess rules. This program is a good start in a chess game, but we should consider the following:

- *More error checking:* Error checking is good, especially for web programs—the last thing we want is a user to come to our website, run a program, and have that program fail. One thing we should do is handle the failure of opening the file when we read and when we write. This requires more than simply using the `die()` function because the output from `die()` goes to standard error, which does not end up in the browser. There are several ways to address this including a helpful module called `CGI::Carp`.

- *The design of the web page:* This page is OK, for geeks. But for consumption by the general public, we will want a slick, professional-looking website that is easy to navigate and pleasant to look at. This requires the help of a graphic artist and web designer—more art than HTML. To illustrate the difference, check out www.bware.org—that is a web page designed by a geek. Compare that to www.onsight.com, which was developed by a graphic artist.[3]

- *An even more appealing design:* Speaking of an appealing web page, it would be nice to replace those letters with pictures. Wouldn't it be cool if instead of seeing BP we saw a picture of a black pawn? Again, we need an artist!

- *Every user gets their own game:* As this program is written, there is only one game. If you are playing, and you make a move, your friend can run the program and see the result. He can then make a move, which you will see the next time you run the program. Then another friend can come along, run the program, and you and your initial friend would see this new move. Not such a great thing. To resolve this we could add authentication with a username/password and store a unique copy of the game state for each user.

Hopefully this example has shown how easy it is to write CGI scripts in Perl. By adding a little bit of code, we were able to transform a program that ran in a shell to a program that has a web interface. Not only was it easy, it was fun! Speaking of fun, it's time to play some chess . . .

What We Did Not Talk About

Since this chapter is not meant to cover everything there is to know about CGI programming (if it were, it would end up being its own book), there are several things that we did not talk about. They are very important topics that you should take time to learn about, eventually:

- *Web security:* Running a webserver that is connected to the Internet allows anyone who can reach your site to run your program. If the program is written insecurely, then anyone with the mind to can execute that insecure program, possibly doing nasty things. And there are individuals in the world that like to try to break CGI scripts and crack into

---

3. Brought to you by the fine folks at BDGI (www.bdgi.com).

machines—that is the reality of the world we live in.[4] The good news is that it is possible to write secure CGI programs applying just a few techniques. For a thorough discussion of this topic, check out *CGI Programming with Perl* by Scott Guelich, et al. (O'Reilly & Associates, 2000).

- *HTML:* This chapter is not meant to be a primer on HTML, so we did not discuss all the available tags and form widgets. There are many books and websites devoted to HTML— read one and learn all about it. Then check out *Official Guide to Programming with CGI.pm* written by Lincoln Stein, the author of `CGI.pm`, to see how to use `CGI.pm` to build any HTML you want.

- *Many other features:* There are lots of other features of CGI and HTTP that we didn't cover including JavaScript, SSL, authentication, and `mod_perl`.

- *Database access:* Most modern websites contain content that is generated dynamically by reading the data out of a database. In order to achieve any level of sophistication with Perl and databases, we need the excellent Perl module `DBI`. And that is the topic of the next chapter.

- *Templating:* Most modern websites have a consistent look and feel. In other words, every page in the website has the same general layout—perhaps the same logo and links along the top, the same navigation links on the left side of the page, and the same information on the bottom of the page. If this were hard-coded for each page, then changing the look and feel of the website would require a change to every single CGI script on the website. The solution is to create a template, or a general layout for every page. Each CGI script would then use the template for the basic look of the page, then add the specific content for its purpose. Then, when the look and feel changes (it probably will, eventually), the changes are made in one place—the template—and they are immediately applied to every CGI program. Perl offers many ways to template your website including `HTML::Template`, the Template Toolkit, Mason, and Embperl.

Summary

CGI is the cornerstone of programming for the web, and Perl is *the* language to use to write CGI programs. In this chapter we discussed the CGI protocol, `CGI.pm`, forms, and form data. We learned that CGI programs are essentially a bunch of `print()` functions that generate standard output. We learned that `CGI.pm` can help make our life easier by providing helpful methods to generate this output.

Form data can be processed using the `param()` function. Dynamic CGI scripts generate the form and/or process the form, depending on how they were invoked: without form data or with form data.

---

4. These individuals are often called *hackers*, but that is a misuse of the term. A hacker is one who creates a useful program, usually quickly, in an artistic way—what many of us programmers aspire to be. A person who breaks into other computers is called a *cracker*.

You now know enough about CGI programming to get started. So get started! And happy hacking.

Exercises

1. Write a CGI script that asks a user to enter their name, address, and phone number. Respond to them with a nice message thanking them for filling out the form, and append their information to a file.

2. Make the changes to webchess.pl that were made to chess.pl in the exercises at the end of Chapter 11.

CHAPTER 15

■ ■ ■

Perl and DBI

It is now time to talk about one of Perl's best modules: the Database Independent (DBI) module. DBI provides an easy-to-use and portable (both across operating systems and across databases) application programming interface (API) that allows us to connect to a wide variety of databases including Oracle, Sybase, Informix, MySQL, mSQL, Postgress, ODBC, and many others, even files with comma-separated values (CSV). With this module we can access and administer databases from our Perl programs, combining the power and enjoyment of Perl with the usefulness of databasing information.

In this chapter we will introduce the concept of SQL and discuss the most common ways to use it. Then we will discuss DBI and the related DBD (Database Driver) modules. We will then write some Perl code to access and update a MySQL database. Finally, we will take our newfound knowledge and connect it with our topic from the last chapter and create a simple web interface to a database by combining Perl, DBI and CGI. This sounds like fun, so let's get to it.

Structured Query Language (SQL, pronounced as "EssQueueEl" by most and "Sequel" by some) is a language allowing a programmer access to a *relational database*. It is relatively easy to use—compared to Perl, learning SQL is a snap. We will talk about some of the most common SQL *queries*, or commands that access a database, and in talking about them we will describe the language to the point that learning the remaining details will be simply a matter of referring to an SQL book or website.

But we are getting ahead of ourselves. Before we can talk about SQL we need to discuss relational databases.

Introduction to Relational Databases

In order to talk about SQL, we will need to start by talking about relational databases. There are two important facts about relational databases. First, the content in a relational database is *persistent*—the data continues to exist after the execution of the program that accesses or modifies it. This is much like writing the data to a file on disk that will stay on the disk after the file is created, read from, or modified. The second important fact is that relational databases, unlike files on disk, allow concurrent access and updates from multiple users and processes. This means that more than one user can access the database at the same time—the database server takes care of making sure the changes are made to the data in a safe way.

A relational database, simply put, is a database of *tables* that can relate to one another in some way. A table is a collection of *rows* of data. Every row of data has the same basic pieces of information, called *fields*. There are a lot of buzzwords here, so let's describe each of these by an example.

Let's say we want to keep some information about our favorite musicians. The information includes their name, phone number (since we often call them up and chat), and the instruments that they play. We might start by creating a list of the musicians like this:[1]

Roger Waters	555-1212
Geddy Lee	555-2323
Marshall Mathers III	555-3434
Thom Yorke	555-4545
Lenny Kravitz	555-5656
Mike Diamond	555-6767

This list of musicians shows six lines of data. These lines are called *rows* in relational database–speak. We would take these six rows and place them together into one collection of data, called a *table*. Normally, when we place data within a table, we want to create a unique identifier for the row, called a *key*—just in case we had two different Marshall Mathers III in our table we could access the one we are interested in using this unique value. We will name the key player_id and name the other columns, or fields, as well:

player_id	name	phone
1	Roger Waters	555-1212
2	Geddy Lee	555-2323
3	Marshall Mathers III	555-3434
4	Thom Yorke	555-4545
5	Lenny Kravitz	555-5656
6	Mike Diamond	555-6767

What we have created here is a table (let's name it musicians) with three fields (player_id, name, and phone) and six rows of information. With this one example we have defined most of our relational database buzzwords, except *relational*.

The Relational of Relational Database

Normally when we create a database of information, we spread the data out among several different tables. These tables will relate to one another in some way, usually by a key or other field in the table.

As an example, let's expand our information about musicians to describe what instruments each of our musicians play and some important facts about those instruments. We could add each instrument to the row in the musicians table, but that would cause a lot of repeated

---

1. These aren't their real phone numbers. Sorry about that.

information. For instance, three of our musicians play the guitar, so any information we provide for a guitar would have to be repeated for each of the three musicians. Also, several of our musicians play more than one instrument (for instance, Thom Yorke plays guitar, sings vocals, and also plays keyboard). If we provide each instrument that Thom plays, our table would become big and difficult to work with.

Instead, let's create another table, named instruments, that will have this information:

inst_id	instrument	type	difficulty
1	bagpipes	reed	9
2	oboe	reed	9
3	violin	string	7
4	harp	string	8
5	trumpet	brass	5
6	bugle	brass	6
7	keyboards	keys	1
8	timpani	percussion	4
9	drums	percussion	0
10	piccolo	flute	5
11	guitar	string	4
12	bass	string	3
13	conductor	for-show-only	0
14	vocals	vocal	5

Now that we have defined some instruments and our opinions of their related difficulties, we somehow need to map the instrument information to the information stored in the musicians table. In other words, we need to indicate how the instruments table *relates* to the musicians table. We could simply add the inst_id value to the musicians table like this:

player_id	name	phone	inst_id
1	Roger Waters	555-1212	12

and so on, but remember that many of our musicians play more than one instrument. We would then need two rows for Roger Waters (he sings, too) and three rows for Thom Yorke. Repeating their information is a waste of memory and makes the database too complex. Instead, let's create another table that will connect these two tables. We will call it what_they_play and it will have two fields: player_id and inst_id.

player_id	inst_id
1	11
1	14
2	12
2	14
3	14
4	7
4	11
4	14
5	11
5	14
6	9

To read all this information and make sense of how it relates, we would first look in the musicians table and find the musician we want, for instance Geddy Lee. We find his player_id, 2, and use that value to look in the what_they_play table. We find two entries in that table for his player_id that map to two instr_ids: 12 and 14. Taking those two values, we use them as the keys in the instruments table and find that Geddy Lee plays the bass and sings for his band.[2]

This example illustrates that the musicians table relates to the instruments table through the what_they_play table. Breaking up the data in our database into separate tables allow us to list the information that we need only once and is often more logical than listing all the information in a single table—this is called *normalization*.

We Need an SQL Server—MySQL

Before we can show examples of SQL, we need an SQL server. There are many available to choose from, some that cost money, some that cost a *lot* of money, and some that are free. Given that we like free, we are going to choose one of the best, most powerful SQL servers available: MySQL.

MySQL (www.mysql.com) is open source and available for many different operating systems. It is relatively easy to install and administer. It is also well documented (http://dev.mysql.com/doc/mysql/en/) and there are many good books available including the excellent *The Definitive Guide to MySQL, Second Edition* by Michael Kofler (Apress, 2003). MySQL is an excellent choice for small, medium, and large databases. And did we mention it is free?

Installing MySQL

If you are a Linux user, the chances are MySQL is installed already. Do a quick check of your system to see. If not, it will have to be installed.

---

2. www.rush.com

Installation instructions can be found at the MySQL website (http://dev.mysql.com/doc/mysql/en/Installing.html). Since it is so well documented there, we will not repeat that information here. You can also check out *The Definitive Guide to MySQL, Second Edition*.

Testing the MySQL Server

Just to be sure all is well, let's enter a few MySQL commands to the shell prompt to see if everything is working. The following examples assume that the MySQL root user (not to be confused with the Unix root user) has been given a password. Giving the MySQL root user a password is a very good idea if your server will be available over the network—you don't want a pesky cracker logging into the server and being able to do devastating and destructive things like modifying or deleting your data. Let's say root's password is "RootDown".[3]

First, this command will show all the tables set up on the server:

```
$ mysqlshow -u root -p
Enter password: RootDown
+------------------+
|    Databases     |
+------------------+
| mysql            |
| test             |
+------------------+
```

This command shows all the tables in the database named mysql:

```
$ mysqlshow -u root -p mysql
Enter password: RootDown
Database: mysql
+--------------+
|    Tables    |
+--------------+
| columns_priv |
| db           |
| func         |
| host         |
| tables_priv  |
| user         |
+--------------+
```

If these commands worked, then all is well with our MySQL server. We can now create a database to store our musician information.

---

3. This is a very bad password for many reasons, the least of which is that it is published in this book. For information on creating good passwords, see *Hacking Linux Exposed, Second Edition*, Brian Hatch, Osborne Press (2002).

Creating a Database

The first step in creating a database is to start the MySQL server and then issue a MySQL command to create the database—let's call the database `musicians_db`, since it will contain information about our favorite musicians. First, let's log into the MySQL command line interface (CLI):

```
$ mysql -u root -p
Enter password: RootDown
```

A few lines of information about the MySQL server will be printed, and then we will see the MySQL prompt:

```
mysql>
```

SQL CASE SENSITIVITY

Before we start working with the MySQL database, we should take a moment and talk about the case sensitivity rules for SQL commands. Unlike Perl, SQL commands are not normally case sensitive; however, the parts of the command that refer to what we programmers have created are. This may sound confusing, but it is quite simple, and best described with an example.

Later on in this chapter we will be working with a table named `musicians`. This table will be named by us—this is the name we have chosen, and it is a good name, since it has information about a number of musicians. One of the fields in this table will be `name`, another good label since it contains the name of the musician for which we have information.

An SQL command to show the names in the table will look like this:

```
SELECT name FROM musicians;
```

The two uppercase pieces of this command are the SQL parts of the command. The lowercase pieces are the parts of the database that we have created. The SQL parts of the command are case insensitive, so the command could have been written as follows:

```
select name from musicians;
```

However, the parts that we have named are not case insensitive (that means they are case sensitive—double negatives are confusing!). So this command would not work:

```
SELECT NAME FROM MUSICIANS;
```

For clarity in this chapter, we will use all uppercase terms for the SQL parts of a command and all lowercase for the parts that we defined.

The CREATE DATABASE Command

The first step in working with a MySQL database is to create one. Creating a database is as simple as executing the CREATE DATABASE command:

```
mysql> CREATE DATABASE musicians_db;
Query OK, 1 row affected (0.01 sec)
```

The USE Command

Now that the database named musicians_db is created, we need to tell MySQL that we want to work with it. That is done with the USE command.

```
mysql> USE musicians_db;
Database changed
```

The CREATE TABLE Command

Now that the database has been created and we have selected it as the one we are using, we need to create some tables. The first table to create is musicians. Recall that it has three fields: player_id, an integer that is the key; name, a character string; and phone, a character string.

The command to create a table is, not unsurprisingly, CREATE TABLE.[4] The syntax for this command will resemble this:

```
CREATE TABLE table_name (field_definition, field_definition...)
```

The value of table_name is up to us—we are using musicians. The field definitions within the parentheses is a comma-separated list of information that follows this basic form:

```
field_name type
```

We get to choose the field names. The type will be one of many different types that MySQL supports including INT. Strings are specified as CHAR(n) where n is the number of characters in the string.

Here is the command to create our table of musicians:

```
mysql> CREATE TABLE musicians (
    ->    player_id INT PRIMARY KEY,
    ->    name CHAR(50),
    ->    phone CHAR(12));
```

The player_id field is an integer that will be the key into the table. Both name and phone are strings.

---

4. This MySQL stuff is easy!

Note There are many different SQL data types and ways in which we can create keys. For all the information on this subject, see the online documentation or the recommended textbook.

The DESCRIBE Command

The DESCRIBE command shows all the fields in the table and their types. This will show us if the musicians table was created correctly:

```
mysql> DESCRIBE musicians;
+-----------+----------+------+-----+---------+-------+
| Field     | Type     | Null | Key | Default | Extra |
+-----------+----------+------+-----+---------+-------+
| player_id | int(11)  |      | PRI | 0       |       |
| name      | char(50) | YES  |     | NULL    |       |
| phone     | char(12) | YES  |     | NULL    |       |
+-----------+----------+------+-----+---------+-------+
3 rows in set (0.00 sec)
```

This looks OK so far. Let's create the other two tables: what_they_play and instruments:

```
mysql> CREATE what_they_play (
    ->    player_id INT,
    ->    inst_id INT);
Query OK, 0 rows affected (0.01 sec)

mysql> CREATE TABLE instruments (
    ->    inst_id INT PRIMARY KEY,
    ->    instrument CHAR(40),
    ->    type CHAR(20),
    ->    difficulty INT);
Query OK, 0 rows affected (0.00 sec)
```

Creating a Non-root User with the GRANT Command

It is important to create a non-root user to access the database—performing normal non-MySQL-admin activities using the root user is a bad idea for security reasons. So let's create a user that will be allowed to perform basic queries on the musicians_db database:

```
mysql> GRANT SELECT, INSERT, UPDATE, DELETE
    ->    ON musicians_db.*
    ->    TO musicfan@localhost
    ->    IDENTIFIED BY "CrimsonKing";
Query OK, 0 rows affected (0.03 sec)
```

You can trust us when we say that this command creates a user named musicfan with a password "CrimsonKing"[5] and grants this user permission to select, insert, update, and delete records from the database. Or, you can check out the documentation and read all about the GRANT command.

We are going to start inserting data into our musicians_db database, so we need to log out as the root user and log back into MySQL as the newly created musicfan user:

```
mysql> quit
Bye
$ mysql -u musicfan -p
Enter password: CrimsonKing

mysql>
```

The INSERT Command

Now comes the time to insert data into the table. We will use the SQL command named INSERT. The basic syntax of this command is

```
INSERT INTO table_name (field1, field2, ...) VALUES (value1, value2, ...);
```

We first tell MySQL into what table we are inserting a row of data. Then, within parentheses, we indicate which fields in the table will be given values. The second set of parentheses after the term VALUES contains a list of values that are plugged in memberwise into the fields indicated in the first set of parentheses.

Roger Waters is deserving of a row of data in our table, so let's insert him as key 1, including his phone number:

```
mysql> INSERT INTO musicians (player_id, name, phone)
    -> VALUES (1, "Roger Waters", "555-1212");
Query OK, 1 row affected (0.01 sec)
```

The SELECT command can tell us if the row was inserted correctly (more on SELECT later).

```
mysql> SELECT * FROM musicians;
+-----------+---------------+----------+
| player_id | name          | phone    |
+-----------+---------------+----------+
|         1 | Roger Waters  | 555-1212 |
+-----------+---------------+----------+
1 row in set (0.00 sec)
```

Let's enter the other musicians:

```
mysql> INSERT INTO musicians (player_id, name, phone)
-> VALUES (2, "Geddy Lee", "555-2323");
Query OK, 1 row affected (0.00 sec)
```

---

5. Another bad password, but a snippet of lyrics from a great song.

```
mysql> INSERT INTO musicians (player_id, name, phone)
    -> VALUES (3, "Marshall Mathers III", "555-3434");
Query OK, 1 row affected (0.00 sec)

mysql> INSERT INTO musicians (player_id, name, phone)
    -> VALUES (4, "Thom Yorke", "555-4545");
Query OK, 1 row affected (0.00 sec)

mysql> INSERT INTO musicians (player_id, name, phone)
    -> VALUES (5, "Lenny Kravitz", "555-5656");
Query OK, 1 row affected (0.00 sec)

mysql> INSERT INTO musicians (player_id, name, phone)
    -> VALUES (6, "Mike Diamond", "555-6767");
Query OK, 1 row affected (0.00 sec)

mysql> SELECT * FROM musicians;
+-----------+----------------------+----------+
| player_id | name                 | phone    |
+-----------+----------------------+----------+
|         1 | Roger Waters         | 555-1212 |
|         2 | Geddy Lee            | 555-2323 |
|         3 | Marshall Mathers III | 555-3434 |
|         4 | Thom Yorke           | 555-4545 |
|         5 | Lenny Kravitz        | 555-5656 |
|         6 | Mike Diamond         | 555-6767 |
+-----------+----------------------+----------+
6 rows in set (0.00 sec)
```

Excellent! Our musicians are entered. Now for the commands to enter data into the other two tables. Read along and follow the bouncing ball . . .

```
mysql> INSERT INTO what_they_play (player_id, inst_id)
    -> VALUES (1, 11), (1, 14), (2, 12), (2, 14), (3, 14),
    -> (4, 7), (4, 11), (4, 14), (5, 11), (5, 14), (6, 9);
Query OK, 11 rows affected (0.00 sec)
Records: 11  Duplicates: 0  Warnings: 0
```

```
mysql> SELECT * FROM what_they_play;
+-----------+---------+
| player_id | inst_id |
+-----------+---------+
|         1 |      11 |
|         1 |      14 |
|         2 |      12 |
|         2 |      14 |
|         3 |      14 |
|         4 |       7 |
|         4 |      11 |
|         4 |      14 |
|         5 |      11 |
|         5 |      14 |
|         6 |       9 |
+-----------+---------+
11 rows in set (0.00 sec)
```

Notice that we used an alternative form of the INSERT command to insert multiple rows, in our case all the rows, at the same time.

```
mysql> INSERT INTO instruments
    ->    (inst_id, instrument, type, difficulty)
    ->    VALUES
    ->    (1, "bagpipes", "reed", 9),
    ->    (2, "oboe", "reed", 9),
    ->    (3, "violin", "string", 7),
    ->    (4, "harp", "string", 8),
    ->    (5, "trumpet", "brass", 5),
    ->    (6, "bugle", "brass", 6),
    ->    (7, "keyboards", "keys", 1),
    ->    (8, "timpani", "percussion", 4),
    ->    (9, "drums", "percussion", 0),
    ->    (10, "piccolo", "flute", 5),
    ->    (11, "guitar", "string", 4),
    ->    (12, "bass", "string", 3),
    ->    (13, "conductor", "for-show-only", 0),
    ->    (14, "vocals", "vocal", 5);
Query OK, 14 rows affected (0.00 sec)
Records: 14  Duplicates: 0  Warnings: 0
```

```
mysql> SELECT * FROM instruments;
+---------+------------+--------------+------------+
| inst_id | instrument | type         | difficulty |
+---------+------------+--------------+------------+
|       1 | bagpipes   | reed         |          9 |
|       2 | oboe       | reed         |          9 |
|       3 | violin     | string       |          7 |
|       4 | harp       | string       |          8 |
|       5 | trumpet    | brass        |          5 |
|       6 | bugle      | brass        |          6 |
|       7 | keyboards  | keys         |          1 |
|       8 | timpani    | percussion   |          4 |
|       9 | drums      | percussion   |          0 |
|      10 | piccolo    | flute        |          5 |
|      11 | guitar     | string       |          4 |
|      12 | bass       | string       |          3 |
|      13 | conductor  | for-show-only|          0 |
|      14 | vocals     | vocal        |          5 |
+---------+------------+--------------+------------+
14 rows in set (0.00 sec)
```

Now that the three tables have been created and populated with data, we can talk about how we can pull information out of the database.

The SELECT Command

The SELECT command allows us to query the database, and it reports back to us the information that matches the criteria we specify from the table we indicate. We have seen several SELECT commands in this form:

```
mysql> SELECT * FROM musicians;
+-----------+---------------------+----------+
| player_id | name                | phone    |
+-----------+---------------------+----------+
|         1 | Roger Waters        | 555-1212 |
|         2 | Geddy Lee           | 555-2323 |
|         3 | Marshall Mathers III | 555-3434 |
|         4 | Thom Yorke          | 555-4545 |
|         5 | Lenny Kravitz       | 555-5656 |
|         6 | Mike Diamond        | 555-6767 |
+-----------+---------------------+----------+
6 rows in set (0.00 sec)
```

This SELECT asks for * from the table named musicians. The * means "all fields" in the order that they are in the table. We can explicitly ask for the fields by listing them comma separated instead of using the star.

```
mysql> SELECT player_id, name, phone FROM musicians;
+-----------+----------------------+----------+
| player_id | name                 | phone    |
+-----------+----------------------+----------+
|         1 | Roger Waters         | 555-1212 |
|         2 | Geddy Lee            | 555-2323 |
|         3 | Marshall Mathers III | 555-3434 |
|         4 | Thom Yorke           | 555-4545 |
|         5 | Lenny Kravitz        | 555-5656 |
|         6 | Mike Diamond         | 555-6767 |
+-----------+----------------------+----------+
6 rows in set (0.01 sec)
```

The fields we select can be in any order.

```
mysql> SELECT name, phone, player_id FROM musicians;
+----------------------+----------+-----------+
| name                 | phone    | player_id |
+----------------------+----------+-----------+
| Roger Waters         | 555-1212 |         1 |
| Geddy Lee            | 555-2323 |         2 |
| Marshall Mathers III | 555-3434 |         3 |
| Thom Yorke           | 555-4545 |         4 |
| Lenny Kravitz        | 555-5656 |         5 |
| Mike Diamond         | 555-6767 |         6 |
+----------------------+----------+-----------+
6 rows in set (0.00 sec)
```

We can request specific fields—we don't need to show all the fields available.

```
mysql> SELECT name, phone FROM musicians;
+----------------------+----------+
| name                 | phone    |
+----------------------+----------+
| Roger Waters         | 555-1212 |
| Geddy Lee            | 555-2323 |
| Marshall Mathers III | 555-3434 |
| Thom Yorke           | 555-4545 |
| Lenny Kravitz        | 555-5656 |
| Mike Diamond         | 555-6767 |
+----------------------+----------+
6 rows in set (0.00 sec)
```

The WHERE Clause

So far, all of our SELECT queries have shown every row in the table. Oftentimes we want only specific rows. The WHERE clause tells the SELECT query to show only the rows that match our criteria. For instance, we may want to see all the information in the musicians table for the musician with player_id having the value 1.

```
mysql> SELECT * FROM musicians WHERE player_id = 1;
+-----------+--------------+----------+
| player_id | name         | phone    |
+-----------+--------------+----------+
|         1 | Roger Waters | 555-1212 |
+-----------+--------------+----------+
1 row in set (0.00 sec)
```

Or, how about selecting only the name of the musician with player_id 1.

```
mysql> SELECT name FROM musicians WHERE player_id = 1;
+--------------+
| name         |
+--------------+
| Roger Waters |
+--------------+
1 row in set (0.00 sec)
```

Here's how to grab Thom Yorke's phone number:

```
mysql> SELECT phone FROM musicians WHERE name = "Thom Yorke";
+----------+
| phone    |
+----------+
| 555-4545 |
+----------+
1 row in set (0.00 sec)
```

Maybe we are interested in all instruments with difficulties of 8 or higher:

```
mysql> SELECT instrument FROM instruments WHERE difficulty >= 8;
+------------+
| instrument |
+------------+
| bagpipes   |
| oboe       |
| harp       |
+------------+
3 rows in set (0.00 sec)
```

Or the easiest instruments:

```
mysql> SELECT instrument FROM instruments WHERE difficulty <= 2;
+------------+
| instrument |
+------------+
| keyboards  |
| drums      |
| conductor  |
+------------+
3 rows in set (0.00 sec)
```

More than one condition can be combined. Here is a SELECT query that returns all the percussion instruments with a difficulty less than or equal to 3:

```
mysql> SELECT instrument FROM instruments
    ->   WHERE type = "percussion" AND difficulty <= 3;
+------------+
| instrument |
+------------+
| drums      |
+------------+
2 rows in set (0.00 sec)
```

▌**Note** There are many different ways to use the WHERE clause in the SELECT. See the docs for all the details.

We could go on forever with describing all the different uses of the WHERE clause, but we should instead mention how to sort the output.

The ORDER BY Clause

The last bit of SQL that we will look at will be how to order the output. The ORDER BY clause allows us to specify on which field the output should be sorted. Let's say we want to show all the musician information, but the output is to be sorted by name.

```
mysql> SELECT * FROM musicians ORDER BY name;
+-----------+---------------------+----------+
| player_id | name                | phone    |
+-----------+---------------------+----------+
|         2 | Geddy Lee           | 555-2323 |
|         5 | Lenny Kravitz       | 555-5656 |
|         3 | Marshall Mathers III | 555-3434 |
|         6 | Mike Diamond        | 555-6767 |
|         1 | Roger Waters        | 555-1212 |
|         4 | Thom Yorke          | 555-4545 |
+-----------+---------------------+----------+
6 rows in set (0.00 sec)
```

How about all the instruments and their difficulty from easiest to hardest.

```
mysql> SELECT instrument, difficulty FROM instruments ORDER BY difficulty;
+------------+------------+
| instrument | difficulty |
+------------+------------+
| drums      |          0 |
| conductor  |          0 |
| keyboards  |          1 |
| bass       |          3 |
| timpani    |          4 |
| guitar     |          4 |
| trumpet    |          5 |
| piccolo    |          5 |
| vocals     |          5 |
| bugle      |          6 |
| violin     |          7 |
| harp       |          8 |
| bagpipes   |          9 |
| oboe       |          9 |
+------------+------------+
14 rows in set (0.00 sec)
```

Let's list all the percussion instruments sorted on the name:

```
mysql> SELECT instrument FROM instruments
    ->   WHERE type = "percussion"
    ->   ORDER BY instrument;
+------------+
| instrument |
+------------+
| drums      |
| timpani    |
+------------+
3 rows in set (0.00 sec)
```

You may be wondering, "Can I reverse that order?" Yup, using the qualifier DESC.

```
mysql> SELECT instrument FROM instruments
    ->   WHERE type = "percussion"
    ->   ORDER BY instrument DESC;
+------------+
| instrument |
+------------+
| timpani    |
| drums      |
+------------+
3 rows in set (0.00 sec)
```

More Complicated SELECTs

Sometimes we want to select information from our database to satisfy criteria that are a bit more complicated than what we have seen so far. For instance, if we use our database for what it was really created for, finding out what instrument a particular musician plays, it is going to be more complex.

As an example, if we wanted to find out what instruments Lenny Kravitz plays, we would have to first find out what his `player_id` is by querying the `musicians` table; then using that `player_id`, select the `inst_ids` out of `what_they_play`; then for each of those `inst_ids`, we can then get the `instrument` name out of the `instruments` table.

First, get Lenny Kravitz's `player_id`:

```
mysql> SELECT player_id FROM musicians WHERE name = "Lenny Kravitz";
+-----------+
| player_id |
+-----------+
|         5 |
+-----------+
1 row in set (0.00 sec)
```

Now, using his `player_id` of 5, grab the `inst_ids` out of `what_they_play`:

```
mysql> SELECT inst_id FROM what_they_play WHERE player_id = 5;
+---------+
| inst_id |
+---------+
|      11 |
|      14 |
+---------+
2 rows in set (0.00 sec)
```

And the last step is, for each of the `inst_ids`, 11 and 14, query the `instruments` table for the instrument:

```
mysql> SELECT instrument FROM instruments WHERE inst_id = 11;
+------------+
| instrument |
+------------+
| guitar     |
+------------+
1 row in set (0.02 sec)
```

```
mysql> SELECT instrument FROM instruments WHERE inst_id = 14;
+------------+
| instrument |
+------------+
| vocals     |
+------------+
1 row in set (0.00 sec)
```

Whew, that seems like a lot of work just to find the instruments that Lenny Kravitz plays, especially since this database was created to do just that kind of query. There must be a better way, right? Yes, there is another way.[6] These four queries can be done in one query using a *table join*.

Table Joins

MySQL is a relational database, so we must be able to query information out of our database using information from more than one table. By joining the tables, we can use multiple tables in a single SELECT.

Again, the best way to talk about table joins is with an example. In the complex SELECT in the previous section, we discovered the instruments that Lenny Kravitz plays. We could have stated that request like this: "Give me all the instrument names in the instruments table that match the inst_ids in the what_they_play table for the player_id in the musicians table associated with the musician with the name Lenny Kravitz."

The field instrument in the instruments table can be indicated in SQL with both the table name and the field name as instruments.instrument. Likewise, inst_id in what_they_play is what_they_play.inst_id. These fully qualified names allow us to use player_id in both the musicians table and the what_they_play table, and SQL can keep them separate because we will call them musicians.player_id and what_they_play.player_id.

Given that bit of good news, let's translate the query we stated in English two paragraphs earlier into SQL:

```
mysql> SELECT instrument FROM instruments,what_they_play,musicians
    ->     WHERE instruments.inst_id = what_they_play.inst_id AND
    ->           what_they_play.player_id = musicians.player_id AND
    ->           musicians.name = "Lenny Kravitz";
+------------+
| instrument |
+------------+
| guitar     |
| vocals     |
+------------+
2 rows in set (0.00 sec)
```

The big difference in this query is that we have listed more than one table in the FROM part: instruments, what_they_play, and musicians. Then, our WHERE clause has several conditions all ANDed together. Since we are using more than one table and are comparing values in one table with the values in another, we are joining the data together. Hence the term *table join*.

Let's do one more table join. Here is a query that will show all the musicians that play percussion instruments:

```
mysql> SELECT what_they_play.player_id FROM what_they_play,instruments
    ->     WHERE what_they_play.inst_id = instruments.inst_id AND
    ->           instruments.type = "percussion";
```

---

6.   TMTOWTDI in SQL too!

```
+-----------+
| player_id |
+-----------+
|         6 |
+-----------+
2 rows in set (0.00 sec)
```

As you can see, the SELECT combinations are endless! SQL is quite flexible—we can pull out exactly the information we need in exactly the order we want from the particular tables in which we are interested. We have only explored a few SQL commands—there are so many more to learn. Check out the documentation and Kofler's book for more information.

Using the MySQL command line interface is enjoyable, but it is much more fun to query our database using Perl and DBI.

Introduction to DBI

DBI is the Database Independent module and was written by Tim Bunce. It is a collection of APIs that allow a programmer to connect to and access a database. As the name implies, the module allows us to write programs to access a database independent of the type of database. We can write a program to query an Oracle database, or a Sybase database, or MySQL, or Postgres, or ODBC, and the list goes on and on. All we need on our computers is the DBI module and the appropriate Database Driver (DBD).

▓Note Each of the mentioned databases has its own dialect of SQL. Most implement the basic commands such as INSERT and SELECT in a similar way, but when it comes to the details of specific commands, they are sometimes implemented slightly differently from database to database. Keep this in mind if you are creating a Perl script that you want to port from one type of database to another—use the common form of each command even if a database has a nifty feature that you can use that is not supported elsewhere.

We are using MySQL server in this chapter, so we need to install DBI and the MySQL DBD modules.

Installing DBI and the DBD::mysql

The first step to using DBI is to install the appropriate modules. The first module we need is DBI. As this is being written, the latest version of DBI on CPAN is 1.42, but as usual this version may not be the same by the time you read this.

Follow the instructions in Chapter 13 on installing modules to install DBI. When successful, it is time to install the MySQL driver. The name of this module is DBD::mysql.

Connecting to the MySQL Database

Our first Perl program will simply connect to the MySQL database. If it works correctly, we know that DBI and DBD::mysql were installed correctly, and the real fun can then begin. Let's look at an example (connect.pl):

```
#!/usr/bin/perl -w
# connect.pl

use strict;
use DBI;

my $dbh = DBI->connect("DBI:mysql:musicians_db", "musicfan", "CrimsonKing");

die "connect failed: " . DBI->errstr() unless $dbh;

print "connect successful!\n";

$dbh->disconnect();
```

After the shebang, comment, and use strict;, we use the DBI module. Then we see a call to the DBI->connect() method. When we talked about object-oriented programming in Chapter 12, we mentioned that most modules use the method new() as their constructor. DBI, however, uses connect(). This is fine—any method name that we choose can be the constructor, and since to construct a DBI object we must connect to a database, connect() seems a logical choice.

There are three arguments to connect(): the DSN, also known as the *data source name*, the username of the user, and their password. In this invocation, the data source name is

```
"DBI:mysql:musicians_db"
```

All data sources will start with DBI, followed by a colon, the term mysql since we are using the MySQL server and DBD::mysql, a colon, and the database to which we are connecting, here musicians_db.

■**Note** Let's say that one day we want to port our database from MySQL to some other database server such as Oracle. In this script, all we need to do is change the text mysql in the data source to oracle. Provided that DBD::oracle is installed on our machine and we don't use any MySQL-specific queries, the script will work perfectly. Talk about portable!

The return value of DBI->connect() is an object that we can use to do things with the database. We call this the *database handler* so we name it $dbh. After the call to DBI->connect(), we check the value of $dbh.

```
die "connect failed: " . DBI->errstr() unless $dbh;
```

This makes sure $dbh has a true value. If DBI->connect() fails, it returns a false value to $dbh, so we die(), complaining that something went wrong with the database connection. The function DBI->errstr() will report the error of whatever just went wrong, so as a help to the user we will include this information in the string that die() prints.

If all is well, we print a cheerful message and disconnect from the database.

```
print "connect successful!\n";
```

```
$dbh->disconnect();
```

We use the disconnect() method to disconnect from the database. This is not really necessary since Perl will disconnect us when the script terminates, but it is still a polite thing to do.

Here is what happens if we execute this program:

```
$ perl connect.pl
connect successful!
$
```

Now that we can connect, it is time to execute an SQL query.

Executing an SQL Query with DBI

The last example, connect.pl, demonstrated how we can connect to the database. Now it is time to talk about how to execute arbitrary SQL queries.[7] We will first look at a program that will connect to the database musicians_db and display all the rows in the musicians table. It is called showmusicians.pl:

```
#!/usr/bin/perl -w
# showmusicians.pl

use strict;
use DBI;

my $dbh = DBI->connect("DBI:mysql:musicians_db", "musicfan", "CrimsonKing");

die "connect failed: " . DBI->errstr() unless $dbh;

# prepare the query to get the data out
# of the musicians table
my $sth = $dbh->prepare("SELECT player_id,name,phone FROM musicians")
            or die "prepare failed: " . $dbh->errstr();

$sth->execute() or die "execute failed: " . $sth->errstr();
```

---

7. As usual, there are a lot of ways to execute an SQL query and retrieve its results using Perl and DBI. We will look at the easiest and most common way, but you can read about all the various ways by typing perldoc DBI at the shell prompt.

```
my($player_id, $name, $phone);

# loop through each row of data, printing it
while (($player_id, $name, $phone) = $sth->fetchrow()) {
    print "$player_id : $name : $phone\n";
}


$sth->finish();


$dbh->disconnect();
```

This program connects as before, prepares and executes an SQL query, and then loops through the result of the query. Here is the code that prepares the query:

```
# prepare the query to get the data out
# of the musicians table
my $sth = $dbh->prepare("SELECT player_id,name,phone FROM musicians")
            or die "prepare failed: " . $dbh->errstr();
```

The database handler, $dbh, executes the prepare() method. This method's job is to take its argument, an SQL query, and compile it and prepare it to execute. The query in this case is "SELECT player_id,name,phone FROM musicians", which will select those three fields from the musicians table. If the prepare() method succeeds, it returns back an object, known as the *state handler*, that is assigned to $sth. If the prepare() method fails, it returns back false, and if so, we die() printing $dbh->errstr(), the reason for the failure.

If all is well at this point, we then execute the query.

```
$sth->execute() or die "execute failed: " . $sth->errstr();
```

The execute() method executes the query, storing the result into the $sth object. If execute() fails, we die(), and explain why by executing $sth->errstr().

The $sth object has the result of the query stored within it, so we have to retrieve that information. The fetchrow() method does this for us.

```
# loop through each row of data, printing it
while (($player_id, $name, $phone) = $sth->fetchrow()) {
    print "$player_id : $name : $phone\n";
}
```

The fetchrow() method returns the next row of information returned by the query. This code takes that row and copies it memberwise into three variables. Since our query asked for the player_id, name, and phone from the musicians table, we take those three pieces of information and store them in $player_id, $name, and $phone, respectively. Those variables are then printed.

After we are done with the state handler, it is good practice to finish it with this code:

```
$sth->finish();
```

Executing this code produces the following:

```
$ perl showmusicians.pl
1 : Roger Waters : 555-1212
2 : Geddy Lee : 555-2323
3 : Marshall Mathers III : 555-3434
4 : Thom Yorke : 555-4545
5 : Lenny Kravitz : 555-5656
6 : Mike Diamond : 555-6767
$
```

A More Complex Example

Remember the complex query we did previously in this chapter when we tried to find out the instruments played by Lenny Kravitz? It was a three-step process: first, we found his player_id from the musicians table. Then we used that player_id to read the inst_ids from the what_they_play table. For each of those inst_ids, we read the instrument name from the instruments table. Here is how we might do this in Perl and DBI:

```
#!/usr/bin/perl -w
# showinstruments1.pl

use strict;
use DBI;

my($who, $player_id, $inst_id);

print "Enter name of musician and I will show you his/her instruments: ";
chomp($who = <STDIN>);

my $dbh = DBI->connect("DBI:mysql:musicians_db", "musicfan", "CrimsonKing");

die "connect failed: " . DBI->errstr() unless $dbh;

# first, grab the musicians player_id
my $sth = $dbh->prepare("SELECT player_id FROM musicians WHERE name = '$who'")
          or die "prepare failed: " . $dbh->errstr();

$sth->execute() or die "execute failed: " . $sth->errstr();

($player_id) = $sth->fetchrow();

die "player_id not found" unless defined $player_id;

# given the player_id, grab their inst_ids from what_they_play
$sth = $dbh->prepare("SELECT inst_id FROM what_they_play
                         WHERE player_id = $player_id")
          or die "prepare failed: " . $dbh->errstr();
```

```
$sth->execute() or die "execute failed: " . $sth->errstr();

# foreach inst_id, grab the instrument name from the
# instruments table and print it
while (($inst_id) = $sth->fetchrow()) {
    my $sth = $dbh->prepare("SELECT instrument FROM instruments
                                    WHERE inst_id = $inst_id")
            or die "prepare failed: " . $dbh->errstr();

    $sth->execute() or die "execute failed: " . $sth->errstr();

    my($instrument) = $sth->fetchrow();
    print "    $instrument\n";

    $sth->finish();
}

$sth->finish();

$dbh->disconnect();
```

Let's look at each step of this process. After connecting to the database as we have been doing in the previous examples and asking for the user to enter the name of a musician, we construct and execute a query to obtain that musician's player_id.

```
# first, grab the musicians player_id
my $sth = $dbh->prepare("SELECT player_id FROM musicians WHERE name = '$who'")
            or die "prepare failed: " . $dbh->errstr();

$sth->execute() or die "execute failed: " . $sth->errstr();

($player_id) = $sth->fetchrow();

die "player_id not found" unless defined $player_id;
```

Notice how the SQL query is constructed using the variable $who. The outer double quotes of the query string are needed to take the value of $who. The SQL query needs to quote the name since it is a string, so wrapped around $who within the query are single quotes.

The query is then executed. This should return only one row (it could return zero rows if the musician is not found in the table) so we only have to call fetchrow() once—we take the return value of that method, a list of one value, and assign it to the assignable list ($player_id). The result is that $player_id will be the player_id of the musician that the user entered at standard input or undef if the musician was not found. The program die()s if $player_id is not defined.

Then we use $player_id and construct a query asking for the inst_ids:

```
# given the player_id, grab their inst_ids from what_they_play
$sth = $dbh->prepare("SELECT inst_id FROM what_they_play
                            WHERE player_id = $player_id")
          or die "prepare failed: " . $dbh->errstr();

$sth->execute() or die "execute failed: " . $sth->errstr();
```

Notice how the query string contains $player_id, the value we just read out of the database. Since the player_id is an integer, it does not need to be quoted within the SQL query. When executed, this should return back all the inst_ids for that player_id. We then loop through the result, each row at a time:

```
# foreach inst_id, grab the instrument name from the
# instruments table and print it
while (($inst_id) = $sth->fetchrow()) {
    my $sth = $dbh->prepare("SELECT instrument FROM instruments
                                WHERE inst_id = $inst_id")
            or die "prepare failed: " . $dbh->errstr();

    $sth->execute() or die "execute failed: " . $sth->errstr();

    my($instrument) = $sth->fetchrow();
    print "    $instrument\n";

    $sth->finish();
}
```

As we loop through each row of output from the previous query, we prepare() another query to read the name of the instrument from the instruments table. Notice that within the while loop, $sth will receive the return value from prepare() and that we have declared this variable with a my(). The my() here is very important—it creates a new copy of $sth within the while loop so we will not clobber the previous value of $sth outside the while loop (the result of the query of the what_they_play table). If we had not declared $sth with a my(), that previous query would have been overwritten and we would have only processed one row of output from the query of what_they_play. An alternative to declaring $sth with my() would have been selecting a different variable name, which would have been fine, but sticking with $sth as the state handler variable is the convention (besides, that new variable would have to have been my()ed as well).

Executing the program looks like this:

```
$ perl showinstruments1.pl
Enter name of musician and I will show you his/her instruments: Roger Waters
    guitar
    vocals
$
```

Excellent! But, not so fast. There is a problem with this program, demonstrated with this example:

```
$ perl showinstruments1.pl
Enter name of musician and I will show you his/her instruments: Chris O'Rourke
DBD::mysql::st execute failed: You have an error in your SQL syntax near
'Rourke'' at line 1 at showinstruments1.pl line 20, <STDIN> line 1.
execute failed: You have an error in your SQL syntax near 'Rourke'' at line 1 at
showinstruments1.pl line 20, <STDIN> line 1.
$
```

Can you see what the problem is? The query that uses $who, the name entered, looks like this:

```
$dbh->prepare("select player_id from musicians where name = '$who'")
```

Since $who is single-quoted in the SQL query string, the single quote in the name "Chris O'Rourke" makes SQL think that the string it is comparing to name is "Chris O". SQL then sees "Rourke", which is totally out of place—this is a syntax error.

You may think the answer is to escape the single quote and turn $who into "Chris O\'Rourke". This is possible, and would work, but there is a better way.

Use Placeholders

Notice how the SQL query strings change in showinstrument2.pl:

```perl
#!/usr/bin/perl -w
# showinstruments2.pl

use strict;
use DBI;

my($who, $player_id, $inst_id);

print "Enter name of musician and I will show you his/her instruments: ";
chomp($who = <STDIN>);

my $dbh = DBI->connect("DBI:mysql:musicians_db", "musicfan", "CrimsonKing");

die "connect failed: " . DBI->errstr() unless $dbh;

# first, grab the musicians player_id
my $sth = $dbh->prepare("SELECT player_id FROM musicians WHERE name = ?")
            or die "prepare failed: " . $dbh->errstr();

$sth->execute($who) or die "execute failed: " . $sth->errstr();

($player_id) = $sth->fetchrow();
```

```
die "player_id not found" unless defined $player_id;

# given the player_id, grab their inst_ids from what_they_play
$sth = $dbh->prepare("SELECT inst_id FROM what_they_play
                             WHERE player_id = ?")
            or die "prepare failed: " . $dbh->errstr();

$sth->execute($player_id) or die "execute failed: " . $sth->errstr();

# foreach inst_id, grab the instrument name from the
# instruments table and print it
while (($inst_id) = $sth->fetchrow()) {
    my $sth = $dbh->prepare("SELECT instrument FROM instruments
                                    WHERE inst_id = ?")
            or die "prepare failed: " . $dbh->errstr();

    $sth->execute($inst_id) or die "execute failed: " . $sth->errstr();

    my($instrument) = $sth->fetchrow();
    print "    $instrument\n";

    $sth->finish();
}

$sth->finish();

$dbh->disconnect();
```

The first call to prepare() and execute() has changed to

```
my $sth = $dbh->prepare("SELECT player_id FROM musicians WHERE name = ?")
            or die "prepare failed: " . $dbh->errstr();

$sth->execute($who) or die "execute failed: " . $sth->errstr();
```

Instead of using the variable $who in the query string, we use a question mark (?). This acts as a *placeholder* for a variable or value that we will provide later. That later ends up being an argument to the execute() method: $sth->execute($who). DBI will take the argument $who and plug it into the question mark in the query string. The nice thing about using this feature is that we don't have to worry about escaping the single quote. Much better!

You may be wondering—what if there is more than one variable in the query string? All of their values are provided in the execute() method and are plugged into the placeholders member-wise as shown in this snippet:

```
$sth = $dbh->prepare("SELECT * FROM data WHERE name = ? AND age = ?");
$sth->execute($name, $age);
```

But wait a minute! Both showinstruments1.pl and showinstruments2.pl are using three SQL queries. We learned earlier in this chapter that we could obtain the same information using one query by using a table join.

DBI and Table Joins

Any SQL query is possible using DBI. This includes table joins. Let's modify the previous example showinstruments2.pl and perform a table join as shown here in showinstrument3.pl:

```perl
#!/usr/bin/perl -w
# showinstruments3.pl

use strict;
use DBI;

my($who, $instrument);

print "Enter name of musician and I will show you his/her instruments: ";
chomp($who = <STDIN>);

my $dbh = DBI->connect("DBI:mysql:musicians_db", "musicfan", "CrimsonKing");

die "connect failed: " . DBI->errstr() unless $dbh;

# use a table join to query the instrument names
my $sth = $dbh->prepare("SELECT instruments.instrument
    FROM musicians,what_they_play,instruments
    WHERE musicians.name = ? AND
        musicians.player_id = what_they_play.player_id AND
        what_they_play.inst_id = instruments.inst_id")
            or die "prepare failed: " . $dbh->errstr();

$sth->execute($who) or die "execute failed: " . $sth->errstr();

# loop through them, printing them
while (($instrument) = $sth->fetchrow()) {
    print "    $instrument\n";
}

$sth->finish();

$dbh->disconnect();
```

The big change is the preparation and execution of the query:

```perl
# use a table join to query the instrument names
my $sth = $dbh->prepare("SELECT instruments.instrument
    FROM musicians,what_they_play,instruments
    WHERE musicians.name = ? AND
```

```
            musicians.player_id = what_they_play.player_id AND
            what_they_play.inst_id = instruments.inst_id")
                or die "prepare failed: " . $dbh->errstr();

$sth->execute($who) or die "execute failed: " . $sth->errstr();
```

Here we construct one large query as we did previously in this chapter. It joins the musicians, what_they_play, and instruments tables. Notice how we are using a placeholder when we compare musicians.name and how the variable $who is provided within the execute() method.

Does this table join work? Yep.

```
$ perl showinstruments3.pl
Enter name of musician and I will show you his/her instruments: Thom Yorke
    keyboards
    guitar
    vocals
$
```

Perl and DBI allow us to easily create programs that query our database. This means we can do anything with Perl that we can do with the SQL database including many SQL commands that we have not talked about in this chapter.

Perl + DBI + CGI = Fun!

Perl and DBI are enjoyable, but now it is time to take it to another level of fun. Let's put our new skill of Perl and DBI together with the topic of the last chapter: CGI.

We will develop a CGI script that will interface to the musicians_db database. It will be a dynamic CGI program that will first present the user with a form, and when the user submits data by clicking a button, the program will then report the response back to the user. The user will be able to make a choice to see one of two responses: either a musician's phone number or the instruments they play.

Let's first have a look at the code. When examined closely, the code follows this general flow of execution:

```
if (param()) {
    if (param('Show phone number')) {
        # query database and show the musicians phone number
    } elsif (param('Show instruments')) {
        # query the database and show the instruments played by the musician
    }
} else {
    # query the database and build the initial form with all the musicians names
}
```

Here is the code in all its glory. We will look at the specific pieces in detail as we talk about them:

```perl
#!/usr/bin/perl -w
# musicians.pl

use strict;
use CGI ':standard';
use DBI;

if (param()) {
    # we have parameters, go grab the musicians
    # name
    my $musician = param('musician') || '';

    if (param('Show phone number')) {
        # the user wants to see the musician's phone number
        # print first part of HTML
        print
            header(),
            start_html("Phone Number for $musician"),
            h1("Phone Number for $musician");

        # query the database and get the phone number
        my $dbh = DBI->connect("DBI:mysql:musicians_db", "musicfan",
                               "CrimsonKing");
        my $sth = $dbh->prepare("SELECT phone FROM musicians
                                        WHERE name = ?")
                    or die "prepare failed: " . $dbh->errstr();

        $sth->execute($musician) or die "execute failed: " . $sth->errstr();

        my($phone);

        ($phone) = $sth->fetchrow();

        # print number and end HTML
        print
            "Call $musician at $phone.",
            end_html;
    } elsif (param('Show instruments')) {
        # the user wants to see the instruments the musician
        # plays, start the HTML
        print
            header(),
            start_html("Instruments played by $musician"),
            h1("Instruments played by $musician"),
            "$musician plays:",
            '<ul>';
```

```perl
        # query the database with a table join and retrieve the
        # instruments played by musician
        my $dbh = DBI->connect("DBI:mysql:musicians_db", "musicfan",
                               "CrimsonKing");
        my $sth = $dbh->prepare("SELECT instrument
                        FROM musicians, what_they_play, instruments
                        WHERE musicians.name = ? AND
                              musicians.player_id = what_they_play.player_id AND
                              what_they_play.inst_id = instruments.inst_id")
                    or die "prepare failed: " . $dbh->errstr();

        $sth->execute($musician) or die "execute failed: " . $sth->errstr();

        my($instrument);

        # print all the instruments in a bullet list
        while (($instrument) = $sth->fetchrow()) {
            print "<li>$instrument</li>";
        }

        # finish the HTML
        print
            '</ul>',
            end_html;
    }

} else {
    # no data was posted, so print the initial form to the user
    # allowing to select the musician and whether they want
    # to see the phone number or the instruments
    print
        header(),
        start_html('My Favorite Musicians'),
        h1('Select a Musician'),
        start_form(),
        '<select name="musician">';

    # grab all the musician's names out of the database
    my $dbh = DBI->connect("DBI:mysql:musicians_db", "musicfan", "CrimsonKing");
    my $sth = $dbh->prepare("SELECT name FROM musicians")
                or die "prepare failed: " . $dbh->errstr();

    $sth->execute() or die "execute failed: " . $sth->errstr();

    my($name);
```

```perl
    # loop through each row of data, printing it as an option
    # in the select widget
    while (($name) = $sth->fetchrow()) {
        print qq{<option value="$name">$name</option>};
    }

    # finish the select widget, print the submit buttons
    # and end the HTML
    print
        '</select>',
        br(),
        submit('Show phone number'),
        submit('Show instruments'),
        end_form(),
        end_html();
}
```

When we run the program the first time (http://localhost/cgi-bin/musicians.pl), we see this initial page:

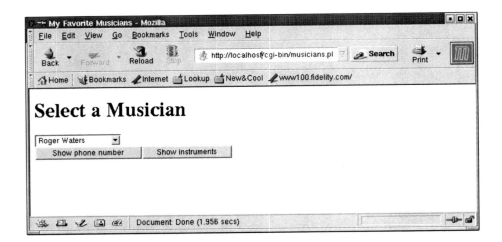

This form allows us to select a musician from the drop-down list. Notice that the menu contains all the musicians that we have inserted into our table—in fact, it is built by reading from the database. Then there are two buttons—one that indicates if we click on it we will see the selected musician's phone number. The other button, when clicked, will show the instruments played by the selected musician. This page is built with the else part of the program starting with

```perl
} else {
    # no data was posted, so print the initial form to the user
    # allowing them to select the musician and whether they want
```

```
# to see the phone number or the instruments
print
    header(),
    start_html('My Favorite Musicians'),
    h1('Select a Musician'),
    start_form(),
    '<select name="musician">';
```

First, the header is printed, followed by the start of the HTML for the page. Within the form we see the creation of a <select> widget—this is a drop-down menu that allows us to select one of the provided options. Then we see

```
# grab all the musicians names out of the database
my $dbh = DBI->connect("DBI:mysql:musicians_db", "musicfan", "CrimsonKing");
my $sth = $dbh->prepare("SELECT name FROM musicians")
            or die "prepare failed: " . $dbh->errstr();

$sth->execute() or die "execute failed: " . $sth->errstr();
```

This code connects to the database and prepares and executes the query to retrieve all the musician names. The code that displays the names is next.

```
my($name);

# loop through each row of data, printing it as an option
# in the select widget
while (($name) = $sth->fetchrow()) {
    print qq{<option value="$name">$name</option>};
}
```

This code loops through all the rows of output (the musician names) and prints them in an <option> widget, adding them to the drop-down menu so that they can be selected. This is followed by

```
# finish the select widget, print the submit buttons
# and end the HTML
print
    '</select>',
    br(),
    submit('Show phone number'),
    submit('Show instruments'),
    end_form(),
    end_html();
}
```

The <select> widget is closed, two submit buttons are printed, and the page is finished up.

Since it has been a while since we talked to Geddy Lee, let's select his name from the drop-down menu and click the button "Show phone number". The following screen is produced:

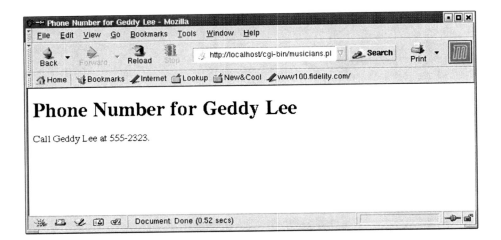

Let's look at the code that built this page. It starts with

```
if (param('Show phone number')) {
        # the user wants to see the musician's phone number
        # print first part of HTML
        print
            header(),
            start_html("Phone Number for $musician"),
            h1("Phone Number for $musician");
```

The `if` determines that the user wants to see the musician's phone number. The HTML is started for the page and then we see the code to access the database:

```
        # query the database and get the phone number
        my $dbh = DBI->connect("DBI:mysql:musicians_db", "musicfan",
                                "CrimsonKing");
        my $sth = $dbh->prepare("SELECT phone FROM musicians
                                    WHERE name = ?")
                    or die "prepare failed: " . $dbh->errstr();

        $sth->execute($musician) or die "execute failed: " . $sth->errstr();
```

This is familiar by now—we connect and query the database using the placeholder for the musician's name. This returns the phone number for the musician, so we need to fetch the row, read the data into $phone, and print it to the browser followed by the end of the HTML:

```
        my($phone);

        ($phone) = $sth->fetchrow();
```

```
      # print number and end HTML
      print
          "Call $musician at $phone.",
          end_html;
```

After calling Geddy Lee, we may want to see the instruments played by Thom Yorke, so we can go back to the initial page where we can select Thom from the drop-down menu and click "Show instruments". When we do so we see this page:

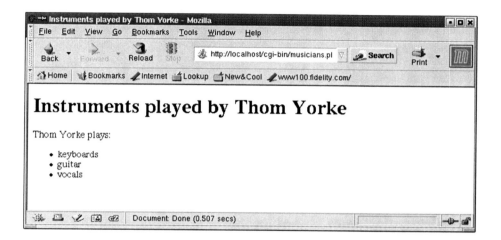

This page is built with this code:

```
} elsif (param('Show instruments')) {
      # the user wants to see the instruments the musician
      # plays, start the HTML
      print
          header(),
          start_html("Instruments played by $musician"),
          h1("Instruments played by $musician"),
          "$musician plays:",
          '<ul>';
```

We see that the user wants to show the musician's instruments, so we start the HTML, print some text, and then start an unordered list (a bullet list). This is followed by the code to query the database:

```
      # query the database with a table join and retrieve the
      # instruments played by musician
      my $dbh = DBI->connect("DBI:mysql:musicians_db", "musicfan",
                             "CrimsonKing");
```

```
my $sth = $dbh->prepare("SELECT instrument
                 FROM musicians, what_they_play, instruments
                 WHERE musicians.name = ? AND
                      musicians.player_id = what_they_play.player_id AND
                      what_they_play.inst_id = instruments.inst_id")
              or die "prepare failed: " . $dbh->errstr();

$sth->execute($musician) or die "execute failed: " . $sth->errstr();
```

Using the table join that we have seen a few times in this chapter, we find all the instruments that the musician plays. Then we see the code that prints the instruments:

```
my($instrument);

# print all the instruments in a bullet list
while (($instrument) = $sth->fetchrow()) {
    print "<li>$instrument</li>";
}
```

Notice that each instrument is printed within an <li> tag, which makes it into a bullet item in the list. Finally we see the end of the unordered list and the end of the HTML:

```
# finish the HTML
print
    '</ul>',
    end_html;
}
```

That was fun! And using Perl, CGI, and DBI it was easy as well. Such is the power and practicality of Perl revealed.

What We Didn't Talk About

This chapter is not meant to be an exhaustive discussion of SQL and DBI. There are many topics we did not talk about that should be learned if the maximum power of SQL is to be harnessed.

First, there are several commands that are essential to use including the following:

- UPDATE: Allows data in a table to be modified. An example might be

```
UPDATE musicians SET phone = "555-9999" WHERE player_id = 3;
```

- DELETE: Deletes a row from a table. An example might be

```
DELETE FROM instruments WHERE inst_id = 13;
```

Be careful! If the WHERE clause is not used, all rows in the table are deleted.

- REPLACE: If the key provided does not exist, the data is inserted; otherwise the row with that key is first deleted, then the new row is inserted. An example might be

```
REPLACE INTO musicians (player_id, name, phone)
       VALUES (1, "Neil Peart", "555-8888");
```

In addition to the preceding SQL commands, another topic that is important to know is *indexing* a table. This can significantly increase the speed of SELECT statements on large tables. See the docs for more information.

Speaking of seeing the docs for more information on SQL, as a reminder, be sure to check out the online documentation for MySQL at http://dev.mysql.com/doc/mysql/en/ and the excellent book *The Definitive Guide to MySQL, Second Edition* by Michael Kofler.

Summary

In this chapter we described how we can access a database using Perl and the DBI module. We started with a description of a relational database and followed that with a brief introduction to SQL.

We then installed MySQL and created a database with three tables. We talked about several SQL commands: INSERT and SELECT were the most important ones. Table joins were discussed as a way to implement the relations in relational databases.

Then we introduced DBI and DBD::mysql, and wrote several Perl scripts to access and query the database.

We ended with an example of how easy it is to create dynamic web content by connecting Perl, DBI, and CGI.pm. And in the middle of that discussion we took time out of our busy day to call one of our favorite musicians.

Exercises

1. Write a Perl script that prompts the user for an instrument and then prints all the musicians that play that instrument.

2. Write a CGI program similar to musicians.pl that is a web interface to the script you created for exercise 1.

■ ■ ■

Exercise Solutions

This appendix contains the answers to the chapter exercises. An important note: each solution is *an* answer, not *the* answer. Remember that in Perl, there is more than one way to do it, and that applies to these solutions as well.

Chapter 1

1.

```
#!/usr/bin/perl -w
# chap01ex1.pl

print "Hi Mom.\nThis is my second program.\n";
```

Chapter 2

1.

```
#!/usr/bin/perl -w
# chap02ex1.pl

use strict;

print "Currency converter\n\n";

print "Please enter the exchange rate: ";
chomp(my $yen = <STDIN>);

print "Enter first price to convert: ";
chomp(my $price1 = <STDIN>);

print "Enter second price to convert: ";
chomp(my $price2 = <STDIN>);
```

```perl
print "Enter third price to convert: ";
chomp(my $price3 = <STDIN>);

print "$price1 Yen is ", ($price1/$yen), " dollars\n";
print "$price2 Yen is ", ($price2/$yen), " dollars\n";
print "$price3 Yen is ", ($price3/$yen), " dollars\n";
```

2.

```perl
#!/usr/bin/perl -w
# chap02ex2.pl

use strict;

print "enter a hex number: ";
chomp(my $hexnum = <STDIN>);
print "converted to an int: ", hex($hexnum), "\n";

print "enter an octal number: ";
chomp(my $octal = <STDIN>);
print "converted to an int: ", oct($octal), "\n";
```

3.

```perl
#!/usr/bin/perl -w
# chap02ex3.pl

use strict;

print "enter a value less than 256: ";
chomp(my $bin = <STDIN>);

print((128 & $bin) / 128);
print((64 & $bin) / 64);
print((32 & $bin) / 32);
print((16 & $bin) / 16);
print((8 & $bin) / 8);
print((4 & $bin) / 4);
print((2 & $bin) / 2);
print((1 & $bin) / 1);

print "\n";
```

4.

```
2 + (6 / 4) - (3 * 5) + 1 = -10.5
17 + ((-3 ** 3) / 2) = -3.5
26 + (3 ^ (4 * 2)) = 37
((4 + 3) >= 7) || (2 && ((4 * 2) < 4)) = 1
```

Chapter 3

1.

```perl
#!/usr/bin/perl -w
# chap03ex1.pl

use strict;

my $target = 12;
print "Guess my number!\n";
print "Enter your guess: ";

my $guess;
while ($guess = <STDIN>) {
    if ($target == $guess) {
        print "That's it! You guessed correctly!\n";
        last;
    } elsif ($guess > $target) {
        print "Your number is more than my number\n";
    } elsif ($guess < $target) {
        print "Your number is less than my number\n";
    }
    print "Enter your guess: ";
}
```

2.

```perl
#!/usr/bin/perl -w
# chap03ex2.pl

use strict;

for (my $i = 1; $i <= 10; $i++) {
    print "$i square is: ", $i*$i, "\n";
}
```

3.

```perl
#!/usr/bin/perl -w
# chap03ex3.pl

use strict;

for (my $i = 1; $i <= 50; $i++) {
    if ($i % 5 == 0) {
        print "$i is evenly divisible by 5\n";
    }
}
```

Chapter 4

1.

```perl
#!/usr/bin/perl -w
# chap04ex1.pl

use strict;

my @a = (2, 4, 6, 8);

foreach (@a) {
    print "$_ ** 2 = ", $_ ** 2, "\n";
}

foreach (reverse @a) {
    print "$_ ** 2 = ", $_ ** 2, "\n";
}
```

3.

Here is a program that illustrates the answer to this question.

```perl
#!/usr/bin/perl -w
# chap04ex3.pl

use strict;

my @a = ('aa' .. 'bb');
print "first array:\n";
print "@a\n";
```

```perl
@a = ('a0' .. 'b9');
print "------------\n";
print "second array:\n";
print "@a\n";
```

Chapter 5

1.

```perl
#!/usr/bin/perl -w
# chap05ex1.pl

use strict;

my %hash = (
    scalar => 'dollar sign',
    array  => 'at sign',
    hash   => 'percent sign'
);

foreach (sort keys %hash) {
    print "$_: $hash{$_}\n";
}
```

2.

```perl
#!/usr/bin/perl -w
# chap05ex2.pl

use strict;

my %phonenumbers = (
    John  => '555-1212',
    Sue   => '555-2222',
    Larry => '555-3232',
    Moe   => '555-4242'
);

print "enter name: ";
while (<STDIN>) {
    chomp;
    if (exists $phonenumbers{$_}) {
        print "$_ has the phone number: $phonenumbers{$_}\n";
```

```perl
    } else {
        print "$_ is not in the phone book\n";
    }
    print "enter name: ";
}
```

3.

```perl
#!/usr/bin/perl -w
# chap05ex3.pl

use strict;

my %jokes = (
    Java   => "None. Change it once, and it's the same everywhere.",
    Python => "One. He just stands below the socket and the world " .
              "revolves around him.",
    Perl   => "A million. One to change it, the rest to try and do it in " .
              "fewer lines.",
    C      => '"CHANGE?!!"'
);

print "enter programming language: ";
while (<STDIN>) {
    chomp;
    if (exists $jokes{$_}) {
        print "How many $_ programmers does it take to change a lightbulb?\n";
        sleep 2;
        print $jokes{$_}, "\n";
    } else {
        print "That language is not funny...\n";
    }
    print "enter programming language: ";
}
```

Chapter 6

1.

```perl
#!/usr/bin/perl -w
# chap06ex1.pl

use strict;

print "enter a number: ";
chomp(my $input_num = <STDIN>);
```

```perl
    if ($input_num < 0) {
        print "please enter a positive number!\n";
    } else {
        my $result = factorial($input_num);
        print "$input_num! = $result\n";
    }

    sub factorial {
        my $num = shift;

        if ($num == 0) {
            return 1;
        } else {
            my $answer = 1;
            foreach (2 .. $num) {
                $answer = $answer * $_;
            }
            return $answer;
        }
    }

    # here is the solution using recursion -
    # a recursive function is a function that calls
    # itself
    sub factorial_recursive {
        my $num = shift;

        if ($num == 0) {
            return 1;
        } else {
            return $num * factorial_recursive($num - 1);
        }
    }
```

2.

```perl
#!/usr/bin/perl -w
# chap06ex2.pl

use strict;

my $number_of_seconds;

prompt_user();
my ($hours, $minutes, $seconds) = secs2hms($number_of_seconds);
```

```perl
print "$number_of_seconds seconds is $hours hours, $minutes ",
    "minutes and $seconds seconds";
print "\n";

sub prompt_user {
    print "please enter the number of seconds: ";
    chomp($number_of_seconds = <STDIN>);
}

sub secs2hms {
    my ($h,$m);
    my $seconds = shift;;      # defaults to shifting @_
    $h = int($seconds/(60*60));
    $seconds %= 60*60;
    $m = int($seconds/60);
    $seconds %= 60;
    ($h,$m,$seconds);
}
```

Chapter 7

1.

Match "hello" followed by zero or more and any character but \n followed by "world"; or, in other words, any string that contains "hello" followed later by "world".

Match one or more digits at the beginning of the string followed by one whitespace character followed by zero or more word characters followed by the end of the string.

Match an uppercase letter at the beginning of a word followed by zero or more lowercase letters to the end of a word; or, in other words, match a word that begins with an uppercase letter followed by any number of lowercase letters.

Match a character, remember it in \1, followed by any number of any characters but \n, followed by the character remembered. In other words, match any string with two occurrences of the same character.

2.

```
/^\d.* \d$/

/^[\s\w]+$/

/^\S*$/
```

3.

```perl
#!/usr/bin/perl -w
# chap07ex3.pl
```

```perl
while (<>) {
    print if /[aeiouy][aeiouy]/i;
}
```

4.

```perl
#!/usr/bin/perl -w
# chap07ex4.pl

while (<>) {
    print if /^[^aeiouy]*[aeiouy][^aeiouy]*[aeiouy][^aeiouy]*$/i;
}
```

Chapter 8

1.

```perl
#!/usr/bin/perl -w
# chap08ex1.pl

use strict;

open(INFH,  '<', 'gettysburg.txt') or die $!;
open(OUTFH, '>', 'ex1out.txt')     or die $!;

while (<INFH>) {
next if /^\s*$/;
    my @words = split;
    print OUTFH "$_\n" foreach @words;
}

close INFH;
close OUTFH;
```

2.

```perl
#!/usr/bin/perl -w
# chap08ex2.pl

use strict;

unless (@ARGV) {
    @ARGV = qw(file1.dat file2.dat file3.dat);
}

print <>;
```

3.

```perl
#!/usr/bin/perl -w
# chap08ex3.pl

use strict;

my $target;
while (1) {
    print "What file should I write to? ";
    $target = <STDIN>;
    chomp $target;
    if (-d $target) {
        print "No, $target is a directory.\n";
        next;
    }
    if (-e $target) {
        print "File already exists. What should I do?\n";
        print "(Enter 'r' to write to a different name, ";
        print "'o' to overwrite or\n";
        print "'b' to back up to $target.old)\n";
        my $choice = <STDIN>;
        chomp $choice;
        if ($choice eq "r") {
            next;
        } elsif ($choice eq "o") {
            unless (-o $target) {
                print "Can't overwrite $target, it's not yours.\n";
                next;
            }
            unless (-w $target) {
                print "Can't overwrite $target: $!\n";
                next;
            }
        } elsif ($choice eq "b") {
            if (-e "$target.old") {
                print "Backup $target.old exists.  Overwrite it? [y|n] ";
                my $choice = <STDIN>;
                chomp $choice;
                if ($choice ne 'y') {
                    next;
                }
            }
            if ( rename($target, $target.".old") ) {
                print "OK, moved $target to $target.old\n";
```

```
            } else {
                print "Couldn't rename file: $!\n";
                next;
            }
        } else {
            print "I didn't understand that answer.\n";
            next;
        }
    }
    last if open(OUTPUT, '>', $target);
    print "I couldn't write to $target: $!\n";
    # and round we go again.
}

print OUTPUT "Congratulations.\n";
print "Wrote to file $target\n";

close OUTPUT;
```

Chapter 9

1.

```
#!/usr/bin/perl -w
# chap09ex1.pl

use strict;

open(FH, '<', 'ex1.dat') or die $!;

while (<FH>) {
    my $name    = substr $_,  0, 24;
    my $address = substr $_, 25, 18;
    my $city    = substr $_, 52, 20;
    my $state   = substr $_, 72,  2;
    my $zip     = substr $_, 75,  5;


    print <<EOT;

Record:
name     : $name
address  : $address
city     : $city
```

```
state    : $state
zip      : $zip
EOT

}

close FH;
```

2.

```perl
#!/usr/bin/perl -w
# chap09ex2.pl

use strict;

while (<>) {
    tr/a-zA-Z/n-za-mN-ZA-M/;
    print;
}
```

Chapter 10

1.

```perl
#!/usr/bin/perl -w
# chap10ex1.pl

use strict;

my $dir  = shift || '';
my $size = shift || '';

die "usage: ex1.pl <dir> <size>\n" unless $dir and $size;

chdir $dir or die "can't chdir: $!";

# first, a file glob
# this gets hidden files too
print "using glob:\n";
foreach (<.* *>) {
    if (-f $_ and -s _ >= $size) {
        print '    ', $_, ' ' x (30 - length($_)), -s _, "\n";
    }
}
```

```perl
# now using a directory handle
print "\n\nusing directory handle:\n";
opendir DH, '.' or die "opendir failed: $!";
while ($_ = readdir(DH)) {
    if (-f $_ and -s _ >= $size) {
        print '    ', $_, ' ' x (30 - length($_)), -s _, "\n";
    }
}
closedir DH;
```

Chapter 11

1.

```perl
#!/usr/bin/perl -w
# chap11ex1.pl

use strict;

my @chessboard;
my @back = qw(R N B Q K N B R);
foreach (0..7) {
    $chessboard[0]->[$_] = "W" . $back[$_]; # White Back Row
    $chessboard[1]->[$_] = "WP";                # White Pawns
    $chessboard[6]->[$_] = "BP";                # Black Pawns
    $chessboard[7]->[$_] = "B" . $back[$_]; # Black Back Row
}

while (1) {
    # Print board
    foreach my $i (reverse (0..7)) { # Row
        foreach my $j (0..7) {        # Column
            if (defined $chessboard[$i]->[$j]) {
                print $chessboard[$i]->[$j];
            } elsif ( ($i % 2) == ($j % 2) ) {
                print "..";
            } else {
                print "  ";
            }
            print " ";  # End of cell
        }
        print "\n";     # End of row
    }
```

```perl
    print "\nStarting square [x,y]: ";
    my $move = <>;
    last unless ($move =~ /^\s*([1-8]),([1-8])/);
    my $startx = $1-1; my $starty = $2-1;

    unless (defined $chessboard[$starty]->[$startx]) {
        print "There's nothing on that square!\n";
        next;
    }
    print "\nEnding square [x,y]: ";
    $move = <>;
    last unless ($move =~ /([1-8]),([1-8])/);
    my $endx = $1-1; my $endy = $2-1;

    # detect if a piece is about to be taken
    if (defined $chessboard[$endy]->[$endx]) {
        print "\n$chessboard[$endy]->[$endx] at (", $endx + 1, ",",
            $endy+1, ") is being taken!\n\n";
    }

    # Put starting square on ending square.
    $chessboard[$endy]->[$endx] = $chessboard[$starty]->[$startx];
    # Remove from old square
    undef $chessboard[$starty]->[$startx];
}
```

2.

```perl
#!/usr/bin/perl -w
# chap11ex2.pl

use strict;

my @chessboard;
my @back = qw(R N B Q K N B R);
foreach (0..7) {
    $chessboard[0]->[$_] = "W" . $back[$_]; # White Back Row
    $chessboard[1]->[$_] = "WP";            # White Pawns
    $chessboard[6]->[$_] = "BP";            # Black Pawns
    $chessboard[7]->[$_] = "B" . $back[$_]; # Black Back Row
}

while (1) {
    # Print board
    foreach my $i (reverse (0..7)) { # Row
        foreach my $j (0..7) {       # Column
```

```perl
            if (defined $chessboard[$i]->[$j]) {
                print $chessboard[$i]->[$j];
            } elsif ( ($i % 2) == ($j % 2) ) {
                print "..";
            } else {
                print "  ";
            }
            print " ";  # End of cell
        }
        print "\n";     # End of row
    }

    print "\nStarting square [x,y]: ";
    my $move = <>;
    last unless ($move =~ /^\s*([1-8]),([1-8])/);
    my $startx = $1-1; my $starty = $2-1;

    unless (defined $chessboard[$starty]->[$startx]) {
        print "There's nothing on that square!\n";
        next;
    }
    print "\nEnding square [x,y]: ";
    $move = <>;
    last unless ($move =~ /([1-8]),([1-8])/);
    my $endx = $1-1; my $endy = $2-1;

    if (defined $chessboard[$endy]->[$endx]) {
        # can't take your own piece
        if (substr($chessboard[$endy]->[$endx], 0, 1) eq
            substr($chessboard[$starty]->[$startx], 0, 1)) {
            print "\nyou can't take your own piece!\n\n";
            next;
        }
        # can't take a king
        if ($chessboard[$endy]->[$endx] =~ /K/) {
            print "\nyou can't take a king!\n\n";
            next;
        }
    }

    # Put starting square on ending square.
    $chessboard[$endy]->[$endx] = $chessboard[$starty]->[$startx];
    # Remove from old square
    undef $chessboard[$starty]->[$startx];
}
```

3.

```perl
#!/usr/bin/perl -w
# chap11ex3.pl

use strict;

my %addressbook;

sub menu {
    print <<EOT;

Please make a choice:
    1   add an entry
    2   view an entry
    3   view all entries
    4   delete an entry
    5   exit

Your choice:
EOT
}

sub add_entry {
    print "Enter name: ";
    chomp(my $name = <STDIN>);
    if (exists $addressbook{$name}) {
        print "Name alread exists in the address book!\n";
    }
    print "Address:     ";
    chomp(my $address = <STDIN>);
    print "Phone:       ";
    chomp(my $phone = <STDIN>);
    $addressbook{$name} = {
        address => $address,
        phone   => $phone
    };
}

sub view_entry {
    print "Enter name to view: ";
    chomp(my $name = <STDIN>);
    if (exists $addressbook{$name}) {
        print "Address: $addressbook{$name}{address}\n";
        print "Phone:   $addressbook{$name}{phone}\n\n";
```

```perl
        } else {
            print "$name is not in address book!\n\n";
        }
    }

    sub view_all {
        foreach my $name (sort keys %addressbook) {
            print "Name:    $name\n";
            print "Address: $addressbook{$name}{address}\n";
            print "Phone:   $addressbook{$name}{phone}\n\n";
        }
    }

    sub delete_entry {
        print "Enter name to delete: ";
        chomp(my $name = <STDIN>);
        if (exists $addressbook{$name}) {
            delete $addressbook{$name};
        } else {
            print "$name is not in address book!\n\n";
        }
    }

    while (1) {
        menu();
        chomp(my $answer = <STDIN>);
        SWITCH: {
            $answer == 1 and add_entry(),    last SWITCH;
            $answer == 2 and view_entry(),   last SWITCH;
            $answer == 3 and view_all(),     last SWITCH;
            $answer == 4 and delete_entry(), last SWITCH;
            $answer == 5 and exit(0);
        }
    }
```

Chapter 12
1.

```perl
#!/usr/bin/perl -w
# chap12ex1.pl

use strict;
use Person8;
```

```perl
my $object1 = Person8->new(
    lastname    => "Galilei",
    firstname   => "Galileo",
    address     => "9.81 Pisa Apts.",
    occupation  => "bombadier",
    phone_no    => "312.555.1212"
);

my $object2 = Person8->new(
    lastname    => "Wall",
    firstname   => "Larry",
    address     => "123 Perl Ave.",
    occupation  => "Programmer",
    phone_no    => "312.555.2323"
);

my $object3 = Person8->new(
    lastname    => "Torvalds",
    firstname   => "Linus",
    address     => "593 Linux Ave.",
    occupation  => "Programmer",
    phone_no    => "312.555.3434"
);

print "There are ", Person8->headcount(), " Person8 objects\n";

foreach my $person (Person8->everyone()) {
    print "\n", '-' x 80, "\n";
    $person->printletter("You owe me money. Please pay it.");
}
```

Chapter 14

1.

```perl
#!/usr/bin/perl -w
# chap14ex1.pl

use strict;

use CGI ':standard';

print
    header(),
    start_html('Exercise 1');
```

```
if (param) {
    my $name    = param('name')    || '';
    my $address = param('address') || '';
    my $phone   = param('phone')   || '';

    print
        h1('Thanks for your information!'),
        'Thanks for entering the following information:',
        br(),
        $name,
        br(),
        $address,
        br(),
        $phone;

    open FH, '>>', '/tmp/ex1.dat';
    print FH '-' x 80, "\n$name\n$address\n$phone\n";
    close FH;
} else {
    print
        h1('Please enter some information'),
        start_form(),
        'Name: ',
        textfield(-name => 'name'),
        br(),
        'Address: ',
        textarea(-name => 'address', rows => 3),
        br(),
        'Phone number: ',
        textfield(-name => 'phone'),
        br(),
        submit(),
        end_form();
}

print
    end_html();
```

2.

The solution to this problem is to include the changes shown previously in the section for Chapter 11, exercises 1 and 2.

Chapter 15

1.

```perl
#!/usr/bin/perl -w
# chap15ex1.pl

use strict;
use DBI;

my($instrument, $musician);

print "Enter instrument: ";
chomp($instrument = <STDIN>);

my $dbh = DBI->connect("DBI:mysql:musicians_db", "musicfan", "CrimsonKing");

die "connect failed: " . DBI->errstr() unless $dbh;

# use a table join to query the instrument names
my $sth = $dbh->prepare("SELECT musicians.name
    FROM musicians,what_they_play,instruments
    WHERE instruments.instrument = ? AND
        musicians.player_id = what_they_play.player_id AND
        what_they_play.inst_id = instruments.inst_id")
            or die "prepare failed: " . $dbh->errstr();

$sth->execute($instrument) or die "execute failed: " . $sth->errstr();

# loop through them, printing them
while (($musician) = $sth->fetchrow()) {
    print "    $musician\n";
}

$sth->finish();

$dbh->disconnect();
```

2.

```perl
#!/usr/bin/perl -w
# chap15ex2.pl

use strict;
use CGI ':standard';
use DBI;
```

```perl
if (param()) {
    my $instrument = param('instrument') || '';

    print
        header(),
        start_html("Musicians who play $instrument");
        h1("Musicians who play $instrument");

    my $dbh = DBI->connect("DBI:mysql:musicians_db", "musicfan",
                           "CrimsonKing");
    my $sth = $dbh->prepare("SELECT name
                    FROM musicians, what_they_play, instruments
                    WHERE instruments.instrument = ? AND
                        instruments.inst_id = what_they_play.inst_id AND
                        what_they_play.player_id = musicians.player_id")
                    or die "prepare failed: " . $dbh->errstr();

    $sth->execute($instrument) or die "execute failed: " . $sth->errstr();

    my($name);

    while (($name) = $sth->fetchrow()) {
        print "$name plays the $instrument.<br>";
    }
    print
        end_html;
} else {
    print
        header(),
        start_html('My Favorite Instrument'),
        h1('Select an Instrument'),
        start_form(),
        '<select name="instrument">';

    my $dbh = DBI->connect("DBI:mysql:musicians_db", "musicfan",
                           "CrimsonKing");
    my $sth = $dbh->prepare("SELECT instrument FROM instruments")
                or die "prepare failed: " . $dbh->errstr();

    $sth->execute() or die "execute failed: " . $sth->errstr();

    my($instrument);

    while (($instrument) = $sth->fetchrow()) {
        print qq{<option value="$instrument">$instrument</option>};
    }
```

```
    print
        '</select>',
        br(),
        submit('Show musician(s)'),
        end_form(),
        end_html();
}
```

Index

Breinigsville, PA USA
15 November 2009
227528BV00004B/15/P